Many scholars of language have accepted a view of grammar as a clearly delineated and internally coherent structure which is best understood as a self-contained system. The contributors to this volume propose a very different way of approaching and understanding grammar, taking it as part of a broader range of systems which underlie the organization of social life and emphasizing its role in the use of language in everyday interaction and cognition. Taking as their starting-point the position that the very integrity of grammar is bound up with its place in the larger schemes of the organization of human conduct, particularly with social interaction, their essays explore a rich variety of linkages between interaction and grammar.

D1536798

Studies in interactional sociolinguistics 13

GENERAL EDITOR
John J. Gumperz

ADVISORY EDITORS
Charles Briggs, Paul Drew, Deborah Schiffrin

Interaction and grammar

Studies in Interactional Sociolinguistics

Interaction and grammar

edited by

ELINOR OCHS
University of California, Los Angeles

EMANUEL A. SCHEGLOFF
University of California, Los Angeles

SANDRA A. THOMPSON
University of California, Santa Barbara

CAMBRIDGE
UNIVERSITY PRESS

Published by the Press Syndicate of the University of Cambridge
The Pitt Building, Trumpington Street, Cambridge CB2 1RP
40 West 20th Street, New York, NY 10011 – 4211, USA
10 Stamford Road, Oakleigh, Melbourne 3166, Australia

First published 1996

Printed in Great Britain at the University Press, Cambridge

A catalogue record for this book is available from the British Library

Library of Congress cataloguing in publication data
Interaction and grammar/edited by Elinor Ochs, Emanuel E. Schegloff and Sandra A. Thompson.
     p.   cm. – (Studies in interactional sociolinguistics ; 13)
ISBN 0 521 55225 7 (hardback) ISBN 0 521 55828 X (paperback)
1. Sociolinguistics. 2. Social interaction. 3. Conversation analysis. I. Ochs, Elinor. II. Schegloff, Emanuel A. III. Thompson, Sandra A. IV. Series.
P40.I55 1996
306.4'4 – dc20   95 – 24891 CIP

ISBN 0 521 55225 7 hardback
ISBN 0 521 55828 X paperback

K W

Contents

Notes on the contributors

Cecilia E. Ford teaches linguistics in the English Department at the University of Wisconsin, Madison. Her research centers on interactional aspects of language use. She is the author and coauthor of a number of articles on conversation and grammar and on spoken and written language, including the recent book, *Grammar in Interaction: Adverbial Clauses in American English Conversations* (1993), in which she uses conversation analysis as a framework for examining interactional functions of adverbial clauses.

Barbara A. Fox teaches in the Linguistics Department at the University of Colorado, Boulder. Her research interests are mainly in the area of interaction and grammar. Her publications in this area include work on anaphora, relative clauses, and self-repair.

Patrick Gonzales is a doctoral candidate in applied linguistics at the University of California, Los Angeles. His research interests include discourse analysis, conversation analysis, language socialization, and the teaching and learning of mathematics and science.

Charles Goodwin is Professor of Anthropology at the University of South Carolina. His research interests include the analysis of conversation, human interaction, multi-party participation frameworks, the ethnography of science, the social organization of talk and perception in professional settings, and aphasia as an interactive phenomenon. Publications include *Conversational Organization: Interaction between Speakers and Hearers* (Academic Press, 1981), *Rethinking Context: Language as an Interactive Phenomenon* (edited with Alessandro Duranti,

Cambridge University Press, 1992), and numerous articles in journals and edited collections (for example "Professional vision" *American Anthropologist*, September 1994).

Makoto Hayashi is a doctoral student in linguistics at the University of Colorado, Boulder. He received his BA from Kyoto University, Japan. His research interests include conversation analysis, interaction and grammar, distributed cognition, and discourse-functional approaches to language.

Sally Jacoby is completing her doctorate in applied linguistics at the University of California, Los Angeles. Her dissertation research on the interactional practices of scientists rehearsing for upcoming conference talks combines cross-disciplinary interests in conversation analysis, scientific discourse, language socialization, and ethnography.

Robert Jasperson is a doctoral student in linguistics at the University of Colorado, Boulder. His research interests lie in the area of interaction and grammar. His dissertation explores aspects of grammar through studies of repair in English conversation.

Gene H. Lerner is Assistant Professor of Sociology at the University of California at Santa Barbara. He has written on the collaborative production and social organization of linguistic forms such as sentences and narratives. Most recently he has been investigating the place of speaker turn design in the organization of participation in instructional activities. He is the author of "On the syntax of sentences-in-progress," "Assisted storytelling: deploying shared knowledge as a practical matter," and "Collectivities in action: establishing the relevance of conjoined participation in conversation."

Marcyliena Morgan is Assistant Professor of Anthropology at the University of California, Los Angeles. She received her Ph.D. in educational linguistics from the University of Pennsylvania. She is the editor of the book *Language and the Social Construction of Identity in Creole Situations* and is North American editor of the journal *Pragmatics*. She has published articles on language use and communicative style in the African American community, language and gender, language and identity, the ethnography of speaking and pragmatics.

Elinor Ochs, Professor of Applied Linguistics at the University of California, Los Angeles, is an interdisciplinary scholar with research interests in the nexus of linguistics, anthropology, and psychology. She is concerned with ways in which language practices organize human life, including ways in which grammar and discourse are resources for constructing and socializing actions, emotions, knowledge, activities, and identities of import to persons as well as communities. These interests have drawn her to analyze grammar and discourse patterns among families, scientists, orators, and the emotionally disabled, based on ethnographic fieldwork carried out in Madagascar, Western Samoa, Italy, and the United States.

Emanuel A. Schegloff teaches in the Department of Sociology at UCLA. His interests revolve around the naturalistic study of interaction and what we can learn about humans and the organization of social life and experience from it.

Bambi B. Schieffelin is Professor of Anthropology at New York University. Her research areas include language socialization, literacy, language ideology, and language change. She has done ethnographic and linguistic fieldwork among the Kaluli since 1967. She is the author of *The Give and Take of Everyday Life: Language Socialization of Kaluli Children* (1990) and with Elinor Ochs has co-edited *Developmental Pragmatics* and *Language Socialization across Cultures* (1986). She is currently completing a Kaluli-English dictionary with Steven Feld, and is working on a monograph on language use, metalinguistics, and social change based on her Kaluli research.

Marja-Leena Sorjonen received an MA in Finnish language from the University of Helsinki. She is currently a doctoral student in Applied Linguistics at UCLA, as well as a researcher in a project on Finnish doctor-patient interaction conducted in Helsinki, funded by the Finnish Foundation for Alcohol Studies. Her dissertation examines meaning and use of a group of particles used as responses in Finnish everyday conversation. Her research interests include the interplay between grammatical forms and interaction and interaction in institutional settings.

Sandra A. Thompson is Professor of Linguistics at the University of California at Santa Barbara. She specializes in discourse and language universals, and is particularly interested in the role of patterns of conversational discourse in shaping morphosyntactic regularities. She is the co-author with Charles Li of *Mandarin Chinese: A Functional Reference Grammar*. She has co-edited *Studies in Transitivity* with Paul Hopper, and *Clause Combining in Grammar and Discourse* with John Haiman.

1

Introduction[1]

EMANUEL A. SCHEGLOFF, ELINOR OCHS, AND
SANDRA A. THOMPSON

One of sociology's ancestral figures, Emile Durkheim, with whom
DeSaussure is often linked, is known (among many other contributions) for the claim that "the social" is not reducible to the psychological or the biological, or the sum of any individual attributes. It
is, he said, an *emergent* phenomenon, a *distinct* level of organization; it is, he said, a reality *sui generis* – unto itself, of its own sort
(Durkheim, 1938 [1895], 1951, among others). Some cynical (or
astute, depending on one's point of view) students of intellectual
history, of the history of sociology and of the social sciences more
generally, and practitioners of the sociology of knowledge have
remarked that this claim needs to be understood as part of a struggle to find a place for sociology in the structure of French academic
life at the turn of the century. To have as the object of one's study a
domain which was *autonomous*, which could not be reduced to
other people's work and subject matter, was arguably one prerequisite for establishing one's own organizational niche, for establishing one's own standards of quality work, of important
problems, of acceptable methods, of distinctive theories, and the
like, and the professional license and mandate – the professional
autonomy – to administer them.

None of this – even if true – has any bearing, of course, on the
theoretical or empirical merit of Durkheim's claim. To hold otherwise would be to commit the so-called genetic fallacy. Yet it can
enrich our understanding to have called to our attention that there
can be secular (i.e., material) as well as sacred (i.e., theoretical)
grounds for insisting on the total autonomy of one's subject matter
from any apparently overlapping or even contiguous domains of
phenomena and inquiry.

Sociology is hardly the only academic discipline to have had to struggle to establish a place for itself within the bureaucratic organization of contemporary academic life. It was not until the 1960s, for example, that Departments of Linguistics began to be established as undertakings with a proper subject matter domain of their own, in which linguists could do "their own thing," rather than serve as marginal adjuncts to Departments of Language and Literature, such as English, French, German, etc. – caught between language teaching and literary scholarship.[2] It is surely no coincidence that this departmental autonomy within the academy was directly linked to the claims of the then newly ascending stance within the discipline that claimed for its subject matter autonomy – autonomy from the humanistic literary disciplines on one side, and from the encroaching behaviorist forms of psychology on the other. The key documents in the latter regard were, of course, Chomsky's review (1959) of B. F. Skinner's *Verbal Behavior* and his attack (1957: 18-25) on information-theoretic models of language use such as Shannon and Weaver's *Mathematical Theory of Communication* (1949). This disciplinary autonomy was grounded theoretically as well, in the claimed autonomy of syntax as the backbone of the biological faculty called "language."

There were, then, diverse resonances – the purely theoretical merits aside – for that approach to language (and to syntax in particular) which took it to be a well-formed structure in its own right, built to stand on its own, with its coherence and structure best understood as self-enclosed integrity. Its proper understanding would then be equally internally shaped, and only marginally affected by our understanding of, for example, other "mental capacities," or the cultures which are irremediably intertwined with the semantics and the lexicon of a language, let alone its pragmatics and the contexts in which language develops and is used.

The contributors to this volume are exploring a different way of approaching and understanding grammar. For them, grammar is part of a broader range of resources – organizations of practices, if you will – which underlie the organization of social life, and in particular the way in which language figures in everyday interaction and cognition. In this view, the involvement of grammar in such other organizations as those of culture, action and interaction has as a consequence that matters of great moment are missed if grammar's order is explored as entirely contained within a single, self-enclosed organization. Grammar's integrity and efficacy are bound up with its place in larger schemes of organization of human conduct, and with social interaction in particular. The contributions to this volume explore a variety of telling linkages between interaction and grammar.

1.1 Background

Three genres of inquiry converge here – one grounded in functional approaches to language concerned with its role in communication and cognition, one grounded in linguistic anthropology and the cultural underpinnings of language, and one grounded in conversation analysis and the interactional matrix of language structure and use.

Functional linguists with interests in language as it appears empirically in conduct have found a potentially attractive resource in work developed in the last thirty years – largely under the aegis of sociology – on the organization of conversational interaction. Conversation analysts have sought input from linguists for at least twenty years to help describe the grammatical shaping of one of the most fundamental units in talk-in-interaction, namely turns; the research efforts of functional grammarians can be a prime source of such input. For at least thirty years, since the introduction of the Ethnography of Communication (Gumperz and Hymes, 1964), if not longer, linguistic anthropologists have appreciated the centrality of careful examination of recorded communicative events, and in recent years have come increasingly to articulate ways in which social order and cultural understandings are constituted and socialized through the moment-by-moment, turn-by-turn organization of everyday conversational interaction. At the same time, conversation analysts have become increasingly concerned with ways in which talk and interaction both organize and are organized by institutions, relationships and culturally specified environments. In addition, while linguistic anthropology has long been interested in the relation of grammatical to communicative competence, recently anthropologists have addressed ways in which grammatical structures have meaning in part by virtue of the social practices and activities which they help to constitute. Each of these budding common interests has continued to expand. This volume presents a sampling of the state of work at their interfaces.[3]

This undertaking is not yet a well-formed enterprise: the topics taken up here are varied and not systematically related to one another; the ways of working at them are equally diverse, and the authors hold themselves (and are held) responsible to quite different audiences and constituencies in the analytic themes which they sound and in the ways in which they address them.

That is where things stand now; little is to be gained by imposing an artificial order. What may be more helpful is briefly to take stock of the recent trajectories of these "feeder streams," so that readers can have a sense of where the authors are coming from. These accounts must, of necessity, be thumbnail sketches, and they are irremediably perspectival – each written from the perspective of the editor's feeder stream (Ochs for linguistic anthropology, Thompson for functional linguistics, Schegloff for sociology/conversation analysis), and not necessarily seen in the same light by the others (although there is a fair degree of consensus among us).

1.1.1 Linguistic anthropology

In the early decades of this century, Franz Boas formulated his program of cultural anthropology on the assumption that linguistic inquiry is necessary to investigating the mental habits and social life of a people (1911). For Boas and his student Edward Sapir (1927, 1933), grammatical analysis is essential to the enterprise of ethnology in that grammatical categories reflect fundamental, unconscious, cultural patterns of thinking and acting. Grammars are deeply socio-cultural and integral to cross-cultural analysis because they illuminate how humans structure the world.

Sapir's writings in particular promoted a radical view of how grammar and the lexicon relate to social life. He suggested that language does not stand apart from experience as a parallel symbolic structure but rather "completely interpenetrates with it" (1974: 49). Sapir proposed that this interpenetration of language and life is pervasive: "For the normal person every experience, real or potential, is saturated with verbalism" (1974: 49-50). Language is not only a tool for thinking, it is also a tool for acting. Language is not only embedded in social intercourse; it is also itself a form of social intercourse.

Boas and Sapir championed the study of language as both thought and action, articulated human similarities as well as differences, foregrounded individual variation within social groups, and conceptualized the relation of grammar to custom as subtle and indirect. However, their ideas became rigidified in the Linguistic Relativity Hypothesis to mean (for many) that the grammar of a language unidirectionally and uniformly molds its speakers into distinct patterns of thinking and behaving (Whorf, 1956). This formulation gave rise to studies relating lexical and grammatical categories within a particular language to distinct conceptual systems of its speakers (Conklin, 1955; Goodenough, 1956; Hoijer, 1951, among others). With some exceptions (e.g. Frake, 1964), linguistic relativists tended to relate linguistic systems to thought without recording and closely examining how such systems actually interpenetrate with activities and become constitutive features of social action. In part because of technological limitations and in part because of a professional disposition to capture underlying cultural patterns, these studies characterized language behavior in social life largely in terms of underlying features, habits, norms, and integrated fashions of speaking, gleaned primarily from participant observations, interviews, and secondary sources.

While a cadre of linguists and anthropologists continued to conduct research on indigenous languages and cultures, urban dialects, and multilingual communities, formal linguistics became increasingly concerned with Universal Grammar rather than grammars as holistic systems and with syntactic structure rather than semantic categories. In the 1960s, Dell Hymes asked, "Is the role of prime collaborator of linguistics among the sciences now to pass to psychology?" (1962/1974: 190). Hymes encouraged linguists to "move outward into the exploration of speech behavior and use" (1962/ 1974: 193). John Gumperz and Dell Hymes (1964) promoted extending linguistic inquiry to units of analysis such as the speech act, the speech event, the speech situation, and the speech community. They redrew the boundaries of linguistic competence to include communicative competence as well as grammatical competence. But these messages fell on deaf linguistic ears; the enterprises of linguistics and anthropology drew rapidly apart. Grammatical analysis faded from the syllabi of most anthropology programs; anthropology departments hired fewer and fewer linguists, rendering linguistics the least represented among the the four perspectives (physical, cultural, archeology, linguistics) that comprise the discipline of anthropology in the United States.

As grammar lost its centrality among cultural anthropologists, social action assumed a more important analytic role in the field. This shift paralleled a sea change across disciplines away from an analytic focus on timeless mental competence and atemporal structural analysis towards a focus on unfolding, socially co-ordinated, temporally and spatially situated "interactional rituals" (Goffman, 1964, 1967, 1974), "practices" (Garfinkel, 1967; Bourdieu, 1977, 1990; Schegloff, 1972), "activities" (Vygotsky, 1978; Leontyev, 1981), and "talk-in-interaction" (Sacks, Schegloff, and Jefferson, 1974; Schegloff, Jefferson, and Sacks, 1977; Schegloff, 1987). In these approaches, people are not visualized as passive bearers of unconscious patterns of language and culture, but rather as active agents whose actions and sensibilities at different moments influence the organization, meaning, and outcome of events. While performance is loosely motivated and organized by conventions, principles, and expectations, it is not predictable from mental scripts of situations. Rather, everyday social life is appropriately characterized by historically positioned, situationally contingent moves and strategies of active participants. Moreover, through these moves and strategies, members actively (re)construct, for themselves and for others, orderly ways of being in and understanding the world. In this sense, competence enters into a dialectical relation with performance in that each impacts the other, each is a resource for the other, each helps to constitute the other.

For linguistic anthropologists, an interest in social interaction is a compatible extension of their concern with speaking as situated action. However, the above mentioned approaches to practices, joint activity, and contingent accomplishments differ from the structuralist *zeitgeist* that characterized much of linguistic anthropology up through the early days of the Ethnography of Speaking. For example, Hymes called for reconfiguring the competence-performance distinction by encompassing communicative as well as grammatical competence and concomitantly shrinking the bounds of what was considered mere performance. However, this redesign preserved the competence-performance dichotomy and privileged competence over performance as the analytic focus of the discipline. Further, in the early 1960s when Hymes launched the study of "the situations and uses, the patterns and functions, of speaking as an activity in its own right" (Hymes, 1962/1974: 191), he advocated utilizing Roman Jakobson's framework of paradigmatic and syntagmatic relations (Jakobson and Halle, 1956) as well as Jakobson's dimensions of a speech event (1960) to analyze the structures and functions of speaking across communities. This methodology inspired comparative research on communicative events, including studies by one of the editors of this volume (e.g. Keenan, 1973, 1974; Ochs, 1984). These accounts, however, generally objectified the communicative event and de-emphasized the subjective experience of moving through these events and collaboratively building actions and meanings with other persons over interactional and historical time.

A more phenomenological turn emerged later in linguistic anthropology – for example, in interactional accounts of cross-cultural miscommunication (Gumperz, 1982), language socialization (e.g. Goodwin, 1990; Heath, 1983; Kulick, 1992; Ochs, 1992a, 1992b; Schieffelin, 1990), intentionality and authorship (Duranti and Brenneis, 1986; Hill and Irvine, 1992), professional discourse (Cicourel, 1992; Goodwin, 1994), and context more broadly (Duranti and Goodwin, 1992; Hanks, 1990). Although varying in focus, these anthropological accounts articulate how in the course of historically situated social interactions participants formulate and co-ordinate their utterances, gestures, and other actions to co-construct understandings, misunderstandings, social personae, relationships, stances, activities, and/or modes of learning, knowing, and controlling the world. For some researchers, an interaction-centered anthropology of language means relating strategies for engaging in verbal interaction to the socialization, maintenance, and transformation of social realities such as the family, the school, work, or community political structures. Others relate verbal interaction to the socialization, maintenance, and transformation of ideologies, including ideologies of spoken and written language. And others have returned to the question of how grammatical and lexical structure relates to society and culture by articulating ways in which linguistic structures are themselves interactional. In his study of deixis in a Mayan community, William Hanks distills the essence of this perspective (1990: 4): "This is the real rub: reference is a kind of communicative action which occurs as part of an interactive manifold." This position is resonant with Sapir's conviction that language is not a symbolic system that runs parallel to experience but rather interpenetrates experience. An anthropology of language in this sense warrants studying not only how linguistic and socio-cultural histories inform social interaction, but also how interactional processes universally and locally motivate, give meaning to, and otherwise organize language, society and culture.

1.1.2 Functional grammar

The area of research which has come to be known informally during the last two decades or so as "functional grammar" has encompassed a wide variety of endeavors. What all these have in common is an emphasis on "grammar," taken generally as morphosyntax, and a commitment to examining grammatical data in terms of functional considerations, that is, in terms of the ways in which language functions as a tool of human communication. It has been clear to all involved that this commitment has consistently stood in opposition to a view of language, and more particularly grammar, as an autonomous faculty of human cognition.

Within this broad conception of "functionalism," a number of important contributions to our understanding of language as it functions in communication have emerged, most densely in four or five roughly demarcated areas of work. One intensively worked area is that of typology and universals (e.g., Comrie, 1989; Givón, 1984, 1990; Greenberg, 1978; Li, 1976; Nichols and Woodbury, 1985; Shopen, 1985, inter alia). A continuing emphasis on cross-linguistic generalizations throughout this period has greatly increased the degree of sophistication with which languages are described with respect to almost every aspect of "grammar." Comparison across languages has enhanced the capacity to generalize e.g., about how tense-aspect systems get grammaticalized (e.g., Bybee, 1985; Bybee et al., 1994; Cole and Sadock, 1977; Comrie, 1976, 1985; Hopper, 1982 inter alia), what possible types of grammatical relations systems there are (e.g., Comrie, 1978; Croft, 1991;

Dixon, 1979; Foley and Van Valin, 1984; Hopper and Thompson, 1980; Mithun, 1991; Shibatani, 1988, inter alia), how classifiers work in languages that have them (e.g., Craig, 1986), how number can be expressed (e.g., Mithun, 1988), what types of clause-combining strategies languages can have (e.g., Austin, 1988; Haiman and Thompson, 1988), what the possible ways of expressing causation are (e.g., Comrie and Polinsky 1993; Shibatani, 1976), and how grammaticalization works by converting lexical resources into grammatical ones (e.g., Bybee, 1985; Bybee et al., 1994; Hopper and Traugott, 1993; Heine, Claudi, and Hünnemeyer, 1991).

During the same period, work in lexical semantics and cognitive models – such as that by Fillmore, Kay and their associates (e.g., inter alia, Fillmore, 1988, 1989; Fillmore, Kay, and O'Connor, 1988), by Lakoff and his associates (e.g., Lakoff and Johnson, 1980; Lakoff, 1987), by Langacker and his associates (e.g., Langacker, 1987, 1991), and by Van Valin and his associates (e.g., Van Valin, 1990, 1993) – has brought to light a number of insights into regularities in word "meanings" and constructions. This work, often associated with the rubrics "construction grammar," "cognitive grammar," and "role and reference grammar," focusses on naming and categorization processes, the nature of grammatical constructions, prototype theory, and the operation and effects of metaphor. A related effort has been mounted under the rubric "functional grammar," associated with the name of Simon Dik (1981, 1983) and his associates, and a more socially oriented semantically based model of grammatical structure has been the focus of attention for a group centered around M. A. K. Halliday and his associates, known as "systemic functional grammar" (e.g., Halliday, 1985).

Within psycholinguistics since the mid-1970s, several lines of work have most directly been preoccupied with the ways in which language figures in social interaction. In psycholinguistic research on communication per se, the work of H. Clark and his associates (e.g., Clark and Wikes-Gibbs, 1986; Clark and Schaeffer, 1987; Clark and Gerrig, 1989; Clark and Brennan, 1991) is perhaps the most sustained and visible. In the area of child language, functionally oriented work – done as much by psychologists (e.g., Bates et al., 1988; Bloom, 1973; Bruner, 1983; Ervin-Tripp, 1979; Garvey, 1984; Greenfield et al., 1985; MacWhinney, 1987, inter alia) as by linguists (e.g., Clancy, 1986; E. Clark, 1978; Halliday, 1975, inter alia) – has shown how children acquire grammatical constructions and learn to use them in appropriate contexts – constructions such as classifiers, questions, relative clauses, tense-aspect markers and other aspects of verb morphology, etc., and this work has been enhanced by cross-linguistic work by developmental psychologists (see especially the contributions to Slobin, 1985, 1992) and by anthropologists such as Ochs (1988) and Schieffelin (1990).

Arising from, and centered around, a recognition of the importance of approaching grammar in terms of its natural contexts of use, in the late 1970s a new area of functional linguistics began to emerge, which could be called discourse-and-grammar.[4] A central tenet of the researchers defining this area has been that, if we take seriously the claim that the function of language as a tool of human communication is the central motivation for observed grammatical patterns, then the study of grammar entails both taking actual discourse as one's primary data, and explicitly relating the structure of grammar to the structure of discourse (cf., for example, Halliday, 1978, 1985; Quirk, 1960; Quirk et al., 1972). Notable proponents of this view include those outlining the relation between grammar and narrative structure (e.g., Chafe, 1980 inter alia), as well as many pursuing the study of grammatical phenomena in written texts (e.g., Firbas, 1971; Fox, 1987; Halliday, 1985; Thompson, 1985; Thompson and Matthiessen, 1989, inter alia), comparisons between written and spoken texts (such as Biber, 1988; Chafe and Danielewicz, 1987; Firbas, 1992; and the survey in Chafe and Tannen, 1987), and interactions among children and caregivers (cf. selected citations above regarding child language). Additional stimulus was imparted to this theme by the rapid development of computational linguistics (cf., for example, Grosz and Sidner, 1986). Later, inspired in part by the work of Sankoff and Brown, 1976, even more explicit claims began to be made regarding the way in which grammatical structure is deeply related to, and explainable in terms of, discourse structure (e.g., Du Bois, 1985, 1987; Givón, 1984). Hopper, 1988 captured this relationship with the phrase *emergent grammar*, showing that in fact grammar must be seen as *emerging* from discourse.

A partially overlapping research tradition with functionalist commitments has been that stream of sociolinguistics associated with the names of Labov (1972a, 1972b), D. Sankoff (1978), G. Sankoff (1980) and their associates. To be sure, the bulk of this work, under the "variationist" rubric, has tried to relate grammar to context in a *demographic* sense, focussing on communities ranging from New York to Montreal (Laberge and G. Sankoff, 1979; G. Sankoff and Vincent, 1980), from Britain (e.g., Milroy, 1980; Trudgill, 1978) to Papua New Guinea (Sankoff, 1980). On the other hand, another component of sociolinguistic work has had a more situational flavor, examining the linguistic construction of stylistic variation (Labov, 1966), ritual insult exchanges (Labov, 1972c), therapeutic discourse (Labov and Fanshel, 1977), and narratives of personal experience (Labov, 1972d). This work reflects both the interest in working with texts and a concern for how grammar is deployed to achieve particular outcomes.

While precedents existed in psycholinguistic and sociolinguistic studies and in work such as that of Crystal, 1969; Fries, 1952; and Pittenger et al., 1960, only recently has functional linguists' attention focussed on the close examination of grammatical data from social interactions *in real time*. One could say that out of the study of discourse-and-grammar, we are now seeing the development of studies of interaction-and-grammar. Intriguingly, for linguists immersed in this endeavor, real-time data have inspired a radical shift in the kind of question being asked. These data are now prompting functional linguists to ask in what ways an understanding of the profoundly interactional nature of spoken language can be brought to bear on our understanding of what we take grammar to *be*. These scholars are beginning to examine the probability that categories of grammatical description need to be made responsible to the categories appropriate to describing communicative interaction. As Hopper (1988) has suggested, (interactionally) emergent grammar may well not be grammar-as-linguists-know-it. These questions and directions guide several of the contributions in this volume, especially Ford and Thompson, Fox, Hayashi and Jasperson, and Sorjonen.

1.1.3 Conversation analysis

Although informed by input from disciplines ranging from anthropology to classics, communications to philosophy, linguistics to psychology, conversation analysis emerged within the academic context of American sociology. The place one might expect to find a concern with grammar in sociology would be sociolinguistics. It is symptomatic of the disciplinary remoteness between sociology and matters linguistic, however, both that sociolinguistics has been a relatively minor branch of American sociology, and that grammar has not been near the center of its attention.

Although there has been intermittent work in sociolinguistics for some fifty years, its roots in sociology are not deep, in the sense that it has not been as close to core concerns of the field as language has been in anthropology; it has not commanded a broad interest within the discipline; nor has it preoccupied the central figures in the field, in spite of arguable involvement by such major classical sociologists as Durkheim (in his concern with embodiments of cultural conceptions of space, time and causality, or other aspects of cultural classificatory schemes; Durkheim, 1954 [1915]; Durkheim and Mauss, 1963) and Mannheim, whose sociology-of-knowledge analysis of the elective affinity of conservative thought for the image of society as organism and the consequences of this usage (Mannheim, 1953a, 1953b, 1986) might strike some readers as anticipatory of the kind of metaphor analysis associated at present with the name of George Lakoff (e.g., Lakoff and Johnson, 1980).

For some sociological sociolinguists (e.g., Hughes, 1969, 1970; Lieberson, 1970, 1981; Fishman, 1966, 1972, 1989), a concern with language has been in substantial measure prompted by, and a focus for studying aspects of, ethnicity and nationality; but whether for this or other purposes (e.g., Cicourel, 1974a, 1974b, 1980; Grimshaw, 1981; Mehan, 1979), the language was often more or less invoked tout court, rather than having its forms registered differentially in a technically specified manner, and was explored as either dependent or independent variables (to adopt, for the moment, the kind of methodological paradigm with which the field generally conceived projects), rather than as process or practice.

But sociological sociolinguistics gets only cursory mention here, for that was not really the source of the conversation-analytic impulse in sociology. Sociological sociolinguistics was on the whole of a piece with (and *at peace* with) mainstream sociology both theoretically and methodologically (although not politically, if one locates work on gender within sociolinguistics rather than gender studies, e.g., Thorne and Henley, 1975; Thorne, Kramarae, and Henley, 1983). It sought to extend the reach of sociology to a neglected dimension of social life, and to bring into view the relevance of language as a sometimes defining component of the identity and collective life of sub-groups of a society. By contrast, CA was engendered in important respects by developments in sociology which were substantially at odds with its contemporary tenor.

The two key "forebear" figures here are Erving Goffman and Harold Garfinkel. Although they have on occasion been referred to as sociolinguists, and Goffman on occasion so characterized some of his own writing, their work was of such a different character as to make the appellation virtually misleading. Both were rather preoccupied with the fundamentals of sociality, social interaction and social order, and are now appreciated much more as theorists than as sociolinguists.

Goffman (who had studied, as it happens, with Everett Hughes at the University of Chicago) had launched a distinctive program of studies of the organization of conduct in face-to-face interaction in the early to mid-1950s in a modality which was somehow both anthropological and social psychological. By the mid-1960s this work was converging with anthropological work sufficiently that Goffman was a contributor to the special issue of the *American Anthropologist* in which the Ethnography of Communication came to substantially greater professional visibility. One key linkage was the very topic of Goffman's contribution to that publication, "the situation" (his paper was entitled, "The neglected situation," 1964).

A critical component of the stance emerging from linguistic anthropology – in dialectic with the preoccupation in "autonomous linguistics" with universal grammar and ideal speaker/hearers – was the contextual specification of linguistic "performance." The social situation – a unit which Goffman was elaborating in a series of publications (1961, 1963, 1971) around that time and subsequently – was admirably suited to serve as the most proximate context for uses of language, however the situation might otherwise be "located" by reference to other, "larger-scaled," social and cultural structures. Although one of Goffman's main points in "The neglected situation" was that the contingencies of "situations" were *not* specific to language, and were socio-interactional rather than linguistic in character, the most ready and relevant exploitation of this line of inquiry focussed on the bearing of "the situation" – or particular situations – on the behavior of language deployed in it. But although Goffman was in increasingly dense scholarly contact with both linguists (especially, in the last decade and a half of his career, William Labov and associates) and linguistic anthropologists (such as John Gumperz and Dell Hymes), he was cautious about himself taking up a scholarly stance on the details of linguistic matters. Indeed, the closest he came was in his paper "Felicity's Condition" (1983), which he withheld from publication even after it was accepted by the journal in which it was eventually published posthumously, for fear that he lacked adequate technical understanding himself, and that he had not been briefed with sufficient critical edge by his linguistic colleagues. The exigencies of language and interaction were thus brought into contiguity, but not to interpenetration.

Garfinkel's development through the 1950s and 1960s of the program of inquiry he called "ethnomethodology" (Garfinkel, 1967; Heritage, 1984) was importantly informed by considerations about language, but not about language distinctively, or in the ways then central to linguistic thinking or theorizing. A few key points will have to suffice here.

Garfinkel's undertaking – although quite distinct from phenomenology per se – took some inspiration from a number of figures writing in the phenomenological idiom (e.g., Husserl, Schütz, Gurwitsch, Merleau-Ponty, Heidegger), and shared a focal interest in the practices by which the world is apperceived by the sentient being. This included how signs and sign systems were interpreted and understood, and, consequently, how language – as one important system of signs – was interpreted and understood.

Early in his studies, Garfinkel was at pains to show the inadequacy of a device common in the sociological and anthropological theorizing then current – the notion of a common culture as a guarantor of shared understanding and/or of social order. He showed in various demonstrations that "common" or "shared" could *not* mean that sets of the same contents, same meanings, same norms or rules, were inscribed in the minds/brains of separate persons, and were independently triggered and brought to bear on the production and decoding of signs, whether linguistic or other-wise. Garfinkel discerned a profound indexicality about *all* sign systems that made the privileged treatment of proterms and demon-stratives in this regard appear shallow and impoverished. He drew attention instead to the practices of common-sense theorizing in particularized local contexts of practical action by which the mean-ing or import of actions, signs, symbols, and other vehicles of com-munication, action and appearance were convergently and contingently established.

Although there is much which differentiates CA from many cen-tral features of ethnomethodology along these lines, the local deter-mination of action and understanding has ethnomethodology as its most substantial and proximate source. However, although some would disagree with this assessment, the emphasis in ethnometho-dology – perhaps as a consequence of the phenomenological idiom in which it was conceived – was on the uptake, interpretation and understanding of apperceivable elements of the surround, and much less on their production. The resources which it made available for an exploration in depth of the reflexive relationship between situa-tional particulars and "the situated" (including situated language), were thus somewhat asymmetrical resources. The practices it brought to attention (and ethnomethodology was among the first lines of inquiry in American social science to feature the notion of "practice" as a key analytic and interpretive tool) were most likely to be *interpretive* practices, leaving under-addressed the contingen-cies by reference to which the conduct to be interpreted had come to have the features and character which it did. This has so far turned out to be an asymmetry difficult to redress within the terms of those forms of ethnomethodology itself.

Conversation analysis is by no means a straightforward product of the combination of ethnomethodology and Goffmanian interac-tion analysis, however much it has profited from the new directions of inquiry both have opened. (On the relationship between conver-sation analysis and ethnomethodology, cf., inter alia, Clayman, frth.; Clayman and Maynard, 1995; Goodwin and Heritage, 1990; Heritage, 1984; Maynard and Clayman, 1991.) Its exploita-tion of recorded episodes of quotidian interaction – both as an object of inquiry supporting its empirical bent, and as a source of disciplined control on analysis – is but one of many contrasts with these sources, but one which has issued in marked differences in its directions of inquiry and in the character and "texture" of its products.

While the disciplinary origins of the contributors to this volume, and the *intra*-disciplinary variations which inform the intellectual ferment which fuels it, are diverse, there are commonalities. More often Wittgensteinian family resemblances than Aristotelian criteria of category membership, there are common themes, similar orientations and presuppositions, common departures from much that is taken for granted in contemporary linguistics, and – of most immediate import – distinct ways for readers to examine the materials presented here to be properly appreciated. In what follows, we try to sketch at least some of this "common ground" as a point of reference by which the reader can position the several contributions which follow.

1.2 Convergences

Perhaps the first thing to be said is that, whatever their disciplinary starting point, all the papers hold themselves accountable to recorded data of naturally occurring episodes of interaction of one sort or another – from literacy lessons in Papua New Guinea to laboratory meetings of university physicists, from airport ground operations to Finnish telephone conversations, among others.

This common point of departure is by no means incidental or arbitrary. It is deeply consequential for how the work of the papers gets done, for how their analytic and theoretical contribution is to be extracted and assessed, for how the papers must be read to be properly understood, and we will turn to those matters below. But there is another sense in which this starting point is non-arbitrary, and that is historical.

Although in the most recent period the detailed examination of recordings of mundane interaction has been most closely associated with conversation analysis, it is worth recalling (cf. the chapter by Schegloff below) that over forty years ago, some linguists had already begun to move in this direction. In his *The Structure of English: An Introduction to the Construction of English Sentences* (1952) Charles Fries proposed to base his account on an "entirely different kind of evidence" (identified as telephone conversation at p. 37). Regarding this evidence he wrote (pp. 3-4),

With the recent development of mechanical devices for the easy recording of the speech of persons in all types of situations there seems to be little excuse for the use of linguistic material not taken from actual communicative practice when one attempts to deal with a living language. Even though the investigator is himself a native speaker of the language and a sophisticated and trained observer he cannot depend completely on himself as an informant and use introspection as his sole source of material. He has a much more satisfactory base from which to proceed with linguistic analysis if he has a large body of mechanically recorded language which he can hear repeated over and over, and which he can approach with more objectivity than he can that which he furnishes from himself as informant.

Within five years, of course, other "developments" were to supersede this one in shaping the course of linguistics, and deflected it away from taking as its empirical constraint how people actually talk. Even among those who remained committed to goals other than those engendered by the generativist transformation of the discipline, however, few took up Fries' charge. (Notable exceptions included Charles Hockett, as in Pittenger, Hockett, and Danehy (1960), and Norman McQuown, as in McQuown, Bateson, Birdwhistell, Brosin, and Hockett (1971); cf. the accounts in Kendon, 1990; Leeds-Hurwitz, 1987; and Winkin, 1981.) The notion that there was promise in doing so has hovered over the study of language for quite a while, waiting to be allowed to land. Though there have been some efforts along these lines in more recent years (e.g., by Labov and his associates), most interest in actual talk (which is what recorded data are of interest for) has been consigned to psycholinguistics, where it is largely confined within the impoverished environment of experiments and testing sessions (here again with exceptions, as in the work of H. Clark and his associates).

To be sure, there are important differences between Fries' vision of the function of recorded data and the ones that inform the papers in this volume. For example, Fries was little concerned with how the language he was describing was part and parcel of the interaction in which he found it, either generically or episodically. There is a sense, nonetheless, in which the enterprise this volume seeks to advance is one which had begun to come to maturity some decades ago.

Its historical resonances aside, the naturalistic commitment to address the observable, situated ways in which people actually talk, as preserved for repeated and detailed examination, is one of the distinctive features of the reorientation of inquiry which this book advocates. A common feature of these papers is their intense focus on the data of talk-in-interaction which composes the quotidien experience of the participants in whatever social worlds and settings they inhabit, frequent or construct. Extensive, careful and detailed specimens of such materials in their respective contexts are what we believe students of grammar must most importantly come to terms with, and extensive detailed accounts of this material is a primary product of such coming-to-terms.

For the reader, this means that there will be in these papers long stretches of data, accompanied in some instances by substantial ethnographic background which permits the data extract to be examined intelligently, and analytic explication of those data more detailed – and differently detailed – than will be familiar to many readers. *It is key to the serious understanding of the vision informing the volume that readers engage the data citations in detail and with care*, and familiarize themselves with the notational conventions made available in the Appendix to make this possible. To understand what the authors' texts are claiming, the reader must stand shoulder to shoulder with them, examine the data with them, understand what they are claiming about it and about the language structuring to be learned from it, and then assess those claims and their grounding in those data. No reading that detours around the data excerpts can properly support a reader's assessment of the result. On the other hand, if readers have taken the data seriously, they have at least partially engaged the project being prosecuted here, even if they find the author's take on it faulted. To find it faulted, the reader should (in principle, at least) undertake to wrest her/his understanding in engagement with the same recalcitrant reality of what is on the tape/transcript as challenged the author.

But this is not a fetishism of tape per se. The materials which furnish the authors their challenges are all records of naturally occurring scenes in the lives of their participants. They are not pretenses or role plays; they are not tests or experiments, in which the actual fabric of the interaction is treated as an invisible and property-less film through which other matters – ones of academic interest to the investigators – may be observed. Three interrelated features of such material (out of a rather larger set) may be mentioned here to alert the reader to their relevance, and to the different terms of inquiry in this arena: temporality, activity-implication, and embodiment.

1.3 Some differences the data make

1.3.1 Temporality

The passage of tape past the heads of the playback machine is both physical and symbolic representation of the temporality of talk-in-interaction – "physical" because the tape reading is also a process in real/reel time, "symbolic" because that process is iconic with that which is recorded on the tape. Temporality figures in talk-in-interaction in multiple ways, among them the sheer distribution of elements of conduct across passing time (including hiatuses in that distribution) and directionality.

The passage of time, and the distribution of that which a grammar organizes in that real time, figures in a number of the papers in this volume. Among the more telling appearances of real time in grammar is the import of "0," the null or zero value. The idea of no surface realization for some grammatical variable is familiar enough – so-called "zero anaphora" for example. But that zero does not itself have a physical representation; it denotes the absence of an occurrence made potentially relevant by reference to the theory being employed. But no "zero" can be detected in the talk.

On the other hand, in temporal terms, the distribution of elements of an utterance in real time can include moments at which no utterance element is realized – silence. "Zero" here is detectable, and potentially meaningful. Depending on its positioning or sequential context, it can convey uncertainty about what is to follow or reluctance to produce it, or even embody its inaccessibility; it can project what follows as being "dispreferred;" it can begin or collaborate in the constitution of a lapse in the interaction, etc. (In Schegloff's paper below, the possibility is accordingly entertained of such silences themselves being "elements" organized by a grammar.) But these "zeros" are discernable, palpable occurrences, time allowed – by all the parties convergently – to elapse with "nothing which counts" occurring in it, and whose actual duration thus matters, and emerges as a necessarily collaborative production. The notion of an utterance as the sole product of a speaker, or of a mind, could hardly have been entertained had real talk-in-interaction been what investigators had to come to terms with.

But what kind of time is this? The time of seconds, and tenths of seconds and milliseconds? Perhaps, but surely not that alone. Those are units of standardized time, or chronometric time, of the time captured by the underlying Greek root, "chronos." But Greek offered another conception of time, captured by the root "kairos." This is meaningful, or meaning-implicated time. One prototype of its application is in Christian theology, where historical time is composed not so much of decades and centuries which follow one another evenly, as by anticipatory time leading up to Christ and a very different trajectory thereafter. Kairotic time, then, is *directional*, and the real time in which talk-in-interaction occurs, in which grammar operates, is kairotic time; kairotic time converges with chronologic time via the relevance of the structures of the occasion, including grammar. Just as (pace Gertrude Stein) a century is not a century is not a century, so are half seconds strikingly contrastive in import depending on where they materialize (so to speak) in the developing structure of the occasion – in the midst of a grammatical construction like a phrase, after a question has come to possible completion, after an answer has, after its acknowledgement has, after the silence following such acknowledgement has already begun, after the second last participant has left the scene (Goffman, 1963).

And so a second relevance of temporality for the sort of grammar which figures in interaction is *directionality*, for, of course, directionality matters for much besides silence. Much of what is involved here is captured simply by the notion of structuring distributed in a shaped, differentiated manner over time, and this seems deeply implicated both in grammar and in interaction. It is what underlies the projectability which figures in many of the papers here (Ford and Thompson; Fox, Hayashi, and Jasperson; Lerner; Schegloff), but this is not the only way in which temporality enters into these papers (see, for example, the way in which the moment-by-moment structuring of activity figures in the papers of Goodwin; and Ochs, Gonzales, and Jacoby).

1.3.2 Activity-implication

One consequence of drawing empirical materials from the actual life of the society is that the grammar at work in deployments of the language is "at work," that is, engaged in the activities that compose the quotidien life of the society and the quotidien experience of its members, in all its actual consequentiality. Although it is true that participants in experiments and testing situations, in role plays and academically instigated demonstrations, are also participating in real activities of the society (such as cooperating in the production of "science," at the very least, as the literature on the demand characteristics of experiments showed long ago, e.g., Orne, 1959, 1962; Rosenthal, 1966), this is so only in a highly skewed and specialized sense, and not one which makes such settings illuminative of how language figures in activities not devoted to securing samples of "language use."

Once we register that language figures in the actual, practical activities of the lives of people and societies, and that how the language is configured is more than incidentally related to its involvement in those activities, it is readily apparent that, at the very least, attention must be paid to what the relationship is between activity, action and the orderly deployment of language called grammar. For many of the papers in this volume that relationship is utterly central to understanding the grammar itself, the activity itself, or how the grammar interpenetrates with its context of activity (cf. especially the papers by Goodwin; Morgan; Ochs, Gonzales, and Jacoby; Schieffelin; and Sorjonen). Accordingly, it is regularly the case in these papers that what is being said about grammar cannot be divorced – *should* not be divorced – from what is being said about the interactional dynamics implemented by that grammatical construction, or precipitated by that grammatical usage (cf. chapters by Morgan, Schieffelin).

Here again there are consequences for the reader. Because grammatical accounts are intercalated with accounts of interactional trajectory, of the texture of activity, of the shape of sequences and the emergent upshot of the interactional episode, materials enter these accounts which may appear extraneous to those readers accustomed to more traditional linguistic texts. Some such readers may find themselves asking what level of "nitty gritty details" are "sufficiently relevant to get such lengthy treatment," – "whether," as one reader put it, "they are of sufficient generality."

However, the issue is not the generality of this or that detail, but rather how the details of the context of any particular bit of talk bear on its grammatical composition and shape. There is no question but that the materials in this book go far beyond current conceptions of the bearing of "nitty gritty details" of an interactional or ethnographic sort on the understanding of grammar; that is just the point. The challenge to readers who find themselves reluctant or unable to grasp how some detail – or *order* of detail – is relevant, is to rethink what orders or senses of "relevance" might need to be entertained, which are currently not being entertained.

1.3.3 Embodiment

Just as activities and their implementing utterances are inextricably built for and with one another, so are the products of vocalization and other bodily processes. Here we encounter another inescapable feature of the materials to which the authors hold themselves responsible, and that is the embodied character of most talk-in-interaction.

"Most" because, although talk on the telephone is also embodied (speakers on the telephone continue to gesture, to shift posture, to engage in other simultaneous projects), its non-vocal elements are ordinarily unavailable to interactional co-participants. In that sense they do not enter into the interaction, and are not deployed resources and practices in it, requiring analytic attention from investigators. Those bits of body behavior which *do* get conveyed on the telephone – one can often hear the breathing, the turning away to address someone in the room, the so-called "smile voice" – testify even in this specialized medium of interaction to the relevance of the embodied character of talk-and-other-conduct-in-interaction. (Of course, as the mention of breathing in the preceding sentence should make clear, vocalization itself is an embodiment of embodiment.)

The bearing of the embodied character of talk on the relationship between grammar and interaction is key to a range of concerns of grammar not so far mentioned here. Most notable here are anaphora, deixis, and indexicality more generally. Perhaps nowhere in grammar is there a more pointed display (so to speak) of the relevance of the embedding context of surrounding discourse and coordinate bodily practice. In a number of the papers in this volume, the very deployment of some vocalized components of the conduct, and their import, is predicated on the coordinate bodily action and is complementary with it (in particular the papers of Goodwin, and of Ochs, Gonzales, and Jacoby).

1.4 On theoreticity

These few observations about some prima facie features of the data to which the authors hold themselves accountable and which constrain the terms of their examination should suggest substantial differences in the disciplined inquiry directed to them. And, indeed, very different sorts of observations, analytic methods, problems, and notions of theoreticity characterize these undertakings than are common in most contemporary linguistic work, and surely than inform inquiry into the grammaticality of abstract sentences.

It is the latter, in particular, which has come to dominate – indeed, to define – what is to be understood as "theoretical" in contemporary inquiry into language. By reference to that default template of theoreticity, the papers included here may be found to be theoretically inexplicit, or even irrelevant. Indeed, one reader of an early version of this collection characterized the manuscript as "hav[ing] a non-theoretical character," and complained that the papers do not "really go into the issue of how their observations regarding the effect of interaction on features of language could be integrated into linguistic description, or in models of linguistic structure (i.e., in grammar)." But such a view underestimates the scope and degree of reorientation of inquiry which this book is meant to advance. Many of the papers in this volume embody in the conduct of their analyses a theoretical take on the organization of language – and grammar in particular, and not a few of them discuss this explicitly. They do not, it is true, undertake to integrate their observations into "linguistic description" or "models of linguistic structure," but this is because they do not accept current ideals of linguistic description or models of linguistic structure as a basis into which matters of interaction can be, or should be, "integrated."

Rather the import of the volume is that the interactional matrix of grammar requires a different understanding of what should enter into a linguistic description and/or a different model of linguistic structure. We do not aim to integrate *into* them; we aim to transform current understandings *of* them. And this thrust underlies every contribution to the volume, though it is not shouted from each of their rooftops. Each raises the issue of the bearing of interaction on our understanding of what observable events in the world a grammar operates on and organizes, and how the elements traditionally comprehended in/by a grammar find a place in a re-theorized grammar for interaction.

Note that there are at least two matters being called under review here: the scope and range of elements, practices and organizations properly understood under the rubric of grammar, and the terms in which such components are properly to be understood. The second of these raises the issue as to whether there is a uniquely adequate or uniquely relevant descriptive apparatus for whatever is comprehended by "grammar." This issue is not wholly new; alternative terminologies, embodying alternative conceptions of what is being named and for what, call to mind reflections on the status of "noun" and "verb" (Hopper and Thompson, 1984), "subject" and "predicate," "agent" and "action" and "patient," "adjective" and "modifier," etc. But once set in an interactional matrix, still other characterizations recommend themselves, more attuned to what an element is being used to do in the *utterance* than what it does in the *sentence*. What may be a "modifier" of a "noun" under one dispensation may invite treatment as a "descriptor" for a "referrer" under another. This is part of what we mean by being cautious regarding "integration" into linguistic description, as compared to reorienting it.

1.5 A note on formalism

There is a virtually inescapable tension in inquiry between the formalist impulse in analysis and the substantivist commitment to the particularizing panoply of detail, or, as it used to be called, between the nomothetic and the idiographic (though the former is often interpreted within a positivist framework as aspiring to "generalization" rather than formalism). And that tension is not resolved in the present undertaking.

In invoking the inextricable co-implication of activity and utterance, or of speech and bodily activity, we can hardly be denying in principle the possibility of describing practices of utterance construction abstracted from, or transcending, particular activities, or divorced from temporally coordinate gesticulation. For how, in that case, could one be proposing to speak, for example, of "turn organization" across the universes of possible projects undertaken in turns? No, anti-formalism by itself is *not* what this is about.

One thing one *can* question, however, is the adoption of practices of inquiry and analysis which themselves engender a whole genre of results which are then attributed to the natural world, and not to the procedures of inquiry which produced them.

Consider, for example, Levelt's account of the role of syntax in the ordering of self-initiated repair (Levelt, 1983). This otherwise thoughtful and careful work was done on the speech of subjects in a psycholinguistic experiment, in which there was no active co-participant serving as interlocutor with whom the subject was in real-time interaction. The materials were drawn, then, from a setting in which the operation of interactional organization – and of ordinary interactional activities – had been eliminated by design. In the absence of interactional organization, syntactic organization can be claimed to play a key role. But it is quite another matter to show that syntax plays that role when the full range of naturally occurring features of talk-in-interaction is in effect. This is especially ironic in view of the transparently interactional motivation of the whole *organization of repair*, even if these particular episodes have been stripped of their interactional context. That is, the resources, practices, and organization of repair are built not only to effect changes in the ongoing talk of a speaker, but to do so in a way accessible to systematically organized parsing and understanding by the recipient(s) in the framework of an ongoing interaction.

But proceeding in this fashion is the product of largely invisible premises underlying much linguistic and psycholinguistic work at present – in which the primary organization of language is situated at the syntactic, semantic, lexical, and phonological levels, with only the surviving, unordered "details" – the "residual variation" – being referred to pragmatic or sociolinguistic or interactional "factors." But given the thoroughgoing situatedness of language's observable engagement with the world, and its role as an instrument in the effecting of real worldly projects, does it not make more sense, is it not theoretically more plausible, to suppose that interactional and pragmatic organizations play a *primary and formative role*, rather than a residual one, in the organization of conduct, including talk, and that grammar and syntax are, if not *sub*ordinate, then not more than *co*-ordinate with them, for example, by being among the available resources and practices informing the interactional and pragmatic organizations?

The critique of much in the contemporary linguistic enterprise implicit in the stance of this volume is aimed not at formalism per se, but at a formalism which has "stacked the deck" by holding itself responsible only (or largely) to data – whether intuitive or experimental – which exclude from the outset those features, forces, and possible organizations which are then claimed to be of lesser importance (or are ignored and omitted altogether) as a matter of empirical and theoretical fact.

Such formalism as is part of the present undertaking is meant to avoid these pitfalls. By working with naturally occurring materials, the authors give themselves – and their readers – a chance to be forced into a confrontation with whatever might have been at play in the production of those materials. With naturally occurring materials, that is a production which invites understanding solely (or almost solely; cf. the following paragraph) by reference to properties of the natural/cultural world we aim to understand, and not by reference to techniques of experimentation, testing, or other investigatory intrusion (including consensually validated judgments of acceptability) which claim to open windows to nature, only to fill them with distorting or filtering glass.

Not that there is no glass in *our* windows, or that it is entirely devoid of its own refractory effects. The authors are not unaware of the consequentiality of camera angles and microphone placement and sensitivity, and the sensory restriction to sight and sound at the expense of touch and smell (let alone the attenuation of such sight and sound as are made available). They are not unaware of the disparities of knowledge and experience and perceptual reach or access that discriminate the existential position of the researcher (and even more so the reader) from that of the participants in the events being examined. They are not unaware of the frailties of notational convention, of graphic reproduction, etc. which further attenuate the robustness of the data that can be made available to the reader.

But they are under no illusions that all these obstacles – and the many others which come with the complexity of this undertaking – can be somehow magically dispelled by ignoring them in efforts of theoretical imagination and intuition, or by holding them constant in artificially created experimental worlds whose methods of creation add *complications* rather than simplifications to the analytic task.

1.6 Extending the familiar, anticipating the unknown

Whatever the reservations about simply integrating into past models of linguistic structure, wholesale iconoclasm is not the point, nor is reorienting for the sake of novelty per se. We have a healthy respect for our co-workers, past and present; much of what we inherit will support continued work, either as its basis or as its point of departure. Our reconsiderations are prompted by taking seriously the nature of the material with which we believe grammar must come to terms, and its consequences for inquiry. The papers in this volume (collectively, and in some cases singly) thus proceed on two tracks – one grounded in not unfamiliar understandings of grammar, the other reaching for new conceptions which are at some variance with past work. The shape of the second of these impulses cannot be formulated a priori and is best left to the several contributions. But it may be useful to offer, in advance of the contributions of the volume's papers, a sample of some interplay between grammar in a not unfamiliar sense and one class of concerns related to interaction.

The essays in this volume (and, in some instances, *parts* of the essays) vary in the degree to which they explore the mutual bearing of interaction and grammar conceived in some more-or-less familiar form, on the one hand, and, on the other, the ways in which the intersection of interaction and grammar prompts a rethinking of what sort of thing grammar might be thought to be and how it might be configured. For the time being, both enterprises are worthy of pursuit, even though the latter must remain especially tentative, at the current stage of development. In this Introduction, we can give no more than a premonitory sketch of some lines of inquiry of each sort as a kind of orientation to the more detailed treatments in the papers themselves.

Consider three lines of informed speculation on the potential reflexive relationship between grammar in a relatively traditional sense and the organization of turns and turn-taking. One concerns German, a second Italian, the third Japanese.

Begin with the observation that the account of turn-taking which informs several of the papers in this volume (namely, Sacks, Schegloff, and Jefferson, 1974 – henceforth SSJ; for a different view of turn-taking cf. Duncan, 1972, 1974; Duncan and Fiske, 1977) was developed in the first instance while working with materials in English. A key element of the turn-taking organization on this view is the projectability of possible turn completion in advance of its actual arrival (an element focussed on in the paper by Ford and Thompson, but figuring as well in those of Lerner and Schegloff). It seems clear that one key contribution to projectability is grammatical structure. It is plausible to entertain the possibility that projectability will vary with different grammatical resources and structures, and with it the contingencies of turn-taking and accordingly of turn construction. It may matter, then, that English grammar gives rather more weight to word order than to morphological inflection, and that it is – within the word-order languages – a so-called SVO language. *How* might it matter?

Although it is common to assign so-called "given" information to early ("left") positions in grammatical units and "new" information to late ("right") ones, by the time ordinary English clauses and sentences approach their ends, their last elements have often been substantially adumbrated, and may appear well nigh fully determined. Their projectability can then be very high. Among the apparent consequences of this is their vulnerability to "anticipatory completion" by a co-participant (cf. Lerner, this volume) or to terminal overlap – the sort of simultaneous talk produced by another *in anticipation* of the projected imminent completion of current turn, rather than *to precipitate* it.

Consider, by way of contrast, the grammatical structure of German. Its richer morphological resources aside, its word order structure differs from that of English in a way consequential for the point under discussion: the verbal expression is commonly discontinuous. While an auxiliary or other finite verb form may occur in clause-second position, a non-finite verb form, often expressing the semantic heart of the verbal expression, may occur in final position. In many utterance constructions, therefore, the sense or upshot of what is being said may be substantially *under*-determined (if not indeterminate) until the verb appears in clause-final or sentence-final position. The structure of projectability would, accordingly, appear to be quite different than it is in English, and with it the placement of possible completions within the structure of the utterance. Although some sorts of anticipatory completions should remain unaffected because they are articulated around phrase or clause boundaries (the ones carried through on "compound turn-constructional units," Lerner, 1991, this volume),[5] the possibility of terminal overlaps should be attenuated because the "casualties" they would inflict on the ongoing-turn would be more consequential to its understanding, and would not yet have occurred in German, as they would have in English, thus constraining the potential overlapper's readiness with a response. When this possibility was first discussed with a native speaker of German interested in this area some years ago, his response was to remark that he had in fact been puzzled, in reading SSJ, by the discussion of terminal overlap, which he said he found relatively infrequently in his German conversational materials. We were of a mind that verb-final position was key here.

Examination of such materials, however, quickly revealed that matters were somewhat more complicated. For example, many German verbs are formed by combining a stem with a prefix, and not uncommonly, contrastive pairs of verbs are formed by combining a stem with contrasting prefixes – for example, "an/ab" (toward/away from). A preliminary examination of some interactional materials suggested that regularly only one such verb from a contrastive pair is in use at a time. When combined with the grammatical usage that has the prefix occupy the clause- or sentence-final position, that final element may be virtually fully determined well in advance of articulation, a result quite the opposite of the previously sketched line of conjecture.

The key substantive analytic work remains to be done to establish empirically the bearing of German grammar on turn-construction and turn-taking practices. German's verb-final character has often been credited (or blamed) for the multiple center-embedding that can make for very long sentences, at least in written uses of the languages. Does that feature have the same consequences in talk-in-interaction? Or are there countervailing practices of talk-in-interaction which limit that outcome? (For one account of the ramifications of such facts for the study of interaction and grammar in German, see Schuetze-Coburn, to appear.)

If German raises the possibility of keeping entry by an interlocutor at bay, Italian may raise the possibility – in a confluence of grammar, culture and turn-taking organization – of early entry by interlocutor as a common practice, with a variety of possible attendant problems. Of course it is part of a common stereotype about Italian speakers that they talk simultaneously a great deal. Italian conversation is occasionally offered as grounds for questioning whether conversation's organization is designed for one-speaker-at-a-time in the first instance. But no detailed research of which we are aware documents this supposedly massive overlapping, or specifies what in the organization of Italian conversation allows us to understand it (if it occurs) as an orderly product of Italian conversational practices.

One possibility is suggested by a passing observation in a recent paper on testing the oral proficiency of learners of Italian as a second language (Filipi, 1994). The setting is an oral examination, in which two assessors interact with the examinee. Although the author notes that the assessors "come in" while students are still talking, she also remarks about particular junctures that "the assessor is holding back thereby creating opportunities for the student to continue talking..." She goes on to note that "the assessor 'created' a tolerance for redundant talk by withholding a response until the student had a chance to complete his utterance," and that we have here "a greater tolerance for redundancy of talk," presumably greater than in natural settings involving native speakers.

Trying to think through what systematic practices of talking-in-interaction might underlie such observations (as well as other, more impressionistic claims about Italian conversation), the following conjectures present themselves:

(a) what SSJ treated as a speaker's and hearer's *right* and *obligation* – that speaker bring, and be permitted to bring, a so-called turn-constructional unit to possible completion, is here treated as an *optional practice* by recipient;

(b) "redundancy" here is being used to refer to a speaker saying at the end of a turn-constructional unit what earlier parts of it more or less projected, and this fits with the treatment (by the author, and, if she is right, by speakers and hearers of Italian) of actual completion as merely an option;

(c) if it is an option, where does it set in? At the sorts of points which Lerner (1991, this volume) analyzes as providing an opportunity place within a turn-constructional unit, where for example anticipatory completions are launched? Or does it have a broader provenance than that?

(d) if it is (only) an option for speaker to complete a TCU, how do speaker and recipient coordinate on what is going to be done? If they do not arrive at the same option, is *this* the source of claimed greater incidence of overlap in Italian, i.e., the speaker chooses to exercise the "option," while the recipient treats it as dispensable? If so, then it is not just that Italians allow an even earlier early start of next turns than Americans do; it is that they organize the talk differently. That is a difference not in the values of the variables plugged into a working organization, but a difference in the organization itself. But, if that is the claim, we need a characterization of where that differing organization comes into play.

(e) And we need to ask whether it has consequences for how Italian speakers organize the talk in a turn. If projecting aspects of the talk-to-follow makes that talk appear potentially redundant and thereby vulnerable to pre-emptive next turn starts, then does projection get differently implemented in the design of turns and turn-constructional units in Italian?

If German appears initially to offer some *protection* against "premature" starts by next speakers, the conjecture here is that Italian may *institutionalize the possibility* by changing some of the modus operandi of its turn-taking organization in ways which further exploit possibilities made available by the grammar. (On a nice fit between the phonemic inventory of a language and its practices for initiating same-turn repair, cf. Schegloff, 1987.)

Another way of conceiving the relationship between grammar, turn organization and turn-taking organization is prompted by Fox, Hayashi, and Jasperson's treatment of repair in Japanese and English (this volume). Early in their paper they suggest that "differences in repair organization (and...turntaking) arise...from larger differences in syntactic resources": Although not everyone will wish to subscribe to this apparent claim of linear causality in which syntax seems to determine practices of turn-taking and repair, taken more broadly the line suggests that there can be various ways in which syntax, turn-taking, turn organization and repair practices co-organize the sequential organization of talk-in-interaction. Then features managed by turn-taking organization or turn organization in some settings (e.g., in some languages) are managed by grammar in others, and vice versa. The suggestion in the paper by Fox, Hayashi, and Jasperson relates the often remarked-on practices of aizuchi to features of Japanese grammar. The interpolations which in English conversation ordinarily come at the boundaries of larger chunks of extended turns understood to be not yet complete (Schegloff, 1982) are produced – and solicited – for much smaller chunks of utterance in Japanese, in part to offset otherwise potentially problematic indeterminacies built into Japanese grammar, indeterminacies which are problematic precisely because of the exigencies of recipient parsing in real time.

We have then several variations on a theme that sets grammar (in a rather traditional usage of the term) in a complementary relationship to other organizations of practices in talk-in-interaction, and prompts a search for the details of that complementarity, the trade-offs between various orders and types of organization, and the differential products of such trade-offs – from the lengths of German sentences to the multi-vocality of Italian conversation to the density of understanding and co-construction (aizuchi) tokens in Japanese.

1.7 The papers

As is not uncommon in thematically motivated volumes such as this, the several chapters relate to the theme in three main ways. Some take the volume's theme as *their* theme, more or less (Schegloff; Ford and Thompson; Lerner). Some address themselves explicitly to the theme intermittently, while otherwise being organized around a more specific project, with more or less transparent bearing on the theme (Fox, Hayashi, and Jasperson; Goodwin; Ochs, Gonzales, and Jacoby). Some have their own project and pursue it, the project in principle having a perspicuous bearing on, or in some fashion embodying in its very constitution, the underlying theme of the volume (Morgan; Schieffelin; Sorjonen). Each of these types invites a somewhat different introductory setting.

But juxtaposing each paper to the title of the volume is only one way of understanding their separate and intersecting contributions. Laced through this introduction have been various other allusions to the way in which various of the papers fit together. In the end, it is the mosaic which each reader fashions from the resources of their own analytic resources and taste which will be most useful. So it is not to pre-empt such individualized integrations that we offer here a preliminary orienting overview of the contributions to this volume, but to offer provisional guidance until the readers come to a view of their own.

The contributors to this volume explore the notion that grammar and social interaction organize one another. Within this overarching endeavor, each of the chapters can be read for promoting (in varying ways and emphases) three arguments: (1) grammar organizes social interaction; (2) social interaction organizes grammar; and (3) grammar is a mode of interaction. These arguments vary in the conceptualization of grammar and its vulnerability to the exigencies, potentialities, and architecture of social interaction.

1.7.1 Grammar organizes social interaction

The first argument – *that grammar organizes social interaction* – preserves a relatively traditional notion of grammar. Grammars are abstract mental structures that organize linguistic elements within utterances that in turn comprise social interaction. All of the contributors to this volume treat grammar as a resource par excellence for doing social interactional work. All examine the interactional potency of particular linguistic structures that form part of a speaker's grammatical knowledge.

Several contributions examine ways in which grammar organizes "turn constructional units," i.e. components that compose a turn (Sacks, Schegloff, and Jefferson, 1974). Emanuel Schegloff proposes a key role of grammar to be precisely this – to provide an orderliness to the shape of interactional turns and to facilitate the calibration of possible turn endings and turn-taking. Cecilia Ford and Sandra Thompson find that syntax alone is not an adequate guide to projecting when a speaker is completing a turn, but rather that interlocutors rely as well upon intonational and pragmatic structures in making such projections. Gene Lerner's chapter observes that interlocutors who anticipate the remainder of a turn before a current speaker has completed his utterance characteristically do so at grammatical boundaries. Clause boundaries, for example, are routinely a resource for interlocutors to take a turn that anticipatorily completes an utterance-in-progress.

In addition to turn construction and speaker transition, grammar influences the management of "repair" in conversation (Schegloff, Jefferson, and Sacks, 1977; Schegloff, 1987). As noted earlier, while repair is a universal means for handling sources of trouble in the production, hearing, and understanding of utterances, grammars of languages organize this conversational practice somewhat differently. In this volume, Barbara Fox, Makoto Hayashi, and Robert Jasperson document how English and Japanese provide different grammatical resources for accomplishing same turn self-repair. Among other influences, the grammars of these two languages differentially impact which linguistic constituents are repaired, which are recruited as place holders in word searches, and which are recycled as part of same turn self repair.

Grammatical constructions are also resources that constitute particular types of activities. For example, Elinor Ochs, Patrick Gonzales, and Sally Jacoby analyze how working physicists recurrently use "indeterminate constructions" in their collaborative interpretive activity. These constructions, accompanied by gestures, allow physicists to take interpretive journeys in multiple, constructed worlds and iconically experience the physical dynamics they are struggling to understand. At these moments, the physicists use grammar to interact not only with one another but also, facilitated by graphic displays, with inanimate physical constructs. Marcyliena Morgan examines how members of the African American community routinely draw upon members' awareness of dialect differences to accomplish conversational activities. Using lexical and grammatical features that distinguish African American English and standard American English, these interlocutors engage in particular types of assessment activity such as "reading" (as in "I READ her!") and "conversational signifying." This study captures the important notion that grammatical *oppositions* rather than the grammatical features of a particular variety can be the relevant resource for constituting social activity.

Long a theme in conversation analytic studies, grammatical forms organize not only current but also past and future social behavior. In this volume, the contributions by Schegloff; Ford and Thompson; and Lerner discuss the use of grammar in projecting and/or anticipating possible turn endings. The grammatical orchestration of future activity is also richly analyzed in Charles Goodwin's study of collaborative sense-making among airport personnel. Goodwin illuminates how co-workers use "prospective indexicals" to direct interlocutors' cognitive and visual attention to a phenomenon and to signal that (they should anticipate that) the meaning of this phenomenon will become clearer in subsequent interaction. As such, prospective indexicals are resources for inviting participation in an upcoming focal activity and for outlining how participants should perceive (i.e. see) some phenomenon.

Grammatical forms can also be used to constitute past social realities, as emphasized in the studies of Marja-Leena Sorjonen and Bambi Schieffelin. Sorjonen examines how Finnish conversational partners use the particles *niin* and *joo* to frame past (and future) conversational actions. The analysis focuses on one particular conversational environment for these particles, namely in response to a turn that repeats some portion of the preceding turn. Sorjonen suggests that interlocutors use *niin* to retrospectively frame the repeat as a request for confirmation, in which case *niin* is used to constitute the current turn construction unit as a confirmation. *Joo*, on the other hand, is used to frame the repeat as an acknowledgment (a "receipt" of information), in which case *joo* constitutes the current turn construction unit as a re-confirmation or verification. Sorjonen's point is that while the repeats may be intended as confirmations or receipts by their producers, these are possible meanings. When interlocutors respond with *niin* and *joo*, they imbue the repeats with heard meanings. Positioned strategically at the beginnings of turns, *niin* and *joo* are resources for complex renderings of past, current, and future utterances.

Grammatical forms can reach beyond a past conversational turn to reconfigure how members of a community acted and thought in the historical past. Schieffelin documents the historical emergence and interactional deployment of a new evidential particle among Kaluli speakers (Papua New Guinea). Marking information as new, true, and only known from the written word, this particle appears in instructional materials and talk of missionary personnel in the context of teaching Kaluli people about past and current views of religion and health. Instructors and the institutions they represent use this particle along with pictures and photographs to establish factivity of mission beliefs. Schieffelin's study of the import of grammar and visual media to missionizing interactions parallels Goodwin's study of the import of grammar and visual media to establishing factivity and socializing a world view among airport personnel. Both situations involve participants in the activity of "virtual witnessing," wherein linguistic and visual representations simulate for readers/audiences the experience of actually witnessing an event, thereby authenticating information as true (Shapin and Schaffer, 1985).

1.7.2 *Social interaction organizes grammar*

The second theme of this volume – that *social interaction organizes grammar* – positions grammar as an outcome of lived sociality. In this interpretation, grammar stands in a relatively intimate relation to social interaction. It is designed for interactional ends and as such must reckon with the architecture and dynamics of turns, sequences, activities, participant frameworks, stances, trouble, expectations, contingencies, and other relevant interactional actualities. Grammar is vulnerable to social interaction in that social interaction is the universally commonplace medium for language acquisition, language maintenance, and language change. As Schegloff notes, "It should hardly surprise us if some of the most fundamental features of natural language are shaped in accordance with their home environment in copresent interaction, as adaptations to it, or as part of its very warp and weft."

Schegloff's chapter charts a paradigmatic vision of "syntax-for-conversation," including how grammar is shaped by the position of a turn construction unit within a turn and the position of a turn within a sequence. Grammatical forms such as prospective indexicals in English (Goodwin, this volume) and particles in Finnish (Sorjonen, this volume) may be positioned not only with respect to sentence structure but with respect to turn and sequence structure. Prospective indexicals, for example, are designed to project upcoming turn construction units. And it may be no accident that particles in many languages come at or near the start or possible end of a turn, as many of these particles are responsive to preceding and/or upcoming turn construction units or turns at talk. Indeed Fox, Hayashi, and Jasperson propose that sentence-final particles in Japanese evolved in part to mark possible turn completions. Similarly, forms such as tag questions in English may be designed as turn extensions, units which recreate a possible interactional place for speaker transition (Sacks, Schegloff, and Jefferson, 1974; Schegloff, this volume; Ford and Thompson, this volume).

In addition to the impact of turn organization, special social activities may give rise to linguistic innovations, both novel forms and novel amalgams of existing forms. In Papua New Guinea, missionary practices such as the creation of literacy materials produced new varieties of Kaluli language – amalgams of different dialects, syntactic simplifications, and non-canonical forms. As discussed above, rapid social change engendered by missionization also involved innovation within the evidential system. This form both arises from social change and facilitates that change in marking past practices as unenlightened and present-day, mission-generated practices as what we now know as truth. In a radically different locus, the practices of physicists give rise to novel constructions that amalgamate a personal pronominal subject (e.g. "I"), which generally presupposes animacy and a predicate that presupposes inanimacy (e.g. "am breaking up into domains.") These constructions emerge as part of routine interpretive activity involving physicists moving through graphs and symbolically experiencing physical processes. Fox, Hayashi, and Jasperson also speak of grammatical amalgams that arise from conversational repair. Repair across languages allows interlocutors to "splice together" otherwise ungrammatical syntactic units. Such amalgams provide opportunities for interlocutors to convey a complex concatenation of information before a possible point of speaker transition.

1.7.3   *Grammar is a mode of social interaction*

The third thematic focus addressed in this volume – that *grammar is a mode of social interaction* – more radically realigns how we think about grammar. Closely associated with conversation analytic research (e.g., Goodwin, 1981; Sacks, 1992; Sacks, Schegloff, and Jefferson, 1974; Schegloff, 1979), this vision also has anthropological and linguistic roots that go back to Sapir's notion that language interpenetrates experience. Grammar is not only a resource for interaction and not only an outcome of interaction, it is part of the essence of interaction itself. Or, to put it another way, grammar is inherently interactional.

In this perspective, grammar is imbued with subjectivity and sociability: grammar is viewed as lived behavior, whose form and meaning unfold in experienced interactional and historical time. For example, Kaluli evidential particles (Schieffelin, this volume) embody modes of experiencing the world. These and other linguistic forms compose the fabric of missionizing interactions that attempt to socialize Kaluli into new truths. A Kaluli grammar of these evidentials comprehends their existential condition. Similarly the Finnish particles *niin* and *joo* (Sorjonen, this volume) are quintessential interactional entities. They constitute interactional configurations that link current to just past and just next conversational moves. Tacit understandings of Finnish particles incorporate just this sort of situatedness. Likewise in the world of working scientists, indeterminate, semantically disjunctive constructions (Ochs, Gonzales, and Jacoby, this volume) form the interactional crucible for linking scientists and the physical constructs they are examining. Part of a physicist's grammar of these constructions is this experiential potentiality. Indeed the syntactic conjoining of a personal pronominal subject with an inanimate-presupposing predicate is itself an iconic representation of the experiential conjoining of physicists with the objects of their study. Not only specific constructions, but also codes can be visualized as modes of interaction. For example, code-switching between African American English and American English dialects (Morgan, this volume) itself is an interactional move that may count as a bid to formulate identities of participants and activities such as signifying, reading, or other kinds of assessment. For members of the African American community, a grammar of these varieties encompasses such contrapuntal, interactional work.

An important dimension of linguistic structures is their moment-by-moment, evolving interactional production. Sacks (1974); Sacks, Schegloff, and Jefferson (1974); Schegloff, Jefferson, and Sacks (1977); Sacks and Schegloff (1979); and Goodwin (1981) stand out as classic demonstrations that the linguistic shaping of an utterance is intertwined with changing relationships among participants over interactional time. As an utterance proceeds, its lexical and grammatical structuring may open up, narrow down, or otherwise transform the roles of different participants to the interaction. In this volume, several studies articulate how the unfolding structuring of a single utterance shifts the statuses of participants as speakers and recipients. Lerner speaks of linguistic structures as temporally unfolding interactional opportunities for reorganizing (indeed for pre-empting) who takes a conversational turn. Schegloff invites us to re-perspectivize approaching a (possible) turn boundary not as an interim between events but rather as a central interactional event that has shape and duration, and implications for subsequent talk and speaker transition. Goodwin illuminates how in the course of a current utterance, a prospective indexical "unleashe[s}. . interactive processes" by drawing co-workers together as co-participants in extended problem-solving.

That linguistic forms manifest a progression of interactional arrangements renders them interactional structures *par excellence*. As interactional structures, linguistic forms can be understood as collaborative achievements of different interlocutors (Duranti and Brenneis, 1986; Goodwin, 1981, 1987, this volume; Keenan and Schieffelin, 1976; Lerner, 1987, 1991, this volume; Ochs,

Schieffelin, and Platt, 1979; Schegloff, Jefferson, and Sacks, 1977; Schegloff, 1979; Schegloff, this volume; Scollon, 1976). In some cases, as in anticipatory completions and certain types of repair, different participants produce linguistic forms that comprise a linguistic construction. In other cases, the joint activity generating a construction is discernible only by attending to eye gaze, body orientation, or non-occurrence of verbal uptake at some relevant moment in the course of producing a construction. Interlocutors who do not display recipientship through eye gaze, for example, may lead speakers to redesign their utterances for other recipients (Goodwin, 1981). And, as noted earlier, tag questions may be inspired by the non-occurrence of speaker transition at a point of possible turn completion (Sacks, Schegloff, and Jefferson, 1977; Ford and Thompson, this volume; Schegloff, this volume). In all of these cases, the resulting constructions are co-authored by multiple participants. The meaning of any single grammatical construction is interactionally contingent, built over interactional time in accordance with interactional actualities. Meaning lies not with the speaker nor the addressee nor the utterance alone as many philosophical arguments have considered, but rather with the interactional past, current, and projected next moment. The meaning of an entire utterance is a complex, not well understood, algorithm of these emergent, non-linear, sense-making interactions.

The present volume offers an intellectual springboard for a transformative synthesis – an *aufhebung* – from a separately conceived interactional grammar and grammar of interaction to an as-yet-only-dimly-perceivable conjunction. In it, grammatical structures are revisualized as interactional structures that have their own interactional morphology and syntax within and across turns (see especially chapters by Schegloff, Goodwin, and Lerner). Strips of talk make sense within a more encompassing orderliness of historically situated, social encounters. Of central import are turn construction units, turns, sequences, collaborative completions, participant frameworks, endogenous activities, the built environment, gestures, visual representations and other interactional resources.

Applying the lens of interaction, the contributors to this volume see grammar as a contingent and concerted accomplishment, symbiotic with the setting of social interaction which is its home base. This vision in turn inspires an analytic lexicon of possibility, preemption, non-occurrence, reformulation, and achievement. What it will at some future retrospect turn out to have inspired is itself contingent on what others – what you, the readers – make of the efforts offered here.

Notes

1   This introduction has benefited from the comments and help of Chuck Goodwin, John Heritage, Adam Kendon and Barrie Thorne.
2   Even then, linguistic anthropologists – or anthropological linguists – continued to be housed in Departments of Anthropology, where they were largely answerable to the central thematics of the larger discipline, whether regarding culture, evolution, or other such general disciplinary preoccupations.
3   The proximate sources of this sampling were two mini-conferences on Grammar and Interaction, held at UCLA under the auspices of the Center for Language, Interaction and Culture in the Spring terms of 1992 and 1993, organized by Elinor Ochs with the support of the Division of Humanities of the College of Letters and Sciences. We are indebted to then-Dean Herbert Morris for his support. Earlier versions of the papers by Ford and Thompson; Goodwin; Morgan; Ochs, Gonzales and Jacoby; and Schegloff were presented at one or the other of those conferences, as were parts of the present introduction. Several other of the contributors to this volume (Fox, Sorjonen) participated in the conferences, but not through their contributions to this volume. Other contributors to the volume (Lerner, Schieffelin) were present in spirit, if not in body. Others who attended the conferences have contributed to this volume through their participation in the discussions and their comments on the papers, and papers by several of them could not be incorporated in this volume because of constraints on either their time or our space. The point is that this volume indexes a larger community of workers and a more extensive body of work than are overtly presented here in print.
4   To some extent the importance of grammar-in-context had been addressed in those corpus-based linguistic descriptions, from the time of Boas and Sapir, which were based on texts, typically myths and legends.
5   For a suggestion that in a strongly verb-final language, Japanese, anticipatory completions – of the type discussed in Lerner, 1991; Ono and Thompson, forthcoming; and Sacks, 1992 – appear to occur only under very restricted interactional circumstances, see Ono and Yoshida, forthcoming. For a different view, see Lerner and Takagi, forthcoming.

References

Austin, P. (ed.) (1988). *Complex Sentence Constructions in Australian Languages*. Amsterdam: John Benjamins.

Bates, E., Bretherton, I., and Snyder, L. (1988). *From First Words to Grammar: Individual Differences and Dissociable Mechanisms*. New York: Cambridge University Press.

Biber, D. (1988). *Variation Across Speech and Writing*. Cambridge: Cambridge University Press.

Bloom, L. (1973). *One Word at a Time*. The Hague: Mouton.

Boas, F. (1911). Introduction. In F. Boas (ed.) *Handbook of American Indian Languages*, Washington, DC: Smithsonian Institution, Bureau of American Ethnology.

Bourdieu, P. (1977). *Outline of a Theory of Practice* (translated by Richard Nice). Cambridge: Cambridge University Press.

(1990). *The Logic of Practice*. Stanford: Stanford University Press.

Bruner, J. (1983). *Child's Talk: Learning to Use Language*. New York: W.W. Norton.

Bybee, J. (1985). *Morphology: A Study of the Relation Between Meaning and Form*. Amsterdam: John Benjamins.

Bybee, J., Perkins, R., and Pagliuca, W. (1994). *The Evolution of Grammar*. Chicago: University of Chicago Press.

Chafe, W. (ed.) (1980). *The Pear Stories*. Norwood, NJ: Ablex.

Chafe, W. and Danielewicz, J. (1987). Properties of spoken and written language. In R. Horowitz and S. J. Samuels (eds.) *Comprehending Oral and Written Language*. pp. 83–113. New York: Academic Press.

Chafe, W. and Tannen, D. (1987). The relation between written and spoken language. In B. J. Siegel, A. R. Beals and S. A. Tyler (eds.) *Annual Review of Anthropology*, pp. 383–407. Palo Alto: Annual Reviews, Inc.

Chomsky, N. (1957). *Syntactic Structures*. The Hague: Mouton.

(1959). Review of *Verbal Behavior* by B. F. Skinner. *Language* 35: 26–58.

Cicourel, A. (1974). *Cognitive Sociology*. New York: Free Press.

(1980). Three models of discourse analysis: the role of social structure. *Discourse Processes* 3: 101–32.

(1992). The interpenetration of communicative contexts: examples from medical encounters. In A. Duranti and C. Goodwin (eds.) *Rethinking Context: Language as an Interactive Phenomenon*, pp. 291–310. Cambridge: Cambridge University Press.

Cicourel, A. et al. (1974a). *Language Use and School Performance*. New York: Academic Press.

Clancy, P. (1986). The acquisition of communicative style in Japanese. In B. Schieffelin and E. Ochs (eds.) *Language Socialization Across Cultures*, pp. 213–50. Cambridge: Cambridge University Press.

Clark, E. V. (1978). Awareness of language: some evidence from what children say and do. In A. Sinclair, R. Jarvella, and W. J. M. Levelt (eds.) *The Child's Conception of Language*, pp. 17–43. New York: Springer.

Clark, H. H. and Wilkes-Gibbes, D. (1986). Referring as a collaborative process. *Cognition* 22: 1-39.

Clark, H. H. and Schaefer, E. F. (1987). Concealing one's meaning from overhearers. *Journal of Memory and Language* 26: 209–55.

Clark, H. H. and Gerrig, R. J. (1990). Quotations as demonstrations. *Language* 66(4): 764–805.

Clark, H. H. and Brennan, S. E. (1991). Grounding in communication. In L. B. Resnick, J. Levine, and S. Teasley (eds.) *Perspectives on Socially Shared Cognition*, pp. 127–49. Washington, DC: American Psychological Association.

Clayman, S. (1995). The dialectic of ethnomethodology. *Semiotica* 107 (1/2): 105–123.

Clayman, S. and Maynard, D. (1995). Ethnomethodology and conversation analysis. In P. Ten Have and G. Psathas (eds.) *Situated Order: Studies in the Social Organization of Talk and Embodied Activities*. pp. 1–30. Washington, DC: University Press of America.

Cole, P. and Sadock, J. (eds.) (1977). *Grammatical Relations*. New York: Academic Press.

Comrie, B. (1976). *Aspect*. Cambridge: Cambridge University Press.

    (1978). Ergativity. In W. Lehmann (ed.) *Syntactic Typology*, pp. 329–94. Austin: University of Texas Press.

    (1985). *Tense*. Cambridge: Cambridge University Press.

    (1989). *Language Universals and Linguistic Typology*. Chicago: University of Chicago Press.

Comrie, B. and Polinsky, M. (eds.) (1993). *Causatives and Transitivity*. Amsterdam: John Benjamins.

Conklin, H. (1955). Hanunoo color categories. *Southwestern Jounal of Anthropology* 11: 339–44.

Craig, C. (ed.) (1986). *Noun Classes and Categorization*. Amsterdam: John Benjamins.

Croft, W. (1991). *Syntactic Categories and Grammatical Relations*. Chicago: University of Chicago Press.

Crystal, D. (1969). *Prosodic Systems and Intonation in English*. Cambridge: Cambridge University Press.

Dik, S. (1981). *Functional Grammar*. Dordrecht: Foris Publications.

    (ed.) (1983). *Advances in Functional Grammar*. Dordrecht: Foris Publications.

Dixon, R. M. W. (1979). Ergativity. *Language* 55: 59-138.

Du Bois, J. (1985). Competing motivations. In J. Haiman (ed.) *Iconicity in Syntax*, pp. 343–65. Amsterdam: John Benjamins.

    (1987). The discourse basis of ergativity. *Language* 63: 805–55.

Duncan, S., Jr. (1972). Some signals and rules for taking speaking turns in conversations. *Journal of Personality and Social Psychology* 23: 283–92.

(1974). On the structure of speaker-auditor interaction during speaking turns. *Language in Society* 2: 161–80.

Duncan, S., Jr. and Fiske, D. W. (1977). *Face-to-Face Interaction: Research, Methods, and Theory.* Hillsdale, NJ: Lawrence Erlbaum Associates.

Duranti, A. and Brenneis, D. (eds.) (1986). The audience as co-author, special issue of *Text* (6-3): 239–347.

Duranti, A. and Goodwin, C. (eds.) (1992). *Rethinking Context: Language as an Interactive Phenomenon.* Cambridge: Cambridge University Press.

Durkheim, E. (1938 [1895]). *The Rules of the Sociological Method.* Glencoe, IL: Free Press.

(1951). *Suicide, A Study in Sociology.* Glencoe, IL: Free Press.

(1954 [1915]). *The Elementary Forms of the Religious Life.* Glencoe, IL: Free Press.

Durkheim, E. and Mauss, M. (1963). *Primitive Classification.* Chicago: University of Chicago Press.

Ervin-Tripp, S. (1979). Children's verbal turn-taking. In E. Ochs and B. B. Schieffelin (eds.) *Developmental Pragmatics*, pp. 391–414. New York: Academic Press.

Filipi, A. (1994). Interaction or interrogation? A study of talk occurring in a sample of the 1992 VCE Italian Oral Common Assessment Task (CAT 2). Paper delivered at the Annual Meetings of the Applied Linguistics Association of Australia, Melbourne, Australia, July, 1994.

Fillmore, C. J. (1988). The mechanisms of "construction grammar." *Berkeley Linguistics Society* 14: 35–55.

(1989). Grammatical construction theory and the familiar dichotomies. In R. Dietrich and C. F. Graumann (eds.) *Language Processing in Social Context*, pp. 17-38. Amsterdam: Elsevier.

Fillmore, C. J., Kay, P., and O'Connor, M. C. (1988). Regularity and idiomaticity in grammatical constructions. *Language* 64: 501–38.

Firbas, J. (1971). On the concept of communicative dynamism in the theory of functional sentence perspective. *Sbornik Praci Filosoficke Fakulty Brnenske University* A 19: 135–44.

(1992). *Functional Sentence Perspective in Written and Spoken Communication.* Cambridge: Cambridge University Press.

Fishman, J. A. (1966). *Language Loyalty in the United States: The Maintenance and Perpetuation of Non-English Mother Tongues by American Ethnic and Religious Groups.* The Hague: Mouton.

(1972). *Readings in the Sociology of Language.* The Hague: Mouton.

(1989). *Language and Ethnicity in Minority Sociolinguistic Perspective.* Clevedon: Multilingual Matters.

Foley, W. and Van Valin, R. (1984). *Functional Syntax and Universal Grammar*. Cambridge: Cambridge University Press.

Fox, B. (1987). *Discourse Structure and Anaphora*. Cambridge: Cambridge University Press.

Frake, C. O. (1964). How to ask for a drink in Subanun. *American Anthropologist* 66, no.6, part 2: 127–32.

Fries, C. C. (1952). *The Structure of English: An Introduction to the Construction of English Sentences*. New York: Harcourt, Brace and World.

Garfinkel, H. (1967). *Studies in Ethnomethodology*. Englewood Cliffs, NJ: Prentice-Hall.

Garvey, C. (1984). *Children's Talk*. Cambridge, MA: Harvard University Press.

Givón, T. (1984). *Syntax I*. Amsterdam: John Benjamins.

(1990). *Syntax II*. Amsterdam: John Benjamins.

Goffman, E. (1961). *Encounters: Two Studies in the Sociology of Interaction*. Indianapolis: Bobbs-Merrill.

(1963). *Behavior in Public Places: Notes on the Social Organization of Gathering*. New York: Free Press.

(1964). The neglected situation. In the ethnography of communication. John J. Gumperz and Dell Hymes (eds.) *American Anthropologist* 66, 6, pt. II: 133–36.

(1967). *Interaction Ritual: Essays in Face to Face Behavior*. Garden City, New York: Doubleday.

(1971). *Relations in Public: Microstudies of the Public Order*. New York: Harper and Row.

(1974). *Frame Analysis: An Essay on the Organization of Experience*. New York: Harper and Row.

(1983). Felicity's condition. *American Journal of Sociology* 89: 1–53.

Goodenough, W. H. (1956). Componential analysis and the study of meaning. *Language* 32: 195–216.

Goodwin, C. (1981). *Conversational Organization: Interaction Between Speakers and Hearers*. New York: Academic Press.

(1987). Forgetfulness as an interactive resource. *Social Psychology Quarterly* 50, No. 2: 115–30.

(1994). Professional vision. *American Anthropologist* 96,3: 606-33.

Goodwin, C. and Heritage, J. (1990). Conversation analysis. *Annual Reviews of Anthropology* 19: 283–307.

Goodwin, M. H. (1990). *He-Said-She-Said: Talk as Social Organization among Black Children*. Bloomington: Indiana University Press.

Greenberg, J. (ed.) (1978). *Universals of Human Language* (4 volumes). Stanford: Stanford University Press.

Greenfield, P. M., Reilley, J., Leaper, C., and Baker, N. (1985). The structural and functional status of single-word utterances and their relationship to early multi-word speech. In M. Barrett (ed.) *Children's Single-Word Speech*, pp. 233–67. Chichester: John Wiley.

Grimshaw, A. D. (1981). *Language as Social Resource*. Stanford: Stanford University Press.

Grosz, B. and Sidner, C. (1986). Attention, intentions and the structure of discourse. *Computational Linguistics* 12: 175–204.

Gumperz, J. J. (1982). *Discourse Strategies*. Cambridge: Cambridge University Press.

Gumperz, J. J. and Hymes, D. (eds.) (1964). The ethnography of communication. Special issue of the *American Anthropologist* 66, 6, part II.

Haiman, J. and Thompson, S. A. (1988). *Clause Combining in Grammar and Discourse*. Amsterdam: John Benjamins.

Halliday, M. A. K. (1975). *Learning How to Mean*. London: Edward Arnold.

  (1978). *Language as Social Semiotic: The Social Interpretation of Language and Meaning*. London: Edward Arnold.

  (1985). *Introduction to Functional Grammar*. London: Edward Arnold.

Hanks, W. F. (1990). *Referential Practice: Language and Lived Space Among the Maya*. Chicago: University of Chicago Press.

Heath, S. B. (1983). *Ways with Words: Language, Life and Work in Communities and Classrooms*. Cambridge: Cambridge University Press.

Heine, B., Claudi, U., and Hünnemeyer, F. (1991). *Grammaticalization: A Conceptual Framework*. Chicago: University of Chicago Press.

Heritage, J. (1984). *Garfinkel and Ethnomethodology*. Cambridge: Polity Press.

Hill, J. and Irvine, J. T. (eds.) (1992). *Responsibility and Evidence in Oral Discourse*. Cambridge: Cambridge University Press.

Hoijer, H. (1951). Cultural implications of some Navaho linguistic categories. *Language* 27: 111–20.

Hopper, P. (ed.) (1982). *Tense-Aspect Between Semantics and Pragmatics*. Amsterdam: John Benjamins.

  (1988). Emergent grammar and the a priori grammar constraint. In D. Tannen (ed.) *Linguistics in Context: Connecting Observation and Understanding*. Norwood, NJ: Ablex.

Hopper, P. and Thompson, S. A. (1980). Transitivity in grammar and discourse. *Language* 56: 251–99.

  (1984). The discourse basis for lexical categories in universal grammar. *Language* 60,4: 703–51.

Hopper, P. and Traugott, E. (1993). *Grammaticalization*. Cambridge: Cambridge University Press.

Hughes, E. C. (1969). Comment on Lieberson's statement about measurement of bilingualism. In L. G. Kelly (ed.) *Description and Measurement of Bilingualism*, p. 422. Toronto: University of Toronto Press.

  (1970). The linguistic division of labor in industrial and urban societies. *Proceedings of the Georgetown University 21st Round Table of Linguistics*, Washington, DC, Georgetown University School of Languages and Linguistics.

Hymes, D. H. (1962). The ethnography of speaking. In T. Gladwin and W. C. Sturtevant (eds.) *Anthropology and Human Behavior.* Washington, DC: Anthropological Society of Washington, pp. 13–53. Reprinted in B. Blount (ed.), *Language, Culture and Society: A Book of Readings*, pp. 189–223. Cambridge, Mass: Winthrop, 1974.

Jakobson, R. (1960). Closing statement: linguistics and poetics. In T. A. Sebeok (ed.) *Style in Language*, pp. 398–429. Cambridge, MA: MIT Press.

Jakobson, R. and Halle, M. (1956). *Fundamentals of Language.* The Hague: Mouton.

Keenan, E. O. (1973). A sliding sense of obligatoriness: the poly-structure of Malagasy. *Language in Society* 2: 225–43.

  (1974). Norm-makers, norm-breakers: uses of speech by men and women in a Malagasy community. In R. Bauman and J. Sherzer (eds.) *Explorations in the Ethnography of Speaking*, pp. 125–43. Cambridge: Cambridge University Press.

Kendon, A. (1990). Some context for context analysis: a view of the origins of structural studies of face-to-face interaction. In A. Kendon, *Conducting Interaction: Patterns of behavior in focussed encounters*, pp. 15–49. Cambridge: Cambridge University Press.

Kulick, D. (1992). *Language Shift and Cultural Reproduction: Socialization, Self, and Syncretism in a Papua New Guinean Village.* Cambridge: Cambridge University Press.

Laberge, S. and Sankoff, G. (1979). Anything "you" can do. In T. Givón (ed.) *Syntax and Semantic, Volume 11, Discourse and Syntax*, pp. 419–40. New York: Academic Press.

Labov, W. (1966). *The Social Stratification of English in New York City.* Arlington: Center for Applied Linguistics.

  (1972a). *Language in the Inner City: Studies in the Black English Vernacular.* Philadelphia: University of Pennsylvania Press.

  (1972b). *Sociolinguistic Patterns.* Philadelphia: University of Pennsylvania Press.

  (1972c). Rules for ritual insults. In Labov, *Language in the Inner City*, pp. 297–353.

  (1972d). The transformation of experience in narrative syntax. In Labov, *Language in the Inner City*, pp. 354–96.

Labov, W. and Fanshel, D. (1977). *Therapeutic Discourse: Psychotherapy as Conversation.* New York: Academic Press.

Lakoff, G. (1987). *Women, Fire and Dangerous Things.* Chicago: University of Chicago Press.

Lakoff, G. and Johnson, M. (1980). *Metaphors We Live By.* Chicago: University of Chicago Press.

Langacker, R. W. (1987). *Foundations of Cognitive Grammar, Volume 1.* Stanford: Stanford University Press.

  (1991). *Foundations of Cognitive Grammar, Volume 2.* Stanford: Stanford University Press.

Leeds-Hurwitz, W. (1987). The social history of "A natural history of an interview": a multidisciplinary investigation of social communication." *Research in Language and Social Interaction*, 20: 1–51

Leont'ev, A. N. (1981). *Problems of the Development of the Mind.* Moscow: Progress Publishers.

Lerner, G. H. (1987). Collaborative turn sequences: sentence construction and social action. Unpublished Ph.D. dissertation, Psychology, University of California at Irvine.

 (1991). On the syntax of sentences-in-progress. *Language in Society* 20: 441–58.

Lerner, G.H. and Takagi, T. (frth). On the place of linguistic resources in the organization of talk-in-interaction. *Journal of Pragmatics.*

Li, C. (ed.) (1976). *Subject and Topic.* New York: Academic Press.

Lieberson, S. (1970). *Language and Ethnic Relations in Canada.* New York: John Wiley.

 (1981). *Language Diversity and Language Contact.* Stanford: Stanford University Press.

MacWhinney, B. (ed.) (1987). *Mechanisms of Language Acquisition.* Hillsdale, NJ: Lawrence Erlbaum Associates.

Mannheim, K. (1953a) Conservative thought. In P. Kecskemeti (ed.) *Essays on Sociology and Social Psychology*, pp. 74–164. London: Routledge and Kegan Paul.

 (1953b). The history of the concept of the state as an organism: a sociological analysis. In P. Kecskemeti (ed.) *Essays on Sociology and Social Psychology*, pp. 165-82. London: Routledge and Kegan Paul.

 (1986). *Conservatism: A Contribution to the Sociology of Knowledge.* London and New York: Routledge and Kegan Paul.

Maynard, D. W. and Clayman, S. E. (1991). The diversity of ethnomethodology. *Annual Review of Sociology* 17: 385–418.

McQuown, N. A. (ed.) (1971). The natural history of an interview. Microfilm collections of manuscripts. Joseph Regenstein Library, University of Chicago.

Mehan, H. (1979). *Learning Lessons.* Cambridge, MA: Harvard University Press.

Milroy, J. (1980). *Language and Social Networks.* Oxford: Blackwell.

Mithun, M. (1988). Lexical categories and the evolution of number marking. In M. Hammond and M. Noonan (eds.) *Theoretical Morphology*, pp. 211–34. New York: Academic Press.

 (1991). Active/agentive case marking and its motivations. *Language* 67: 510–46.

Nichols, J. and Woodbury, A. (eds.) (1985). *Grammar Inside and Outside the Clause.* Cambridge: Cambridge University Press.

Ochs, E. (1984). Clarification and culture. In D. Shiffrin (ed.) *Georgetown University Round Table in Languages and Linguistics*, pp. 325–41. Washington, DC: Georgetown University Press.

(1988). *Culture and Language Development: Language Acquisition and Language Socialization in a Samoan Village*. Cambridge: Cambridge University Press.

(1992). Indexing gender. In A. Duranti and C. Goodwin (eds.) *Rethinking Context: Language as an Interactive Phenomenon*, pp. 335–58. Cambridge: Cambridge University Press.

Ochs, E., Schieffelin, B. B. and Platt, M. L. (1979). Propositions across utterances and speakers. In E. Ochs and B. B. Schieffelin (eds.) *Developmental Pragmatics*, pp. 251–68. New York: Academic Press.

Ochs, E., Taylor, C., Rudolph, D., and Smith, R. (1992). Story-telling as a theory-building activity. *Discourse Processes* 15,1: 37–72.

Ono, T. and Thompson, S. A. (frth.). Interaction and syntax in the structure of conversational discourse. In E. H. Hovy and D. Scott (eds.) *Interdisciplinary Perspectives on Discourse*. Heidelberg: Springer Verlag.

Ono, T. and Yoshida, E. (frth.). A study of co-construction in Japanese: we don't "finish each other's sentences". In N. Akatsuka and S. Iwasaki (eds.) *Japanese/Korean Linguistics 5*. Stanford: CSLI.

Orne, M. T. (1959). The nature of hypnosis: artifact and essence. *Journal of Abnormal and Social Psychology* 58: 277–99.

(1962). On the social psychology of the psychological experiment: with particular reference to demand characteristics and their implications. *American Psychologist* 17: 776–83

Pittenger, R. E., Hockett, C. F., and Danehy, J. J. (1960). *The First Five Minutes*. Ithaca, NY: Paul Martineau.

Quirk, R. (1960). Towards a description of English usage. *Transactions of the Philological Society* : 40–61.

Quirk, R., Greenbaum, S., Leech, G., and Svartvik, J. (1972). *A Grammar of Contemporary English*. London: Longman.

Rosenthal, R. (1966). *Experimenter Effects in Behavioral Research*. New York: Appleton-Century–Crofts.

Sacks, H. (1974). An analysis of the course of a joke's telling in conversation. In R. Bauman and J. Sherzer (eds.) *Explorations in the Ethnography of Speaking*, pp. 337–53. Cambridge: Cambridge University Press.

(1992). *Lectures on Conversation*. Two volumes. Edited by G. Jefferson, with Introductions by E. A. Schegloff. Oxford: Blackwell.

Sacks, H. and Schegloff, E. A. (1979). Two preferences in the organization of reference to persons and their interaction. In G. Psathas (ed.) *Everyday Language: Studies in Ethnomethodology*, pp. 15–21. New York: Irvington Publishers.

Sacks, H., Schegloff, E. A., and Jefferson, G. (1974). A simplest systematics for the organization of turn-taking for conversation. *Language* 50: 696–735.

Sankoff, D. (ed.) (1978). *Linguistic Variation: Models and Methods*. New York: Academic Press.

Sankoff, G. (1980). *The Social Life of Language.* Philadelphia: University of Pennsylvania Press.

Sankoff, G. and Brown, P. (1976). The origins of syntax in discourse: a case study of Tok Pisin relatives. *Language* 52: 631–66.

Sankoff, G. and Vincent, D. (1980). The productive use of "ne" in spoken Montreal French. In G. Sankoff (ed.) *The Social Life of Language*, pp. 295–310. Philadelphia: University of Pennsylvania Press.

Sapir, E. (1927). The unconscious patterning of behavior in society. In E. S. Dummer (ed.) *The Unconscious: A Symposium.* New York: Alfred Knopf, pp. 114-142. Reprinted in B. Blount (ed.), *Language, Culture and Society: A Book of Readings.* pp. 32-45. Cambridge, MA: Winthrop, 1974.

(1933). Language. In E. R. A. Seligman and A. Johnson (eds.) *Encyclopaedia of the Social Sciences*, pp. 155–69. New York: The Macmillan Company, Volume 9.

Schegloff, E. A. (1972). Notes on a conversational practice: formulating place. In D. N. Sudnow (ed.) *Studies in Social Interaction*, pp. 75–119. New York: Free Press.

(1979). The relevance of repair for syntax-for-conversation. In T. Givón (ed.) *Syntax and Semantics 12: Discourse and Syntax*, p. 261–88. New York: Academic Press.

(1982). Discourse as an interactional achievement: some uses of "uh huh" and other things that come between sentences. In D. Tannen (Ed.) *Georgetown University Roundtable on Languages and Linguistics 1981; Analyzing Discourse: Text and Talk*, pp. 71–93. Washington DC: Georgetown University Press.

(1986). The routine as achievement. *Human Studies* 9: 111–51.

(1987). Between macro and micro: contexts and other connections. In J. Alexander, B. Giesen, R. Munch, and N. Smelser (eds.) *The Micro-Macro Link*, pp. 207-34. Berkeley: University of California Press.

Schegloff, E. A., Jefferson, G., and Sacks, H. (1977). The preference for self-correction in the organization of repair in conversation. *Language* 53(2): 361–82.

Schieffelin, B. B. (1990). *The Give and Take of Everyday Life: Language Socialization of Kaluli Children.* Cambridge: Cambridge University Press.

Schuetze-Coburn, S. (frth.) *Prosody, Grammar and Discourse Pragmatics: Organizational Principles of Information Flow in German Conversational Narratives.* Amsterdam: John Benjamins.

Scollon, R. (1976). *Conversations with a One Year Old: A Case Study of the Developmental Foundation of Syntax.* Honolulu: The University Press of Hawaii.

Shannon, C. and Weaver, W. (1949). *The Mathematical Theory of Communication.* Urbana, IL: University of Illinois Press.

Shapin, S. and Schaffer, S. (1985). *Leviathan and the Air Pump: Hobbes, Boyle and the Experimental Life*. Princeton: Princeton University Press.

Shibatani, M. (ed.) (1976). *The Grammar of Causative Constructions*. New York: Academic Press.

(1988). *Passive and Voice*. Amsterdam: John Benjamins.

Shopen, T. (ed.) (1985). *Language Typology and Syntactic Description* (3 volumes). Cambridge: Cambridge University Press.

Slobin, D. I. (ed.) (1985). *The Cross-Linguistic Study of Language Acquisition, Volumes 1 and 2*. Hillsdale NJ: Lawrence Erlbaum Associates.

(ed.) (1992). *The Cross-Linguistic Study of Language Acquisition, Volume 3*. Hillsdale, NJ: Lawrence Erlbaum Associates.

Thompson, S. A. (1985). Grammar and written discourse: initial vs. final purpose clauses in English. *Text* 5(1/2): 55–84.

Thompson, S. A. and Matthiessen, C. (1989). The structure of discourse and "subordination". In J. Haiman and S. A. Thompson (eds.) *Clause Combining in Grammar and Discourse*, pp. 275–329. Amsterdam: John Benjamins.

Thorne, B. and Henley, N. (1975). *Language and Sex: Differences and Dominance*. Rowley, MA: Newbury House.

Thorne, B., Kramarae, C., and Henley, N. (1983). *Language, Gender and Society*. Rowley, MA: Newbury House.

Trudgill, P. (1978). *Sociolinguistic Patterns in British English*. London: Arnold.

Van Valin, R. D. (1990). Layered syntax in role and reference grammar. In J. Nuyts, A. M. Bolkestein, and C. Vet (eds.) *Layers and Levels of Representation in Language Theory: A Functional View*, pp. 193–231. Amsterdam: John Benjamins.

(1993). A synopsis of role and reference grammar. In R. D. Van Valin (ed.) *Advances in Role and Reference Grammar*, pp. 1-164. Amsterdam: John Benjamins.

Vygotsky, L. S. (1978). *Mind in Society: The Development of Higher Psychological Processes*. Cambridge: Harvard University Press.

Whorf, B. L. (1956). *Language, Thought, and Reality*. Cambridge, MA: MIT Press.

Winkin, Y. (1981). *La Nouvelle Communication*. Paris: Seuil.

2

Turn organization: one intersection of
grammar and interaction[1]

EMANUEL A. SCHEGLOFF

2.1 Introduction

From early in its development, conversation-analytic work on
interaction has declined to accord language any principled primacy
as an object of inquiry (e.g., Schegloff and Sacks, 1973: 290).
Although not derived from them, this view was in accord with
the stances of such intellectual forbears as Garfinkel's ethnomethodology (1967) and Goffman's several approaches to interaction. It
may be recalled, for example, that in "The neglected situation"
Goffman (1964) injected into the "coming-out party" of the
embryonic subfield known as the ethnography of speaking or communication the observation that speaking occurs most proximately
in "situations," in which it *need not* occur; speaking, then, had to
be understood by reference to exigencies of contexts not designed
for speaking in particular (as elaborated, for example, in the earlier
Goffman, 1961, 1963, and the later Goffman, 1971). In both of
these modalities of work, and in *their* predecessors, language was
not a *privileged* object of inquiry, however *interesting* an object of
inquiry it might be.

Still, the accessibility of conversation (and talk-in-interaction
more generally) to systematic inquiry has brought with it a need
to explore the mutual bearing of the various organizations of
"language" on the one hand (whatever that notion might turn
out to refer to; cf. Schegloff, 1979: 282) and the organizations of
interaction and talking-in-interaction on the other. For linguistics,
the promise has been to situate language relative to the social/inter-
actional matrix in which it is to be understood as inescapably as it is
relative to the organization of the mind/brain. For sociologists, the

prospect has been the satisfaction of needs akin to the needs of a carpenter to understand the properties of different kinds of wood.

From early on it seemed clear that some parts of the enterprise of understanding conversation would rest heavily on the contributions of linguists (Sacks, Schegloff, and Jefferson, 1974: 703, fn. 12, 721, 722, 723). On the whole, their exploration of this interface has been disappointing, perhaps because the point of articulation between language organization and interaction has been insufficiently explicated on the interactional side. Nothing comparable to the logical substructures of predication and proposition underlying other linguistic projects seemed available to linguistic students of actual talk-in-interaction. This paper is addressed to that possibility, and to its remedy.

Although there are a number of fronts along which the relationship between language and interaction can be fruitfully explored, the relationship between grammar and the organization of the turn-at-talk offers as attractive a prospect as any.[2] One reason is that, in conversation and many other forms of talk-in-interaction, turns-at-talk are the key proximate organizational niche into which bursts of language are introduced, and to which they may be expected to be adapted. And grammar is one of the key types of organization shaping these bursts. More on this in a moment.

As with other conversation-analytic work, satisfying results should have certain features and payoffs. The account which we develop of turn organization should be adequate to the analysis of single turns-at-talk on the one hand, and to observable features of aggregates of turns on the other; to the particulars of situated instances on the one hand, and to the formal structuring of talk on the other; to the projects both of academic analysts on the one hand, and (more precisely, "by virtue of its adequacy for") the projects of parties to interaction on the other.

Here, then, I hope to provide resources for parsing single turns (as implicated in larger structures of conversation), both as a post hoc analytic undertaking for professional inquiry and as an account of a real-time undertaking by participants (as well as, necessarily, a resource and constraint on speakers' construction of the talk). At the same time, we should find here guidelines to the organizational devices for the structuring of talk in turns and especially the units from which turns are constructed (so-called "turn constructional units" or TCUs, as per Sacks, Schegloff, and Jefferson, 1974: 702-3, 720-3; henceforth SSJ) – that is, grammatical structuring as language's counterpart, fitting to the organizational exigencies of turns as the "host space" in which language deposits are accommodated.

I am not unaware of the detailed relevance of contextual particulars – whether of culture, language structures, situation, relationship, immediate interactional contingency and import, and all the other things under the generic rubric of context which one can be found to have disattended. In much of what follows below, I will try to attend to some such contextual detail. Not enough, I am sure. And in some instances, hardly any at all. The underlying project is to explore, to ask: are there general contingencies of talking in interaction – or of conversation in particular – that in a recurrent, orderly way seem to shape the organization of a turn-at-talk and the units of which it is built– either its actual articulation or the relevancies by reference to which it is shaped.

2.2 Points of departure

Let me begin with a point of departure on which I have relied before. In many respects, the fundamental or primordial scene of social life is that of direct interaction between members of a social species, typically ones who are physically co-present. For humans, talking in interaction appears to be a distinctive form of this primary constituent of social life, and ordinary conversation is very likely the basic form of organization for talk-in-interaction. Conversational interaction may be thought of as a form of social organization through which the work of most, if not all, the major institutions of societies – the economy, the polity, the family, socialization, etc. – gets done. And it surely appears to be the basic and primordial environment for the use and development (both ontogenetic and phylogenetic) of natural language.

Therefore, it should hardly surprise us if some of the most fundamental features of natural language are shaped in accordance with their home environment in copresent interaction, as adaptations to it, or as part of its very warp and weft (Schegloff, 1989: 142-4; 1991: 153-5). For example, if the basic natural environment for sentences is in turns-at-talk in conversation, we should take seriously the possibility that aspects of their structure – for example, their grammatical structure – are to be understood as adaptations to that environment. In view of the thoroughly local and interactional character of the organization of turn-taking in conversation (SSJ, 1974), the grammatical structures of language should in the first instance be understood as at least partially shaped by interactional considerations (Schegloff, 1979). And one locus of those considerations will be the organization of the turn, the organizational unit which "houses" grammatical units.

But what shall we call those units? A moment ago I referred to "the basic natural environment for sentences [being] in turns-at-talk in conversation," but the grammatical units which occur in turns are not all sentences; and it is not obvious that it is their "sentence-ness" that is criterially relevant for those that are (though it may well be so in particular cases). The same applies to the clause.

The components of which turns-at-talk are composed we have in the past (SSJ, 1974: 702-4) termed "turn constructional units." By "turn-constructional unit," it may be recalled, we meant to register that these units *can* constitute possibly complete turns; on their possible completion, transition to a next speaker becomes *relevant* (although not necessarily accomplished).[3] So perhaps we can begin by thinking of grammar as the – or one – basic organization for the turn constructional unit. Of course, grammar is not the only way of organizing the materials of language. Poetics – with its metrics, rhyming, sound patterning, tropes, etc., for units such as its lines, stanzas, verses, etc. – is another way of putting linguistic elements together – for poetry. And logic is another – with its propositions, arguments, operations, etc. – for analyses, demonstrations and proofs.

But the (or one) key unit of language organization for talk-in-interaction is the turn constructional unit; its natural habitat is the turn-at-talk; its organization we are calling "grammar." And we are beginning with the premise that grammar as an organizing device is expectably formed up by reference to the habitat, "the turn." N.B.: the issue here is not one of terminologies: the aim is not to replace terms like "sentence" or "clause" with "turn constructional unit." Talking in turns means talking *in real time, subject to real interactional contingencies.* Whether articulated fluently or haltingly, what results is produced piece by piece, incrementally, through a series of "turns-so-far." These features support the openness of talk-in-progress to considerations of interactional import and reactivity, recipient design, moment-to-moment recalibration, reorganization and recompletion, and to interactional co-construction (cf., for example, Goodwin, 1979). When the grammar we attempt to understand inhabits actually articulated talk in interaction (rather than constructed prototype sentences), as it does in the habitat of a turn-at-talk in a series of turns through which a sequence may develop embodying a course of action, its realization in structured real time for both speaker and recipient(s) is inescapable.[4] If "sentences," "clauses," and "phrases" should turn out to be implicated, they will be different in emphasis, and perhaps in kind, from the static syntactic objects of much linguistic theorizing.

The central prospect, then, is that grammar stands in a reflexive relationship to the organization of a spate of talk as a turn. On the one hand, the organizational contingencies of talking in a turn (a turn in a *series* of turns, with sequence potential; SSJ, 1974: 722) shape grammar – both grammar as an abstract, formal organization[5] and the grammar of a particular utterance. On the other hand, the progressive grammatical realization of a spate of talk on a particular occasion can shape the exigencies of the turn as a unit of interactional participation on that occasion, and the grammatical properties of a language may contribute to the organization of turns-at-talk in that language and of the turn-taking device by which they are deployed.

Such a beginning orientation points us in two directions of inquiry: the organization of the turn (i.e., the habitat in which turn constructional units – henceforth TCUs – are housed) and the characteristics of the grammar – or grammar*s* – which organizationally constitute the TCUs for this habitat.

2.3   Some initial payoffs of shifting from sentences to TCUs

One consequence of re-framing the object of our attention as TCUs rather than sentences is that objects which might otherwise be taken as sentence-initial particles, interjections, etc. – that is, virtual appendages pre-positioned to the core unit – now invite treatment as possible TCUs in their own right. And the sentence, for which such an object might otherwise have been seen to be preliminary, can now be re-cast as itself a contingent accomplishment. This

recasting results from the introduction of temporality and structured interactional contingency into the analysis, by way of the
implication of TCUs in the practices of turn*taking* in ordinary conversation, specifically the systematic relevance of transition to
another speaker at the possible completion of a TCU. Let me pursue
this for a bit to see if we can quickly get some payoff from this way
of starting, and thereby some encouragement.

It seems to me that some aspects of prosody provide evidence for,
and may need to be understood by reference to, just such considerations;[6] what could be seen in some approaches as a sentence-initial
particle has quite different resonances when understood as a possible TCU in its own right. The excerpt below is drawn from a
telephone conversation between two young women who had been
close friends and attended the same school, but who now attend
different colleges and have apparently not talked to one another for
quite a while.[7]

```
(1)    TG:4:35 - 5:03

Bee:    Eh-yih have anybuddy: thet uh:? (1.2) I would know from the
        English depar'mint there?
Ava:    Mm-mh. Tch! I don't think so.
Bee:    °Oh,=<Did they geh ridda Kuhleznik yet hhh
-->  Ava:    No in fact I know somebuddy who ha:s huh [now.
Bee:                                               [Oh my got hh[hhh
Ava:                                                             [Yeh...
```

I do not command the technical language which would nowa-
days be used to describe the prosody of the target turn here, but I
hope it will suffice for present purposes to say that the flat intonation contour and the breath deployment are such as to interdict
(literally) the possibility of another – of *the* other, Bee – starting
to talk at the possible juncture between "No" and "in fact." I think
that this is best understood by reference to the speaker Ava's orientation to the status of "No" as a possible TCU, and its end as a
possible turn completion, and thus as a place at which Bee would
relevantly locate a possible start for a next turn.[8]

Although I wish to minimize the amount of analysis of sequential
context and interactional import to be included here in the interest
of keeping the size of the paper under control, let me sound the note
early, if not often, and exemplify it at least here. The relevance of an
intervention by Bee after "No" is informed not only by its status as
a possible TCU, but also by the sequence which is in progress, of

which this turn is a next increment, and in which it implements a next action.

I take this to be a topic-proffering sequence. It is a recurrent feature of such sequences that *two* tries or proffers are put forward, each of which can be taken up and embraced or declined by its recipient. Taking up a topic proffer is ordinarily done as a preferred response – i.e., with no delay *of* its turn or *in* its turn, with no qualification, account, etc., and as more than a minimal response (cf. Pomerantz, 1984; Sacks, 1987[1973]); Schegloff, 1988a). Declining a topic proffer is ordinarily done as a *dis*preferred response – delayed, minimal, and if expanded, then expanded with accounts bearing adversely on the topic, etc. Positive terms ("yes") recur in embracings, negative ones ("no," "mm mm") in declines. Most importantly, taking up a proffered topic generally involves *claiming* access to it; declining involves *denying* access.

Note then that in Excerpt (1), Ava's first turn declines the proffered topic (on the delivery of this declining as a *preferred* response, cf. Schegloff, 1988a: 454), and the "No" at the start of her second turn (the arrowed one) is at risk of being taken as a declining of the second try, although (as the sequel in the turn shows) she is actually moving to *embrace* this second topic proffer. The "No" thus is to be understood not only by reference to the TCU in its turn, but by reference to the turn within its sequence. (Below I will return to the theme that some things which occur in turns require analysis by reference to other than turn-organization.) The point is that it is by reference to *Ava's orientation* to such a systematically grounded *possible orientation by Bee* that the "No" is delivered with a prosody designed to block such a hearing and to interdict such an otherwise projectable possible next turn start, which would respond to such a rejection.[9]

The themes broached in the preceding analysis are generic to conversation, and potentially to much other talk-in-interaction. At every possible completion of a TCU, the turn-so-far will have amounted to – will be analyzable as – some possible action or actions. Management of the production of the turn or TCU – both by the speaker and by recipients (e.g., whether to start or withhold a next turn) – is in substantial measure conducted by reference to the action(s) analyzable out of the turn-so-far. Management of the interface or conjunction of action and imple-

menting utterance is a key task of the parties and a key topic for
disciplinary analysis of talk-in-interaction.[10]

Parsing a stretch of talk by reference to its TCU properties can
lead to analyses distinct from those of sentential grammar not only
at apparent utterance beginnings, but at the "other end" of the talk
as well. The videotape of a backyard picnic in early 1970s Ohio
begins like this: [11]

```
(2)   Automobile Discussion 1:01-12

      Carney:  (..'hear the same story),
-->   Pam:     'hh Oh yeah you've gotta tell Mike tha:t. Uh-cuz they
-->            [want that on fi:lm.
      Carney:  [Oh: no: here we go ag(h)[(h)ain o(h)o(h)o] 'hh=
      Curt:                             [Huh huh huh huh.]
      Gary:    =I[don't thin[k it's that funny.
      Carney:    [ O  h  :  [:,
      Pam:                  [I gotta go t'the
               joh[n before I hear tha[t again.
      Carney:     [You'll like it, you'[ll rilly like it.
      Curt:                            [You do too y[ou laugh like hell you
               hhuh!                               [
      Phyllis:                                     [°ehheh huh
```

Leaving aside the turn-initial "Oh yeah," which can constitute a
TCU in its own right, we can note that in *sentence*-structural terms
the rest of the turn is composed of a single unit, "You've gotta tell
Mike that 'cuz they want that on film." In *turn-constructional unit*
terms, the turn is built to come to possible completion – to designed
and realized completion – at "...tell Mike that." It is syntactically
possibly complete; it is "pragmatically" complete (i.e., it recognizably implements an action); its intonation contour comes to a full
fall, and the stretch or drawl on "tha: t" is common on turn-term-
inal items. So this utterance is different from a "syntactically iden-
tical" sentence that lacked the implementation of a possible
completion after "that."

When Pam moves to extend the talk in this turn, the added talk
can be executed in two different relationships to the prior talk – as
an increment within the same TCU or as a new TCU.[12] In a while
we will turn to the grammar, by reference to which just such dis-
tinctions are differentially implemented – i.e., how does one *do*
"TCU start?" Or *do* "TCU continuation?" But here we note as a
pre-analytic observation that Pam does *this* extension as a continuation. (It seems plausible that she could have done it as a new,
separate TCU just by not beginning with "uh-cuz;" the connector

here is not what one might call "anchored" in the objects being connected.)[13] The continuation is a post-positioned "because-clause," of the sort (together with other adverbial clauses pre- and post-positioned) described in Ford (1993). Such post-positioned accounts – in this case, grounds or justification – seem oriented to incipient disalignment by recipient(s) from what the speaker has just said, proposed or done. Here a proposal to have someone retell a joke or story to a newcomer to the gathering – a proposal embodying an assessment of its worth as a tellable – is buttressed, when not immediately taken up, by a conversationally extrinsic justification – the taping. (And, indeed, a question is raised in its aftermath – in Gary's first turn following – about its worth as a "re-tellable.") Consider the likely construction of the utterance in the first instance if the filming were the primary grounds for the re-telling proposal.

If the grammar at issue in our exploration of "grammar and interaction" is the grammar of turn-constructional units in the organization of the turns which they compose, then what I have just been describing have been grammatical alternatives, or even "choices" and "practices" fitted to *interactional contingencies*, which do not enter into the grammar of sentences. The line between the grammar of TCUs and the construction and organization of turns, then, may be permeable, and perilous to draw. And it appears that there are analytic results to be achieved by examining the talk by reference to the unit "TCU" which are not available by reference to "sentences" or "clauses."

Because the boundaries of the grammar may extend *beyond* those of a single TCU in their contexts of relevance, I propose to begin with a consideration of *multi-unit* turns, even though it might seem more cogent to take those up only after a consideration of the grammar of the single TCU. The grammar of a TCU may be related to its *position in its turn* – as sole TCU or one of several, and if one of several, in various positions. So we entertain first what may characterize TCUs by virtue of their joint incumbency of a turn, and how they may be constructed so as to fit together and complement one another as parts of its construction – or fail to do so.

2.4   Single- and multi-unit turns

Register as an observation – rather than as a presupposition – that it is an organizational and perhaps even a grammatical fact about turns that they can accommodate more than one TCU, although there are interactional contingencies (in conversation) biasing turn size to one, and then few, TCUs (cf. SSJ, 1974: 709). It can take "work," i.e., praxis, to get more than one TCU into a turn (Schegloff, 1982). That work – that practice – can itself occupy a TCU, e.g., the "story preface" described by Sacks (1974), or the "pre-pre" described by Schegloff (1980).[14]

One relevance of the possibility of multi-unit turns is that some TCUs can be designed for their position in the turn. It may well be that many – perhaps most – TCUs are constructed in ways which are *not* indicative of their position in their turn; but some *are*, and it is that possibility which I want to explore for a moment, for it has a bearing on the issue whether it is *one* grammar whose relation to interaction needs to be described, or *multiple* grammars (as does the subsequently discussed issue of position of the turn in a sequence).

For example, a first unit in its turn can be built to project that there will be (a) subsequent one(s). Excerpt (3) is taken from the source of Excerpt (1), at an earlier point in the conversation.

```
(3)     TG:03:01-04

Bee:      =[(Mnuh,)]
Ava:      =[ Oh my ] mother wannduh know how's yer grandmother.
-->  Bee:      ˙hhh Uh::, (0.3) I don'know I guess she's aw- she's
           awright she went to thee uh:: hhospital again tihda:y,
Ava:      Mm-hm?,
Bee:      ˙hh t! ˙hh A:n:: I guess t'day wz d'day she's supposetuh
           find out if she goes in ner not.=
Ava:      =Oh. Oh::.
Bee:      Becuz they're gonna do the operation on the teeuh duct.
           f[fi: rs]t. Before they c'n do t[he cata]ract ]s.
Ava:       [Mm-hm,]                        [ Right.]Yeah,]
Bee:      ˙hhh So I don'know I haven:'t yihknow, she wasn' home
           by the t-yihknow when I lef'fer school tihday.=
Ava:      =Mm hm,
Bee:      Tch! .hh So uh I don't kno:w,
```

Leaving aside for now the initial delay of the arrowed turn by inbreath, and then of the initial TCU by "uh," and silence, the first unit of Bee's turn, "I don'know" is designed here to project "more to come." Although this syntactically possibly complete unit could be deployed in a fashion that fully denies knowledge of the answer to the question which Ava has conveyed (i.e., it could be "I don't

kno<u>w</u>: .", with up-down terminal contour and carrying primary
stress, roughly as in the last utterance reproduced in Excerpt 3)
and could then invite analysis as the whole of its turn, here it is
produced as a kind of prefatory epistemic disclaimer. This is done
largely prosodically, by a combination of the primary stress on the
"I," the non-falling (or so-called "continuative") intonation contour on "know," and the phrasing (in the musical sense) across
the juncture into the next unit of talk.

Non-first TCUs can also be built to project additional unit(s) to
follow. For example, Excerpt (4) is taken from a college dormitory
room conversation in the mid-1970s. Mark has come by the residence shared by Sherri, Ruthie, and Karen. The excerpt follows a
brief exchange about the planning for Sherri's forthcoming wedding.

```
(4)    SN-4: 02:23-33


      Sherri:   [Look once a quarter et school is enough.=That's uh:: (·)
                finals.
      (??):     (huh-)
-->   Mark:     I know whutcha mean. Me t[oo.<that's why I came here d'night.=
      (??):                              [°(Wha-)°]
-->   Mark:     ='hh I came tih talk tuh Ruthie about borrowing her:-
                notes.fer (·) econ.
                (0.8)
      Ruthie:   [Oh.
      Sherri:   [You didn't come t' talk t' Kerin?
                (0.4)
      Mark:     No, Kerin: (·) Kerin 'n I 'r having a fight.
```

Here I mean to take note of the third TCU in Mark's turn, "that's
why I came here d'<u>night</u>," and specifically the "that." By use of
what I have elsewhere called a "dummy term" (Schegloff, 1982)
and what Goodwin (this volume) more felicitously terms a
"prospective indexical," Mark projects that there will be more to
follow, which the syntax of the construction shapes toward being a
new TCU. Note as well the second TCU in the target turn in
Excerpt (3) above, "I guess she's aw- she's aw<u>right</u>," whose self-
interruption seems directed to a re-doing of the prosody to make
this TCU also prefatory rather than conclusory, i.e., to project
another (at least) to follow.

Not only can first, and subsequent, TCUs be designed and/or
delivered in a fashion which projects additional ones to follow;
non-first TCUs can be designed and/or delivered as
"subsequents." Looking again at the target turn in Excerpt (1),
"No in fact I know somebuddy who ha: s huh [now," I mean only

to remark that the "in fact" construction here (in common with many "actually" and "as a matter of fact" constructions) serves to relate the TCU which it initiates to its predecessor; this practice can be used to indicate that what follows has a contemporary relevance to the speaker other than that created by the question just asked, and that what it is about has a reality and "facticity" independent of the circumstance prompting the talk which it introduces. Its effect is often to register a so-called "coincidence."

So one consequence of the organizational possibility of multi-unit turns is the possibility of recognizable differentiation, and potentially of positionally specific grammars, by reference to TCU position within a turn,[15] as I will later suggest ones sensitive to position in a sequence. And indeed there may be structural affinities between "position in a turn" and particular TCU types, employing various "typologies" of TCU. For example, the TCU typology that entered prominently into the formulation of a turn-taking organization for conversation (SSJ, 1974) made reference to "lexical, phrasal, clausal and sentential" units. By reference to these types of units, lexical TCUs occur overwhelmingly (I think) as first – or only – TCU in their turns. Their occurrence elsewhere is, I suspect, limited and marked, i.e., doing something special when they occur.[16] Such a differential distribution can offer one kind of evidence for positionally sensitive grammars.

To note this is not to understand it. We need studies that will examine such lexical TCUs (and perhaps phrasal ones as well) in their sequential and interactional context to see what they are and how they work. Such studies may bring into focus a sense of how sequence-specific and positionally specific grammars might work together, i.e., be organizationally related. For example, many lexical and phrasal TCUs will turn out, I suspect, to be first in *turns follow-ing questions*, and will be a way of designing answers to be sym-biotic with, and (to use a less pleasant metaphor) parasitic on, their questions. Indeed, by reference to this different "typology," Sacks observed (1987[1973]: 57-58) that if there is a multi-unit turn with a "question" in it, the question will be likely to occur last (and if there is an "answer," one place it is likely to be is first in its turn).[17] Although the term "question" can be taken to refer both to gram-mar and to action (Schegloff, 1984a; Heritage and Roth, 1995), either way some sort of link between position and grammar seems clearly to be involved.

Or, using still another typology of components, we can note that, if the types of TCUs are cast as "agreements" and "disagreements," then the former come early (first?) in their turns and the latter are delayed (non-first?); that disagreements may be done as "exceptions," and it turns out that there is "a place" for exceptions, i.e., late (last?) in the turn (Sacks, 1987[1973]: 62). To be sure, here we seem clearly to be talking about the distribution of activities or actions in turns, but activities can have elective affinities with turn constructional unit types in which they are embodied, and these grammatical units can have distributional properties, as has already been noted. So there are several inquiries here: whether and how types of TCUs are positionally sensitive – to being sole TCUs or with distinctive placements in their turns, and in what terms such placements or positions are most aptly understood; whether and how TCUs are built to relate to others – to project further TCUs, to position themselves relative to prior TCUs; whether there is describable orderliness between *types of positions* in a turn and *types of units* occupying those positions.[18]

But here programmatic speculation should yield to empirical inquiry. One basic task of analysis in this area is to examine the succession of TCUs that occur in turns and ask whether or not such examination reveals recurrent, oriented to, and interactionally consequential constructional types – what we might come to formulate as recognizable turn formats, with bearings on the production and recipient parsing of component TCUs. Let me suggest just a few, with some exemplary displays. Once such recurrences are empirically registered, we can ask as well how (if at all) they should be characterized as grammatical.

Look first at excerpts 5a–d

(5a)   TG:01:26-30

```
        Bee:     ˙hh You [sound sorta] cheer[ful?]
        Ava:            [°(Any way).]       [˙hh ]  How'v you bee:n.
        Bee:     ˙hh Oh:: survi:ving I guess, hh[h!
  -->   Ava:                                    [That's good, how's (Bob),
        Bee:     He's fine,
        Ava:     Tha::t's goo:d,
```

(5b) TG:02:30-40

```
Ava:     En, I had- I wz- I couldn't stop laughin it wz the funniest
         thing b't y'know you get all sweaty up'r en evrything we
         didn' thing we were gonna pla:y, 'hh en oh I'm knocked out.
Bee:     Nhhkhhhh! 'hhhh
Ava:     Ripped about four nai:ls, 'n okhh!
Bee:     Fantastic.=
-->  Ava:     =B't it wz fun-You sound very far away
         (0.7)
Bee:     I do?
Ava:     Nyeahm.
Bee:     mNo? I'm no:t,
```

(5c) MDE:MTRAC:60-1/2, 01:01-22

```
Marsha:  Hello:?
Tony:    Hi: Marsha?
Marsha:  Ye:ah.
Tony:    How are you.
Marsha:  Fi::ne.
         (0.2)
Marsha:  Did Joey get home yet?
Tony:    Well I wz wondering when 'e left.
         (0.2)
Marsha:  'hhh Uh:(d) did Oh: .h Yer not in on what ha:ppen'.(hh)(d)
Tony:    No(h)o=
Marsha:  =He's flying.
         (0.2)
Marsha:  En Ilene is going to meet im:.Becuz the to:p wz ripped
         off'v iz car which is tih say someb'ddy helped th'mselfs.
Tony:    Stolen.
         (0.4)
Marsha:  Stolen.=Right out in front of my house.
-->  Tony:    Oh: f'r crying out loud,=en eez not g'nna eez not
         g'nna bring it ba:ck?
Marsha:  'hh No so it's parked in the g'rage cz it wz so damn
         co:ld. An' ez a matter fact snowing on the Ridge Route.
```

Each of the arrowed turns in 5a–5c is composed of two TCUs. In each, the first TCU completes closure of a preceding sequence, and the second TCU initiates a new sequence. In each case, the first TCU closes the prior sequence with an assessment, but as 5d shows, this need not be criterial (though assessment closures may have distinctive features), for here as well the first TCU moves to close the preceding sequence, and the second moves to initiate a new sequence:

(5d) MDE:MTRAC:60-1/2, 02:22-28

```
Marsha:  'hhhh So: yer ba:ck.
Tony:    Yah.
         (1.0)
-->  Marsha:  I see. So you'll- you'll hear fr'm im,
         (0.2)
Tony:    Oka:y, well: if there's any prob'm w'l letche know. But
         I'm sure he'll be here ok[ay.
```

As it happens, such linkages between the end of one sequence and the start of another can be done in a response turn (or "second position"), following such a response in third position (as in 5a, 5c and 5d, and cf. Schegloff, 1986: 130-33) or in a less clearly defined position in a larger sequence (as in the "story evaluation" exit in 5b).

Or consider the multi-unit turns in 6a–d, which display another recurrent format:

```
(6a)   TG:01:01-23

       Ava:    H'llo:?
       Bee:    hHi:,
       Ava:    Hi:?
       Bee:    hHowuh you:?
       Ava:    Oka:::y?hh
       Bee:    =Good.=Yihs[ou:nd ] hh
       Ava:               [<I wan]'dih know if yih got a-uh:m
               wutchimicawllit. A:: pah(hh)khing place °th's mornin'.`hh
       Bee:    A pa:rking place,
       Ava:    Mm hm,
               (0.4)
       Bee:    Whe:re.
       Ava:    t! Oh: just anypla(h)ce? I wz jus' kidding yuh.
       Bee:    Nno?=
       Ava:    =[(°No).]
-->    Bee:    =[W h y ]whhat'sa mattuh with y-Yih sou[nd HA:PPY,] hh
       Ava:                                          [ Nothing. ]
-->>   Ava:    u- I sound ha:p[py?]
       Bee:                   [Yee]uh.
               (0.3)
       Ava:    No:,
       Bee:    Nno:?
       Ava:    No.


(6b)   SN-4:05:18-32

       Carol:  =No they [didn' even have any Ta:(h)b.
       ?Ruth:           [°hheh
       Carol:  This is all I c'd find.
               (·)
       Ruth:   Well then there's ez many calories ez that prob'ly in en ice
               cream sa:nwich=so yih jis':, yih know.
               (·)
-->    Carol:  I know(,) an icecream sanwich is better, but I di'n feel like
-->            going down tuh P* an seeing all those wierd people.an have them
-->            st[a:re at me. ]
-->>   Ruth:     [In yer slipper]s¿        ((*"P" refers to the "Parking
               (0.2)                         Level" in a building.))
       Carol:  Yes.
               (0.8)
       Carol:  I don't want them tih see me when I l(h)ook t(h)is good.
```

```
(6c)  SN-4:02:19-34 (cf. excerpt 4 above)

        Mark:    (Y')haven't been 'n school in five weeks doesn' matter.
        Sherri:  hhmh hih hmh=
        Ruthie:  =heh he[h  heh  heh]
        Mark:           [mmh heh heh] ˙hi:h
        Mark:    [hee hee
        Sherri:  [Look once a quarter et school is enough.=That's uh::(·)
                 finals.
        (??):    (huh-)
  -->   Mark:    I know whutcha mean. Me t[oo.<that's why I came here d'night.=
        (??):                             [°(Wha-)°
  -->   Mark:    =˙hh I came tih talk tuh Ruthie about borrowing her:-
                 notes.fer (·) econ.
                 (0.8)
        Ruthie:  [Oh.
 -->>   Sherri:  [You didn't come t' talk t' Kerin?
                 (0.4)
        Mark:    No, Kerin: (·) Kerin 'n I 'r having a fight.


(6d)  SN-4:02:10-20

        Mark:    W'll (jat'll) jus' be fanta:stic.˙hh So what've y'called any
                 other hotels ('r) anything?
                 (·)
  -->   Sherri:  Y:eah I called thee Embassader 'n stuff. I've go so much
  -->            work that I don't believe it.so I'm j'st not even thinking
  -->            about that [°now.
 -->>   Mark:              [In schoo:l yih mea[:n?
        Sherri:                               [Ye:ah,
                 (0.2)
        Mark:    (Y')haven't been 'n school in five weeks doesn' matter.
        Sherri:  hhmh hih hmh=
```

Without undertaking a detailed analysis, let me just note that in each of these single-arrowed multi-unit turns, a step-by-step topic shift is managed. In each, the first turn-constructional unit links back to preceding talk (although the several segments display different types of "back-linking"), and the ensuing TCUs shift the topic step by step, ending the turn with a topical focus different from the beginning, with separate TCUs constituting the "steps" in this shift. That co-participants are oriented to this use of the turn is displayed by the occurrence in each of the segments (at the double-headed arrow) of a next turn, of regular form (a sort of request for confirmation for a candidate understanding), which engages and "co-operates with" the multi-TCU turn by addressing itself to the proposed new topic focus. These four instances are disparate not only in the sorts of connections made to the prior talk, but also in the types of TCUs through which the step-by-step topic shift is implemented, and in the interactional agenda being served by the shift. Each of these may, however, itself be the locus of order.[19]

I have displayed several small collections of exemplars of distinctive multi-unit turn formats. But it is not necessary to have collections to begin with; indeed, one *cannot* have collections to begin with. Collections begin with a noticing of an apparent orderliness, sometimes in a single occurrence, sometimes in a second occurrence ("I've seen something like that before!"). Consider Excerpt (7):

```
(7)    TG:02:06-11

       Ava:     [°B't asi]de fr'm that it's a'right.
       Bee:     [So what-]
                (0.4)
       Bee:     Wha:t?
-->    Ava:     I'm so:: ti:yid. I j's played ba:ske'ball t'day since the
                firs' time since I wz a freshm'n in hi:ghsch[ool.]
```

This develops into a story telling, but it begins with a TCU sequence which readily invites prima facie characterization as "state description + account," the account here turning out to be realized in a story, which may be quite a contingent outcome (but recall excerpt (3) above, "she's alright + she went to the hospital again today" + more story).[21] Indeed, having noticed "state description + account," one may well become alert to other possibilities, such as "state description + ?" and "? + account" as consecutive TCU types which regularly supply formats of multi-unit turns, and do so via their serving as the vehicles for orderly and significant courses of action.

And here in Excerpt (8) (which incorporates the earlier excerpt 2) is a page of transcript – the very start of the "Automobile Discussion" tape – that I happened to examine with a seminar largely as a matter of convenience, i.e., for reasons incidental to the current topic. Just begin looking at the multi-unit turns (which I have arrowed).

```
(8)    Automobile Discussion:01

       Carney:   (..'hear the same story),
-->    Pam:      'hh Oh yeah you've gotta tell Mike tha:t. Uh-cuz they
                 [want that on fi:lm.
-->    Carney:   [Oh: no: here we go ag(h)[(h)ain o(h)o(h)o] 'hh=
       Curt:                             [Huh huh huh huh.]
       Gary:     =I[don't thin[k it's that funny.
       Carney:    [ O h :  [:,
       Pam:                 [I gotta go t'the
                 joh[n before I hear tha[t again.
-->    Carney:      [You'll like it, you'[ll rilly like it.
-->    Curt:                             [You do too y[ou laugh like hell you
                 hhuh!                              [
       Phyllis:                                     [°ehheh huh
       Gary:     Well I[:,
       Curt:           [Y-
```

```
Gary:       hat'n hadda [b e e r   y e: t.]=
Pam:                    [ You  don'like it][becuz=
Gary:                                      [=eh-heh-heh-[-huh-hah-huh!
Curt:                                                   [ehhh!
Carney:     =you didn't thin[k of it!
Curt:                       [ehh-heh at's ri[h) g h (h) [t nnn ˙hh
Phyllis:                                    [˚hehhhhuhh [
-->  Gary:                                              [I:a-n' adda
        bee[r ye:t.I:c'n laugh ['t anything gi[t a bee:r,
-->  Curt:   [nh huh huh. huh,   [ huh-huh      [
Phyllis:                         [ ˚ehhu::n     [
Curt:                                           [eh-heh
Ryan:       ˚Bo[::.
Gary:          [heh-heh-[-heh-heh-[-heh-ha-ha-ha-ah! ah! ah! ah!=
Curt:                   [That's ri[(h) : g ht.[(huh!),
Mike:                             [hah:hah:hah[hah huh huh,
        huh huh [hah huh                      [
Phyllis:        [                             [˚hnnn n-hn-hn
Curt:           [=(h)You wan'ano[ther beer y[ou better[(keep laughing)=
Carney:                         [˚ahhhhah    [          [
Gary:                                        [e h h i h[ha ha
Carney:                                                [˙hahh!
```

Look for instance at the first of these turns (as this is where the tape and transcript begin, we lack the just preceding context of talk). We may initially dismiss the "Oh yeah" as "just" backlinking to the (or to some) prior turn. But what is the range of ways by which backlinking is done? It appears to be the initial job of a turn, but is it done differently in a one unit turn than it is if there is a separate TCU dedicated to doing it? Ought we then to collect and examine "turn starts" as a distinct object (i.e., distinct from TCU starts)? Perhaps some aspects of turn constructional *units'* starts may "belong" to the TCU, whereas others "belong" to the turn?

2.4.1 *Excursus*

I have spent a bit of time on the parsing of turns into TCUs and on a few of the organizational themes which such parsing may bring into view. The components of the turn formats examined here present themselves as having a "natural" fit to one another, as composing a coherent joint incumbency of a turn, with parts constructed so as to fit together and complement one another as parts of its construction: the end of one sequence and the start of a next; the succession of elements in a "train of thought" which leads from one topic to another. Before leaving this initial consideration of the multi-unit turn, I want to register a cross-cutting theme, one which can usefully inform the analytic parsing of a multi-unit turn. It is that some things, including some whole TCUs, which occur in a turn "belong" not so much to the turn as to a sequence; they are "housed" in the turn, but are made to cohere with its other incumbents only super-

ficially. That is, some components of turns are initially, and differentially, to be understood by reference to extra-turn considerations
such as sequence, interactional juncture, and the like.

To be sure, virtually everything that is said occurs in a turn; and
much of what is said in turns will occur at the same time in a
sequence, although not everything will constitute an organizationally relevant "move" at some other level. "Cuz they want that on
film" in Excerpt (2) above is at one and the same time an increment
to the turn and a response to a potential rejection of a proposal, and
thereby a pointed component in the trajectory of the sequence. But
the particular grammatical practice adopted for adding *to the turn*
may or may not have import for what the increment is doing *to the
developing sequence* (just as the grammatical practice may not be
properly understandable without reference to what that component
of the talk is doing in a "larger" structure, such as a sequence or a
story-telling).

But let me linger for a moment with an excerpt in which the
"belonging" of a TCU to a different level of interactional organization is of a more distinctive character.

In Excerpt (5c), reproduced below as Excerpt (9), Marsha and
Tony are the separated/divorced parents of the teen-aged Joey, who
lives with his father but has just spent the holidays with his mother,
some 500 miles away. The father calls on the day on which Joey is
scheduled to return to him.

```
(9)    MDE:MTRAC:60-1/2, 01:01-19

      Marsha:   Hello̱:?
      Tony:     Hi̱: Marsha̱?
      Marsha:   Ye̱:ah.
      Tony:     How are you.
      Marsha:   Fi̱::ne.
                (0.2)
      Marsha:   Did Joey get home yet?
      Tony:     Well I wz wondering when 'e left.
                (0.2)
      Marsha:   ˙hhh Uh:(d) did Oh: .h Yer not in on what ha:ppen'.(hh)(d)
      Tony:     No(h)o=
  --> Marsha:   =He's flying.
                (0.2)
  --> Marsha:   En Ilene is going to meet im:.Becuz the to:p wz ripped
                off'v iz car which is tih say someb'ddy helped th'mselfs.
      Tony:     Stolen.
                (0.4)
      Marsha:   Stolen.=Right out in front of my house.
      Tony:     Oh: f'r crying out loud,...
```

There is an issue here about Joey's return and its timing. As is
apparent even from this much of the conversation (and it is taken

up in what follows), there has been trouble "on Marsha's watch,"
in the first instance with the car (Joey's car? Tony's car?), but as a
consequence also with Joey's trip home. Marsha's pre-announce-
ment/pre-telling – "Oh, Yer not in on what happened" – suggests
yet another trouble; no one has informed Tony about the "news,"
the change in travel plans, and the possible consequences for *him*.

Note then the composition and construction of Marsha's turn at
the arrows. "He's flying" is the telling which the pre-announcement
had projected. It is built to be complete, syntactically, prosodically,
and pragmatically.[22] It receives no uptake whatsoever – no registering of it as indeed *news*, no assessment of it for the *kind of news*
that it is, these being the two recurrent, virtually canonical types of
response to announcements.

Note that Marsha then adds to her turn two sorts of continuations. One of these is an account for Joey's mode of travel, an
account which extends beyond the fragment which I have reproduced here, and includes an account of the weather (which would
forbid driving without a car top) and of the contingencies of getting
a ticket or standby status at the airport. This continuation is linked
to the initial part of the turn with "Becuz."

To note that "becuz" links the account to "He's flying" is also to
note that it does not link it to what immediately precedes it. Indeed,
"En Ilene is going to meet him" appears in various respects oddly
placed in the developing course of this turn. The turn has been
projected as being about "what happened," and most of it is indeed
in the past tense, but the "Ilene" segment is in the future. There is no
further reference to Ilene (Joey's girl friend) elsewhere in this
sequence, which is otherwise concerned with Joey, Marsha, the
car, the airport, etc. "En Ilene is going to meet him" is an island
(if I may put it that way without generativist echoes) in this
sequence (the "telling sequence") and in this turn, as is shown by
the "becuz" linking around it to "He's flying."

I take it that Marsha has introduced this TCU at the first sign of a
negative interactional stance being taken up by Tony to her news
(displayed here in the 0.2 seconds of silence following "He's flying")
– and before pursuing the rest of her account – for the work it does
in addressing the consequences of the change of travel plans for
Tony's own circumstances. The work it does is reassurance; Tony
need do nothing; Ilene will meet Joey at the airport.

So this TCUs occurrence here is to be understood not as a "natural" way in which this turn can develop, as is the case with other continuations we have examined, including the "becuz..." which follows here. Quite the contrary; it is topically disparate from what surrounds it; it is virtually designed as out-of-place. It is initially to be understood by reference to the larger sequence in progress ("where's Joey?"), and to the interactional and practical concerns which that sequence engenders and carries, and not by reference to its proximate predecessor in the turn. That it is out-of-place is a way of making it high priority; it is not merely out of place, it is made to be "as early as possible." In this sense, it is *in* the turn, but not *of* the turn.[23]

Nonetheless, it is incorporated into the turn into which it is interpolated. Even if the conjunction is pro forma, it is linked to the preceding TCU with an "En." And at its ending, it is phonologically run right into what will follow it. Note that the "m" of "(h)im" is stretched, that there is no break at all as the intonation contour falls to terminal level, and that the lips still closed for the "m" immediately move without opening into the "b" of "becuz." Although this strategically inserted TCU is thus incorporated (virtually "stitched") into the developing turn organization, the work which this has taken is marked and set off by specially registerable turntaking practices ("noticeables") at either end (the gap at its start and the boundary blur at its end). There are practices, then, for managing a unit being *in* the turn whose major locus of relevance is elsewhere.

Still most components of most multi-unit turns are produced in a more felicitous relationship to one another. The preceding discussion of the potentially diverse "organizational roots" or loci of components of turns was introduced as an alert worth bearing in mind in the parsing of turns into TCUs.

So much for now on the turn as an environment for turn constructional units. In some respects I have proceeded backwards, taking up first what might have followed the unit whose organization grammar provides for – the turn constructional unit. Perhaps there were payoffs from beginning with the turn as habitat, not least of which I hope to have been a suggestion about how analysts might proceed in examining turns-at-talk – namely, by locating TCUs *within* the turn. That is, one way to begin to parse a turn is to size up what is in it. What is in it will be (in one respect) one

TCU or several, perhaps with increments – increments added following possible completion of a TCU. But to come to the grammar of the TCU in this fashion is to come to it with the analytic operating field prepared, so to speak – prepared by having laid bare the organizational matrix of the turn and the interactional engines driving the talk. In any case, it is time to turn attention to the TCU itself.

2.5 Turn constructional units

Recognizing some spate of talk as a TCU is itself an accomplishment. That is, some stretches of talk by a speaker are taken (by us as analysts and by co-participants in the setting) not as TCUs, but, for example, as increments of talk to some other, prior talk – either by that same speaker or by another.[24] Here are some cases in point.

```
(10)   TG:08:19 - 09:02

       Bee:    I'nna tell you on:e course.
               (0.5)
       Ava:    [(          ).]
       Bee:    [The mah-    ] the mah:dern art. The twunnieth century a:rt
               there's about eight books,
       Ava:    Mm[hm,
       Bee:      [En I wentuh buy a book the other day I [went] 'hh went=
       Ava:                                              [(mm)]
       Bee:    =downtuh N.Y.U. tuh get it becuz it's the only place thet
               car[ries the book.
       Ava:       [Mmm
       Ava:    Mmh
       Bee:    Tch! En it wz twun::ty do::lliz.
       Ava:    Oh my god.
               (0.4)
XX     Bee:    Yeuh he- ez he wz handing me the book en 'e tol' me twunny
XX             dolliz I almos' dro(h)pped i(h)[t 'hh 'hh
       Ava:                                   [hhunh.
XX     Bee:    'hhh I said but fer twunny dollars I bettuh hh 'hh yihknow,
               (0.2)
       Bee:    'hhh h[hold o:nto i(h)hh] huhh huh] 'hh!
-->    Ava:          [not    drop   it. ] huhh huh]
               (0.2)
       Bee:    Ih wz, (0.2) y'know (fun).=...
```

In Excerpt (10) Ava's "not drop it" appears to be designed as a potential continuation – a collaborative completion (Sacks, 1992: I: 144-7, 321-3, 651-5; II: 57-60 et passim; Lerner, 1991, this volume) – of Bee's ongoing turn, one which, as it happens, gets produced in overlap with Bee's own completion of it. In Excerpt (11), Bee's talk at the arrows is built as an apparent continuation of her own prior talk at the lines marked XX, talk which may indeed be understood *not* to have come to possible completion. (For discussion of this segment, cf. Schegloff, 1987a[1973].) The talk at the three arrows in Excerpts (12)[25] and (13) is in each case built as a continuation of the same speaker's prior talk, talk which *had* otherwise apparently been brought to possible completion.

```
(11)   TG:18:14-27

       Bee:    t! We:ll, uhd-yihknow I-I don' wanna make any- thing
XX             definite because I-yihknow I jis:: I jis::t thinkin:g
XX             tihday all day riding on th'trai:ns hhuh-uh
               ˙hh[h!
       Ava:       [Well there's nothing else t'do.<I wz
               thingin[g   of   taking   the   car  anyway.] ˙hh
-->    Bee:           [that  I would  go  into the  ss-uh-]=I would go into
-->            the city but I don't know,
       Ava:    Well if I do ta:ke it, this way if- uh-if- y'know uh::
               there's no pa:rking right away I c'n give you the car
               en you c'n look aroun a li'l bit.
       Bee:    Mye::[:m ,   ]
       Ava:         [y'know] en see what happens.
               (0.4)

(12)   MDE:MTRAC:60-1/2, 02:11-17

XX     Marsha: ˙hhh Bu:t u-hu:ghh his friend Steve en Brian er driving up.
-->            Right after:: (0.2) school is out.En then hi'll drive do:wn
               here with the:m.
       Tony:   Oh I see.
       Marsha: So: in the long run, ˙hhh it (·) probly's gonna save a
               liddle time 'n: energy.
       Tony:   Okay,

(13)   MDE:MTRAC:60-1/2, 02:32-03:15

       Marsha: Bu:t it wasn't too crowded when we go:t there, so,
               (0.9)
XX     Tony:   Yeh he'll probly get uhp uh one of the planes (too:)
               (0.3)
       Marsha: [˙tch
a->    Tony:   [before too long otherwise y'll be hearing from im et the
               airport y'd probly'd'v heard fr'm im already.
               (0.7)
       Marsha: Wha:t?
XX     Tony:   Y'd of probly heard fr'm im already.
               (0.9)
       Marsha: i-Ya:h.
               (0.4)
b->    Tony:   If 'e hadn' gotten a li:ft
               (0.2)
       Marsha: Ri:ght.
       Tony:   Yeah.
```

The talk indicated at each of these arrows is parsable as not a new turn constructional unit, but as an increment to prior talk by same or other speaker, at least in part because it *does not start with a recognizable beginning*. Spates of talk then (like other organized interactional units, such as whole single conversations) can be recognized as having *starting places* which may or may not have *beginnings* in them (SSJ, 1974: 719 ff.). Turn constructional units – and turns – can start with a "beginning" or with something which is hearably *not* a beginning.[26] And, as was noted concerning Excerpt (11), spates of talk can apparently end not only with recognizable possible completions, but with something which is *not* a recognizable possible completion (indeed, there is a distinct recognizable type of turn closure built around this feature – the "trail off"). An exploration of the organization of turn constructional units – as with many other units of sequential and interactional organization – aptly begins, then, with attention to their beginnings and endings. And I will try to say a few things about what comes in between as well.

There is nothing intrinsic to the arrowed talk in the preceding segments which marks them as continuations and not beginnings. In each case, it is in their relationship to the preceding talk – in the way their relationship to the preceding talk is designed and constructed by their speaker – that (if so heard by recipient) they achieve being a continuation. And so it is with recognizable beginnings as well. Recall Excerpt (9) above, partially reproduced as (14) below:

```
(14)   MDE:MTRAC:60-1/2, 01:10-19

       Marsha:  ˙hhh Uh:(d) did Oh: .h Yer not in on what ha:ppen'.(hh)(d)
       Tony:    No(h)o=
       Marsha:  =He's flying.
                (0.2)
       Marsha:  En Ilene is going to meet im:.Becuz the to:p wz ripped
                off'v iz car which is tih say someb'ddy helped th'mselfs.
  -->  Tony:    Stolen.
                (0.4)
  -->  Marsha:  Stolen.=Right out in front of my house.
       Tony:    Oh: f'r crying out loud,...
```

Although both of these "stolen"s are TCUs, neither of these arrowed utterances, or parts of them, is *intrinsically* a TCU, or "a beginning." Each is designed for the sequential and interactional juncture in which it is positioned.

Indeed, designing a spate of talk as a continuation is itself not necessarily incompatible with its being a TCU in its own right. Consider, for example, Excerpts (15a) and (15b), each taken from talk in therapy sessions. Excerpt (15a) is taken from a group therapy session with teenagers, in which the "dropping out" of the sole female patient has been under discussion.[27]

```
(15a) GTS 4:3

Roger:     She's workin?
           (0.4)
Ther:      (Yeah. She just started a job.)
Roger:     So we lack feminine attendance.
Ther:      ((clears throat)) Does seem so. (Unless) we
           can get some more in.
Ken:       But the girls- any girl that comes in hasta
           take all those tests and stuff don't they?
           (0.6)
Ther:      (Won't be for several weeks now)
Roger:     They make miserable coffee.
Ken:       hhhh hhh
-->  Ther: Across the street?
Roger:     Yeh
Ken:       Miserable food hhhh
           (0.4)
Ken:       hhhh So what'djudo East-er-over Easter Vacation?
```

Here, the arrowed utterance is specifically built as a continuation of
the prior – indeed, that is key to the job the utterance is doing; but it
clearly constitutes a turn-constructional unit – and a turn – in its
own right.[28] So, starting with a non-beginning can be a way of
starting a TCU as well – depending on the form of that non-beginning and what it starts, and its relationship to its context. This is
underscored by Excerpt (15b), taken from a family therapy setting
(Jones and Beach, 1994, in press).

```
(15b) Jones and Beach, 1994 (FAM:A2, simplified)

Ther:      What kind of work do you do?
Mother:    Ah food service
-->  Ther: At?
Mother:    (A)/(uh) post office cafeteria downtown main post office on
           Redwood
Ther:      °Okay° so if you...
```

Here the TCU at the arrowed turn – which does accomplish an
action and is recognized as possibly complete – is designed specifically to have neither a beginning nor an ending in the usual syntactic sense. Implementing the practice of "prompting," it is designed
to be grammatically continuous with what preceded and to provide
for its recipient to provide in next turn a contribution which will be
grammatically continuous with it, and will bring the (now
expanded) whole to possible completion.

Here is part of one sense of the grammar(s) of TCUs being *positionally sensitive*. If an early organizational issue for an incipient
speaker is whether to begin a next installment of talk with a beginning or a non-beginning, and if each of these requires design by
reference to the immediate sequential context, then the selection of a

grammar for turn-construction is context-sensitive in the sense of positionally specified at the praxeological point of departure.

2.5.1   TCU beginnings

Once we have registered that a speaker's contribution of talk in a possible turn position can be designed from its outset to be a separate TCU or not, and that this can turn (if I may put it that way) on whether it starts with a beginning(-in-context) or not, then we are afforded a starting point for analysis. One direction for inquiry into grammar and interaction, into the organization of turn constructional units and turns, concerns beginnings. Here are some practical queries for analysis:

(A)   Beginnings. For any TCU, or – given the preceding considerations – for any initial talk in what could be a turn position, we can ask:

(1) Does it start with a beginning?

(2) Is there more than one beginning?

(3) By reference to what is/are the beginning(s) constituted as beginning? What form does the beginning take?

(4) If there is more than one beginning, are they the same or different?

(5) If the same, how are we to understand the redoing? (cf. Goodwin, 1980, 1981; Schegloff, 1987a[1973].)

(6) If different, are the several beginnings different beginnings for a "recognizably same" TCU, or for different TCUs?

(7) If for a "recognizably same" TCU, what does the new beginning do relative to the prior beginning?

(8) If a new beginning is for a "new" TCU, is there a recognizable shift target, i.e., a recognizable (or conjectural) basis for shifting from the prior to the new TCU?

Here I can offer only a rough indication of how some of these inquiries might be pursued. Consider a few instances of different beginnings for a "recognizably same" TCU:

```
(16)   SN-4:01:05-30

Mark:     Hi Sherry, hi Ruthie,
Ruthie:   Hi Ma:rk.
Sherri:   Hi Ma:rk.=
Mark:     =[How're you guys.
          =[((door slams))
          (0.2)
```

```
        Ruthie:   Jis' fi:ne.
                  (0.2)
        Sherri:   Uh:: tired.
        Mark:     Tired, I hear yih gettin' married.
                  (0.6)
        (??):     °((sniff))
                  (0.3)
        Sherri:   Uh:: you hear right.
                  (0.2)
        Mark:     (Ih) shah-I hear ri:gh[t.
        ?Shrri:                         [mmhh [(heh  hh])
-->     Mark:                                [Didja e-] by the way didja ever
                  call up uh: Century City Hotel 'n
                  (1.0)
        Sherri:   Y'know h'much they want fer a wedding¿  It's incredible.
                  (0.5)
        Sherri:   We'd 'aftuh sell our house 'n car 'n evryt(h)hing e(h)l(h)se
                  [tuh pay fer the wedding .]
        Mark:     [Shhh'er house 'n yer car.]
        (17) Wong:TJ:4:4

        Tang:     Yeah, for the temple you know then the children grow up, you
                  know
                  (0.4)
-->     Tang:     Oh d- by the way did you get the tapes?
        Jim:      Oh yeah I did.

        (18)  Auto Discussion:03:26-40

        Carney:   Thanks hon,
                  (0.1)
        Carney:   W'make a good=
        Gary:     ME::=
X       Phyllis:  =°Go sit by [Curt.
        Carney:                =[couple.
        Gary:     Yer the one thet did it!
                  (0.5)
X-->    Curt:     C'mmere Bo,kih-jus' kick im Phyllis,
        Gary:     hhOh m[y  G o:d.hh]=
X       Curt:           [C'mon! Hey!]=
        Gary:     =hh I've got m[y, sacroilliac twisted all the way arou[:n
X       Curt:                   [`pw! Comon,                            [
X       Curt:                                                           [Comon
                  Bo,=
X       Mike:     =°G'wan.=
```

At the arrowed turn in each of these instances, a TCU is started with
a candidate beginning, is cut off, and some new element is inserted
before the first beginning is re-employed. It is the re-employment of
the initial beginning which allows recognition of the new element as
an "insertion," allows the insertion to be recognized as what the
cut-off was designed to permit, and provides for the whole configuration to be recognized as a re-beginning of the "same" TCU with
a new turn-initial element.

In (16), what invites retro-construction as "Didja ever call up..."
is self-interrupted for the insertion of "By the way," a usage which

in other contexts appears to be used as a "misplacement marker"
(Schegloff and Sacks, 1973: 319-20; also in Baugh and Sherzer,
1984: 92-3). In the present context (roughly), Sherry has discour-
aged Mark's move to initiate topic talk on her forthcoming wedding; Mark's question appears to be pursuing the topic nonetheless,
and the misplacement marker appears to register his orientation to
the question's apparent out-of-order-ness. As well, it can be taken
as marking the question as disjunctive with what preceded, rather
than in line with it.

A similar usage seems to figure in (17), but here the initial start of
the TCU "Oh d-" already incorporates a change-of-state token
(Heritage, 1984), a touch-off marker which can signal disjunction
(Jefferson, 1978a). But in this context, the speaker finds misplacement marking enough in order as to warrant self-interruption in
order to insert "by the way" (I take "by the way" to be inserted, not
to replace the "oh"). In both these instances, the turn's beginning is
redone ostensibly to secure inclusion of a revised indication of the
turn's relationship to prior talk, and of the propriety of its placement.

In Excerpt (18), a backyard picnic gathering has schismed
(Egbert, 1993) into two participation frameworks – Carney and
her husband Gary engaging in assessing responsibility for
Carney's fall from Gary's lap, and – in the exchange of interest
here (marked by Xs) – Phyllis and Mike trying to get host Curt's
dog Bo to move closer to his master and farther from them. In the
arrowed turn, Curt responds to Phyllis' directive to the dog first by
issuing one of his own ("C'mmere Bo"), and then by inviting Phyllis
to "get physical" rather than issuing instructions. The shift from the
reconstructible "Kih[ck him Phyllis]" to "Just kick him Phyllis"
appears designed first to relieve her of a burden of restraint
("just" marking in this regard a "lesser" course of action, i.e., less
self-disciplined), but also (perhaps by virtue of the comparative
tenor which "just" introduces) to relate the directive (or the permis-
sion) he is giving her to the preceding course of action. It thus has
an effect related to, but different from, the "by the way"'s of the
preceding excerpts.

These three excerpts permit another feature to be noted. Earlier it
was useful to remark that some things which occur in turns have
their organizational locus or origin not in the turn but in the
sequence. Here a related observation may be in order. The "By

the way"'s in (16) and (17) *belong to the turn*; they relate the turn –
given what is incipiently being said/done in it – to the talk which
came before and that is the job they seem introduced to do. By
contrast, the "just" in (18) *belongs not so much to its turn as to
its TCU*; it marks the nature of the action Curt is doing; if not
directing Phyllis to kick the dog then permitting her to do so.
That it marks a relationship to earlier elements of the course of
action (and that they were addressed to the dog, though Curt is
now responding) is a by-product, rather than central.

In contrast to multiple beginnings for a "recognizably same"
TCU, consider a candidate instance of a new beginning for a
"new" TCU, and the issue it may be seen to pose concerning the
grounds for the shift. It is drawn from the earlier examined Excerpt
(9), reproduced below.

```
(9)    MDE:MTRAC:60-1/2, 01:01-19

Marsha:   Hello:?
Tony:     Hi: Marsha?
Marsha:   Ye:ah.
Tony:     How are you.
Marsha:   Fi::ne.
          (0.2)
Marsha:   Did Joey get home yet?
Tony:     Well I wz wondering when 'e left.
          (0.2)
-->  Marsha:   'hhh Uh:(d) did Oh: .h Yer not in on what ha:p  pen'.(hh)(d)
Tony:     No(h)o=
Marsha:   =He's flying.
          (0.2)
Marsha:   En Ilene is going to meet im:.Becuz the to:p wz ripped
          off'v iz car which is tih say someb'ddy helped th'mselfs.
Tony:     Stolen.
          (0.4)
Marsha:   Stolen.=Right out in front of my house.
Tony:     Oh: f'r crying out loud,...
```

Marsha's turn at the arrow is begun "tentatively," i.e., after multiple "delays" by an inter-turn gap of silence, then a hearable in-
breath, then an "uh: " which ends in a possible allusion to the initial
sound of the first word – "d", and finally a beginning to the TCU,
"Did."[29] The initial projection which this beginning adumbrates is,
minimally, that a question may be being initiated, and very likely a
"yes/no"-type question. But the "did" is followed not by a possible
next component of the just-launched TCU but by "Oh," which
serves here both as a self-interruption marker and initiator, as a
change-of-state token (here, specifically, what one might call a
"realization" marker), and as a disjunction marker, alerting recipi-

ent that what follows might be not more of what preceded, but something disjunctive with what preceded (compare Jefferson, 1974), including potentially a new start, and potentially a new start of a new "product." And indeed what follows (unlike the self-interruptions in the three excerpts previously examined) does not include the re-appearance of the first beginning.

The new beginning offers at least one immediate contrast with the prior one: it projects a possibly declarative construction (only "possibly" because it can be prosodically shaped to end by being "released" as an interrogative). With such new beginnings which offer an immediate contrast with a prior beginning, one issue they may pose (for recipients as well as professional analysts) is whether something "entirely disjunct" is being done, or whether some type of systematic alternative is being done – i.e., some TCU which stands in an orderly relationship to the one which had been initiated and incipiently projected – for example, a re-ordering with a shift to something which should be said "first," or an alternative tack to what the turn was beginning to take. And often this can be conjecturally retro-constructed from a juxtaposition of the abandoned beginning and the finally realized replacement.

Here in Excerpt (9), for example, one can conjecture that Marsha was beginning to ask "Did Joey call you?" (or even *"Didn't* Joey call you?") but "realizes" that Tony's question belies the relevance of such an inquiry, and delivers the product of that realization instead, in what amounts to an *epistemic upgrade* from an *inquiry* about the current distribution of knowledge about Joey's itinerary to an *assertion* about it. Here then the "new" TCU may not be very remote from the initially begun one, but that clearly can vary.

These few observations can be but the barest indication of two strategic orders of relevance of the starts of spates of talk, and of (initial) TCUs as the predominant form of such talk: the relationship of the talk being launched to what has *preceded* (whether talk, or other conduct, or features of the context) and a *projection* of aspects of what is being launched.

With respect to the former, there are virtually always generic jobs to be done with regard, for example, to prior turn – e.g., showing that it was heard, understood, that its selection of next speaker was registered either in the observance or in the breach. But there can also be particular types of jobs precipitated or made relevant by particular prior turns or actions, or particular *types* of prior turn or action, e.g., stance-taking of various sorts (aligning with or against, registering surprise or familiarity), laughing, doing sequentially appropriate nexts, etc. or disengaging from the sequential projection of prior turn. Such jobs may on occasion be best done in a TCU dedicated to something else (like "just kick him"), on occasion in a TCU-initial component dedicated to back-linking (like "by the way"), or sometimes by a full turn-initial TCU dedicated to back linking, like the pro forma agreement token or expression which may precede a disagreement or account.[30]

With respect to projection by the beginning of a TCU of aspects of what is being launched, we need to consider the "internal" organization of TCUs themselves. (By "internal" I mean the organization that relates the parts of a TCU to one another, however we conceive and formulate those parts.) This is at least one traditional sense of the term "grammar." But before doing so, I want to focus for a short while on TCU *possible completions* and *achieved turn closure*, because TCUs are not symmetrical, are not balanced on some grammatical midpoint, but – and this is one import of temporality and sequential structure – are directional. And what they are directional toward is possible completion.

Recall again that this structural, grammatical asymmetry is – in conversation – *interactionally enforced.* Co-participants will properly be oriented to possible completions as places where they may have rights or obligations to talk, and speakers accordingly will be oriented to them as resources for drawing others in and exiting the turn themselves, or holding others off so as to extend what is being said. We must always keep in mind that, although as post-hoc students of talk-in-interaction it is possible for us (however analytically ill-considered it may be) to look for possible completion by working backwards from where a turn actually ended, *for the participants* possible completion is always oriented to, reckoned and encountered from the start of the turn or the TCU, *forward* in real time. And so it will be useful to have directionality toward possible completion, and the transition-relevance of possible completion, on the table before turning directly to the internal – grammatical – organization of the TCU.[31] As quickly becomes obvious, however, it is not so simple; we can hardly talk about possible completion and achieved closure without invoking the internal grammar of the TCU – and, it turns out, without consideration of beginnings.

2.5.2   TCU endings

Recall how we got here. It was via the observation that we come to construct and to recognize a spate of talk as a TCU, at least in part, by having it start with a beginning (which it need not do) and finish with an ending. These then are significant loci of organization in the production of talk in interaction, and we have just addressed ourselves partially to the "starts with beginnings."[32] What I want to focus on next are possible completion and turn-constructional-unit endings as a locus of organization. In particular, I want to offer some reflections not only on possible completion itself, but also on "pre-possible completion" as one strategic place in the organization (the *grammatical* organization?) of a TCU, and on "post-possible completion" as an underexplored terrain that is still within the boundaries of the turn, and potentially of the preceding TCU. I will have to be brief and compressed; I will rely to a greater extent on past work and less on the examination of data fragments. Let me begin by offering a series of analytic themes which can be brought to the parsing of any TCU in any turn, much as I did for beginnings, and then explore just a few of the issues which these themes reflect.

(B) Endings. For any TCU, we can ask:

(1) Does it end with an ending, i.e., does it come to a recognizable possible completion, on the several dimensions which together constitute possible completion – syntactic, prosodic, and action/pragmatic (cf. Ford and Thompson, this volume)?

(2) Does it come to more than one recognizable possible completion? If so, what are they, and how are they to be understood?

(3) How are some (projectable) possible completions circumvented? For example, (a) how are they marked as "not-designed-to-be-ending"? (b) How are they by-passed (e.g., cut-off, trail-off, restructuring, etc.) or (c) overridden (e.g., rush-through)?

(4) How are non-uptakes of projected-possible-completions/designed-endings dealt with? By an increment to the same TCU? By addition of a new TCU?

(5) If by an increment to the same TCU, how does the prior talk shape the new increment? How does the increment display orienta-

tion to the sequential and interactional import of the non-uptake? Of the talk preceding the non-uptake?

(6) If by the addition of a new TCU, what orderliness obtains between the new TCU and the unresponded one? Here, the set of issues raised earlier about multi-unit turns becomes relevant.

One product of focusing on the intersection of grammar and interaction is the specification of loci of strategic organizational import possibly not otherwise analytically accessible. One such locus I want to take notice of is "pre-possible completion." One way my own concern with it arose was with the query, where does the transition space begin? It is clear that sometimes next turns begin in so-called terminal overlap with prior turns which are (it appears to the participants) coming to an end. But how far back into an "expiring" turn can a next speaker go in getting an early start while still not, in effect, doing an interruption? And *how* does it appear that an ongoing turn is coming to an end? A number of *syntactically* possible completions may have passed without being targeted as possible turn completions; how is some incipient next one made the occasion for an early start? Recall that for the parties, these syntactically possible completions are encountered forward in real time; it is not given in advance (as it is to post-hoc analysts looking at or listening to a tape, or looking at a transcript) which possible completions will be passed and which acted upon.

I am sure that there are various resources, and that we know relatively few of them (for one account, cf. Jefferson, 1984b). One usage that I have noticed and examined a bit is a pitch peak in grammatical environments which remain to be characterized. But when the syntactic and pragmatic conditions have been met (e.g., some recognizable action has been projected), a pitch peak can adumbrate "designed possible completion at next grammatically possible completion." Just after such a pitch peak is the locus for various orderly phenomena: it is where early-starting next turns regularly come in; it is where speakers initiate a "rush-through" (Schegloff, 1982) if they mean to extend their talk through the transition-space into a new turn-constructional unit; it is where continuers and other forms of interpolation into otherwise projectably extended spates of talk are placed if they overlap with the otherwise ongoing talk (cf. Goodwin, 1986). Consider, for example, the earlier Excerpt (7), reproduced below with the ensuing turns:

```
(7)   TG:02:06-21

       Ava:   [°B't a si]de fr'm that it's a'right.
       Bee:   [So what-]
              (0.4)
       Bee:   Wha:t?
       Ava:   I'm so:: ti:yid. I j's played ba:ske'ball t'day since the
 -->          firs' time since I wz a freshm'n in hi:ghsch[ool.]
 -->>  Bee:                                                [Ba::]sk(h)et=
              b(h)a(h)ll? (h)[(°Whe(h)re
       Ava:                  [Yeah fuh like an hour enna ha:[lf.]
       Bee:                                                 [`hh] Where
 -->   Bee:   didju play ba:sk[etbaw.  ]
 -->>  Ava:                   [(The) gy]:m.
       Bee:   In the gy:m? [(hh)
       Ava:                [Yea:h. Like grou(h)p therapy.Yuh know
              [half the grou]p thet we had la:s' term wz there en we=
       Bee:   [ O h : : : . ]`hh
```

Directly after the pitch peaks marked by the underlinings on the single-arrowheaded lines ("hi:ghsch[ool" and "ba:sk[etbaw") come the "responses" of the double-arrowheaded lines.

But aside from marking where next turns by others might "prematurely" start and where pre-emptions of them must therefore be initiated, this location of "pre-possible completion" can be organizationally strategic in other respects.

For example, within the organization of repair, there is a key positioning principle for the initiation of repair, and that is by reference to its target – the repairable or trouble-source. The familiar position typology of "same turn initiation, next turn initiation, third position," etc. (Schegloff, Jefferson, and Sacks, 1977 – henceforth SJS) are all positions of repair-*initiation* relative to the trouble-source. Within same turn, the general principle appears to be, "as close to the repairable (i.e., as early) as possible," although the work of Levelt (1983) – if applicable to ordinary conversation – suggests that grammatical structure may in some respects qualify this principle (see also Fox and Jasperson, frth; Fox, Hayashi, and Jasperson, this volume). But there appears to be at least one other conditioning environment for same turn repair initiation and it is *not* relative to the trouble-source – and that is "pre-possible completion." Thus, a few years ago I examined the utterance reproduced in Excerpt (19) below in some detail (Schegloff, 1987b, also 1988b).

```
(19)  Auto Discussion 5:35-36

Curt:     [He- he's about the only regular <he's about the
          only good regular out there'z, Keegan still go out?
```

The point relevant in the present context concerns the self-repair
which inserts the word "good" into an utterance otherwise constructed as "He's about the only regular out there." If we ask
where the repair is initiated, then one account would locate it just
before possible completion of the TCU, for we see that what follows
"regular" in the final delivery of the TCU is "out," which is the
carrier of the pitch peak which adumbrates upcoming possible completion. Any later and the TCU is vulnerable to incipient talk by a
next speaker; before that position, i.e., before "pre-possible completion," seems to be a strategic place for same turn repair initiation.

   Here is another evidence of the relevance of "pre-possible completion." When two speakers find themselves talking at the same
time, one or both of them may begin to speak "competitively," i.e.,
to produce their talk in ways designed to "drive the other out," or
alternatively to outlast the other's competing production. One of
these devices is the "sound stretch," that is, the prolongation of a
component sound of the speaker's ongoing TCU (cf. Jefferson and
Schegloff, 1975 for an early version). If we ask where in the talk of
an overlap this competitive practice is deployed, then one of the
most prominent loci is pre-possible completion in the competing
(the *other* party's) turn. I offer but a single exemplar here, taken
from Excerpt (11), reproduced below.

```
(11)  TG:18:14-27

Bee:      t! We:ll, uhd-yihknow I-I don' wanna make any- thing
          definite because I-yihknow I jis:: I jis::t thinkin:g
          tihday all day riding on th'trai:ns hhuh-uh
          'hh[h!
Ava:          [Well there's nothing else t'do.<I wz
-->       thingin[g  of   taking   the   car  anyway.]  'hh
-->  Bee:         [that I would  go  into the ss-uh- ]=I would go into
          the city but I don't know,
Ava:      Well if I do ta:ke it, this way if- uh-if- y'know uh::
          there's no pa:rking right away I c'n give you the car
          en you c'n look aroun a li'l bit.
Bee:      Mye::[:m , ]
Ava:           [y'know] en see what happens.
```

At the arrows Bee and Ava are talking in overlap. Note that Bee
abandons the saying of "that I would go into the city," only to
resume it and bring it to completion before continuing "but I

don't know." Note as well that, just before abandoning the first saying, she begins the word "city" (it appears in the transcript excerpt as "ss-uh-") and holds its first sound, before starting the resaying. Note finally that she begins this sound stretch just as Ava is beginning the word "anyway," projectably the designed ending of her TCU. It is at pre-possible completion of Ava's TCU that Bee initiates the sound stretch which "absorbs" the remainder of her overlapping talk. (For a further account of this episode, cf. Schegloff, 1987 [1973].)

There are other forms of talk whose organization and placement must be understood, it seems to me, by reference to what seems to be a *grammatical position in the turn constructional unit – pre-possible completion*, among them trail-offs, some of the collaborative completions described by Lerner (1987, 1991), the "pregnant pause" adopted by some speakers during which "planning" for a next TCU and preparation of a rush-through to get there can appear to be prepared, etc.[33]

"Pre-possible completion" is but one of several loci of organizational relevance arrayed around endings of TCUs and turns. Another, obviously key, one is the possible completion point itself. *From the point of view of the organization of talk-in-interaction, one of the main jobs grammar or syntax does is to provide potential construction- and recognition-guides for the realization of the possible completion points of TCUs, and potentially of turns.* And here, therefore, is another major contribution (of the many) which students of grammar can make to our understanding of talk-in-interaction. The grammatical constitution of possible completion is what is "played with" or flouted by trail offs: in the trail off, just what is needed to arrive at a possible completion point is projected, and then left unarticulated. It is worth registering the converse possibility as well – that is, that a point of grammatical possible completion can be reached (including prosody), but the turn not yet be possibly finished – if its "activity" or pragmatic constraints are not met (cf. also Ford and Thompson, this volume). In Excerpt (20) (from which the earlier Excerpt (1) was taken), Bee is proffering as a topic talk about the college which she and Ava had attended together before Bee transferred to another school.

```
(20)  TG 04:35-06:01

     Bee:   Eh-yih have anybuddy: thet uh:? (1.2) I would know from the
            English depar'mint there?
     Ava:   Mm-mh. Tch! I don't think so.
     Bee:   °Oh,=<Did they geh ridda Kuhleznik yet hhh
     Ava:   No in fact I know somebuddy who ha:s huh [now.
     Bee:                                           [Oh my got hh[hhh
     Ava:                                                        [Yeh=
     Ava:   =en s' he siz yihknow he remi:nds me of d-hih-ih- tshe
c--> reminds me, ˙hhh of you, meaning me:.
            (0.4)
     Bee:   Uh-ho that's [a- that's a s[wee:t co:mplimint, ]  ˙hh-
     Ava:                [Kuhleznik.=  [=I said gee:, tha:n]ks a
            lo:[t honeh,
     Bee:      [ hhhhhhhuh huh=
     Ava:   =˙hh [ Said ] yih all gonna gitch' mouth shuddup fih you=
     Bee:        [˙hhhh!]
     Ava:   =yih don't sto:p i[t.]
     Bee:                     [°M]mmyeh,
     Bee:   I think evrybuddy's had her hm[hhh!
     Ava:                                 [Ohh, [she's the biggest=]
b--> Bee:                                       [-fih    something, ]
     Ava:   =pain in the a:ss.
            (0.3)
     Bee:   °Yeh,
     Ava:   .T She's teaching uh English Lit too, no more composition,
     Bee:   Oh:::, She's moved up in the wor[ld ]
     Ava:                                   [She] must know somebuddy
            because all those other teachers they got rid of.hhhh
            (0.3)
     Bee:   Yeh I bet they got rid of all the one::Well one I had, t!
            ˙hhhh in the firs' term there, fer the firs'term of
            English, she die::d hhuh-uhh [˙hhh
     Ava:                                [Oh:.
     Bee:   She died in the middle of the te:rm?mhhh!=
     Ava:   =Oh that's too ba:d hha ha!=
     Bee:   =Eh-ye:h, ih-a, She wz rea:lly awful, she ha-duh, (˙hh)
            she's the wuh- She ha:duh southern accent too.
     Ava:   Oh:.
     Bee:   A:nd, she wz very difficul'tuh unduhstand.
a--> Ava:   No, she ain't there anymoh,
     Bee:   No I know I mean she, she's gone a long t(h)ime
            (h)a'rea(h)[dy? hh
     Ava:              [Mm, [hhmh!
     Bee:                   [˙hhh
            (0.2)
     Bee:   nYeeah, ˙hh This feller I have-(nn) "felluh"; ((etc.))
```

Note here that at the "a"-arrowed turn, "No" taken by itself
cannot constitute the full turn. And because by "turn constructional
unit" we mean units of talk which *can* constitute the whole turn,
"No" here is not only not the possible completion point of a TCU;
it may not be a TCU at all – not in this environment, even though
elsewhere it is. Indeed, in the very next turn it is. I must limit myself
to a brief explication.

In the immediately preceding talk, Bee has been providing an account of a teacher she "had" whom they did *not* "get rid of," because she had died in the middle of the term – this as an installment in the ongoing topic of a search for mutual acquaintances (including instructors) from the past, a search which Ava has been discouraging. In the turn just preceding the "a"-arrowed one, Bee is bringing her characterization of this teacher to a close in a common way – with a summary assessment. This was (apparently) not an instructor whom Ava had shared with Bee, and she (Ava) is in no position to agree or disagree with this assessment. The turn-initial "No" is then potentially anomalous; it cannot be all of what Ava is going to say (and, indeed, she goes on to provide a linkage back to *that* prior talk to which her talk *is* addressed). By contrast, in the following turn, after Ava has remarked (presumably ironically, given the reported death) that this teacher is no longer at the college, a turn-initial "no" *can* be all of the turn – the negative being a form of agreement token with a preceding negative assertion.

As it happens, this "no" is not all of its turn either. But note that in the arrowed turn, where the "no" *cannot* be the possible completion, the speaker has the luxury of pausal prosody, being little vulnerable to a start up of a next turn by the other; whereas in the following turn, where the "no" *is* a possible completion, there is no prosodic juncture marked, but the talk is pressed through to a next TCU (as in Excerpt (1), which reappears here in (20) as the second turn by Ava).

The more general point here (whose relevance extends beyond turn closure to the form of the grammar more generally, and to the positional variability of grammar) is this. Because what it will take for a turn's work to be possibly done can vary with its position in a sequence (e.g., the question vs. the answer turn, the first assessment or the response to it, etc.), the grammar can also vary, and with it, *what can constitute possible completion*. In composing a turn, then, a speaker can – perhaps, must – consult "place in sequence" – indeed, must consult "place in the set of organizational frameworks in which the moment is lodged" – and the composition of the immediately preceding talk as a resource for constructing the present turn, including its grammatical form. And recipients will then have to do the same in parsing and grasping it. I will return to this theme.

If "pre-possible closing" and "possible completion point" are loci of organizational import for TCU closure and thereby potentially for turn ending, so is *"post-possible completion."* And here I want to discriminate two different *sorts* of things which can occupy post-possible completion position. One sort is composed of elements of talk added to the TCU and the turn which re-occasion possible completion; that is, which constitute extensions to the TCU or the turn (the two are different) and which themselves come to another possible completion of the TCU or turn.[34] The other sort is composed of elements which are positioned post-possible completion, but do not represent extensions of the prior talk, but rather retrospective or retroactive alignments *toward* it, or consequences *of* it – what I will term below "post-completion stance markers."

First, grammatically structured extensions of, or increments to, the talk. Various sorts of elements can follow possible completion. Some of these appear to add a new grammatical unit (often a phrase or a clause) to what preceded and thereby to extend it in some fashion, often "specifying" it, as in Excerpt (3) ("Stolen. Right out in front of my house."). or Excerpt (21) below:

```
(21)   TG 16:22-31

Ava:      Yeh w'l I'll give you a call then tomorrow.when I get in
          'r sumn.
          (0.5)
Bee:      Wha:t,
Ava:      <I'll give yih call tomo[rrow.]
Bee:                              [Yeh: ] 'n [I'll be ho:me t'mor]row.
-->  Ava:                                    [When I-I  get  home.]  I
     Ava:      don't kno-w- I could be home by-'hh three, I c'd be home
               by two [I don't] know.]
Bee:              [ Well  ] when ]ever. ((etc.))
```

Here "when I get home" is a clause added post-possible completion of Ava's prior TCU (and turn), a possible completion testified to by Bee's taking it as the occasion for initiating a next turn.

But the post-possible completion element can be an "add-on" which does not add a new grammatical construction but complements a grammatical construction with which the prior TCU had apparently come to closure, as in Excerpt (20), above at the "b-" arrowed turn (where "fih something" appears to complement "...everybody's had her,") or Excerpts (22) and (23) below.

```
(22)  TG 11:01-09

Bee:      Mm, tch! I wz gonnuh call you. last week someti(h)me
          'hhh[hh!
Ava:          [Yeh my mother a:sked mih I siz I don'know I haven't
          hea:rd from her.I didn' know what day:s you had.'h[hh
Bee:                                                       [Yeh
          en I[: didn' know w-]
-->  Ava:      [ cla:sses 'r   ] a[nything,
Bee:                             [I didn'know when you were hh[ome=
Ava:                                                         [Tch


(23)  TG 14:02-11

Bee:          [Dihyuh have any-cl- You have a class with
          Billy this te:rm?
Ava:      Yeh he's in my abnormal class.
Bee:      mnYeh [ how-]
Ava:            [Abnor]mal psy[ch.
Bee:                          [Still not gettin married,
-->  Ava:      'hhh Oh no. Definitely not.[married.]
Bee:                                      [No  he's] dicided[defin[itely?]
Ava:                                                        ['hhh [O h   ]
          no.
```

In both (22) and (23) Ava appears (syntactically, prosodically, and pragmatically) to have brought a TCU (and with it the turn) to possible completion (i.e., "appears" to her interlocutor Bee, whose next turn beginnings display such an analysis), but Ava then produces an add-on to that talk, which grammatically complements what had otherwise appeared to be possibly complete – "...what days you had" being complemented by "classes or anything" in (22), and "definitely not" being complemented by "married" in (23).[35]

Post-possible completion is also one of the structurally provided and recurrently exploited positions for initiating repair, i.e., "transition-space repair" (cf. SJS, 1977: 366, 374 et passim), as, for example, in Excerpt (20) above at the "c"-arrow ("...meaning me."). Indeed, as a distinctive locus of repair initiation it is defined/constituted by its placement "post-possible completion." As with the previously mentioned additions, it re-engenders a possible completion at its end.

And there is a variety of usages which have post-possible completion as one of their environments of possible occurrence – such as address terms, courtesy terms, and the like (cf. Jefferson, 1973; SSJ, 1974: 707-8), and at least one designed specifically for post-possible completion position – the tag question.[36] The last has as one of its signal jobs (though not necessarily the only one on any particular occasion of use) the decisive completion of the turn to which it is appended (SSJ, 1974: 718). (More generally, many of these elements appear to be extensions of a turn, not a TCU; they are attached to a TCU by virtue of the TCU's completion being the turn's completion. In this regard they are not unlike "uh" as the first element of a turn, which is best understood as beginning a turn without beginning a TCU – cf. above, pp. 61, 79-80 and note 29.)

We have already had occasion to remark (in examining Excerpt (2) early on) that when a TCU has come to possible completion and its speaker moves to add to it (whether by reference to non-uptake by another or – as Excerpts (21)-(23) show – independent of non-uptake), the two major grammatical and sequential alternatives are the initiation of a new TCU or a grammatical extension of the prior, and this is perhaps one of the most common exploitations of post-possible completion by the addition of further talk.

But I want to register as well the occurrence of a second sort of element following the possible completion of a TCU or a turn, one which does not appear to constitute, or be taken as, an extension of it nor another possible completion of it, but is *specifically after* its completion. I have in mind a variety of what can be called "post-completion stance markers." They take such forms as post-completion nodding, facial expressions (e.g., smiles or grimaces), shrugs, posture shifts, disclaimers ("I dunno"), laugh tokens, coughs, exhalations and sighs, in-breaths, and I know not what else.[37] They occupy the same space occupied by other post-possible completion possibilities, and may serve as alternates to them (as delays of them?) – in any case, they are elements in the configuration by which TCUs (and, with them, turns) get brought to closure with endings.

2.5.3   A reprise on TCU beginnings

It is striking that among the "inventory" of possible post-completion elements are bits of conduct that can serve as *beginning* elements. Or, more precisely, now that we have registered sorts of occurrences which are *post-possible completion*, we need to return to our treatment of beginnings, and add to them what we should call "*pre-beginning*" elements – elements which project the onset of talk, or the beginning of a (next) TCU or a turn, but are not yet proper recognizable beginnings. They occupy a position just outside the beginning, much as there is a position just outside the possible ending. I have in mind such elements of conduct as turning the head toward (or redirecting gaze at) a potential recipient, the onset of gesture deployment and often its full realization (Streeck and Hartge, 1992 – one of several citations in the present paper suggesting the relevance of its themes to languages and grammars other than English), incipient facial expression (e.g., smile), lip parting, cough or throat clear, (hearable) in-breath (sometimes exaggerated), as well as "uh(m)," which can serve to initiate a turn, while not yet initiating a TCU within it. I will return in a moment to the observation that some of the same bits of conduct appear as elements which occur post-possible completion and pre-beginning of a TCU.

But having been prompted (by post-possible completion) to register the pre-beginning position, it turns out that there is a position just *inside* the beginning boundary as well, which is the structural locus for determinate activities – what might be termed "post-beginning" position. I will mention only a few such activities.

One is the phenomenon described by C. Goodwin (1980, 1981) as a "phrasal break." Goodwin noted that the basic organization of gaze orientation around turns involved an orientation by beginning speakers to find recipient's gaze already on them as they brought their gaze to recipient. Should they not find that, then one practice which they adopt introduces a break in their talk – a "phrasal break" – which regularly serves to attract the gaze of recipient. Although the locus of this practice can vary, for readily apparent reasons its most likely occurrence is just after turn beginning – where the talk can already have attracted recipient's eyes so that speaker can turn to recipient expecting to find them, and can introduce the practice of the phrasal break if they are not there. Just post beginning. (Note that this would be a structured location for initial TCUs in a turn, or sole TCUs, but not in other TCUs, except as a resource for retrieving recipient's wandering attention; cf. Goodwin, 1987.)

Another is related to a phenomenon I have described previously (Schegloff, 1982) as a rush-through. A speaker approaching possible completion of a TCU can speed up the talk, shape the prosody not to come to even temporary closure at the grammatical possible completion point and proceed immediately into the start of new TCU. Then it is common for the speaker to allow the break which might otherwise have occurred at possible completion to develop just after the start of the new TCU, at a place which could be characterized as one of "maximum grammatical control,"

e.g., after a preposition but before its object, after the infinitive
marker but before the verb, etc., but at such a place just after the
start of the new TCU. (Note that this would be a structured location
in specifically *non*-initial or sole TCUs!)

Yet another activity whose locus is just inside the beginning boundary of the TCU or turn is the phenomenon of the "post-failed-joke
hitch." Although the failed joke is its most common (or perhaps its
most obtrusive) site, other "performance" infelicities can induce this
perturbation in the talk. Speakers may essay a variety of "special
productions" – jokes, cute sayings, wisecracks, self-deprecations,
special bits of physical performance (pirouettes, etc.), unusual stories
– in short, productions designed to elicit determinate, *marked* recep-
tions from interlocutors – of which laughter for a joke is only the most
familiar exemplar. If they have done the "special production" and fail
to achieve the marked response or appreciation it makes relevant,
then just after the start of a next turn or TCU they may register a
noticing of the failure by a hitch or perturbation in their talk.

Thus in Excerpt (24) (which is an expansion of Excerpt (12)
above), drawn from the conversation between Marsha and Tony
about the changed travel plans of their son Joey because of the
damage to his car, Marsha responds to Tony's expression of
anger at the stealing of the convertible top from Joey's car by
recounting her reaction with the adolescent drug users whom she
counsels at a local agency:

```
(24)   MDE-MTRAC 60-1/2, 01:35 - 02:13

       Tony:     W't's 'e g'nna do go down en pick it up later? er
                 somethin like (       ) [well that's aw]:ful
       Marsha:                          [H i s   friend ]
       Marsha:   Yeh h[is   friend Stee- ]
       Tony:          [That really makes] me ma:d,
                 (0.2)
       Marsha:   ˙hhh Oh it's disgusti[ng ez a matter a'f]a:ct.
       Tony:                          [P o o r  J o e y ,]
       Marsha:   I- I, I told my ki:ds. who do this: down et the Drug
a->              Coalition ah want th'to:p back.h ˙hhhhhhhhh ((1.0 breath))
a->              SEND OUT the WO:RD.hhh hnh
                 (0.2)
       Tony:     Yeah.
b->    Marsha:   ˙hhh Bu:t u-hu:ghh his friend Steve en Brian er driving
                 up. Right after:: (0.2) school is out.En then hi'll
                 drive do:wn here with the:m.
```

Marsha, who is an outgoing and dramatic speaker at her most
restrained, here gives full vent to her enacted emotion. The empha-

tic delivery of "I want the top back" (at the "a" arrow) is brought to crescendo by its dramatically delayed follow up. She follows with a post-completion stance marker (the laugh tokens), but Tony initially withholds any response, and when he does register uptake, it is only that, with a highly restrained "yeah," in dramatic contrast with the preceding context. Just into the start of her ensuing turn, this failed uptake is registered (though hardly adequately reproduced in the transcript here) by Marsha's "u-h<u>u</u>: ghh." "Just post beginning" is here again the locus of relevance for a distinctive type of activity.

In fact, this is also the locus for a variety of repair initiations (cf. Fox and Jasperson, frth.), as well as a kind of "delayed" or "last check" position by a speaker on prior turn by other, and its adequacy as a response to *its* predecessor (cf. Whalen, 1995, 206-7, and see note 51 below).

2.5.4   TCU beginnings and endings and complications

Having reflected on the organization of the beginnings of TCUs and turns, and on the endings of TCUs and turns, which has led to the noticing of pre- and post- phases for each, it is in point now to connect the two. For they are, of course, inextricably connected...and in a variety of ways. For example,

(a) if a speaker has brought a TCU to possible completion and there is no uptake, should that speaker choose to deal with the incipient silence, TCU beginning organization and TCU ending organization provide alternative sets of resources – either resume with an increment to the possible completion of the prior TCU or begin a new TCU;

(b) most generally, beginning a turn with the beginning of a TCU is occasioned by the recognizable ending of a prior TCU/turn by another;

(c) indeed, generally the starts of turns are designed to connect to their prior turns, and their ends are designed to provide projections and connections for their following turns (SSJ, 1974: 722-3);

(d) there is often a semantic, lexical and/or phonological connection between the terminal elements of one turn and the initial elements of the next (i.e., there is a direct, achieved linkage between beginnings and preceding endings);

(e) in some instances, beginnings deal with the ending of the prior turn *by same speakers* – across, or by reference to, the intervening talk by another, as in the post-failed joke hitch, or the practice which Sacks termed (1992: II: 349-51, 356-7, et passim in volume I) "skip-tying," in which a speaker links a next utterance to their own prior, skipping over the intervening talk by another;

(f) on the possible completion of a turn, a next speaker may begin a next turn with "uh" or some other element to delay the actual start of the first TCU in the new turn, and this can occasion a resumption by prior speaker of preceding turn, realized through a continuation of the otherwise complete prior turn and TCU.

Let me note, then, that I have so far been taking up these beginnings and endings from the perspective of the turn, or the turn-constructional unit. That seems natural enough: they are after all the beginnings and ending of TCUs and turns. The beginnings regularly project aspects of what it will take for the TCU's endings to be achieved. And we have been working our way towards a focus on the grammar which organizes the talk between the beginning and the endings (though we have unavoidably already been discussing it). And we have (until points a–f just above) taken it that we were dealing with beginnings and endings of *same TCUs*.

But we have also seen that the endings of TCUs live under the shadow of the incipient beginnings of next turns, and that beginnings of turns can be thoroughly preoccupied with the ends of their preceding turns. Which is to say that the entire picture as we have been conceiving it can be inverted: for, taken together, the two sets of practices – of turn and TCU beginnings and turn and TCU endings constitute the major factors shaping *the social and interactional organization of the transition space.*

While from the point of view of the "talk itself" the turns themselves are the key elements and the transition spaces merely their boundaries, from the point of view of the organization of the interaction as an event realized *in situ* in real time, it is at the transition spaces that the determination of next chunks is accomplished, amid dense interactional considerations. Transition spaces are objects too – with their own shape, duration, import and limits – starting somewhere in a prior turn or TCU and lasting until somewhere in a next turn or TCU.[38] Taking the turns-at-talk as focal (as is the usual stance), the transition spaces are "negative space," – what comes in between instances of the units. Taking the transition spaces as focal, the *turns* become negative space – mere respites between episodes of determination of when the action shall pass to another, to whom, and for what.

The "beginnings" and "endings" can then be seen as boundaries not only of turns, but of transition spaces – another exemplar, perhaps, of the aphorism about chickens being seen as the device by which eggs reproduce themselves. But this is not only a joke; it is clear that transition spaces are as organizationally strategic as turns are in the organization of talk in interaction. One should not dismiss on grounds of plausibility (or implausibility) the degree to which the talk in the turns (which we are prepared to treat as central) is shaped by the organization of their interstices (which we sometimes are not prepared to so treat).

Having just sprung a "gestalt switch"[39] on our consideration of grammar and interaction, let me now project the whole matter onto a three-dimensional grid. Any utterance in conversation may be understood to go through three phases: as (incipient) next, as current, and as prior. That is, as a current-recipient-of-some-talk/potential-next-speaker parses it in the course of its progressive articulation, potential response types and lines are engendered, subject to revision and replacement as the current talk is further produced bit by bit. This is the first phase of an utterance's development;[40] it may be the *only* phase, should someone else get next turn and use it in a fashion which permanently supersedes the relevance of the one which was *in statu nascendi*. But should the "current-recipient/potential-next-speaker" to whom I was referring *get* the next opportunity to talk, then what had been an "incipient or potential next turn" may begin to be articulated, and thus progressively take on the cast of "current turn." And on its completion, a completion sealed by the start of a following turn which is itself then making the transition from "incipient next" to "current," what *was* current turn becomes "prior turn."[41]

Of course, it is not so simple. For example, while some current turn is coming to possible completion and verging on becoming prior turn, incipient next turn may begin to show itself, for example, by features of its pre-beginning. And this pre-beginning of the potentially next turn may then induce changes in the turn which was lapsing from current into prior; for example, its speaker may take measures to override a projected imminent possible completion and extend the turn into a hitherto "unplanned" direction. And the consequence of this extension may be that the incipient next turn whose pre-beginnings prompted this may be rendered irrelevant, and be replaced by a "new" next turn, which displays a new pre-beginning and passage into "current turn" status.

Indeed, elsewhere I have described an empirical instance of just this story (Schegloff, 1987b, 1988b (and cf. Excerpt (19) above and its discussion)). A speaker, Curt, proposes about the car races and one of the drivers, Al, that "He- he's about the only regular he's about the only good regular out there," and as he projects upcoming possible completion with a pitch peak on "out," his recipient Mike displays aspects of the incipient next-turn-in-formation, with a lateral shaking of the head which adumbrates disagreement. Thereupon the speaker, Curt, shifts into a rush-through, and anticipates the grounds of the incipient disagreement by adding another TCU, "Does Keegan still go out?" And, indeed, recipient Mike now shifts the shape of his pre-beginning gesture to a vertical, agreeing nod, and responds, "Keegan's out there..."etc.

The point is that whatever understanding we wish to develop about the interface between grammar and interaction for the organization of turns and turn-constructional units will need to be triply considered. We will need to understand what happens to the grammar of an utterance as it passes from being an incipient next turn (indeed, from a *history* of incipient next turns, as the current turn progressively reveals itself) to being a current turn or TCU in the course of *its* progressive development through a series of turns-so-far, to being a/the prior turn or TCU, whether as a "revivable" or for its interest as the object to which *its next turn* must be adapted.

Another order of consideration which is relevant here again concerns the possible usefulness of our thinking not of "a grammar" or "the grammar" but of a set of positionally sensitive grammars. I mentioned this earlier in the present paper and will return to it briefly in a moment. But the relevance here is this. If utterances pass through the phases of next/current/prior, then all those phases may be positionally specified. For example, hearing an assessment being offered, its recipient's embryonic next turn may be shaped up as a second assessment (Pomerantz, 1984), a second assessment which is then delivered as a current turn, and becomes something to be dealt with by another as it passes into prior turn status. But if, as in the case I just described, the current turn which our incipient next speaker is parsing and forming a response to is not only changed but is sequence-structurally transformed – for example, into a question – then the sort of positional specification of the next turn is transformed as well, and with it the grammatical resources which are relevant for what is incipient next/current/prior.

I have introduced a number of reconfigurations of the discussion here: from turn organization to its obverse – transition space organization; from the talk which we can actually hear, to phases that are not quite as "tangible;" from just a turn-at-talk – or a unit from which it is constructed – to a situated opportunity to talk at a particular interactional and sequence-structural juncture. But it seems to me that all of these have to be entertained in considering the interface of grammar and interaction.

And so far, the focus has taken beginnings and endings of TCUs and turns as the point of departure. But surely there is more to the grammar than that, even if by grammar we mean only the way in which the component elements of a TCU can be selected and configured.[42] So let me say just a little bit about the grammar other than beginnings and endings.

2.5.5   The grammars themselves

What *are* the elements that compose TCUs? What kinds of configurations do they take to compose TCUs, or to compose unmarked forms of TCUs? Here there is room for only a few reflections on these matters.

When we ask "what are the elements of which TCUs are composed" we are in search of such an account of what enters the talk as is built afresh – one that has not already presupposed that some sorts of elements are part of "the language" and others not; that some are components of the TCU whereas others are by-products of the process of its construction – a kind of psycholinguistic detritus. Initially we need to take a simple inventory: what actually occurs in a turn, in what order, in what configurations, by what practices. Then we can sort out what does, and what does not, belong in an account of turn and TCU construction.

For example, unless I am mistaken, "uh" is ordinarily not considered an element of the language of which a grammar must take account. It is a psycholinguistic artifact, likely to occur at important information-theoretic decision points, etc. Yet over twenty years ago Jefferson (1974) showed that the gearing of selection between alternative realizations of the indefinite and definite articles (between "ay" and "uh" and "thee" and "thuh") to the initial sound of the following word incorporated sensitivity to "uh." That is, the "initial sound of the following word" regularly referred not to the next word that "counted" by official standards of what a word is, but to the "uh" that intervened between the article and that word. "Uh" then needs to be counted as among the elements from which a TCU is constructed, for it figures in the construction of the turn even in a traditional sense, and affects the realization of other elements of its construction.[43] Our inventory of elements of TCUs needs to be assembled in the first instance in a generously inclusive fashion – to err on the side of inclusion; there will be ample opportunity subsequently to exclude occurrences which are better understood as other than constructional resources, but in the course of grounding their exclusion explicitly we stand to learn about the underlying constitution of the grammatical and the extra-grammatical.

Implicit in the earlier discussion of such key structural locations as pre-beginnings and pre-possible completion is an underlying organizational shape to the organization of the TCU which we can term "directionality." In large measure this is prompted by the inescapably temporal character of talk-in-interaction, but it is reinforced by the organizational consequentiality of possible completion (and orientations to it by others) for all the participants.[44] About each next bit (including elements, but also bits of elements) of a turn-in-progress a recipient may be oriented to (not necessarily in this order) (a) its projection – i.e., what further course it adumbrates; (b) its realization – i.e., how it contributes to the realization of previously projected courses; and (c) its re-direction – i.e., how it operates to modify previous projections in new directions. These recipient interests can be directed to "elements" such as words, or bits of them such as syllables, sounds, breaths, etc., or the absence of these in silences-in-context, as well. TCUs and turns must be taken in the first instance to be designed and constructed by reference to such an orientation by recipient(s). Grammar is, in large measure, one organizational framework for such construction and receptive orientation.

This is one important reason for including such units of conduct as "same turn repair initiations" (such as glottal or dental stops, for example, or some sound stretches) as grammatical elements, even though apparently not phonemic for English. Serving as they do as possible alerts to a recipient that what follows may not be more of the trajectory which had preceded in the TCU-so-far (Jefferson, 1974; Schegloff, 1979), and often as the operation which marks an actual disjunction between what preceded and what follows, cut-offs operate as organizational operations relating elements of the TCU to one another – albeit productionally rather than propositionally.

That observation, however, leads to another. Repair is one of several types of strips of activity which may be launched in the course of a turn or TCU-in-progress (replacing, or running simultaneous with, its continuing course) which have an organizational shape of its/their own. For example, word searches have a characteristic organizational trajectory, beginning with a series of "uh"s and pauses, followed by an interjection, and clues which might allow the recipient to aid in the search (though not each of these elements is present in every search), which composes the activity of "searching for a name/word/etc.,"[45] and which is launched as its own organization of elements inside the TCU in which a word search is undertaken. Similarly, speakers who believe they can recognizably refer to someone by name while speaking to their current recipient but are unsure of success (that is, are unsure that recipient will achieve recognition from the reference-by-name) may employ the name with "try-marked" intonation (Sacks and Schegloff, 1979: 18-20) and pause for evidence of recognition; in its absence they may produce a (further) clue to the identification of the intended referent, etc. Again, there is a characteristic course to the activity of achieving possibly problematic "recognitional reference" which may be introduced into a turn or TCU-in-progress, and (like the word search) "take over" the next stretch of talk. And some elements will properly be understood as positioned within this activity-based strip of talk, rather than within the organization of the TCU in which the strip was launched.[46]

But there are other activities which commonly overlay the talk and co-occur with it, rather than displacing or deferring it, which may inform and complement the construction and import of the talk, and figure in its upshot and understanding together with the otherwise ongoing TCU. There are varieties of evidence, for example, that gesture is co-organized with the talk which it regularly accompanies. Some hand gestures may, for example, be co-organized with the distribution of stress and accent in the talk (what Ekman and Friesen, 1969 termed "batons"). Some head gestures may do the work which verbal components may also be doing, or in lieu of them (e.g., on lateral headshakes as "intensifiers" cf. Schegloff, 1987b: 106; 1988b: 142-43). Hand gestures may have more or less transparent iconic, semantic or graphic relationships to lexical components of the ongoing talk, and these gestures undergo a characteristic trajectory of delivery, from launching in advance of the word tokens to which they are affiliated, through deployment of the gesture or "gesture phrase" (Kendon, 1972), through the speaker's gaze at the achieved gesture which underscores its interactional significance to recipient (Streeck, 1988), through decay of the gesture to its extinction or retraction (Kendon, 1972, 1979 as well as a number of more recent papers; Schegloff, 1984b). But gestures do not only map on to words; words may be selected in a finely calibrated relationship to the gesture with which they are co-produced, as with choices between the indexicals "this" and "that," sensitive to the at-that-moment current state of the coordinate pointing gesture (Schegloff, 1984b: 291-94).

Here as well figure the unarticulated facial expressions (e.g., frowns and eyebrow flashes; cf. Ekman, 1979),[47] the partially articulated ones such as smiles ("partially articulated" because of the phenomenon known as "smile voice"), and the more decisively and unarguably immanent ones such as laughter (e.g., Jefferson, 1979, 1984c, 1985; Jefferson, Sacks, and Schegloff, 1977, 1987), This last is a systematically produced acoustic component of the "speech stream," which surely contributes to the "meaning" and "import" and "understanding" of the speech production of which it forms a part (sometimes crowding it out, sometimes intercalated into its sounds), but so do the acoustically less obtrusive forms of conduct. All of them have beginnings, courses, and decays – sometimes discrete, sometimes imperceptibly shaded (this is itself a property of these elements), and these are introduced into the talk of a turn or TCU at some point, held for some duration, transformed into other elements and dissolved at some point. They are full-fledged candidates for inclusion in a grammar – or relative to a grammar.

Finally, we must explore the possibility that grammar(s) is/are built to provide for in-course incorporation of, and adaptation to, input from the environment (e.g., Goodwin, this volume) – most centrally, observable uptake and alignment by recipient(s). Various accounts of the production of what are unquestionably grammatical units – from the Goodwins (C. Goodwin, 1979, 1980, 1981; M. Goodwin, 1980; Goodwin and Goodwin, 1987) to Ford (1993), with many others in between and since – have shown that we may not be correctly understanding even apparently integral, single speaker productions if we do not understand all or part of those productions as informed by the speaker's orientation to what recipient has done or not done (Schegloff, 1995, frth.) in its course, or by other elements of the speaker's context. So accounts of the grammar organizing the talk which composes the TCUs which constitute turns-at-talk in interaction will need to provide analytic guidelines to the organization of speaker orientation to the environment of talk (is it organized by reference to the production of the TCU-in-progress?), as well as an account of how the talk may be reshaped by reference to what the speaker finds to be going on in that environment.

So we can add to our guidelines for parsing turns another set of specifications:

(C) The grammars. For any TCU, we can ask:

(1) What are the successive elements of each TCU, including (in however adjunct a status) pre-beginning and post-completion elements? In this inventory, we include such elements as: breaths and other aspirations including laughter and laugh tokens; recognizable contexted-silences, coughs, "y'know," "uh" in all its varieties, etc., cut-offs, sound stretches, – i.e., all perceivable elements.

(2) Where do such elements occur? What sorts of elements occupy determinate structural positions in a TCU?

(3) Which elements count as "advancing" the progress of the TCU? Which count as "impediments?" These are, of course, in the

first instance vernacular "readings" of the contribution of an element to a turn; what is taken vernacularly to "retard" the turn's progress can nonetheless be taken technically as its next component – a component whose "vector" (as one might put it) is retardive. Are there other ways in which elements relate to progressivity? How are they distributed relative to one another?

(4) What are the grammatical relations among successive elements? Among elements further removed? Are there different orders of grammatical relations, such that some operate on others? How does any of this vary by the position of the talk being constructed in its sequential, interactional, social, ecological, etc. context?

(5) Do "productional values" count as elements, i.e., pitch peaks and other prosodic features, qualities such crispness/mushiness (cf. Jefferson, 1978b), etc.? If so, how are they positioned relative to others? Otherwise, how are they distributed *on* other elements?

(6) How are non-vocal production elements, values and shifts in them distributed relative to other elements? I have in mind such components of conduct as speaker's gesture, posture, gaze direction, facial expression, smiling, and the course of their respective deployments etc.? How do these bear on TCU construction and organization?

(7) How are the elements of other ongoing activities incorporated in TCU construction and reflected in it – both activities by speaker (e.g., if eating, then ingesting, chewing, swallowing, etc., work activities in all their varieties, etc.) and by others (especially targetted recipients)?

(8) What kinds of grammatical structures provide for, or constrain, internal or boundary TCU expansion? (e.g., self-initiated same-turn repair as an organization for TCU expansion, truncation, and transformation; parentheticals; interpolation of sequences into TCUs such as the earlier-mentioned "try-marked recognitional reference;" cf. Sacks and Schegloff, 1979). Where do such expansions, etc. occur relative to other elements?

(9) How do different kinds of grammatical organizations and structures interface differentially with interactional contingencies, and how do different kinds of interactional contingencies (such as different turn-taking organizations in setting-specific speech exchange systems) differentially shape deployments of grammatical resources?[48]

Here I can pursue only a few of these, and only minimally.

First, to provide just a sense of one kind of payoff of such examinations of data, examine the first page of the transcript of Auto Discussion (Excerpt (8) above) under the auspices of Query #2 above, asking only with what element(s) the TCUs begin. Here are the findings:

oh yeah; you've...; oh no; here we...; I...; I...; you'll...; you'll...; you...; you...; Well I...; Y-; you...; 'at's right; I...; I...; That's right; you....

In sum: 4 agreement markers, 14 starts referring to speaker, recipient or the party of the whole. (I have omitted laughter, of which there is a considerable amount.) Surely not every conversation will show such a distribution, but what are the terms of the alternatives? And do we learn something about this occasion – or this moment in it – by noting the elements out of which its TCU beginnings are constituted?

Second, to provide a sense of the payoff of asking about the possible relationship between elements, I want to recall the earlier discussion of "pre-possible completion" as an organizationally relevant place in a TCU. This locates a sort of structural – grammatical – place with consequences that I suspect are not otherwise brought to our attention – for example, in accounts of the syntax of sentences.

Or consider the import of the placement of breathing. It is tempting to dismiss breathing as merely a physiological prerequisite to talking, but this distracts from a variety of orderly practices which can inform the "doing of breathing" in ways which achieve differing outcomes for the turn's construction and hearing. Thus, for example, a hearable "deep" in-breath at the pre-beginning of a turn or a TCU can foreshadow an "extended" spate of talk to come – whether a lengthy TCU or more than one TCU. But the placement of inbreaths in Excerpts (26) and (27) are doing something different, and this turns on their (grammatical?) placement. These extracts are taken from telephone conversations in which a physician working as a reviewer for an insurer is discussing the preauthorization of a surgical procedure (a tympanostomy, in which tubes are inserted in the ear to treat persistent or recurrent ear

infections) with the physician who has recommended it – a recommendation at risk of being rejected.

```
(25)  Heritage/Kleinman, 2222:4/22/91

Review:   And she's ha:d uh: history: of an effu:sion, (0.2) but
          the information I have is that she's recently had a hearing
          test which was normal.
          (0.2)
Review:   An:d uh::- and I know she's had some effusion but I don't know
          how long °th'° it's been documented for.
Doctor:   .hh (.) Wh- what- (.) when: did she have a normal hearing test?
Review:   I don't have the da:te,=it just says here hearing test within
          normal limits. [hh An' I don't know if that was ju[st-
Doctor:                  [(M-)                                 ['Cause we
--> did an audiogram on th' hh ninth of April which was .hhh
--> abnormal.
Review:   Oh. Okay, (0.3)...
```

Here the inbreath comes (grammatically speaking) in the middle of
a predication, between the verb and the descriptor which it is
reporting. Interactionally, it is placed at a point which can – by
the momentary delay which it introduces – strategically invite a
collaborative completion (Lerner, 1991, this volume) by the recipient, here potentially a reversal by the reviewer of the claim that
child-in-question's hearing is normal.[49] The point here is that
breathings – whether in or out – are practices; they can be done
in various modalities (e.g., designed to be heard or not, of different
"sizes" or "depths"); they can be placed variously in the developing
structure of the TCU. They (and various other traditionally "non-
linguistic" objects) are deployable elements of its construction, and
thus candidate building blocks for its grammar.

Fourth, and in particular, I want to reflect on the potential positional variability of the grammatical constitution of what composes
a TCU in a way that might avoid promiscuous reliance on the
notion of ellipsis. I find problematic that use which takes a one
word or one phrase utterance, reconstructs from it a larger matrix
sentence, of which the original utterance is then said to be a reduction by ellipsis. Some ellipsis may be demonstrably a member's – a
speaker's – practice, and that status underwrites our academic
account of it as such. But are not other lexical or phrasal TCUs
directly constituted by a grammatical resource that recognizes their
sequential position, and uses that position in the construction and
parsing of the utterance by co-participants? (Note that the point
here is different from one taken up earlier; "sequential position"

here refers not to the position of a TCU within a multi-unit turn, but to the position of a turn within a sequence.)

Consider the following sequence.

```
(26)  Auto Discussion 5:16-26

Curt:    (W-)/(Oh-) how wz the races las'night.
         (0.8)
??:      (Ha-[ u h ) ]=
Curt:        [Who w'n][th'feature.]
-->  Mike:            =[A l  w o n,]
         (0.3)
Curt:    [(Who)]=
Mike:    [ A l.]=
Curt:    =Al did?
Gary:    ((hoarse whisper)) Go get im Bo!
Curt:    Dz he go out there pretty regular?
```

When I have worked on this episode with students, a question has routinely come up about the arrowed turn by Mike. Is it produced as an answer to the question by Curt, in whose course it is articulated?[50] Or is it a part – a delayed part – of a multi-part answer to the *initial* utterance in the excerpt, an addition to what is visible in the videotape but not in the transcript during the 0.8 second which follows that initial question – some head nodding by Mike.[51]

This can be sequentially and interactionally consequential. Curt has asked a question which carries a further action beyond a request for an assessment (in response to which Mike's nodding can constitute a "positive assessment"): it is proffering as a topic the automobile races which Mike had attended the previous evening. As was noted earlier, in response to topic proffers, minimal responses can be ways of declining the proffer, or at least of not embracing the topic which has been proffered. Expanded responses, on the other hand, can be ways of "buying into" them, and one basic way that expansion is done is by producing a multi-component response. So the interactional question here can be, is Mike discouraging or encouraging the topic which Curt has put on the table?

This question, and the entire segment in which it comes up, implicates a range of interesting details about the interaction, including ones which support both potential answers, though this is not the place to develop them. What is germane here is the possibility that later in the sequence we find evidence of a grammatical sort which has a bearing on the matter.

Note then that following the overlap between "Al won" and Curt's follow-up question and second topic proffer ("Who won the feature"), there is a 0.3 second gap. Such gaps are not uncommon following overlapping talk which issues in simultaneous ending. Since neither speaker ended as "speaker of record" in the prior turn, it can be indeterminate who should be next speaker. And, in the manner of persons walking in opposite directions on a narrow path and seeking to get around one another, each can go in a direction in which the other also chooses to go, reproducing the blockage which prompted the move in the first place. And so also here. Each having waited for the other to talk next, each finds the other not to have done so, and himself then moves to take the turn, only to find the other arriving at the same place, at the same moment, by the same route. And so after the gap, there is another overlap.

But we – and they – can/could hear what is in those overlaps. Note then that Curt shows that he heard what Mike was saying in the previous overlap; at least he heard that there was a person reference in Mike's turn, although (claimably) not who the reference was to, and he displays this with his category-specific repair initiator, "Who."

Just as Curt is engaged in overlap retrieval on Mike's contribution in the preceding overlap, so is Mike engaged on Curt's. Mike heard through the overlap the question that Curt was asking, and grasps as well that the overlap may have impaired Curt's ability to hear the answer – which he happened to be giving (as, indeed, it did). And so he here responds to the question which Curt asked, "Who won the feature." And in doing so, he displays the form which an answer to that question takes. And it is "Al" – not "Al won" (or "Al did," or "Al won the feature").

Exchanges such as this seem to me relevant resources for exploring the notion of positionally sensitive grammars. Should we not understand "Al" as the proper grammatical form for an utterance doing an "answer" in this position – perhaps even as *the* way there is of showing that he is doing "answering?" Indeed, when Curt does a second other-initiated repair to deal with Mike's part in the second overlap, he shows by the form he employs that he understood "Al" to be the answer to his question, "who won the feature?" Note that he does not offer just a questioning repeat for confirmation (not "Al?"), but rather "Al did?," in which the "did" specifically incorporates reference to "won the feature," i.e., to the question which he takes it "Al" is the answer to. "Al" is, then, *the form* such an utterance takes – in an answer-to-question position like this, and is not an elliptical reduction of some other form.[52]

Not that the other forms *cannot* be used; they simply *are* not used, here. Perhaps one can then be in a position to ask when they *are* used. We might then be able to speak not of "Al" as an elliptical form of "Al won" or "Al won the feature," but of the latter as having some special use when they occur, given that the basic grammatical form in that sequential position is "Al" (if, that is, there *is* a "basic grammatical form").[53]

The general point about positionally sensitive grammars, then, is this.

When the object of traditional inquiry has been taken to be the utterance of a sentence, and investigators have asked how its composition or production is to be understood, it has seemed natural to begin with what the utterance is meant to convey or to do. Whether thought of in terms of information transmission or speech acts in the traditional sense, the analysis has begun with some sort of intention – because the *speaker* is understood to begin with some intention. That intention has then been tracked through subsequent stages in a production process – in which the intention is given some propositional form (perhaps with pragmatic operators as well), the proposition is furnished some specific semantic composition, a syntactic shaping is provided for the embryonic product, its slots are filled with lexical items, and so forth through phonological, intonational, articulatory, operations, through to final production of the utterance as enacted realization of the sentence. With some such conception of speech production, the notion of a single grammar by which the utterance/sentence is shaped is plausible enough, for it is well adapted to other elements of this conception – such as the single proposition.[54]

This view – in the beginning was the intention – is an aspect of a larger strategy of inquiry which takes single sentences, single utterances, single actions or single composites – the single sentence/utterance/action – as the object of inquiry. If one begins with the singular, disengaged, sentence/utterance/action, then where else *could* one locate its origin if not in the impulse or disposition to act/talk? Surely (it has seemed) it is with that that an impending speaker/actor begins.

But if one takes as one's object of inquiry an utterance/action which occurs on an actual occasion, in an actual context, at an actual moment, that is *not* where its speaker begins; that is *not* the point from which the composition or production of the utterance departs. With the exception of initial utterances on an occasion (a class whose form is in general quite distinctive, and in substantial measure for just this reason), any utterance – and its speaker – begins at just the end of what precedes it.[55] A speaker finds her/himself situated at the moment following the possible completion of some other utterance or action by self or another, or at some point in the ongoing production of one – such as the possible completion of a TCU in a turn, or the incipient start of a non-first TCU in a turn. If we are to entertain intentions, then surely they are situated by reference to such moments.[56]

If what lies at the origin of a next increment of conduct in interaction is the state of the interaction which has just been arrived at, then the just-current *sequential* state of the interaction is part of that starting point. And just as possibly relevant next actions, or possibly coherent next utterances, can be shaped by reference to the immediately preceding talk and action, so can a possibly relevant organizational form for a next contribution – a relevant *grammar* – be shaped by the immediately preceding talk and action. If one has been just asked a question, then what one inherits at the next moment is not only the relevance of an answer as one (central) possible action/utterance to do next, but with it one or more candidate or eligible grammatical formats for doing an answer, or doing an answer *to such a question*, or doing an answer to *that* question, and so on. On this line (and whatever may be the case for written or other "textual" language deployments), one does not have "a grammar" for sentences, whose products get whittled away to satisfy discourse or pragmatic considerations in an operation conventionally termed "ellipsis."[57] One has a range of grammatical resources, grammars if you will, whose relevance is positionally sensitive to organizational features and contingencies of the sequential and interactional moment in which the conduct is situated.[58]

If some such view captures the practices of talking in interaction, then the formulation with which this paper began (its title), and which underlies the very title of the volume, can itself occlude our vision. For the domain to be explored may not be the interface between some monolithic grammar and interaction per se, but rather between the sorts of junctures and contingencies which the organizations of interaction engender on the one hand, and the forms of grammatical structure and practice which get deployed at those junctures and in those contingencies on the other. Such an exploration needs to make room, in principle, for the possibility of multiple, positionally sensitive grammars, with the related search for the sorts of positions they are sensitive to.

2.6   The challenge

These last considerations can strike linguists as perplexing in ways which call into question the viability of the entire undertaking being entertained here.

On one view, without a fundamental notion of predication underlying language, linguists do not have anything on which to hang grammar, or anything to count as units. As one linguist put it (p.c.):

> In what sense can we see the TCU forming an initial, superseding category similar to the S in the transformational grammar? All Ss, as it has been defined in grammars through the ages, have had the one thing in common that they are predications. But what can we say that TCUs have in common, other than the possible intonation curve (prosodic completion), and the possibility of the turn ending in the end of the TCU (pragmatic completion)?

Here we encounter again the underlying presence of truth-conditional identity, of language as description, of the logical structure and identity of the proposition as the fundamental constitutive grounding for language. It is this propositional, predicative core which makes the sentence or clause – with its "arguments" – central; makes smaller units ("fragments") invite treatment as reduced versions of units with propositional, predicative import, which can be reconstructed from them, to be reduced again to "fragments" by rules of ellipsis.

What is needed then, is to relax the stranglehold of predication on our understanding of language, and especially on talk-in-interaction. What can we say TCUs have in common, aside from

intonation (if that) and possible completion? The key may be that
they are productions whose status as complete turns testifies to their
adequacy as units for the participants, units which are addressable
with the generic issue for practical actors (Schegloff and Sacks,
1973: 209): "why that now?" Overwhelmingly this issue is
grounded for practical actors as parties to interaction by some version of the *action(s)* the unit is doing (Schegloff, 1995, frth.).
Because "telling" and "describing" are among the actions which
get undertaken, predication is among the structures recurrently
underlying the construction of TCUs, and available for elaboration
in other deployments of language – in monologue, in writing, in
logic and science, and so on. But the counterpart to predication in
talk-in-interaction is the move, the action, the activity, and it is that
which gives a TCU (without respect to its size or mode of realization) its recognizable unit status, the consequentiality of its possible
completion, and the omnirelevant action thematics of its analysis –
why that now.[59]

In this regard, it appears that Austin's (1962) "revolution" was
too conservative not only in retaining the single sentence/utterance
as the analytic target and a set of "conditions" as the format for
analysis (albeit felicity conditions rather than truth conditions), but
in another respect as well. It undershoots the mark to insist that
language is used not only for description but also for action. In its
home environment, it is for action in the *first* instance; it is
"description" which is the "also," in its capacity as one type of
action. In this regard, Wittgenstein (1953) was nearer the mark.

There may be domains (e.g., logic and science) for which the
narrower commitment of language as a tool of description may
be taken as a satisfactory basis for establishing a framework for
analysis, and the proposition/sentence may be the key resource. But
for the more inclusive domain of language's range, especially as it
figures in the quotidien settings of interaction, it is the parameters of
action – not proposition – which need to be formative. If it is this
larger domain of language which sets the horizon of our analytic
ambition, then we must call into question all those versions of
pragmatics which apply "pragmatic operators" or "function indicating devices" to underlying propositional forms, or detect "tacit"
underlying performative verbs attached to them, or other tacks of
this sort (as in such early work as Searle, 1965, 1969; Gordon and

Lakoff, 1971, 1975; Ross, 1970, etc., and many subsequent efforts which proceed along basically similar lines) as ways of reconciling the analysis of a reality composed of *actions* with an underlying analytical format of *propositions* built for *descriptions*.[60]

Rather than starting with propositional forms and overlaying action operators, our primary characterizations need to capture the action(s) embodied in a burst of language. For those actions and on those occasions in which something like a proposition seems to be involved, we need analytic accounts of how these propositions are formatted and associated with the actions which occasion their relevance. There is every reason to suspect that grammar for talk implementing action is quite different from grammar for talk expressing propositions.[61] That we may not yet have much of a clue as to what such grammar(s) look(s) like does not change the suspicion, but may encourage the sort of reaching that promotes the possibility of grammars rather than *a* grammar.

One can take the full range of environments of what can be called "the use of language" – oratory, conversation, technical writing, advertisements, poetry, bureaucratic memoranda, scholarly books, pornography, etc. and make one's account of "grammatical (and other linguistic) structure" answerable to that full range. An alternative strategy is to take those environments to be neither equivalently relevant nor temporally or analytically commensurate, and to take ordinary talk-in-interaction to be the constitutive environment, with writing a further adaptation along lines pioneered by oratory and monologue – that is, the textual (Schegloff, 1995: 202, fn. 1; frth.). This is compatible with every known society and culture having institutions for talk-in-interaction, and not all having writing.[62]

Contemporary (and most, if not all, past) linguistics appears to have adopted the first strategy and has then exploited the license thereby afforded to seize on the most convenient materials to do its work – whether imagined constructions, written texts or the dicta and performances elicited from authoritative informants/consultants. The result has been, as Sacks remarked over twenty-five years ago (in his lectures for Fall, 1967; cf. Sacks, 1992: I: 622-3; cf. also Schegloff, 1992a: lv-lvi), that

By and large, the specific interest of linguistics in the utterance is that study of the utterance which involves detecting those features of it which are handleable without reference to such considerations as sequencing, i.e., without reference to that it has occurred in conversation . . . Polemically we could be seeing if there is the *possibility* of, say, a fully comprehensive, coherent linguistics *without* such matters.

Arguably, there is not.

We very likely have two enterprises before us. One is stretching an older linguistics – built for predication and writing – to cover action in interaction. But whatever stance one takes towards the linguistics which we have and which we may try (and have tried) to stretch, it seems increasingly clear that we need another, one which captures something inescapable about language for humans, one which *starts* with the domain of talk-in-interaction, and gets the appropriate initial units from that domain. That enterprise may later on have to stretch to accommodate monologue and writing, etc., that is, the textual, as opposed to the interactional. But it will almost certainly from the outset contain within it "predication," for that is one of the things people *do* do in talk in interaction – *but only one*. Received linguistics has treated it as the *only* one, or the main one – the one which sets the first-order terms for the understanding of language, and it is far from clear that it is. It may turn out that much in this paper, and in this volume, is stretching the old linguistics to meet the challenge of talk-in-interaction. Perhaps we need to search even farther for new beginnings, or search with fresher eyes and ears, in the details of the talk with which we must, in the end, come to terms.

Notes

1 Prepared for the Second Grammar and Interaction Workshop, UCLA, March, 1993. I want to thank participants in one of my seminars with whom I tried to think through some of these matters: Elizabeth Boyd, Byron Burkhalter, Maria Egbert, Patrick Gonzales, Kyu-Hyun Kim, Geoff Raymond, Andy Roth, and Marja-Leena Sorjonen, and those in another seminar who aided in spotting places where the text needed clarification: Elizabeth Boyd, Irene Koshik, Anna Lindström and Geoff Raymond. I am indebted to Elinor Ochs and Sandra Thompson who helped me give voice to this effort in various, sometimes unanticipated, ways. Chuck Goodwin, Auli Hakulinen, Makoto Hayashi, John Heritage, Gene Lerner, Junko Mori and Jürgen Streeck contributed helpful comments on earlier drafts.

What I am doing with the collection of observations and themes worked through here is, in part, something I undertook not to do some twenty-five to thirty years ago, and that is programmatics. I do not do it without some empirical grounding, but I also do not do it without misgivings. I do it because I increasingly think that much of this work needs to be done by people with training, knowledge, and skills that I lack, but needs to be done in a manner which benefits from, and is grounded in, what we already have learned from examining conversation. This is then, a contribution to collaboration but one which is tentative and still in development.

Publication conventions vary among disciplines. In some, notes hold largely supplementary bibliographical information. In the present paper, notes contain substantive material, ordinarily important to the overall theme, but not directly on line with the argument then ongoing in the main text. Material in the notes is of a piece with the main text.

2 And it was at this interface that some of the early linguistic explorations of grammar and interaction were focussed, e.g., Duranti and Ochs, 1979, and my own earlier effort, in Schegloff, 1979.

3 What sorts of entities (described in grammatical or other terms) will be used and treated as turn-constructional units is determined by those who *use* the language (broadly understood – that is, to include gesture, facial expression, when/where relevant), not those who study it academically. Calls for formal definitions of a TCU – beyond their status as units which can constitute possibly complete turns as above – are therefore bound to be disappointed, but empirical inquiries to explore such issues should be expected to yield interesting results.

4 It is worth recalling that, until Chomsky's (1957: 18–25) attack on "left-to-rightness" or linearity, it was not unusual for temporality to be addressed in linguistic treatments of grammar. Bolinger's "Linear Modification" (1965: 281; first published in 1952), for example, depicts the progressive structuring of talk from "the moment of pre-speaking, followed by the first word and each additional word in course." "Linearity" is, in substantial measure, the written or visual analogue of temporality. Bolinger's reference to "the moment of pre-speaking" (a moment which is taken up below in the section entitled "A Reprise on TCU Beginnings") may remind us of the focus still current among linguists at that time on actual occurrences of language use, among them speaking. The same year as Bolinger's "Linear Modification" first appeared, Charles Fries based his *The Structure of English: An Introduction to the Construction of English Sentences* on an "entirely different kind of evidence" (identified as telephone conversation at p. 37). Regarding this evidence he wrote (pp. 3–4),

With the recent development of mechanical devices for the easy recording of the speech of persons in all types of situations there seems to be little excuse for the use of linguistic material not taken from actual communicative practice when one attempts to deal with a living language. Even though the investigator is himself a native speaker of the language and a sophisticated and trained observer he cannot depend completely on himself as an informant and use introspection as his sole source of material. He has a much more satisfactory base from which to proceed with linguistic analysis if he has a large body of mechanically recorded language which he can hear repeated over and over, and which he can approach with more objectivity than he can that which he furnishes from himself as informant.

Within five years, of course, other "developments" were to supersede this one in shaping the course of linguistics. Although the import of the present paper is not to revive the structuralist linguistics of the early 1950s, it is worth recalling that serious efforts to deal with real talking, and contingencies such as temporality, have had a place in relatively recent linguistic inquiry.

5 I should make clear that I do not use these terms here to indicate particular commitments among currently practiced views of grammar – whether conceptual, cognitivist, symbolic, formalist, etc. Rather I mean to juxtapose generic resources, abstracted from particular realizations and available as deployable practices, on the one hand, with particular instantiations, always realized in and particularized to an idiosyncratic moment, on the other, – and embrace both as relevant to the discussion.

6 Note that the concern here is with the bearing of turn-taking contingencies on certain deployments of prosody, rather than the bearing of prosody on turn-taking organization (on which more below, and inter alia, SSJ, 1974: 721, and Ford and Thompson, this volume).

7 For the notational conventions employed in the transcript excerpts in this chapter, cf. the Appendix to this volume. Cf. also SSJ, 1974: 731–4, or Atkinson and Heritage, 1984: ix-xvi.

8 It may be useful to clarify the usage in this paper (and in some other conversation-analytic writing) of the term format "possible X," as in the text above: "...understood by reference to the speaker Ava's orientation to the status of 'No' as *a possible TCU*, and its end as *a possible turn completion*, and thus as a place at which Bee would relevantly locate a *possible start for a next turn.*"

The usage is not meant as a token of analytic uncertainty or hedging. Its analytic locus is not in the first instance the world of the author and reader, but the world of the parties to the interaction. To describe some utterance, for example, as "a possible invitation" (Sacks, 1992: I: 300-2; Schegloff, 1992a: xxvi-xxvii) or "a possible complaint" (Schegloff, 1988c: 120–2) is to claim that there is a describable practice of talk-in-interaction which is usable to do recognizable invitations or complaints (a claim which can be documented by exemplars of exchanges in which such utterances were so recognized by their recipients), and that the utterance now being described can be understood to have been produced by such a practice, and is thus analyzable as an invitation or as a complaint. This claim is made, and can be defended, independent of whether the actual recipient on this occasion has treated it as an invitation or not, and independent of whether the speaker can be shown to have produced it for recognition as such on this occasion. Such an analytic stance is required to provide resources for accounts of "failures" to recognize an utterance as an invitation or complaint, for in order to claim that a recipient *failed* to recognize it as such or respond to it as such, one must be able to show that it was *recognizable* as such, i.e., that it was "a possible X" – for the participants (Schegloff, 1995, frth.). The analyst's treatment of an utterance as "a possible X" is then grounded in a claim about its having such a status for the participants. (For an extended exploration of how a form of turn construction – repetition – can constitute a practice for producing possible instances of a previously undescribed action – "confirming allusions," cf. Schegloff, 1996.)

This discussion requires modification in various respects for different values of the variable "X" in the phrase "a possible X;" one might wish to phrase the discussion differently for "a possible name," "a possible TCU," or "a possible completion." For now the reader shoud try to adapt this rough abbreviated account to particular "possibles" in what follows.

9   Cf. the discussion of Excerpt (20) below at pp. 88-90 for a contrasting analysis of a turn-initial "no."

10   Goodwin, 1979 offers a beautifully analyzed case in point. Labov and Fanshel (1977) were right to see that the organization of action was key to the coherent use of language, but not in counterposing it to the organization of the linguistic usage itself; they are intertwined. Grammar and action are each subject to both autonomous and interdependent organization.

11   Because this is the very beginning of the videotape reel, the immediately preceding context is not available, beyond the observation that Carney appears to have just referred to a story which has recently been told, and Pam either suggests, or endorses the suggestion, that the story be told again for the benefit of both the recently arrived guests and the ethnographers (Charles and Marjorie Goodwin) recording the occasion on tape. Pam and Curt are hostess and host, Carney is Curt's cousin and Gary is her husband, Mike and his wife Phyllis have just arrived.

12   Although this is, in a sense, a choice between continuing and restarting, it is different from the occurrences which Local (1992) examines under the auspices of "continuing vs. restarting," which involve utterances abandoned before completion and then taken up again.

13   Some might take yet another view, namely, that the utterance as produced should be understood as a new TCU, built to be grammatically continuous with what preceded. Cf. for example, note 26 below for such a view of similar data. However it is important to recognize that

the possible completion at "tha: t" is just that – a *possible* completion. One import of the construction of turns and TCUs in conversation around *possible* completions is that, if their sequelae are not felicitous (e.g., if they do not engender appropriate talk next, or *any* talk next), subsequent conduct by the same speaker can treat them to have *not* been completions after all. One key way this is done is by producing further talk as an organic continuation of the talk which preceded, as an increment of talk within the *same* TCU, which is thereby presented as having not been complete at all, and therefore not ready to engender sequelae or responses, and therefore not a failure in having not done so. And that is the analysis being proposed of Pam's turn in Extract (2). More generally, that is a possibility for TCU construction and its (interactionally) contingent extension which is important for the claims of this paper. (For analysis of another interactional episode along such lines, cf. Schegloff, 1995, frth.)

14 How much work, and what kind of work, will be involved in getting more than one TCU into a turn can itself be positionally variable. Second position turns (in a sequence) may be more expansible than first position turns; for example (many) turns following questions appear to provide for multi-unit answers (at the same time as they may permit/require single TCU responses to be packaged in sub-sentential, sub-clausal TCUs). This may be one theme bearing on the grammar of some TCUs – how they figure in providing for additional TCUs, as per the discussion following in the text. Note as well that some practices (such as the story preface) work not to get an additional TCU in the turn, but to neutralize the "transition-relevance" of the possible completion of ensuing TCUs until some projected feature is articulated, e.g., until something analyzably "funny," "strange," or the like has been told (cf. Sacks, 1974; Schegloff, 1992; Goodwin, this volume). This is a key feature of the production of many so-called discourse units or discourses in conversation (and not only narratives), but may vary in other speech-exchange systems, if different turn-taking practices are in effect, with associated differences in turn organization.

15 This possibility is surely resonant with the current interest in "text grammars," but is here meant for the specific context of talk-in-interaction.

16 Preliminary examination by Andrew Roth of a small corpus of material encourages this line of inquiry. There are particular forms whose deployment and import reinforces their apparent positional restriction; "oh," for example, occurs overwhelmingly in turn-initial position (and I do not mean to refer only to the "touch-off oh" or to the "oh" which Heritage (1986) studies under the rubric "oh-prefaced responses to inquiries," but to free-standing "oh" (Heritage, 1984; Schiffrin, 1987).

17 See also his lectures for Spring, 1972 in Sacks, 1992: II: 521–70.

18 Although raised in the context of a discussion of the organization of multi-unit turns, all of this has direct bearing on the grammar or

grammars by which TCUs are constructed and recognized, and their shaping by reference to the organization of the turn as the host environment. Aside from the Sacks reference above (1987[1973]), see also Pomerantz, 1984 which is directly concerned with turn shapes, the activities being prosecuted and sequential position.

19   On such topic shifting elsewhere see Jefferson's (1984a) account of stepwise topic shift as a device for exiting "troubles talk," though the steps there are not necessarily constituted by successive TCUs in a turn.

20   For an extended discussion of a virtually canonical multi-unit turn format, cf. Schegloff, 1992c: 1304–17.

21   For an extended treatment of the material from which Excerpt (7) is taken which pursues a different theme in its analysis cf. Mandelbaum, 1991/92.

22   The last of these is open to question, for the "preface" – "you're not in on what happened" – could be taken to project not (only) an announcement but a story, in which case there is projectably more (more *telling*, that is) to come after "He's flying."

23   For another type of exemplar of "in but not of" cf. Schegloff, 1979: 272, fn. 15.

24   Indeed, the very reference to a "stretch of talk" or "spate of talk" presumes recognition of some object not yet well defined. By it I will mean, loosely, some talk by a speaker, often but not always one who has not just been speaking.

25   I mean to refer specifically to "Right after (0.2) school is out."

26   These points are both arguable and not fully specified. On the first count, my colleague Chuck Goodwin (p.c.) wants to speak of the arrowed talk in Excerpts (10)-(13) as *new* TCUs constructed to be grammatically continuous with preceding talk. Whether this involves substantive differences in analysis or merely stylistic preferences remains to be elucidated. But see also note 13 above. On the second, much remains unspecified and unexplored. Is what constitutes a recognizable beginning itself positionally specific or sensitive? Or does one (the talk's recipient, the academic analyst) recognize first "not a beginning," and then (therefore?) search for symbiosis with (a) prior turn?

27   For a nice, context-informed account of this fragment, cf. Sacks, 1992, Volume I: 659–64 (Fall, 1967, Lecture 5).

28   Sacks (ibid.) makes the point that such "appendor questions" virtually always constitute the whole of their turn. He remarks as well (663) that it is just the continuative syntax that is of key importance to their realization *as* "appendor questions: "

there is a specific machinery whereby the transition from speaker to *non-speaker* is made a transition that ought to be from speaker to *hearer*. Where being a hearer involves, for one, having available to you an analysis of the syntax of the utterance after yours, and its possible relation to the syntax of your own utterance. That is, you have to see that this prepositional phrase is not the begin-

ning of some puzzling utterance, but that it can possibly be latched onto your
own. (I leave aside the issue that it involves you in having listened to what you
yourself said.)

29   Note that (except for the last) these are all organizationally features of
     the start of the *turn*, though not of the TCU; "uh" in particular can be
     a way of starting a turn with other than a TCU beginning.
30   Here again the relevance of positional sensitivity insists itself, for the
     sort of issue posed by starting a turn with a display of its relationship
     to what precedes is very different if what just precedes has initiated a
     new sequence than if it has possibly closed one. Heritage and
     Sorjonen's "And-prefacing" (1994) – often invoking "external" agen-
     das and constraints on the talk – is a feature of sequence-initiating but
     activity-continuing questions for good reason; there is little place for
     "and-prefaced" answers.
31   This is, of course, one of the major points in bringing the theme of
     grammar and interaction to *talk in turns*.
32   The treatment is rudimentary at best, as is the discussion of endings
     which follows, and both notions remain arguably quite vague. But the
     solution is not to provide (as one reader suggested) definitions of
     "beginning" and "ending." Rather, we register observationally that
     there are recognizable alternative ways in which spates of talk by a
     speaker are bounded, and they are deployed differentially, as imple-
     mentations of different practices, with differing uptakes by their reci-
     pients. The solution is the progressive empirical specification of what
     practices of talking accomplish recognizable beginnings and endings
     for the participants, rather than the stipulation of definitions by inves-
     tigators.
33   The locus of "pre-possible completion" described here is almost cer-
     tainly only one of a number of organizationally relevant loci, depend-
     ing on the level of granularity oriented to by the parties in doing the
     talk and the professional analyst in providing accounts of it. For exam-
     ple, speakers may cut off an utterance which is virtually complete, i.e.,
     just before its possibly last sound, and launch a new TCU, thereby
     exploiting a more fine-grained metric for pre-possible completion than
     is described in the text. Some of these metrics are described in the early
     parts of Jefferson, 1984b. If "pre-possible completion" is a gramma-
     tically strategic place in a TCU, then it is potentially a set of such
     places.
34   I only mention here the work of Davidson (1984: 115–25) who, build-
     ing on Jefferson (1973), examines utterances in which there is "a
     possible sentence completion point that is not actual utterance comple-
     tion, such that components occur after this possible completion point,"
     and focusses on the possibility that "the components occurring after a
     possible completion point may be providing the [speaker] with a *moni-
     tor space* in which he or she can examine what happens or what does

not happen there for its acceptance/rejection implicativeness" (117; emphasis in original).

35   Actually, in Excerpts (22) and (23) the increments do not so much complement what preceded as they restructure it. In (22) "days" which is initially the object of "had" is replaced in that grammatical role by "classes" and becomes something of a prepositional phrase ("[on] what days..."). In (23), the "not" in "definitely not" is an intensified replay of the "not" in Bee's preceding turn, "Still not getting married," and what it is negating is the activity "getting married." With the addition of "married," the scope of the "not" is recast to the state "married," rather than the activity "getting married." So post-completion increments can not only add new grammatical units to the previously complete TCU, and complement what are retrospectively cast as incomplete constructions; they can restructure the grammatical roles and relations as well.

36   Some British "tag questions" seem different, not least in being placed not after possible completion of a TCU but at a place analyzably *not* that. In such cases they obviously are not being used for "decisive completion of the turn." Some such usages appear to being doing "recipient design" work, marking the assertion or assessment to which they are (quite often) affiliated as designed to express what the recipient is figured *already* to know or feel, and hence not something the speaker figured the recipient(s) *needed* to be told. But this is not the place to document or explore this claim. I should also note that some so-called "tag questions" in American English are not designed as post-completion elements, but are indigenous parts of the construction of the clause to which they are appended, as in "You're not leaving, are you?" The familiar term "tag question" may thus refer to usages whose structural character and positioning are diverse.

37   As this list makes clear, in English this post-completion stance marking is not grammaticalized, and is often accomplished by what are conventionally taken to be non-linguistic resources. In languages such as Korean, Japanese, and some languages of China, grammaticalized resources such as particles are used to similar ends.

38   Jefferson, 1984b: 11–28 can be understood as, in effect, an examination of one aspect of the organization of the transition space.

39   I refer here to the familiar drawings to which gestalt psychologists drew attention, in which, in one instance, a figure looked at in one way is a cup or goblet but looked at in another way is two faces oriented to one another; in another instance, the drawing can be seen as either a duck or a rabbit. In such instances, one sees it one way or the other, but not both simultaneously. The shift from seeing one configuration (or, in German, *Gestalt*) to seeing the other may be termed "a gestalt switch."

40   I believe that it is this which is conventionally (and rather blandly) referred to in the speech production literature as "the planning stage,"

as if the planning was going on in a temporal and sequential vacuum, and a stable and unchanging one at that.

41 Cf. Sacks, 1992, vol. 2: 554–60 [Spring, 1972]; Schegloff, 1992b: xlvii; Sacks and I were pursuing related lines in the mid-1970s.

42 There is, of course, even more to grammar – deixis, anaphora, reference, tense and aspect, modality, voice, as well as the resources and practices by which spates of talk get analyzably put together, and these too will be productive when examined in the materials of talk-in-interaction under the auspices of an interest in grammar and interaction.

43 That it does not count as advancing the progress of the construction of the turn – that it counts as retarding progressivity (Schegloff, 1979: 272-80), is another kind of fact about it, maybe even a *grammatical* fact about it, but that should not be taken to discount the validity of the object as an element of the TCU. And perhaps it is not even a fact; from various sources – Sacks (1992: II: 495-98, et passim), the Goodwins separately and together (M. H. Goodwin, 1983; Goodwin and Goodwin, 1986; C. Goodwin, 1987); Gene Lerner, (1987, 1991) – we can learn things about searches and "forgetfulness" which can allow us to see that some "uh"s may in fact promote the progressivity of a TCU in some respects – the progressivity of a distinct type of turn, or one which is made to embody distinctive features or activities.

44 This is without prejudice to the possible co-operation of hierarchical organizations in the talk.

45 The text summarizes parts of an account which Sacks and I were preparing to write up shortly before his death in 1975, based largely on work which he had done. See also M. Goodwin, 1983 and M. Goodwin and C. Goodwin, 1986, as well as Lerner, 1987.

46 Some such interpolations into a TCU, for example, parentheticals, can themselves engender sequences, entirely encapsulated within the TCU, as in the following exchange (taken from Schegloff, 1979: 266), in which the sequence is encapsulated between a prepositioned conditional clause and its "main" clause:

```
      KC-4, 16:23-31

      Kathy:   That is if the warp has sixteen greens an two
               blacks an two light blues and two blacks an sixteen
               greens an: sixteen blacks on sixteen blues an so on,
-->            'hh y'know the warp are the long pieces.
               (0.5)
-->   Frieda:  Mhhm
      Kathy:   The weft has exactly tha:t.
      Frieda:  Yah.
               (0.5)
```

47 I give no more than a mention here to other features of conduct which can figure comparably in the design and understanding of the turn, such as posture. For example, a speaker may bracket a whole utterance or sequence as being in a side or subordinate focus of attention and involvement (Goffman, 1963: 43–44), this bracketing being embodied

via "body torque," in which only the upper reaches of the body are oriented to the recipient, while the trunk and torso remain directed toward a competing main or dominant interactional focus (Schegloff, 1990), thereby placing the talk under constraints not to expand.

48 On the first score, morphologically inflected languages would seem to contrast with predominantly word order languages in the strength and medium by which projection of the shape of the TCU works. So also do differences between SVO and SOV languages invite examination in these terms. We should anticipate a variety of specific mechanisms by which such robust features of turn-taking organization as local organization, interactional management and party administration (SSJ, 1974: 724–27) are implemented, and different detailed empirical outcomes as the result. Regarding the bearing of setting-specific turn-taking organizations on the grammatical constitution of the talk, see the discussion of the news interview in sources such as Clayman, 1988, Greatbatch, 1988; Heritage and Greatbatch, 1991; Heritage and Roth, 1995.

49 Such occurrences are not idiosyncratic. Here is an excerpt from another reviewer and another doctor, with at least three inbreath placements of possible interest, whose examination I leave to the reader's consideration.

```
         Heritage/Kleinman, P2:5:4

      Review:    No I- I would not see it because the nurses that eh- do the
                 initial screening they have our same crite:ria  .h an' they
                 only refer cases to u:s that don't meet the initial criteria
                 .h an' I'm telling you what the criteria a::re  .hh uh for-
-->   Doctor:    for tha:t. It's  .hh [with the hi- if there was no hear:ing=
                                      [Okay.
      Review:    =lo:ss do:cumented we would wanna see three months  .h of
                 effusion  .h [so you know: you might wanna just (.) .h uh::=
      Doctor:                 [Okay.
      Review:    =find out when they repeated that hearing test just to
                 confirm that it's still present.
      Doctor:    [Yeah
      Review:    [.h B't I- yih'know i- that- that's our criteria so it
-->              shouldn't have any problem if- if you do: .hh fi:nd
-->              that this effusion is still present in another uh::
-->              .hh you know after two mo:nths.
      Doctor:    Tch. O::hka:y....
```

50 It clearly can constitute such an answer semantically or propositionally; but was it produced as hearably responsive to that question?

51 I might mention that the phenomenon being examined – an answer partially simultaneous with the question it could be answering – is not idiosyncratic, although the route by which it is produced obviously varies. Consider, for example, the following fragment, taken from Whalen (1995: 188, 207) on the work of a 911 Emergency call-taker (CT in the transcript below) in interaction with a citizen caller. This caller has reported confronting two men. Both the overlapping "answer" and the response to it via other-initiated repair appear

directly cognate with the fragment under examination in the text, although their interactional import and sequential origins are quite different. Reservations about the capacity of recipients to respond this quickly should be assessed against the background of the analysis in Jefferson, 1973 which displays compelling evidence of comparable capacities.

```
            Whalen, 1995

    CT:     =what(r) they doing?
    Caller: Well they had uh (.) concealed
            weapon (.) they had a pistol and
            wuz shootin'
            (1.0)
    CT:     [How long ago? ]
    Caller: [and what I: con-] (0.5) wha:at?=
    CT:     =ho:w-=
    Caller: =just about ten minutes ago
    CT:     And where- (.) [di- you see      ]
--> Caller:                [Willow Crick Road]
--> CT:                Whe:re?
    Caller: On Willow Crick Roa[d
    CT:                        [Did you see the gun?
```

52 The relevance of this theme is by no means restricted to the "answer-to-question" position. See, for example, Ono and Thompson, to appear, which excludes answer-to-question instances, and explicitly considers the "ellipsis" analysis and finds it wanting.

53 Elsewhere (Schegloff, 1996), for example, I have examined confirmatory responses which repeat all (or virtually all) of that which they are confirming – exchanges such as the following, between a late-arriving supervising physician and a medical resident who is reporting at a hospital case conference about a case they have both worked on:

```
    Super:  You talked abou'what happened at thee other hospital?
    Res:    I talked about what happened at thee other hospital.
```

The basic grammatical form(s) for response here might be thought to be "yes," or "I did," rather than this full sentence repeat of the question. The paper in which this practice is treated shows that one use it has is to claim that what is being confirmed had previously been conveyed inexplicitly. This full form, then, is not the "basic" one; its use is marked, and is designed to accomplish a particular action in the sequence.

54 Perhaps the most comprehensive account along these general lines may be found in Levelt, 1989, whose very title and subtitle celebrate the analytic commitment.

55 Indeed, it may go back further yet, to the implicativeness of the prior talk for what should follow it, which itself follows the developmental course of that prior talk; cf. the earlier discussion of the "incipient-next" phase of an utterance's triple phase life, at pp. 97–99.

56 For a related, methodological take on this theme, cf. Heritage, 1990/91.

57   What is being proposed here is thus an alternative to the tack taken by Labov (1966, 1970), who sought to reconcile then-developing syntactic accounts of "the sentence" with actual speech data. His assessment of how much of ordinary speech is actually grammatical, or separated only slightly from grammaticality, led him to formulate "rules of ellipsis and certain editing rules to take care of stammering and false starts" (Labov, 1970: 42). As noted above in the text, where it captures interactants' orientations and practices in talking and hearing/understanding, precisely formulated and empirically grounded accounts along these lines are just what is wanted. However, this tack can be extended to "handle" deviations from stipulated sentence forms on behalf of linguistics taken as an island unto itself, or as one of a group of islands called "cognitive sciences." But the effects of treating such "deviations" as anomalies and "disposing" (or "taking care") of them with a few rules of ellipsis and editing are to mask and suppress relations between grammar as *one* form of organization and other forms or orders of organization with which it interacts in the production and understanding of talk-in-interaction, and whose points of articulation (the plate techtonics of talk-in-interaction, if you will) these departures partially index.

58   Consider, for example, the assertion (in the context of an exchange on "pro-drop" of subject and auxiliary on an electronic scholarly "hot line") that "the auxiliaries that can be eroded are exactly those auxiliaries that are greatly reduced phonetically – to a single consonant, obligatorily (in non-emphatic contexts)," but that "You CANNOT get rid of similar but less reduced auxiliaries, like WAS: Was eatin' an apple./*Eatin' an apple." (Stemberger, 1993; Linguist Hot Line, 08 Mar, 1993, emphasis in original.) Put into the second turn of an adjacency pair, e.g., after a question such as "What were ya doin'?" "Eatin' an apple." is not starred, but is exactly right.

Or consider an empirical instance drawn from a classroom setting with young children, for whom the alternatives pose an issue for explicit instruction; answering with full sentences is something they have to be told to do (taken from Lerner, 1995: 124).

The production of stand-alone complete-sentence answers represents a "marked" form in contrast with elliptical (i.e., sequentially tied) responses ordinarily used in talk-in-interaction. Spoken answers need not be produced as complete sentences (as [the excerpt below] shows) nor do answers ordinarily repeat their originating question (or only reference it indexically) because answerers can rely on their turn's proximity to the question's original production and the projected relevance of answering as a next action for their turn.

```
Simson:   If you were big, if you were big, bigger than
          anybody in this whole classroom (. ) how could you
          solve (.) that problem.
Erica:    um
Juan:     cutting your legs ((laughs)) no huh huh
Erica:    bend dow::n::?
Juan:     get on your knees
Daniel:   (to exercise)
Juan:     get on yr knees
```

In contrast, producing stand-alone answers requires the construction of an utterance that is markedly disengaged from its local sequential environment. Yet, the construction of that utterance is always situated within a particular course of action using practices designed in the first place for situated conduct and copresent recipients. Complete-sentence answers that repeat elements of the question introduce a marked redundancy into the reply that is nonetheless an unmarked (and non-redundant) element of an eventually written sentence that is to be designed to stand on its own, independently of the question. Students must counteract ordinary conversational practices to produce stand-alone, complete and unabridged sentence responses. Yet, this teacher-mandated response-form can itself provide resources for answering questions

Do we not see here a juxtaposition of textually and interactionally grounded grammars, posed, as Lerner puts it (p.c.), "as a member's problem of talking vs. writing?"

59 Curiously, as Goffman (1964) argued that the place of talking was in "situations," in which talking need not occur, so does grammar for talk-in-interaction operate on units which (like nods and shrugs and compliant actions) need not be actually realized in language – actions or activities. It is this (in part) which grounds the withholding of principled primacy from language in CA studies.

60 Indeed, the whole conception of "speech acts" may be understood as an effort to make a propositionally based conception of language – whether linguistic, logical or philosophical – available to satisfy the requirements of the analysis of action. For one thoroughgoing critique of speech act theories, cf. Levinson, 1980, 1981, 1983: Chapter 5.

61 The issue does not involve including such categories as functional grammar's "agent" and "patient," for these are still categories for aspects of propositions.

62 It may be relevant as well to understanding troubles like dyslexia, where a whole component of language resources presumed by the constitutive environment for language (i.e., sound) is dropped out and replaced by a non-constitutive feature – written representation, and such key dimensions as temporality are neutralized by orthographic stasis, with consequent transformations of directionality, the consequentiality of possible completion, the availability of help via repair organization, etc.

References

Atkinson, J. M. and Heritage, J. (eds.) (1984). *Structures of Social Action: Studies in Conversation Analysis*. Cambridge: Cambridge University Press.

Austin, J. L. (1962). *How To Do Things With Words*. Cambridge, MA: Harvard University Press.

Baugh, J. and Sherzer, J. (eds.) (1984). *Language in Use: Readings in Sociolinguistics*. Englewood Cliffs, NJ: Prentice Hall.

Bolinger, D. L. (1952). Linear Modification. *Publications of the Modern Language Association* 67: 1117–44. (Reprinted in Bolinger, 1965: 279-308.)

(1965). *Forms of English: Accent, Morpheme, Order*. Cambridge, MA: Harvard University Press.

Chomsky, N. (1957). *Syntactic Structures*. The Hague: Mouton.

Clayman, S. E. (1988). Displaying neutrality in television news interviews. *Social Problems* 35(4): 474–92.

Davidson, J. (1984). Subsequent versions of invitations, offers, requests, and proposals dealing with potential or actual rejection. In J. M. Atkinson and J. Heritage (eds.) *Structures of Social Action: Studies in Conversation Analysis*, pp. 102–28. Cambridge: Cambridge University Press.

Duranti, A. and Ochs, E. (1979). Left-dislocation in Italian conversation. In T. Givón (ed.), *Syntax and Semantics, Vol. 12: Discourse and Syntax*, pp. 377–418. New York: Academic Press.

Egbert, M. (1993). Schisming: The transformation from a single conversation to multiple conversations. Unpublished Ph.D. Dissertation, Department of Applied Linguistics, University of California, Los Angeles.

Ekman, P. (1979). About brows: emotional and conversational signals. In M. von Cranach, K. Foppa, W. Lepenies and D. Ploog (eds.), *Human Ethology*. Cambridge: Cambridge University Press.

Ekman, P. and Friesen, W. V. (1969). The repertoire of nonverbal behavior: categories, origins, usage, and coding. *Semiotica* 1: 49–98.

Ford, C. (1993). *Grammar in Interaction: Adverbial Clauses in American English*. Cambridge: Cambridge University Press.

Fox, B. and Jasperson, R. (frth.). A syntactic exploration of repair in English conversation. In P. Davis (ed.) *Descriptive and Theoretical Modes in the Alternative Linguistics*.

Fries, C. C. (1952). *The Structure of English: An Introduction to the Construction of English Sentences*. New York: Harcourt, Brace and World.

Garfinkel, H. (1967). *Studies in Ethnomethodology*. Englewood Cliffs, NJ: Prentice-Hall.

Goffman, E. (1961). *Encounters: Two Studies in the Sociology of Interaction*. Indianapolis: Bobbs-Merrill.

(1963). *Behavior in Public Places: Notes on the Social Organization of Gathering*. New York: Free Press.

(1964). The neglected situation. In J. J. Gumperz and D. Hymes (eds.) The Ethnography of Communication. *American Anthropologist* 66(6), Part II: 133–36.

(1971). *Relations in Public: Microstudies of the Public Order*. New York: Harper and Row.

Goodwin, C. (1979). The interactive construction of a sentence in natural conversation. In G. Psathas (ed.) *Everyday Language: Studies in Ethnomethodology*, pp. 97–121. New York: Irvington Publishers.

(1980). Restarts, pauses, and the achievement of mutual gaze at turn-beginning. *Sociological Inquiry* 50: 272–302.

(1981). *Conversational Organization: Interaction Between Speakers and Hearers*. New York: Academic Press.

(1986). Between and within: alternative treatments of continuers and assessments. *Human Studies* 9: 205–17.

(1987). Forgetfulness as an interactive resource. *Social Psychology Quarterly* 50, No. 2: 115–30.

Goodwin, C. and Goodwin, M. H. (1987). Concurrent operations on talk: notes on the interactive organization of assessments. *IPrA Papers in Pragmatics* 1(1): 1–52.

Goodwin, M. H. (1983). Searching for a word as an interactive activity. In J. N. Deely and M. D. Lenhart (eds.) *Semiotics 1981*, pp. 129–38. New York: Plenum Press.

Goodwin, M. H. and Goodwin, C. (1986). Gesture and coparticipation in the activity of searching for a word. *Semiotica* 62(1/2): 51–75.

Gordon, D. and Lakoff, G. (1971). Conversational postulates. In *Papers from the Seventh Regional Meeting of the Chicago Linguistic Society*, pp. 63–84. Chicago: Chicago Linguistic Society.

(1975). Conversational postulates. In P. Cole and J. Morgan (eds.) *Syntax and Semantics*, Vol. 3, pp 83–106. New York: Academic Press.

Greatbatch, D. (1988). A turn-taking system for British news interviews. *Language in Society* 17(3): 401–30.

Heritage, J. (1984). A change-of-state token and aspects of its sequential placement. In J. M. Atkinson and J. Heritage (eds.) *Structures of Social Action: Studies in Conversation Analysis*, pp. 299–345. Cambridge: Cambridge University Press.

(1986). Oh-prefaced responses to inquiry. Unpublished ms.

(1990/91). Intention, meaning and strategy: observations on constraints on interaction analysis. *Research on Language and Social Interaction* 24: 311–32.

Heritage, J. and Greatbatch, D. (1991). On the institutional character of institutional talk: the case of news interviews. In D. Boden and D. H. Zimmerman (eds.) *Talk and Social Structure*, pp. 93–137. Cambridge: Polity Press.

Heritage, J. and Sorjonen, M. L (1994). Constituting and maintaining activities across sequences: *and*-prefacing as a feature of question design. *Language in Society* 23: 1–29.

Heritage, J. C. and Roth, A. L. (1995). Grammar and institution: questions and questioning in the broadcast news interview. *Research on Language and Social Interaction* 28(1): 1–60.

Jefferson, G. (1973). A case of precision timing in ordinary conversation: overlapped tag-positioned address terms in closing sequences. *Semiotica* 9: 47–96.

(1974). Error correction as an interactional resource. *Language in Society* 2: 181–99.

(1978a). Sequential aspects of storytelling in conversation. In J. Schenkein (ed.) *Studies in the Organization of Conversational Interaction*, pp. 219-48. New York: Academic Press.

(1978b). What's in a "Nyem"? *Sociology* 12, No. 1: 135–39.

(1979). A technique for inviting laughter and its subsequent acceptance/declination. In G. Psathas (ed.), *Everyday Language: Studies in Ethnomethodology*, pp. 79–96. New York: Irvington Publishers.

(1984a). On stepwise transition from talk about a trouble to inappropriately next-positioned matters. In J. M. Atkinson and J. Heritage (eds.) *Structures of Social Action: Studies in Conversation Analysis*, pp. 191–221. Cambridge: Cambridge University Press.

(1984b). Notes on some orderlinesses of overlap onset. In V. D'Urso and P. Leonardi (eds.) *Discourse Analysis and Natural Rhetorics*, pp. 11–38. Padova: CLEUP Editore.

(1984c). On the organization of laughter in talk about troubles. In J. M. Atkinson and J. Heritage (eds.) *Structures of Social Action: Studies in Conversation Analysis*, pp. 346-69. Cambridge: Cambridge University Press.

(1985). An exercise in the transcription and analysis of laughter. In T. A. van Dijk (ed.) *Handbook of Discourse Analysis*, Vol. 3, pp. 25–34. New York: Academic Press.

Jefferson, G. and Schegloff, E. A. (1975). Sketch: Some orderly aspects of overlap in natural conversation. Unpublished ms.

Jefferson, G., Sacks, H. and Schegloff, E. A. (1977). Preliminary notes on the sequential organization of laughter. *Pragmatics Microfiche*. Cambridge: Cambridge University Department of Linguistics.

(1987). Notes on laughter in the pursuit of intimacy. In G. Button and J. R. E. Lee (eds.) *Talk and Social Organisation*, pp. 152–205. Clevedon, England: Multilingual Matters.

Jones, C.M. and Beach, W.A. (1994). Therapists' techniques for responding to unsolicited contributions by family members. Paper presented at the Annual Meetings of the American Sociological Association, Los Angeles. To appear in G. H. Morris and R. J. Chenail (eds.) *The Talk of the Clinic*. Hillsdale, NJ: Lawrence Erlbaum.

Kendon, A. (1972). Some relationships between body motion and speech. In A. Seligman and B. Pope (eds.) *Studies in Dyadic Communication*, pp. 177–210. Elmsford, NY: Pergamon Press.

(1980). Gesture and speech: two aspects of the process of utterance. In M. R. Key (ed.) *The Relationship of Verbal and Nonverbal Communication*, pp. 207–27. The Hague: Mouton.

Labov, W. (1966). On the grammaticality of everyday speech. Annual Meetings of the Linguistic Society of America.

(1970). The study of language in its social context. *Studium Generale* 23: 30–87.

Labov, W. and Fanshel, D. (1977). *Therapeutic Discourse: Psychotherapy as Conversation*. New York: Academic Press.

Lerner, G. H. (1987). Collaborative turn sequences: sentence construction and social action. Unpublished Ph.D. dissertation, Psychology, University of California at Irvine.

(1991). On the syntax of sentences-in-progress. *Language in Society* 20: 441–58.

(1995). Turn design and the organization of participation in instructional activities. *Discourse Processes* 19,1: 111–31.

Levelt, W. J. M. (1983). Monitoring and self-repair in speech. *Cognition* 14: 41–104.

(1989). *Speaking: from intention to articulation*. Cambridge, MA: MIT Press.

Levinson, S. C. (1980). Speech act theory: the state of the art. *Language and Linguistic Teaching: Abstracts* 13(1): 5–24.

(1981). The essential inadequacies of speech act models of dialogue. In H. Parret, M. Sbisa and J. Verschueren (eds.) *Possibilities and Limitations of Pragmatics: Proceedings of the Conference on Pragmatics at Urbino*, July 8-14, 1979, pp. 473–92. Amsterdam: Benjamins.

(1983). *Pragmatics*. Cambridge: Cambridge University Press.

Local, J. (1992). Continuing and restarting. In P. Auer and A. Di Luzio (eds.) *The Contextualization of Language*. pp. 273–96. Amsterdam/Philadelphia: John Benjamins.

Mandelbaum, J. (1991/2). Conversational non-co-operation: an exploration of disattended complaints. *Research on Language and Social Interaction* 25: 97–138.

Ono, T. and Thompson, S. A. (1994). Unattached NPs in English conversation. *Proceedings of the Berkeley Linguistic Society* 20: (frth.).

Pomerantz, A. (1984). Agreeing and disagreeing with assessments: some features of preferred/dispreferred turn shapes. In J. M. Atkinson and J. Heritage (eds.) *Structures of Social Action: Studies in Conversation Analysis*, pp. 57–101. Cambridge: Cambridge University Press.

Ross, J. R. (1970). On declarative sentences. In R. A. Jacobs and P. S. Rosenbaum (eds.) *Readings in English Transformational Grammar*, pp. 222–72. Waltham, Mass.: Ginn and Co.

Sacks, H. (1974). An analysis of the course of a joke's telling in conversation. In R. Bauman and J. Sherzer (eds.), *Explorations in the Ethnography of Speaking*, pp. 337-53. Cambridge: Cambridge University Press.

(1987[1973]). On the preferences for agreement and contiguity in sequences in conversation. In G. Button and J. R. E. Lee (eds.) *Talk and Social Organisation*, pp. 54–69. Clevedon, England: Multilingual Matters.

(1992). *Lectures on Conversation*. 2 volumes. Edited by G. Jefferson, with Introductions by E. A. Schegloff. Oxford: Blackwell.

Sacks, H. and Schegloff, E. A. (1979). Two preferences in the organization of reference to persons in conversation and their interaction. In G. Psathas (ed.) *Everyday Language: Studies in Ethnomethodology*, pp. 15–21. New York: Irvington Publishers.

Sacks, H., Schegloff, E. A. and Jefferson, G. (1974). A simplest systematics for the organization of turn-taking for conversation. *Language* 50: 696–735.

Schegloff, E. A. (1979). The relevance of repair for syntax-for-conversation. In T. Givon (ed.) *Syntax and Semantics 12: Discourse and Syntax*, pp. 261–88. New York: Academic Press.

(1980). Preliminaries to preliminaries: "Can I ask you a question", *Sociological Inquiry*, 50(3-4): 104–52.

(1982). Discourse as an interactional achievement: some uses of "uh huh" and other things that come between sentences. In D. Tannen (ed.) *Georgetown University Roundtable on Languages and Linguistics*, pp. 71–93. Washington DC: Georgetown University Press.

(1984a). On some questions and ambiguities in conversation. In J. M. Atkinson and J. Heritage (eds.) *Structures of Social Action: Studies in Conversation Analysis*, pp. 28–52. Cambridge: Cambridge University Press.

(1984b). On some gestures' relation to talk. In J. M. Atkinson and J. Heritage (eds.) *Structures of Social Action: Studies in Conversation Analysis*, pp. 266-96. Cambridge: Cambridge University Press.

(1986). The routine as achievement. *Human Studies* 9: 111–51.

(1987a[1973]). Recycled turn beginnings: a precise repair mechanism in conversation's turn-taking organisation. In G. Button and J. R. E. Lee (eds.) *Talk and Social Organisation*, pp. 70–85. Clevedon, England: Multilingual Matters, Ltd.

(1987b). Analyzing single episodes of interaction: an exercise in conversation analysis. *Social Psychology Quarterly* 50 No. 2: 101–14.

(1988a). On an actual virtual servo-mechanism for guessing bad news: a single case conjecture. *Social Problems* 35(4): 442–57.

(1988b). Discourse as an interactional achievement II: an exercise in conversation analysis. In D. Tannen (ed.) *Linguistics in Context: Connecting Observation and Understanding, Lectures from the 1985 LSA/TESOL and NEH Institutes*, pp. 135–58. Norwood, NJ: Ablex Publishing Corp.

(1988c). Goffman and the analysis of conversation. In P. Drew and A. Wootton (eds.) *Erving Goffman: Exploring the Interaction Order*, pp. 89–135. Cambridge: Polity Press.

(1989). Reflections on language, development, and the interactional character of talk-in-interaction. In M. Bornstein and J. S. Bruner (eds.) *Interaction in Human Development*, pp. 139–53. Lawrence Erlbaum Associates.

(1990). Body torque. Presentation in the invited session on "spacing, orientation and the environment in co-present interaction" at the 89th Annual Meeting of the American Anthropological Association, New Orleans, November 30, 1990.

(1991). Conversation analysis and socially shared cognition. In L. Resnick, J. Levine, and S. Teasley (eds.) *Perspectives on Socially Shared Cognition*, pp. 150–71. Washington, DC: American Psychological Association.

(1992a). Introduction. In G. Jefferson (ed.) Harvey Sacks: *Lectures on Conversation*. volume 1, pp. ix-lxii. Oxford: Blackwell.

(1992b). Introduction. In G. Jefferson (ed.) Harvey Sacks: *Lectures on Conversation*. volume 2, pp. ix-lii. Oxford: Blackwell.

(1992c). Repair after next turn: the last structurally provided defense of intersubjectivity in conversation. *American Journal of Sociology* 97: 5 (March 1992), 1295–1345.

(1992d). In another context. In A. Duranti and C. Goodwin (eds.) *Rethinking Context: Language as an Interactive Phenomenon*, pp. 193–227. Cambridge: Cambridge University Press.

(1995). Discourse as an interactional achievement III: the omnirelevance of action. *Research on Language and Social Interaction* 28(3).

(1996). Confirming allusions. *American Journal of Sociology*, 102: 1 (July 1996), 161–216.

(frth.). Issues of relevance for discourse analysis: contingency in action, interaction and co-participant context. In E. H. Hovy and D. Scott (eds.) *Inter-disciplinary Perspectives on Discourse*. Heidelberg: Springer Verlag.

Schegloff, E. A. and Sacks, H. (1973). Opening up closings. *Semiotica* 8: 289–327. (Reprinted in Baugh and Sherzer, 1984.)

Schegloff, E. A., Jefferson, G. and Sacks, H. (1977). The preference for self-correction in the organization of repair in conversation. *Language* 53: 361–82.

Schiffrin, D. (1987). *Discourse Markers*. Cambridge: Cambridge University Press.

Searle, J. R. (1965). What is a speech act? In M. Black (ed.) *Philosophy in America*, pp. 221–39. Ithaca, NY: Cornell University Press.

(1969). *Speech Acts*. Cambridge: Cambridge University Press.

Streeck, J. (1988). The significance of gesture: how it is established. *IPrA Papers in Pragmatics* 2(1): 60–83.

Streeck, J. and Hartge, U. (1992). Previews: gestures at the transition place. In P. Auer and A. di. Luzio (eds.) *The Contextualization of Language*, pp. 135–57. Amsterdam/Philadelphia: John Benjamins.

Whalen, J. (1995). A technology of order production: computer-aided dispatch in public safety communications. In P. Ten Have and G. Psathas (eds.) *Situated Order: Studies in the Social Organization of Talk and Embodied Activities*, pp. 187–230. Washington, DC: University Press of America.

Wittgenstein, L. (1953). *Philosophical Investigations*. Translated by G. E. M. Anscombe. New York: Macmillan.

3

Interactional units in conversation: syntactic, intonational, and pragmatic resources for the management of turns*

CECILIA E. FORD AND SANDRA A. THOMPSON

3.1 Introduction

The research reported in this chapter is intended as a contribution to an understanding of the basic linguistic units used by speakers in spontaneous communication. Our interest is in the linguistic factors associated with the split-second timing of next turn onset that has been documented in conversation analytic literature (Sacks, Schegloff, and Jefferson, 1974; Jefferson, 1973; Wilson and Zimmerman, 1986).

In the past two decades, conversation analysts have uncovered patterns and principles of interaction, particularly in the areas of turn-taking and the sequential organization of talk. The picture of spontaneous interaction that emerges very clearly from this research depicts a complex and intricately monitored human practice that is maximally sensitive to moment-by-moment input by all parties to a conversation, and is, therefore, characterized by an organization that is locally managed. Turns at talk vary widely in length, and their length is not unilaterally controlled. The extension of a turn at talk has everything to do with the manner in which that turn is being responded to by the other participant(s) in the conversation (e.g., Atkinson and Heritage, 1984; Davidson, 1984; C. Goodwin, 1979, 1981, 1986a, 1986b, 1987; M. Goodwin, 1980; Goodwin and Goodwin, 1986, 1987, forthcoming; Heritage, 1984, 1989; Jefferson, 1973, 1987, 1989; Lerner, 1987, 1989, 1991, in progress; Sacks, et al. 1974; Schegloff, 1979, 1980, 1982, 1986, 1987, 1988, 1989, 1990, 1992; Schegloff and Sacks, 1973; Wilson and Zimmerman, 1986; and Wilson et al. 1984). To understand the syntax and rhetoric of conversational language use, linguists need to take very seriously the situated practices of conversationalists as revealed in the careful work of conversation analysts.

In their highly influential discussion of turn-taking in conversation, Sacks et al. (1974) have proposed that turns can be constructed from what they call "unit-types," or "turn-constructional units" (= TCU):

Unit-types for English include sentential, clausal, phrasal, and lexical constructions. Instances of the unit-types so usable allow a projection of the unit-type under way, and what, roughly, it will take for an instance of that unit-type to be completed. Unit-types lacking the feature of projectability may not be usable in the same way. (p. 702)

Later in the same paper, they say:

whatever the units employed for the construction [of turns], . . . they still have points of possible unit completion, points which are projectable before their occurrence. Since that is the better part of what the turn-taking system asks of the language materials from which its turns are fashioned, it will be compatible with a system of units which has this feature. (p. 72) . . . Examination of WHERE such "next-turn starts" occur in current turns shows them to occur at "possible completion points." (p. 721)

Sacks et al. suggest that the specification of how this projection of unit-types is accomplished, so as to allow "no-gap" starts by next speakers, is an important question to which linguists can make major contributions. The split-second precision of the turn-taking system must rely on a method of prediction on the part of interactants as to where a turn is likely to be terminated, that is, as to where the "transition-relevance place" is. Wilson and Zimmerman (1986) have demonstrated, through the measurement of silences between turns, that conversationalists are able to assess potential points of turn completion before any actual completion or pause has been reached. Sacks et al. acknowledge the role of intonation in projecting the end of a turn-constructional unit and, in the quote above, they suggest that a precise specification of what the actual units are composed of has yet to be given. Wilson et al. (1984: 173) note that:

the weakest aspect of the sequential-production approach [i.e., the Sacks et al. model – CEF & SAT] as it has been developed thus far is the lack of adequate understanding of how transition-relevance places are constructed and recognized by speakers and hearers.

Part of our goal in this paper is to contribute to such an understanding.

Sacks et al. acknowledge that the recognition of TCUs on the part
of speakers must involve the interplay of a number of factors, and
Schegloff (1988, this volume) has noted the importance of pitch
peaks in projecting the imminent end of a TCU. However, the
Sacks et al. quote above, as well as references in the literature to
TCUs, allow the interpretation that they are primarily conceived of
by conversation analysts as syntactic units. Schegloff, 1982: 74-75,
for example, says:

Elsewhere (Sacks, Schegloff, and Jefferson, 1974) it has been argued that
speakers construct utterances in turns at talk out of describable structured
units, with recognizable possible completions. In English, some lexical items
(e.g., "hello," "yes," "who"), some phrasal units, some clausal units, and
sentences constitute such "turn-constructional units." The end of any such
unit is a possible completion of a turn, and possible completions of turns
are places at which potential next speakers appropriately start next turns.

From this it could be, and on occasion has been, inferred that these
syntactic units are in fact what *constitute* "turn-constructional
units.[1]"

In this paper, we wish to pursue the question of the characterization of TCUs and hence of transition-relevance places. Taking seriously the assumption that "aspects of language structure are
designed for conversational use" (Sacks et al. 1974: 722), we take
up Sacks et al.'s challenge to linguists to participate in defining the
character of TCUs. We propose to explore the role of syntax, intonation, and conversational pragmatics in the construction of the
interactionally validated units of talk known as turns. We believe
that the work we present here should mark the beginning of a
collaborative investigation of the nature of turns. This research
program requires the expertise of conversation analysts, discourse
analysts, grammarians, and phonologists. Essential to this enterprise is that researchers have direct experience in analyzing naturally occurring language use, in interaction. While this adds a
measure of complexity to the task at hand, we have found that
idealized data, such as intonation samples read aloud for analysis,
have not yielded theories that can be applied to the situated language use which it is our goal to understand.

We hope to demonstrate that "turn units" are complex, that they include intonational and pragmatic cues as well as syntactic ones, and that speakers design and place their turns according to these complex turn units. By separating intonation, syntax, and pragmatics we do not wish to imply that these systems operate independently. Indeed, we assume that they work together and interact in complex ways. We separate the investigation of these systems in order to measure the degree of association that exists between turn completion and grammatical completion. Our ultimate goal is to contribute to a linguistic investigation in which all three systems, as well as non-verbal communication, are treated as fundamental (see Ford, Fox, and Thompson, in press).

Before reporting on the specific findings of our present research, we would like to situate our investigation within the context of previous research into the nature of turn units.

3.2   Previous discussions of interactional units

An important early contribution to the literature on interactional units is presented by Jefferson (1973), who persuasively argues that speakers are acutely aware of "possible completion points." Jefferson offers evidence in the fact that speakers are able regularly to position an overlapped utterance precisely at a point where an on-going utterance might be finished but is instead continued by an address term, such as *dear* or *sir* in a closing sequence. Jefferson illustrates how the non-observance of the predicted point of completion, through early turn-onset, may be doing strategic interactional work. We take up this point in the analysis of cases of recipient turn beginnings at non-transition points in our data p.159.

In two influential contributions, C. Goodwin (1979, 1981) demonstrates the variety of interactional factors at work in projecting the ends of turns and in extending a turn beyond the first location of potential turn change ("transition relevance place," or TRP hereafter). Goodwin's research suggests that turn completion and turn extension are coordinated through at least a combination of gaze and syntax in face-to-face interaction.

A major contribution to the discussion of interactional units is Goodwin and Goodwin (1987); in a masterful demonstration of the interactive organization of conversation, Goodwin and Goodwin show how participants hear talk as it is emerging, and the consequences of syntactic, intonational, and pragmatic structure for the organization of turns and turn units. Their discussion includes a wealth of examples in which projectable aspects of a turn are confirmed by the time of the completion of that turn. For example, conversational participants can be shown to orient to the intonational, syntactic, and semantic properties of intensifiers like *so* and *really* in utterances like *It was s::o: good* to project the emerging talk as an assessment, and in fact, to produce collaborative assessments of their own just as the intensifier comes to completion. In other words, recipients produce assessments *by making projections* about speech which has not yet occurred (p. 30), and can orchestrate their actions to systematically bring an assessment to a recognizable close (p. 33).[2]

Schegloff (1980), (1982), (1987), (1988) (this volume), addresses the characterization of "turn-constructional units" given in Sacks et al., and suggests ways in which multi-unit turns are achieved. Speakers can indicate an interest in producing a turn consisting of more than one unit; an entire turn may be devoted to such turn-extenders as story prefaces or "pre-pre's" (such as *can I ask you a question?*); or speakers can speed up as the possible completion of a TCU approaches. [3]

Davidson (1984) refers to material that follows a "possible completion point" in an offer or invitation, but she does not define or characterize what she means by this term. Since no mention is made of intonation or pragmatics, we assume that she is referring to syntactic completion. Davidson suggests that:

> the components occurring after a possible completion point may be providing the inviter or offerer with a *monitor space* in which he or she can examine what happens or what does not happen there for its acceptance/rejection implicativeness. (p. 117)

The *monitor space* provides the speaker with a chance to add on to an ongoing turn based on the presence or absence of recipient uptake.

Wilson and Zimmerman (1986), in addition to supporting the projectability of transition-relevance places in connection with the role of silence, also discuss unit-types that are both smaller than and larger than a "sentence." In the case of the former, called "subsentential unit-types," they note that both intonation and sequential context may mark an utterance as "intendedly complete" (p. 172).

Another important paper which considers the ways in which interactants project turn completion is Local and Kelly (1986), who demonstrate, among other things, that all silences are not equal with respect to turn taking. In particular, they show that silences following conjunctionals may be articulated so as to project more talk by the same speaker or may be produced as "trail offs," where speaker change regularly occurs. In the latter instances, a turn is not syntactically complete, but it is produced with phonetic features that are interpretable as compatible with speaker change. In fact, further talk by the same speaker, in such cases, regularly addresses the lack of next speaker uptake during the preceding pause.

Lerner (1987), (1991), (in press) shows how collaborative turn sequences, turn units produced by two or more speakers, provide evidence for projectable completion points. The collaborative turns he analyzes include units whose structures are projected beyond the first point of syntactic completion, such as contrasts and three-part lists. Atkinson (1984) also discusses lists and contrasts as techniques for eliciting audience response in public speaking contexts.

Based on experimental work, Levelt (1989: 34-36) discusses "turn-yielding cues," that is, "means by which a speaker can signal that his turn is over or that he wants to keep the floor in spite of his having completed some unit," including prosodic, rhythmic, syntactic, and lexical cues. Levelt points out that what speakers are projecting is not just "units," but "units that are conversationally relevant," and that "the projectivity of an utterance is probably multiply determined by its prosody, its syntax, and its meaning." He goes on to say that "how a listener combines these sources of information to compute transition-relevance places in actual discourse is largely untouched in the extensive literature on discourse analysis." Our research, which comes from non-experimental conversation, provides support for Levelt's observation that prosody, syntax, and meaning all seem to be involved in projecting the end of a turn unit.

The work to date by conversation researchers documents clearly, then, the regularities in the way speakers construct turn units. Just what these units consist of and how transition-relevance places are constituted, however, remains to be specified.

3.3 Previous discussions of the relationship between syntax and intonation in conversation

Looking at intonation and syntax in spoken English, Quirk et al. (1968) examine two unrehearsed panel discussions of about 10,000 words and find a high degree of correspondence between "tone units" (TU) (auditory units roughly equivalent to "intonation units" (see p. 145 below)) and various types of syntactic units. For example, about half of the TU boundaries coincided with "sentence" and "clause" boundaries.

Levinson (1983: 297), in discussing the Sacks et al. model, also suggests that TCUs are:

determined by various features of linguistic surface structure: they are syntactic units (sentences, clauses, noun phrases, and so on) identified as turn-units partly by prosodic, and especially intonational, means . . . The exact characterization of such units still requires a considerable amount of linguistic work (see C. Goodwin, 1981: 15ff), but whatever its final shape the characterization must allow for the projectability or predictability of each unit's end – for it is this alone that can account for the recurrent marvels of split-second speaker transition.

In an important study addressing the issues, Oreström (1983) notes that one limitation of Sacks et al. is that 'little ... attention is paid to ... the complex nature of a TRP' (p. 29). Oreström goes on to show that TRPs must be thought of minimally as points of intonational completion, syntactic completion, and pragmatic completion.

Oreström's data convincingly show that:

the listener wanting to take the speaker role did so at a point in the discourse which is characterized by a certain combination of features. (p. 68)

Table 3.1 (his Table 11, p. 68) gives these five features, where TU means "tone unit." In evaluating these findings, it is important to note that Oreström's study exclusively involved dyadic conversation, and he only investigated "turns with more than one TU and where there was no simultaneous talk when the transition took

Table 3.1 The linguistic features in turn-final position with the
highest correlation with turn-taking.

```
Prosody; completion of a TU with a non-level nucleus    96.3%

Syntax; completion of a syntactic sequence  95.2%

Semantics; completion of a semantic sequence  95.2%

Loudness; decrease in volume  44.4%

Silent pause; following immediately after end of TU  40.8%
```

place" (p. 61). Given the latter constraint, it is perhaps not surprising that he found that turn-change tended to happen at points of
prosodic, syntactic, and pragmatic completion: Oreström's method
explicitly eliminated from investigation all cases of overlap. Even
with this restriction of the data to multi-TU, non-overlapping turns,
prosody and pragmatics are found to be just as prominent as syntax
in defining TRPs.

From Table 3.1 it is clear that the first three features are critical,
each accounting for more than 95 per cent of the turn changes. As
noted above, then, these data strongly suggest that the notion of
TRP should be expanded to include not just syntactic completion,
but intonational and pragmatic completion as well.

Several other linguistically oriented studies have supported the
roles of both syntax and intonation in the formation of turn
units. Altenberg (1987: chap. 4) provides a lengthy discussion of
the correlations between TUs and various types of syntactic units,
particularly clause types, using two prepared monologic orations.
Duncan and Fiske (1977), (1985) and Denny (1985) suggest that
both "smooth" and "simultaneous" turn exchanges are characterized by a set of cues, including syntactic completion, gaze, gesture,
pitch, syllable length, and intonation. Ford (1993), in a study of
adverbial conjunction in American English conversation, finds that
intonational and syntactic units overwhelmingly coincide in her
data base, and that both syntax and intonation contribute to the
work of signalling that a turn is not yet complete.

A substantial amount of research, then, has pointed to the ability
of conversationalists to project the end of the current speaker's turn.
In our study, unlike that of Oreström, we consider all turns, including those produced in overlap. Furthermore, we include conversations with more than two speakers, a context in which the
possibility of more than one speaker starting a next turn places

an added degree of pressure on the turn-taking system (Sacks et al. 1974). Through our analysis, we further elucidate the resources that language provides and that conversationalists orient to in producing and recognizing turn-completion points. We offer evidence for interactionally validated units in conversational discourse, and we demonstrate the ways in which interactants strategically place turn changes as well as turn continuations relative to these projectable unit completion points.

3.4. Data and methods

3.4.1 Data base

Our data base consists of excerpts from two face-to-face, multiparty conversations in American English, totalling about twenty minutes of talk. The participants, middle class adult native speakers of English, are friends, and one speaker is a member of both conversations. The conversations were audio-recorded and transcribed using the common CA system, as described in the Appendix to this volume. As noted above, unlike Oreström (1983), we analyzed our entire data base rather than a subset which excluded short turns and cases of overlapping talk.

While the contribution of non-verbal communication to the turn-taking process has been well-attested, we chose to limit this study to verbal aspects of the interaction. The expansion of this investigation to include visual cues will be the logical next step in the present research program (Ford, Fox, and Thompson, in press).

3.4.2 Research questions

Two central questions guided our research:

(1) To what extent is syntactic completion a predictor of turn completion as validated by actual speaker change? If intonation and pragmatics are considered, is the prediction stronger?

(2) Where the convergence of syntactic, intonational and pragmatic completion are not associated with speaker change, are crucial interactional factors at work? Can the residue be understood as evidence of the strategic interactional use of a norm?

Recall that in order to test the original conception of the turn-taking system as being strongly tied to syntax, the somewhat artificial separation of syntactic, intonational, and pragmatic completion points is essential. We want to reiterate that this separation is not one we believe is real to the participants. Our goal is to provide empirical grounding for our sense that syntax, as it has been conceived of in traditional linguistics terms, is not the best predictor of turn completion. In the following subsections, we indicate in detail how we operationalized the notions of syntactic, intonational, and pragmatic completion and how we measured points of speaker change.[4]

Syntactic completion. Our purpose in operationalizing the notion of syntactic completion was to test whether the interactants in our data were orienting their turn-taking to the kind of completion point which the Sacks et al. model claims they should be. Syntax, they suggest, provides projectable units. We recognize that the notion of syntax is neither stable nor uncontroversial in current linguistics; however, our use of the term syntactic completion in this study reflects our interpretation of what Sacks et al. conceived of as the projectable units provided by a natural language. For this study, then, we judged an utterance to be syntactically complete if, in its discourse context, it could be interpreted as a complete clause, that is, with an overt or directly recoverable predicate, without considering intonation or interactional import. Syntactically complete utterances can always be extended through further additions, so points of syntactic completion may be incremental. In the category of syntactically complete utterances, we included elliptical clauses, answers to questions, and backchannel responses. Thus, we are not positing that an individual speaker's talk at a given location constitutes an independent grammatical unit in itself, but rather, by "syntactic completion," we mean a point in the stream of talk "so far," a potential terminal boundary for a recoverable "clause-so-far." In operationalizing the notion of syntactic completion, our intention was to give as much benefit of the doubt as we could to the possibility, as suggested by Sacks et al., that syntactic completion alone might be associated with speaker change.

Our definition of syntactic completion clearly diverges from a conception of "sentence" based on invented or decontextualized examples judged for well-formedness. We include preceding context to the extent that it is responsible for the recoverability of reference, as in the case of answers, which do not require the full repetition of previous questions. As anyone who has worked with naturally occurring conversation can attest, without considering previous discourse context in this manner, we would have found it difficult indeed to find any "syntactic" completion points. Our definition of syntactic completion did not, however, include intonation, nor did it include a notion of the completion of a sequentially relevant conversational action (see pp. 145–51 below).

A syntactic completion point, then, is judged incrementally within its previous context. Assuming an utterance to have ended at any one of these points defines the end point of an interpretable clause, though not necessarily a point of intonational or interactional completion. Our syntactic completion points correspond in practice to the ends of what Sacks et al. (1974) termed "unit-types," or "turn-construction units;" our definition clarifies the indeterminacy in their characterization, however, since they provide no criteria for identifying one of these units. So a syntactic completion point will sometimes follow a word, sometimes a phrase, sometimes a clause, and sometimes a multi-clausal unit, as illustrated in Sacks et al. (1974: 702, footnote 12). Examples of utterances containing a series of syntactic completion points (indicated here by slashes) is the following:

```
(1)   (K67)
      V:   And his knee was being worn/- okay/ wait./
           It was bent/ that way/


(2)   (M135)
      D:   I mean it's it's not like wi:ne/ it doesn't taste like wine/ but
           it's
      W:   Fermented./
      D:   White/ and milky/ but it's fermented/


(3)   (K149)
      V:   ...made my Dad feel comfortable//, said that he's gonna have this/
           sa:me operation/ when he's- in about (0.2)  twenty years/ cause he
           had bad knees/ from football/ n-in high school/
```

As mentioned above, then, and as can be seen from these examples, syntactic completion is evaluated incrementally. That is, a marker of syntactic completion does not necessarily indicate that a complete syntactic unit exists between it and the previous syntactic completion point; rather, as is assumed in all the CA literature, syntactic completion is calculated in terms of its relation with a previous predicate if one is available. Thus, for example, in (1), there is no claim that the adverbial expression *that way* constitutes an independent unit by itself; rather, it is understood as being a second possible syntactic completion point, the mark after *it was bent* being the first. By the same token, syntactic *incompletion* is calculated in terms of a projected upcoming predicate.

In contrast to the first three examples, here is an example of a sequence in which the first syntactic completion point is not reached for fourteen words.

(4)   (M148)

D: But what I didn't realize at the time was I had always been

        thinking well a:ll anything alcoholic has been (.) distilled/ and

        is okay/.

Intonational completion. Our starting point for the definition of intonational completion was the prosodic unit which we call the intonation unit (following Chafe, 1979, 1980, 1987, 1992, 1994; Du Bois et al. 1993; and Schuetze-Coburn, 1991, 1993), see also Brazil (1985) and Halliday (1967), roughly characterizable as:

a stretch of speech uttered under a single coherent intonation contour. (Du Bois et al., 1993)

Just as stress judgments are known to be related to a variety of intersecting acoustic properties, so perception of intonation unit boundaries and contours is also influenced by a variety of acoustic features. As discussed in Crystal (1969), Cruttenden (1986), Du Bois et al. (1993), Schuetze-Coburn (1992), (1993), and Schuetze-Coburn et al. (1992), numerous prosodic cues have been identified which are used to determine intonation unit boundaries. The perception of coherence in the pitch pattern is influenced by both the degree and direction of pitch movement on a stressed syllable and by a change in pitch relative to the speaker's preceding utterance (known as "pitch reset"). Timing cues also play a role in the perception of intonation units, including an acceleration in tempo on initial unstressed syllables, prosodic lengthening of final syllables, and a noticeable pause (0.3 second or greater) between intonation units. The identification of intonation units is thus an auditory, perceptual matter.

In making this identification, we did not consider syntactic boundaries. It might be assumed that syntax cannot be disregarded in identifying intonational boundaries in listening to conversational data. However, Schuetze-Coburn et al. (1991) list several factors which reduce the likelihood that the syntax of the utterances determines one's intonational judgments. Important in relation to the present study is the fact that consistent and reliable judgments can be made as to intonation unit boundaries by trained analysts who have never heard the language being analyzed.[5] Furthermore, the portions of the intonation contours relevant for our study are specified only in terms of the binary distinction between "final" vs. "non-final," which increases the reliability of the auditory judgments.[6] Thus, in our transcripts we placed marks to indicate "final" ending contours, and we placed no mark where the contour ending was "non-final" (more on this below).

Intonation units can be compared to units proposed by other researchers. In order to attempt such a comparison, it is useful to point out that the literature on intonation can be broadly grouped into two types: that based on auditory data, as exemplified by Kingdon (1958) and Bolinger (1964, 1972), Crystal (1969), and Cruttenden (1986), and that based on acoustic data, as exemplified by Liberman and Sag (1974), Pierrehumbert (1980), Cooper and Sorensen (1981), Liberman and Pierrehumbert (1984), Selkirk (1984), Beckman and Pierrehumbert (1986), Nespor and Vogel (1986), and Pierrehumbert and Beckman (1988). As noted in Schuetze-Coburn et al. (1991), and Schuetze-Coburn (1993), whose work provides a notable new exception, systematic comparisons between acoustic and auditory data have been absent from the literature.

As noted above, our intonation units are perceptual units, roughly comparable to Crystal's (1969) auditory "tone units" and Cruttenden's (1986) auditory "intonation groups" (Du Bois et al, 1993). Comparing the intonation units we attended to with units proposed in the literature based on acoustic data, however, is difficult because the data for the two types of research are very different. The data for the acoustic studies come from pitch tracings of written English sentences read aloud, while our data consist of tapes of spontaneous conversational language. The acoustic studies thus take isolated constructed sentences as given, and partition them into intonation-based units (Selkirk 1984: 286), whereas in our research, intonation is considered on its own terms and no a priori relationship between intonation and syntax is assumed. Further, in the acoustic studies, contexts and meanings are typically imagined by the readers, whereas in our work, utterances are examined in their contexts.[7]

Among the basic intonation unit types, there are two that are characterized as ending in a contour which signals finality, designated by a period or a question mark in the Chafe (1980, 1987), Du Bois et al. (1993), and Sacks et al. (1974) transcription systems. The period represents a marked fall in pitch at the end of the intonation unit. The question mark represents by a marked high rise in pitch at the end of the intonation unit.[8]

For this project, then, we take the intonation unit as a valid, well-established auditory unit. We marked the ends of intonation units in the transcript only when they exhibited features of finality, according to the criteria just discussed. An intonational completion point was thus a point at which a clear final intonation, indicated by a period or question mark, could be heard. In the examples below, syntactic completions are indicated by '/', as before, and intonational completions are indicated by '.' or '?':

```
(5) (K35)

    V:  Okay/ this is what t-the problem is/.

        My Dad's knee- leg was very bow-legged/.

        It was like thir[teen degrees/]

    C:                 [All his life/.]


(6) (M28)


    J:  Well then he got picked/ up/ by Large Marge/.


(7) (M95)

    W:  They have that/ in San Francisco/. (at Winslows)/.

        It's like a big (wurst factory)/.
```

(8) (M80)

```
W: y'mean just generic fri:ed meat/?
```

To offer an indication of the acoustic correlates of syntactic completion points which do and do not correspond to intonational completion points, we used the CSpeech computerized speech analysis program to produce pitch traces for representative spans of talk (Milenkovic and Read, 1992; Read, Buder, and Kent, 1992). Graphs 3.1 and 3.2 show pitch contours of two parts of the following line from our transcript:

(9) (K188)

```
V: she didn't know/ what was going on/ about why they didn't change the
   knee/.
```

The pitch trace shown in Graph 3.1 represents the words *going on*, which is a point of syntactic completion, but not of intonational completion. The fundamental frequency on these two words can be seen to be relatively level, varying only between 203 and 194 Hertz. In contrast, the pitch trace shown in Graph 3.2 represents the words *the knee* at the end of the intonation unit, a point of intonational completion. The falling pitch is evident; F_0 goes from 195 up to 218, and then down to 178. These data are indicative of the type of difference that is conveyed by syntactic completion in cases where it is or is not accompanied by intonational completion. [9]

Pragmatic completion. The notion of conversational action is basic to the analysis of language use in interaction, as has been demonstrated in the work of Labov and Fanshel (1977), Schiffrin (1986, 1987) and Fox (1987), among others. Whether in a speech act framework or, as in the present case, in the framework of conversation analysis, action completion is conceived of based on the potential that any utterance has for constituting an action in an interactional sequence (for further discussion of conversational actions, see, inter alia, Erikson; 1992; C. Goodwin, 1979, 1981; Goodwin and Goodwin, 1987, 1992a, 1992b; M. H. Goodwin, 1980; Heath, 1992; Schegloff, this volume; and Streek and Hartge, 1992).

While our judgments for syntactic and intonational completion points are easily operationalized and replicated, our judgments of

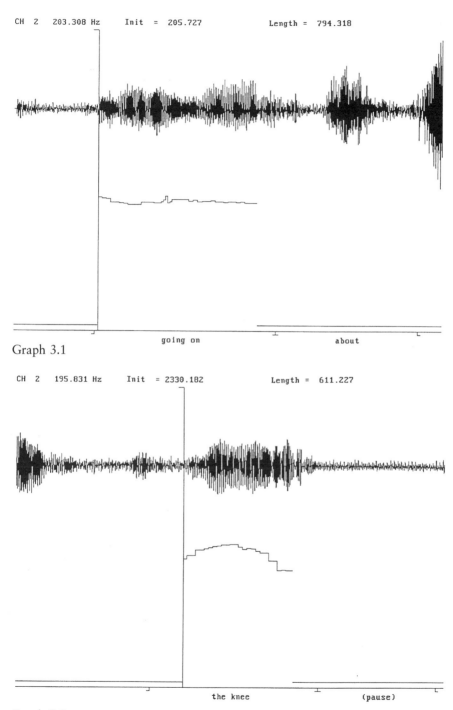

CH 2   203.308 Hz   Init = 205.727   Length = 794.318

going on   about

Graph 3.1

CH 2   195.831 Hz   Init = 2330.182   Length = 611.227

the knee   (pause)

Graph 3.2

pragmatic completion remain intuitive and provisional. However, some such system is certainly involved for the participants, and it would be a mistake to ignore it in our analysis. While we do not base strong claims on the results of this particular measure, we believe it must be included in this study and in further work exploring the resources for projecting turn completion.

In our operationalization of the notion of pragmatic completion, an utterance was required to have a final intonation contour and had to be interpretable as a complete conversational action within its specific sequential context. Note that while this definition contains within it the feature of intonational completion, it is distinct from syntactic completion, since it relies on interactional context rather than merely information recoverability. At the same time, we want to emphasize that pragmatic completion is not the same as intonational completion, since there are points of intonational completion which are not also points of pragmatic completion (see example (10) below as well as Figure 3.1 and the discussion in 3.5.1).

Pragmatic completion can be thought of in both "local" and "global" terms.[10] Local pragmatic completion points are points at which the speaker is projecting more talk, but at which another speaker might reasonably take a minimal turn, such as offering a continuer, display of interest, or claim of understanding. This type of pragmatic completion is thus a location at which another speaker could offer a small, non-floor-taking turn. Example (10) illustrates a sequence containing two examples of this type of pragmatic completion point. K is "leading up to something," but his preliminary points of completion are places where the recipient, C, is given the opportunity to indicate that she is following his "try-marked" utterances (see Sacks and Schegloff, 1979). Again, in these examples, syntactic completion points are marked with a slash, and intonational completion is marked with either a period or a question mark. We have marked the pragmatic completion points with a greater-than sign (>):

(10)   (K1)

    K: It was like the other day/ uh.

                (0.2)

        Vera (.) was talking/ on the phone/ to her mom/?>

    C: Mm hm/.>

    K: And uh she got off the pho:ne/ and she was

        incredibly upset/?>

    C: Mm hm/.>

An utterance was judged to be pragmatically complete in a more global sense if it had the property of not projecting anything beyond itself in the way of a longer story, account, or other agenda. In the following examples, at none of the pragmatic completion points (>) is more talk projected by the current speaker:

(11)   (M101)

    W: They have that/ in San Fransciso/.>   (at Winslows)/.>   It's like a

            big [(wurst factory)/.>]

    C: [oh/ you had veggie - veggie burgers/.>]

                (1.8)

    W: What's a veggie/ burger/?>

    C: (   ) [would be here]

    D: [('s just) a lentil burger/.>

(12)   (K137)

    V: and he said we'll probably have to put an artificial knee in/ in

        five years/.>

                (0.2)

    V: For my Dad/.>

    C: hmm/.>

    V: Because his knees is is deteriorating/ and weak/.>

Pragmatic completion is, then, a combination of intonation and conversational action sequencing. These points of completion emerge not from information recovery aspects of discourse (see pp. 143–45 above), but from the ongoing monitoring of talk for possibly complete conversational actions.

Speaker Change. A speaker change was judged to have occurred at any point where another speaker took a recognizable turn, whether a full turn or a backchannel turn. Like Schegloff (1982), we consider the notion of "primary speakership" to be critical to the definition of "backchannel." We thus considered "backchannels" to be "short utterances produced by an interlocutor who is playing primarily a listener's role during the other interlocutor's speakership." In our coding, we distinguished among several types of backchannel responses, including "continuers" (Schegloff, 1982), displays of interest (C. Goodwin, 1986b), claims of understanding, collaborative finishes (Lerner, 1987, 1989), and help with word searches. The onset of laughter by another speaker was also counted as a speaker change.

We readily acknowledge that these three types of turns (i.e., "full" turns, "backchannel" turns, and laughter) are not equivalent from an interactional point of view, but we have considered them as undifferentiated in this paper because they are similar from the point of view of understanding the units of conversation which are validated by next speaker turn onset. In this way, we are able to test the Sacks et al. (1974) hypotheses regarding the definition of "transition-relevance place".

Speaker change was marked at the completion point in the ongoing turn which was closest to the beginning of the next speaker's utterance. By letting that closest completion point be syntactic, intonational, or pragmatic, we were able to examine whether syntax alone was associated with speaker change (which is what Sacks et al. (1974) have been understood to have predicted, but which we question in our Research Question (1) in 3.4.2). Thus, in (10) above, speaker change would be indicated at each of the first three of the points of pragmatic completion, since a next speaker started at each of those points.

In the case of overlap, we judged a speaker change to have occurred at the closest completion point within two syllables to where the overlapping speaker started, as shown at the arrow in (13).[11] Recall that a slash indicates syntactic completion, a period or question mark indicates intonational completion, and a greater-than sign indicates pragmatic completion. Speaker change is counted as occurring after *anyways*.

(13)   (K35)

    V: Okay this is what t-the problem is./ My Dad's knee - leg was very

        bow-legged./> It was like thirt[een degrees]/

                                        [All his life]./> right?/>

    V: Well, more in old age (h)./>

    C: =Uh huh./>

                    (0.5)

    V: s-Slightly/ anyways./> ve[ry weak knees./>

---> C: [Yeah./> yeah/ I remember/ noticing

        that./>

If there was no completion point within two syllables of the
beginning of the next speaker's turn, then speaker change was
marked at the exact point where it occurred, as in (14):

(14)   (K183)

    V: But- still it covers [eighty percent/.>

    C: [Yeah./>

Having indicated how we determined syntactic, intonational, and
pragmatic completion, and how we determined points of speaker
change, we can now turn to a discussion of our findings.[12]

3.5 Results and discussion

3.5.1 "Complex" TRPs

One of our major findings was the high degree of coincidence
among the three types of completion, as summarized in table 3.2.

Table 3.2 Convergence of types of completion

Total Intonational Completion:	433
Total Pragmatic Completion	422
Total Grammatical Completion:	798
Intonational and Grammatical:	428
Grammatical and Semantic:	417
Total points of convergence of Intonational, Grammatical, and Semantic Completion points.	417

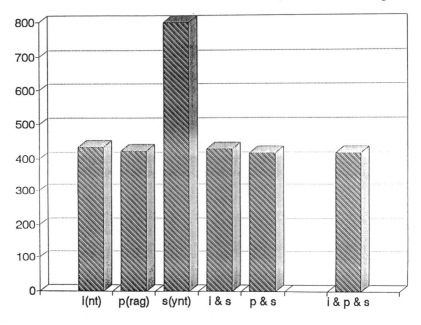

Figure 3.1 Number of completion points by type

Table 3.2 shows that the number of points of convergence of intonational, pragmatic, and syntactic completion in our data is almost the same as the total number of intonational and pragmatic completion points. In other words, intonational and pragmatic completions are nearly always syntactic completions as well. But the reverse was not the case. Syntactic completion points in English, as operationalized for this study, are *not* nearly always intonational and pragmatic completion points; there are in fact many more syntactic completion points than any other kind. In other words, the data show that intonation and pragmatic completion points select from among the syntactic completion points to form what we will call "Complex Transition Relevance Places" (CTRPs). The term "turn unit," then, will refer to a unit which is characterized by ending at a CTRP. Figure 3.1 shows these results in graph form.

An important point to keep in mind in interpreting figure 3.1 is the issue of the interdependence of pragmatic completion and intonation completion. It will be remembered that our determination of pragmatic completion included intonational completion. Therefore, every point of pragmatic completion is also, *by definition*, a point of intonational completion. But this does not imply that they should immediately be collapsed, since it is logically possible that not every intonational completion point is a point of pragmatic completion. And in fact, as table 3.2 shows, there are eleven intonational completion points which are *not* also pragmatic completion points.[13] Because of this, we present figure 3.1 to show the three types of completion separately, though it masks the dependence of pragmatic on intonational completion.

Table 3.2 and figure 3.1 thus show that the number of intonational completion points is similar, though not equal, to the number of pragmatic completion points. Further, the high degree of the coincidence between intonational completion and syntactic completion is striking. As shown in figure 3.2, the vast majority (428/433, or 98.8 per cent) of intonational completion points are also syntactic completion points, but, as shown in figure 3.3, the reverse is not the case: only (428/798, or 53.6 per cent) of the syntactic completion points are also intonational completion points.

Of the three types of completion, then, syntactic completion points alone are the least reliable indicators of any other sort of completion. The first research question for this study concerns the

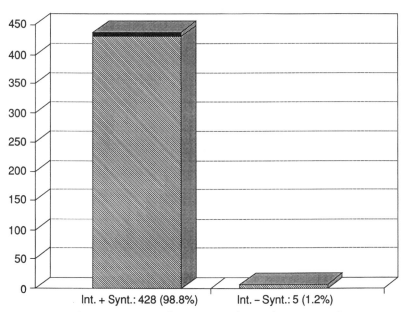

Figure 3.2 What proportion of intonational completions are also syntactic completions?

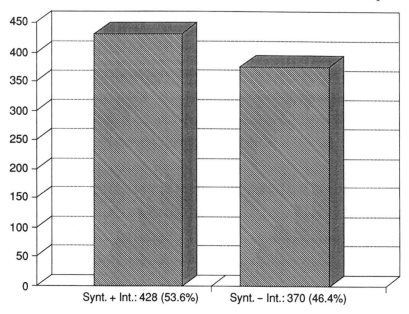

Figure 3.3 What proportion of syntactic completions are also intonational completions?

relative roles of syntax and pragmatics (including intonation) in predicting speaker change. A high proportion of the total speaker changes in our data (198/277, or 71 per cent) occur at CTRPs. Given that syntactic completion points far outnumber CTRPs, we see that syntax in itself is not the strongest predictor of speaker change. Syntactic completion is, however, one of the features associated with, though not definitive of, CTRPs, since intonational and pragmatic completion points regularly fall at points of syntactic completion.

The finding that speaker change coincides best with CTRPs in our data extends the work of Oreström (1983); recall that his study was restricted to multi-tone-unit and non-overlapping turns. We considered multi-party conversations, and all speaker changes, regardless of how long they were or whether they were in overlap. The fact that we still found that the majority of speaker changes, even overlapping and short or backchannel turns, occurred at CTRPs provides even stronger evidence of the multiple features which constitute the points at which speakers consider it appropriate to start a turn.

In line with what Schegloff (1988, this volume) has suggested (as discussed above), we find that intonation plays a major role in determining *which* syntactically complete utterances are being projected by hearers as complete units. Our findings show that in addition to intonation, pragmatics is also involved in determining those syntactic completions that are treated as complete by recipients, although more work needs to be done to further our understanding of its precise role.

What listeners seem to be doing, then, in projecting the ends of another's utterances is paying attention to syntax, intonation, and the pragmatic content of those utterances, that is, to the action the other is doing in the interactional context.[14] [15]

The second question guiding this research concerns the potential orderliness of cases in which speaker changes are not associated with projected completion points. Interestingly, while the majority of speaker changes occurred at CTRPs, only about half of the CTRPs were accompanied by speaker changes, as shown in figure 3.4. Furthermore, 29 per cent of all speaker changes were initiated at non-CTRPs. These apparent exceptions, as has been noted previously in conversation analytic studies, are in fact strategic and patterned interactional achievements. We exemplify the orderliness of both overlaps and same-speaker continuations in section 3.5.2.

3.5.2 Completion points and speaker change

We have seen that patterns of speaker change in our data match best with CTRPs, locations where syntax, intonation, and pragmatics coincide. Turn onset at CTRPs is expectable and, in many contexts, receives no special interactional interpretation. For example, D's turn in (15) comes just at the place where C's turn has reached a point of completion:

(15)   (M72)

C: They never <u>drink</u>/ without it/.>

D: Yeah/ you <u>never</u> have liquor/ without (1.0) fried <u>meat</u>/.>

In terms of their displayed orientation to turn completion, the interlocutors in (15) are treating turn transition as expectable and unproblematic.

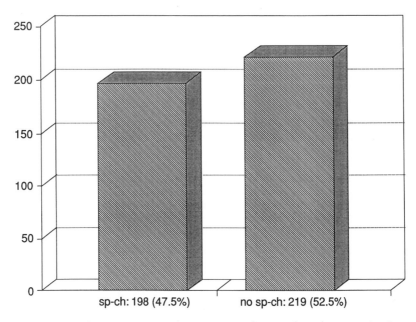

Figure 3.4 What proportion of CTRPs are also speaker change points?

However, there are, as we noted above, instances in which speaker changes do not occur at predictable points of completion. In these cases, as we will see in this section, it is precisely in *not* using CTRPs as locations for speaker change that conversationalists are doing interactional work. We find that when a next speaker starts at a point of non-completion in the prior speaker's turn (pp. 159–64) or when the current speaker takes the opportunity to extend her or his turn past a CTRP (pp. 164–70), this placement is far from erroneous, and is in fact deliberate and meaningful. Observations of the strategic placement of next-turn onset in our data are in line with diverse accounts reported in the conversation analysis literature, particularly in the work of Emanuel Schegloff, Gail Jefferson, Charles Goodwin, Marjorie Goodwin, and Gene Lerner, as we will see. However, our study is the first to articulate these findings in relation to those presented above on the role of syntactic, intonational, and pragmatic factors in defining turn-constructional units.

In what follows, we offer examples of the orderliness of apparent violations of the turn-taking system in cases of early turn onset or same-speaker continuation. Attempting to distribute these cases into discrete categories would be misleading since more than one interactional task is accomplished in any given case. The examples we cite below are representative of the orderliness we find in the collection.

Speaker change at non-CTRPs. Let us first look at next-speaker initiation at non-completion points. When speakers in our data initiate turns in "violation" of the turn-taking rules, we find that these deviations are, in fact, alternative ways of using the turn-taking system. That is to say, a "violation" of turn-taking rules occurs in the service of interaction, and is often associated with the display of affiliation or disagreement with an ongoing turn.

In her paper on precision timing in turn overlaps, Jefferson (1973) demonstrates that certain overlaps are not errors in timing relative to transition relevance places. Rather, they are specifically designed *displays* of prior access to the content of the interrupted turn. Jefferson argues that the "placement at a precise point of 'no sooner and no later' within the talk of an ongoing speaker accomplishes the display of familiarity and the display of co-participant acknowledgement" (1973: 65). Thus, in violating the turn-taking rules by not waiting till the end of a prior turn to initiate a next turn, one may strengthen the basic message of an utterance.

One of Jefferson's examples will be helpful here. In (16), a caller is reporting a fire that the fire department, as it turns out, is already aware of. The prior familiarity with the report is encoded in overlapping turn by the fire department representative (D); the overlap itself is demonstrative of prior access to the information.

(16)   (1973:57)

```
C:   Fire department, out at the Fairview Food [mart there's a-
D:                                             [Yes.
      We've already got the uh call on that ma'am,
```

D could easily have waited until the completion of C's turn to say that the fire had already been reported. However, the overlap, just at the point where the particular location of the fire has been identified, serves to more strongly signal the recognition of prior knowledge.

Jefferson (1983), in an analysis of a large number of instances of overlapping talk, demonstrates that the majority of such cases involve "the recipient/next speakers 'working with' the prior turn, 'showing understanding' of the projected item, or 'taking off from' that turn" (ms. p. 18). Similarly, Tannen (1989) argues persuasively that the notion of "interruption" must be re-examined. She presents a number of instances of simultaneous speech as "cooperative overlapping" (p. 272).

M. Goodwin (1980), C. Goodwin (1986b), and Goodwin and Goodwin (1987) describe the interactive nature of producing assessments and show how the fine tuning of the placement of brief assessments before the end of a current speaker's turn can be taken by the speaker as highly collaborative and supportive, and manifests a well-developed ability on the part of speakers and hearers to time their utterances to display co-participation. Their analysis reveals how the particular kind of talk being done by a recipient (in this case, whether it is an assessment or a continuer) may be relevant to its precise placement *during* rather than *after* the end of the speaker's turn unit. For our data, the analysis of cases in which turns are initiated at non-CTRPs supports these conversation analytic findings.

One regular location for the production of turns in overlap in the present data is when participants are joking and sharing laughter. In such environments, the initiation of a next turn at a non-CTRP represents a display of appreciation or a joining in with the work of the prior turn (see Jefferson et al., 1987). In the following fragment, the interactants are joking about the movie they have just seen together, "Peewee's Big Adventure."

(17)   (M1)


```
      1       D: I did like when he put on his headlight/ glasses/.>

      2       H: Oh G(h)o:d(hh) that was won:derful/.> hh[ hh

      3       D:                                         [hh He was

-->   4          surrounded by uh-heh-heh-heh

      5       J: huh [huh

      6       D:    [[(iz al'eez) going AR[RRahh ((growling)) ani[mals/.>

-->   7       H:                         [All              [All the

      8          animals/ in the wor[ld/.>

      9       D:                     [[(Oh-huh)
```

At line 4, D begins a prepositional phrase, and then breaks into laughter. J begins his laughter at this point, at a non-CTRP (after a preposition); J's overlapping laughter displays alignment with D's ongoing joking turn. At line 6, D continues his turn but is overlapped by H's candidate completion of the original prepositional phrase, *by + all the animals in the world*. The overlaps in this example are by no means mistakenly produced. Not only are these speakers precisely placing their turns, but in doing so they are cooperating in the joint construction of a particular type of interaction. These early onsets are the artful embodiments of interactional cooperation in a laughter and joking sequence (Jefferson, 1984); for discussion of such collaborative alignment, see Lerner, 1987, 1988, 1991, and in progress).

In our data, story-telling sequences are also common locations for the initiation of recipient turns at non-CTRPs. One characteristic of tasks such as story telling is that they require an adaptation of the turn-taking system such that one speaker becomes primary while the other participants tend to restrict their turns to continuers, repair initiators, and cooperative contributions such as words that a primary speaker is having trouble with (Jefferson, 1978). Word searches are thus predictable points for recipient turn onset at non-CTRPs. (18) below is one such example. D is telling about how he got sick after drinking a suspicious alcoholic beverage at a festival in Nepal. After D has displayed problems in characterizing the drink, W offers a candidate term, which she places at a non-CTRP in D's ongoing talk.

(18)   (M132)

D: ... They have a big feast/ an' they <u>drink</u>/ they have these

        <u>big</u> (.) <u>jars</u>/ full of this (.) mm-   (1.0) it's like fer<u>men:</u>ted

        wine/ er- fer<u>men</u>ted ri:ce/. It's like (.) they (.) Y'know ri-

--> W: Rice wine/?>

High points in stories are also environments for interactionally strategic initiation of turns before points of completion. This pattern is in line with the observation in prior studies that assessments are often done in overlap with the ongoing turns to which they are responsive (C. Goodwin, 1986b; Goodwin and Goodwin, 1987). In

the following span of talk, W displays strong reactions to dramatic
points in D's story through turns placed at non-CTRPs:

```
(19)   (M164)

       D: So I drank/ a lo:t/ that day/ an' it [just about
-->    W:                                      [O:h/ Go::d/.>
       D: Oh maybe two or three weeks later it was the tri:ple
          wha:mmy/.>  Y'know/.>
                (0.1)
       D: Wor:ms an:'
-->    W: REA:lly:/?>
       D: Yeah/ [amoe:bas/ y- (giardia) the whole thing/.>
-->    W:       [Oh/.>
          Oh:/ Gho:d/.>  O:h/ Da:niel/.>
```

At the first arrow, W initiates a turn after it is clear that D will be
sick (the projected outcome of the story). W's turn is an assessment,
and, in a pattern consistent with prior findings, it is placed in overlap. At the second arrow, after D has projected that his sickness will
have three parts (*the triple whammy*), he begins his three-part list
with *worms* and the conjunction *and*. Again, at a non-CTRP, W
interjects a reaction of interest and amazement, *REA: lly?* (second
arrow). W's reaction is placed before D has completed his projected
list. Through this early placement W underscores her affiliative
affective response, the response that D's story is designed to elicit.
At the third arrow, W again provides an assessment in overlap with
D's talk.

A recipient can show affiliation with an ongoing turn by providing more than a minimal token of agreement (e.g., *yeah*) at the
completion of a turn. One option for displaying affiliation involves
recipient completion of the ongoing turn. Such collaborative completions of prior speakers' turns are detailed in the work of Lerner
(1991), (in press). In the following example, K is complaining about
his girlfriend's inability to remain detached from her mother's emotional outbursts. C, the recipient, has been siding with the girlfriend,
but now displays an understanding of K's perspective:

(20)   (K253)


```
K:    I mean I understand/ but it- but it see- ya know but
      it [still seems like ya oughta be able to say no-/
C:        [It' still frustrating/.>
```

C's display of understanding is done through an overlapped completion of K's ongoing turn. K is neither syntactically, intonationally, nor pragmatically finished after *but* or *it*. However, the direction in which his talk will move is projectable. Lerner argues that the subunits of turns provide "a systematic (though secondary) place, besides the turn transition relevance space, for the transfer of speakership" (1991: 454).

The examples given thus far in this section have involved early initiation in the service of cooperation and affiliation with another speaker's ongoing talk. However, turn initiation at non-CTRPs is not exclusively used to display affiliation with ongoing turns. In environments of disagreement, the early placement of agreement tokens is interpretable as a kind of grudging acquiescence. By cutting in on a speaker's talk in mid-turn, a recipient can, in effect, agree in a disagreeable way. In (21), which includes (20) above, K is complaining about V's reactions to her mother. At the arrow, V overlaps K's turn and then begins to defend herself for the reaction K is complaining about:

(21)   (K258)


```
K: I mean I understand/ but it- but it see- ya know but
        it [ still seems like ya oughta be able to say no-/
C:         [It' still frustrating/.>
        (0.2)
K: Ya knew befo:re/, how come (0.2) you're lettin'
        this cra[zy person change/ your mind/.> Ya [know/.>
-->  V:         [Right/.>                          [Well s-
        it's like she made me believe that yeah you know the
        doctors are you know horrible/ an' yes this is ridiculous/
        an' ...
```

V's *right* is placed at a non-CTRP, and, although the expression itself is a token of agreement, when it is delivered early, as it is here, it can serve to disrupt the prior turn. We see that what V adds next is a form commonly used as a marker of dispreference, *well*, which is expectably followed by a less than agreeing response. V then gives an account for the behavior which K has been criticizing in his turn.

To summarize what we have discussed in this sub-section, then, we find that cases of turn initiation at non-CTRPs are, in our data, systematic and precisely timed violations of the turn-taking system, violations which in themselves serve communicative ends. Analysis of our data supports previous findings with regard to the interactional work of utterances placed at non-completion points in ongoing turns. It is *relative* to the typical turn-taking pattern, as elaborated in the first part of this paper, that early onset takes on particular, locally interpretable, interactional significance.

Same speaker continuation following CTRPs. We have seen some of the circumstances in which a next speaker may begin a turn at a non-CTRP. We now turn to the cases in our data in which a same speaker continues past a CTRP. How do we account for those CTRPs which were not accompanied by any speaker change?

As shown in figure 3.4, only 47.5 per cent (198/417) of the CTRPs in our data are also points of speaker change, leaving 219 (52.5 per cent) of the CTRPs which are not points of speaker change. At first, it might appear that the percentage of CTRPs accompanied by speaker change (47.5 per cent) is so low as to constitute refutation of our hypothesis that CTRPs play a major role in turn-taking. However, on closer examination, we see that 88 of these 219 CTRPs that are not accompanied by speaker change occur at points where another speaker is already talking in overlap and has not reached a CTRP. An example of this occurs in (22):

(22)   (K106)

```
    C:  B-won't his leg go/ out/ like that/.> now/.>
-->         [instead of in ]/.>
    V:      [Now it's three] degees/.> degrees/.>
```

In this example, C's first utterance comes to a CTRP after both *that* and *now*. The CTRP at *now* is a location of speaker change, with V starting her turn, with *Now*, at that point. It is C's utterance at the arrow, however, that illustrates arrival at a CTRP, at the word *in*, which is not a likely point of speaker change, since the recipient of this utterance, V, is already talking. It is not surprising, then, that no speaker change occurs at these 88 points where a CTRP is reached where another speaker is already talking.

This leaves 131, of the 219 CTRPs, (or 31 per cent of the total CTRPs), then, without any accompanying speaker change. What is most crucial to understanding these cases is the fact that, in offering a model for turn taking, Sacks et al. (1974) explicitly emphasize that transition places (here CTRPs) are option points, and that by one of the possible options, a current speaker may continue to talk. Sacks (1974), (1987), and Schegloff (1980), (1982), (1988), (this volume), discuss ways in which turns longer than one TCU can be projected by speakers. M. Goodwin (1980), C. Goodwin (1986b), Goodwin and Goodwin (1987), and Wilson and Zimmerman (1986) also discuss a number of interactional factors involved in the extension of a turn past a CTRP. All these scholars have shown that both speakers and hearers *orient to* the projection of a completion point, and that conversationalists act jointly in opting either for or against speaker change at points of possible completion.

There are, in fact, strategies for avoiding completion even when syntax, intonation, and pragmatics conspire to signal it. As mentioned above in Section 2, Schegloff (1982), (1987), (1988), (this volume) discusses the "rush through" as one such strategy. We have found a number of examples of this type of avoidance of transition relevance in our data.

In (23), below, V comes to a CTRP after *shorter*, but speeds up her talk in conjunction with reaching this potential point of speaker change. By speeding up, she is able to re-emphasize the contrast between what her mother is saying and what the doctor has said. As discussed by Schegloff, as well as Wilson and Zimmerman (1986), V's rush-through can be interpreted as a way of avoiding the potential for signalling completion. (We mark the rush-through with an arrow above the relevant portion of the turn.)

```
(23)   (K128)

       V: This is what my mom is saying/.>

          (0.4)

       V: Because they took it/ out-/ this is her/.>  The doctor didn't
                                          ------------->
          say his leg's gonna be an inch shorter/.>  She's saying it/.>
```

In this example, the truncation of the word *out* illustrates another way in which a possible point of completion can be manipulated to signal non-completion. *Out* could have been a CTRP, but the cut-off changes the prosody, marking a potential up-coming repair of the turn so far.

Analysis of other cases of the non-coincidence of these points of completion with speaker change reveals a number of interesting facts about the negotiation of turn extension past points of possible completion. As was true with the early turn initiations discussed above, additions made after points of potential speaker change emerge in particular interactional environments. The most common environment for turn extension is found where a speaker is pursuing recipient response (Pomerantz, 1984).

As extensions to the ends of turns, additions past CTRPs are both formally and functionally distinct from units which begin turns. Many cases of turn extension are best understood with reference to the three kinds of work that Sacks et al. (1974) suggest that any given turn must perform. First, a turn must show itself to be relevant to the slot which it fills, that is, it must fit into the sequence of turns so far. Second, it must make its own contribution. And third, on completion, it should provide a context for a relevant next turn by another participant. These three jobs may be done in one piece or they may be presented in serial turn units. In the following example, Sacks et al. analyze the turn at the arrow as having three units that do the three turn jobs.

```
(24)
    A: It would bum you out to kiss me then, [hunh
    B:                                        [Yeah well we all know
       where that's at.
       ((pause))
    A: [ (        )
    B: [I mean you went- you went through a- a long rap on that
       one.=
-->A: =Yeah, so I say that would bum you out then, hunh
          ¦                                            ¦
       FORMAL                                      PROJECTING
       AFFILIATOR                                    LINK
```

Sacks et al. characterize *yeah* as a 'formal affiliator to the last turn,' and *hunh* as "projecting a link," calling for a next turn by B (1974: 722).

Turn extensions in our data are regularly geared toward Sacks et al.'s "projecting a link," creating or modifying relevance for another speaker's response.[16] In pursuing recipient responses, speakers may simply recomplete the previous turn, thereby recreating a transition relevance point. They may add on a tag question, calling more clearly for recipient uptake. They may soften some claim or communicate uncertainty, thus revising the context for agreement or disagreement. They may add support to some prior claim, thereby strengthening the potential for agreement. Or they may treat the lack of response as a failure of understanding, addressing that failure by adding specification or elaboration. Such extensions fill in what could be the development of problematic gaps. In one way or another, an extension past a point of completion provides an additional opportunity for smooth speaker change. These extensions regularly take forms which could only be appropriately placed *non-initially* in a turn; they serve Sacks et al.'s "link-projecting" function.

The following excerpt, from our data, contains two common types of turn extensions in pursuit of recipient response. This excerpt includes example (10) above; K has been reporting an event which he finds dismaying. The recipient, C, does not respond with any sign of affiliation with K's dismay. In the face of K's strongly stated report, to affiliate or agree C would need to join in with K's stance toward what he is reporting. It is in this environment that K extends his turns after several CTRPs, creating additional opportunities for C to give affiliative responses. We would like to focus here on the extensions at the arrows. At the first arrow, C has not given any strong or immediate sign of affiliation, and K adds the extension *or something like that*.

```
(25)   (K1)

 1      K: It was like the other day/ uh.

 2            (0.2)

 3          Vera was talking/ on the phone/ to her mom/?>

 4      C: Mm hm/.>

 5      K: And uh she got off/ the phone/ and she was incredibly

 6          upset/?>
```

```
      6          upset/?>

      7      C: [Mm hm/.>

      8      K: [She was goin' god/ do you think they're performing

-->   9          unnecessary surgery/ on my Dad/.> or something/ like

     10          that/?>

     11              (0.2)

-->12      K: Just cause of something her mom had told her/.>

     13              (0.5)

-->14      K: It was really amazing/.> ('S all) you know like Nazi

-->15          experiments/.> or something/.> (that) God/ he wouldn't be in

-->16          there/ if he didn't need it/.> ya know/?>

     17      C: =Ye[ah/.>

-->18      K:     [If it wasn't something real/.> ya know/.> ss

     19              (0.2)

     20      C: W-Have you met his doctor/?> ((addressed to Vera))
```

Even after K's extension, *or something like that,* in line 9, he gets no
response from C. In further pursuit of uptake, K continues to display the type of stance he is taking toward what he is reporting: one
of dismay and amazement. He continues to extend beyond CTRPs
in lines 12, 14 and 15, and again adds *or something* at line 15. At
lines 16 and 18, K again adds increments past CTRPs; he adds a *ya
know* tag question, another *if*-clause, and another tag. According to
Sacks et al., a tag question is an "exit technique" especially suited to
do turn-taking work (1974: 718). Since questions clearly call for a
speaker change, they remove any ambiguity about whether a recipient response is appropriate. Both tag questions and extensions
such as *or something* are useful as additions in pursuit of uptake.
They do Sacks et al.'s third turn job, creating or modifying a context for a next turn in the interaction.

Another kind of extension represented in example (25), above,
involves elaboration or specification of the content of a previous
turn unit. When K adds the causal phrase at line 12, he is highlighting the cause and effect relationship implicit in the order of
events he has just recounted. K has reported that V was upset
after talking to her mother, and he respecifies this at line 12 as V
being upset *just cause of something her mom had told her.* The
addition displays an interpretation of lack of recipient uptake as
K's indication that his previous turn unit needs to be clarified in
some way to engender appropriate response.

The *if*-clause extension at line 18 is also a respecification, this time of what K has said in a similar clause at line 16. Here, although C has given a response, her response is not aligned with the affective intensity represented in K's delivery of his story. Thus, K's addition at line 18 is not pursuing just any uptake, but a particular type of uptake affiliative with the strong negative assessment he has given the events he has recounted.[17]

The following interchange contains another example of same-speaker continuation in pursuit of recipient response. W, who has been out of the room, asks a question and reaches a CTRP after *about*.

```
(26)   (M13)
     --> W: What are you talking about/?>  Do you mean the (.)
            pet[shop/?>
        H:    [When he put on his headlight/ glasses/ out in the (.)
              [wilds/?>
        C:    [Oh[ huh-
        W:       [Oh.>
```

With no immediate uptake, W adds a further specification of the question. She reformulates the question to offer a candidate response, allowing for a yes/no answer, thus allowing the recipient to simply agree or disagree, rather than have to find a response. W's pursuit of a response is in fact overlapped by H's answer – an answer to the first formulation of the question rather than the second.[18] [19]

In a final example, (27) below, we find two more types of extension. V is responding to a question that has interrupted her longer turn agenda: explaining her father's knee operation. C, the recipient, has just asked whether V's brother has a problem similar to her father's:

```
(27)  (K55)
      21 V: I don't think my- my brother's so a:ctive/.>
  --> 22    I mean I don't know/.>
      23       (0.2)
  --> 24    Anyways his leg turned/ (0.2) thirteen de- he was
      25    bowlegged/... <continuation of talk about father>
```

Note that V continues past one completion point with a claim of lack of knowledge, *I don't know* at line 22. This claim, taken within the larger context,[20] can be interpreted as a move to end the side sequence dealing with the topic of her brother. Lack of certainty here may also reflect a lack of willingness to continue with a line of talk that may seem tangential to the speaker's own purposes. In our data, claims of uncertainty such as this seem to be associated with topic closing, though this corpus is too small to warrant any generalization with regard to the function of such moves.

After completing her response to C's question with this claim of uncertainty, V gets no follow-up turn from C. V takes the opportunity to return to her own original agenda. The return is marked by *anyways*. This exemplifies another type of extension past a point of turn completion. Here the extension does the work of returning to a prior sequence in which a side sequence has now been embedded.

In summary, cases of CTRPs that are not associated with speaker change involve interlocutors choosing one of the options explicitly included in the Sacks et al. model for turn taking, that is, the option of same-speaker continuation. An array of different interactional moves are performed in such cases, depending on the local conversational circumstances. Same-speaker continuations are regularly aimed at dealing with the fact that expected uptake has not been precise and immediate. When uptake does not occur, the original speaker extends the original turn in a manner that will signal or re-signal completion, and, to varying degrees, may also specify or elaborate the content of the turn being extended. The same-speaker extension serves to "project a link" for the recipient. Cases of returning to prior agendas, such as the *anyways* in (27) above also deal with the interactional consequences of the same speaker's prior completion. In these cases, however, rather than pursuing recipient response after a CTRP, the point of completion is optimized as the location for the return to another piece of interactional work that the speaker has temporarily set aside.[21]

Summary. Given that the CTRP is our strongest predictor of speaker change, in this section we have considered the exceptions to this general association in our data. We have seen that the exceptions are systematic: particular interactional work is being done when conversationalists do not wait for a CTRP before taking a turn, and when a speaker reaches a CTRP but no other speaker takes the floor. In this section we have demonstrated that the non-co-occurrence of CTRPs and next-turn initiations is both complex and orderly.

3.6 Conclusions

Conversation analysts generally recognize as true what Sacks et al. (1974) state clearly: turn taking depends on subtle features of the utterance enabling a speaker to project the end of a prior turn. Our goal in this paper has been to examine explicitly the relationship between syntactic completion and speaker-validated turn units, as it was syntax that Sacks et al. originally pointed to as a major linguistic resource deployed and monitored by conversationalists in achieving smooth turn transfer. We have shown that the set of such features must include not only syntactic cues, but also intonational features as well as some notion of pragmatic or action completion, and that, in fact, these three types of cues converge to a great extent to define transition relevance places in conversations, places to which conversationalists orient in sequencing their turns. Intonational completion points turn out to be a major component of Complex Transition Relevance Places, and therefore of the turn-taking system itself. Projecting when a new turn could start must centrally involve the perception of intonation units and pitch peaks within intonation units.

Not only do intonational, syntactic, and pragmatic phenomena cluster at points where transition is relevant, but we suggest that these phenomena provide hearers with resources for projecting *in advance* the upcoming occurrence (or non-occurrence) of such points. With respect to the present findings, the fact that there are intonational, syntactic, and pragmatic points of completion means that people can recognize when they are in the midst of a unit that has not yet come to completion in one or more of these ways; in fact, as we have shown, in the majority of cases, not being completed in one of these respects entails not being completed in the other respects either. At a more profound level, our findings point strongly to the need for a thorough linguistic investigation of the ways that intonation, syntax, and conversational action are all *structured* to permit projection of the future course of the unit in progress, including when it can be expected to come to completion.

We anticipate future research addressing itself to a more precise specification of how the intonational, syntactic, pragmatic, as well as non-verbal, aspects of turn-constructional units embody this projectability.[22]

A major finding of this study is the fact that speaker change correlates with CTRPs. This is evidence that the units defined by the convergence of syntactic, intonational, and pragmatic completion are real for conversationalists; speakers and hearers orient to, and design their own turns in response to, these units. Participants in these conversations treat CTRPs as the basic points relative to which they take and yield turns.

We have noted that syntactic completion does not operate alone in projecting the ends of turns, but that it is a major component of the Complex Transition Relevance Place along with intonation and pragmatics. We hope to have contributed to a deeper understanding of what a TRP is, what its role in conversational interaction is, and to what kind of speaker-validated unit it constitutes the boundary.

Finally, we have shown that speakers not uncommonly place turns at points other than CTRPs or fail to use CTRPs as the locations for next speaker initiation. We have shown how these behaviors involve the strategic use of projectable turn completion points as well as the exploitation of the option of same speaker continuation that was included in the original turn-taking model of Sacks et al. It is relative to the norms of turn transition we document in the quantitative portion of our study that the apparent violations of such boundaries operate. In order for interlocutors to make strategic use of overlap and early turn initiation, they must be able to project upcoming CTRPs prior to their arrival. Likewise, CTRPs which are followed by same speaker continuation are jointly managed interactional achievements.

In addition to providing a clearer understanding of the units speakers orient to in achieving "precision timing" in conversation, one of the implications of this research is the direction it suggests for future research on the relationship between linguistic structure and the dynamics of conversation. Many linguists have become convinced that the only way to fully understand linguistic structure is to consider it as an adaptive response to recurrent habits in the way people talk to each other (e.g., Chafe, 1980, 1987, 1994; Du Bois, 1985, 1987; Durie, 1988; Fox, 1987; Givón, 1979, 1984,

1990; Hopper, 1987, 1988; Hopper and Thompson forthcoming; and Sankoff and Brown, 1976). As Schegloff (1989: 143) suggests,

> If the conduct of language as a domain of behavior is biological in character, then we should expect it (like other biological entities) to be adapted to its natural environment . . . Transparently, the natural environment of language use is talk-in-interaction, and originally ordinary conversation. The natural home environment of clauses and sentences is turns-at-talk. *Must we not understand the structures of grammar to be in important respects adaptations to the turn-at-talk in a conversational turn-taking system with its interactional contingencies?* [Emphasis added CEF & SAT]

We view this study as part of a larger research program that takes the proposition underlying Schegloff's rhetorical question (in italics) as a guiding principle; our findings provide further evidence of the relationship between conversational discourse and language structure, including syntax, intonation, and pragmatics.

Notes

* We are grateful to the following people for valuable discussion of the ideas in this paper: Patti Becker, Wallace Chafe, Patricia Clancy, William Croft, John Du Bois, Alessandro Duranti, Mark Durie, Virginia Evanson, Alan Firth, Barbara Fox, Ronald Geluykens, Talmy Givón, Gene Lerner, Kevin Lesher, Dori Lightfoot, Michael Moerman, Junko Mori, Danae Paolino, Charles Read, Stephan Schuetze-Coburn, Tomoko Sakita, Jakob Steensig, Ryoko Suzuki, Thomas Wilson, Don Zimmermann, and especially Charles Goodwin and Emanuel Schegloff. We also appreciate the input we received from the participants at the Interaction and Grammar Workshop in Los Angeles, May, 1992. None of these people should, however, be held responsible for the shape these ideas take here. We also thank Heidi Riggenbach for providing us with a portion of our conversational data. Authorship of this paper is shared jointly.

1 For example, Denny (1985: 138) explicitly, though, as we have seen, mistakenly, claims that in the Sacks et al. model, "constructional units are syntactic, where the range of unit types is demarcated by grammatical categorization." Power and Dal Martello (1986), in a critique of the Sacks et al. account, also interpret the system as based on syntactic units. However, the only alternative they offer to the syntactic unit is one based on "message" completion. They do not accompany this suggestion with any attempt to elaborate or specify the nature of this unit.

2 Further detailed study of turn-extension and turn-transition can be found in C. Goodwin (1986b) and Goodwin and Goodwin (1986),

where analyses are given of both extended turns that continue beyond the first TRP and turns that designedly occur before the first TRP in the speaker's talk, showing how speakers may modify the emerging structure of the utterance they are producing in response to what the recipient is, or is not, doing.

3 We use these insights in our discussion of local and global pragmatic completion (p. 150).

4 Our technique of marking different points of possible completion was inspired by an exercise assigned by Emanuel Schegloff in an introductory course in conversation analysis at UCLA in 1984.

5 This has been demonstrated repeatedly in seminars at UC Santa Barbara, where linguists trained in identifying intonation units are presented with a tape of conversational data from a language unknown to some members of the group. Judgments consistently agree among those who know the language and those who do not as to intonation unit boundaries at the rate of 85-90 per cent.

6 Further support for the perceptual validity of the "intonation unit" derives from the empirical study of languages with so-called "sentence-final particles," such as the Chinese languages, Japanese, and Korean. In these languages, syntactic criteria appear to be of no value in characterizing the distribution of these particles; the unit that they bound is, in fact, the intonation unit (see Clancy et al. in preparation).

7 In spite of the lack of comparability between these two approaches, though, we can observe that Pierrehumbert (1980: 64 [1987: 34]) proposes that her "intonational phrase" "corresponds to the domain of the "tone unit" in Crystal (1969)". Since "tone units," as we have mentioned, are roughly equivalent to our intonation units, we can reasonably assume our intonation units and Pierrehumbert's intonational phrases to be of the same order of magnitude. Further, Selkirk (1984: 197) defines an intonational phrase as "a unit of prosodic constituent structure with respect to which the characteristic intonational contours of a language are defined," and Nespor and Vogel (1986: 188) define it as "the domain of an intonation contour." Since our intonation units are also units which represent "the characteristic intonational contours of a language," we have another reason to infer that intonation units and intonational phrases are roughly comparable. More recent work, particularly that of Beckman and Pierrehumbert (1986), argues for a level of intonational phrasing below the intonational phrase, called "intermediate phrases." From some of the examples they cite, it is possible to infer that these intermediate phrases more closely resemble our intonation units.

8 For an illuminating discussion of intonation, especially rising intonation, in relation to syntax and meaning, see McLemore (1991).

9 We wish to thank Chuck Read for assisting us in these analyses. We take full responsibility for the use we have made of his advice.

10 This distinction is related to that made by Houtkoop and Mazeland (1985) between "open" and "closed" discourse units.

11 We are well aware that using a number of syllables to determine whether a next turn was an overlap or not is only one way of addressing this issue. Allowing a speaker change to overlap by as much as two syllables without counting as overlap was one way to acknowledge that many such occurrences are not heard as overlap (see Jefferson, 1983). At the same time, we recognize that projecting when a turn will end is probably not done by speakers in terms of number of syllables.

12 For each of our four parameters, intonational completion, syntactic completion, pragmatic completion, and speaker change, we performed our coding independently, and then compared our results. The extent of agreement was high, **impressionistically about 85 per cent**, and we went back to the tapes together to resolve any discrepancies. We then had our intonational completion judgments checked by a third coder, a trained transcriber, and again found high agreement. From our examples, the reader can see samples of our judgments.

13 To provide an idea of what such a situation might involve, we offer an example from our data:

```
(i)
-->V: so the doctor said.  that they would
           (0.3)
       If he:
           (0.5)
   didn''t wanna keep being active and do sports ''n
-->things. right now at his age and with the bad
   condition of his knee, they normally put in a
   plastic knee./>
```

At each of the periods, the speaker produced a final intonation contour, but these are not points of pragmatic (or syntactic) completion. It is not clear why she did this, but the fact that it is possible illustrates well our contention that intonational completion is *in principle* independent of both semantic and syntactic completion. That the vast majority of intonational completion points were in fact also points of both semantic and syntactic completion can thus be taken as a finding.

14 As mentioned earlier, they must also be paying attention to visual cues, but we did not assess the role of these cues might play. Goodwin (1981) provides a persuasive analysis of the role of gaze in projecting the ends of turns. On the role of gesture, see C. Goodwin (1986c), Goodwin and Goodwin (1986), Schegloff (1984), and Streeck (1988) for discussions of the role of gesture in the organization of talk, Kendon (1972), (1980) for a demonstration of co-ordination between

gestures and prosodic units, and Streeck and Hartge (1992) for a discussion of gestures at transition-relevance places. In a current research project (Ford, Fox, and Thompson (in press)), we are examining gesture, intonation, syntax and sequential context in the construction of turns.

15 Preliminary results from a study of Japanese and Mandarin conversations, similarly coded, strongly suggest that these findings are not restricted to English (Clancy et al. frth.).

16 See Auer (1996) for a more information based analysis of turn extensions in German conversation.

17 See Ford (1993) for a discussion of adverbial clause extensions of previously complete turns.

18 One might predict that second versions of questions will generally move from information to polar questions, thus helpfully narrowing the possible recipient responses.

19 Additions of specification may also be accompanied by non-verbal elaboration. In the following excerpt, V and K are explaining the knee operation to C. Since C does not indicate receipt of the explanation so far, V adds elaboration, both verbal and visual:

(i)
```
    V: So they said okay/ in that case (0.2) we will cut
    a we: dge/ out/,      (0.5) and straighten the leg/.:
                (0.2)
    ->V: Glunk glunk glunk.:    ((demonstrating with
    rms))
            (0.5)
      K:  [So-
    ->V: [an'' straighten the leg/.:
      K:  So li[ke-
    ->V:        [They cut a we: [dge-/
    ->C:                        [B-won''t his leg go/ out/
                  like tha: t/.> now/?>
                [instead/ of in/?>
        V:      [Now it's three degees/.> three degrees/.>
```

Note that V reverts to repetition as a means of recompletion in her additions after the visual display (arrows two and three). At the last arrow, we see that C still has problems in responding; she displays puzzlement with a question. This is a further piece of evidence supporting the interpretation that V's turn extensions are oriented to C's lack of response.

20 The larger context is not included due to space considerations, both the space to print it and the space to give a full interpretation. We believe that the problem of how much context to include needs to be seriously addressed by linguists as we move away from presenting

decontextualized language in our scholarly writings. Examples must be presented with more context than we have been accustomed to if we are to look closely at language as it actually occurs in interaction.

21 See Reichman (1978) for a discussion of *anyway* and what she terms a "return relation" in conversation.

22 We pursue this line ourselves in Ford, Fox, and Thompson (in press).

References

Altenberg, Bengt (1987). Prosodic patterns in spoken English: studies in the correlation between prosody and grammar for text-to-speech conversion. *Lund Studies in English 76.* Lund: Lund University Press.

Atkinson, J. Maxwell (1984). Public speaking and audience responses: some techniques for inviting applause. In J. Maxwell Atkinson and John C. Heritage (eds.) *Structures of Social Action: Studies in Conversational Analysis*, pp. 370–409. Cambridge: Cambridge University Press.

Atkinson, J. Maxwell and Heritage, John C., eds., (1984). *Structures of Social Action: Studies in Conversation Analysis.* Cambridge: Cambridge University Press.

Auer, Peter (1996). On the prosody and syntax of turn-continuations. In Elizabeth Couper-Kuhlen and Margaret Selting (eds.), *Prosody in Conversation.* Cambridge: Cambridge University Press.

Beckman, M. and Pierrehumbert, J. (1986). Intonational structure in Japanese and English. *Phonology Yearbook 3.*

Bolinger, Dwight (1964). Intonation as a universal. *Proceedings of the IXth International Congress of Linguists.* The Hague: Mouton.

(ed.) (1972). *Intonation: Selected Readings.* Harmondsworth: Penguin.

Brazil, David (1985). Phonology: intonation in discourse. In Teun A. van Dijk (ed.), *Handbook of Discourse Analysis* volume 2: *Dimensions of Discourse.* London: Academic Press.

Button, G. and Lee, J. R. E. (1987). *Talk and Social Organisation.* Clevedon, Avon: Multilingual Matters.

Chafe, Wallace (1979). The flow of thought and the flow of language. In Talmy Givón (ed.) *Discourse and Syntax.* Syntax and Semantics 12, pp. 159–81. New York: Academic Press.

(1980). The deployment of consciousness in the production of a narrative. In Wallace Chafe (ed.) *The Pear Stories: Cognitive, Cultural, and Linguistic Aspects of Narrative Production*, pp. 9–50. Norwood, NJ: Ablex.

(1987). Cognitive constraints on information flow. In Russell Tomlin, (ed.) *Coherence and Grounding in Discourse*, pp. 21–51. Amsterdam: Benjamins.

(1988). Linking intonation units in spoken English. In John Haiman and Sandra A. Thompson (eds.) *Clause Combining in Discourse and Grammar*, pp. 1–27. Amsterdam: Benjamins.

(1992). Prosodic and functional units of language. In Jane A. Edwards and Martin D. Lampert (eds.) *Talking Data: Transcription and Coding Methods for Language Research*, pp. 33–43. Hillsdale, NJ: Lawrence Erlbaum.

(1994). *Discourse, Consciousness, and Time: the Flow and Displacement of Conscious Experience in Speaking and Writing*. University of Chicago Press.

Clancy, Patricia M., Thompson, Sandra A., Suzuki, Ryoko, and Tao Hongyin. (frth). 'The conversational use of reactive tokens in English, Japanese, and Mandarin.' *Journal of Pragmatics*.

Cooper, W. and Sorensen, J. M. (1981). *Fundamental Frequency in Sentence Production*. New York: Springer-Verlag.

Cruttenden, Alan (1986). *Intonation*. Cambridge: Cambridge University Press.

Crystal, David (1969). *Prosodic Systems and Intonation in English*. Cambridge: Cambridge University Press.

Davidson, Judy (1984). Subsequent versions of invitations, offers, requests, and proposals dealing with potential or actual rejection. In J. Maxwell Atkinson and John Heritage (eds.) *Structures of Social Action. Studies in Emotion and Social Interaction*, pp. 102–28. Cambridge: Cambridge University Press.

Denny, Rita (1985). Pragmatically marked and unmarked forms of speaking-turn exchange. In Starkey D. Duncan and Donald W. Fiske. *Interaction Structure and Strategy*, pp. 135–74. Cambridge: Cambridge University Press.

Du Bois, John W. (1985). Competing motivations. In John Haiman, ed., *Iconicity in Syntax*. Amsterdam: John Benjamins.

(1987). The discourse basis of ergativity. *Language* 63.4: 805–55.

Du Bois, John, Schuetze-Coburn, Stephan, Paolino, Danae, and Cumming, Susanna (1993). Outline of discourse transcription. In Jane A. Edwards and Martin D. Lampert (eds.), *Talking Data: Transcription and Coding Methods for Language Research*. Hillsdale, NJ: Lawrence Erlbaum.

Duncan, Starkey D. and Fiske, Donald W. (1977). *Face-to-Face Interaction: Research, Methods, and Theory*. Hillsdale, NJ: Lawrence Erlbaum.

(1985). *Interaction Structure and Strategy*. Cambridge: Cambridge University Press.

Durie, Mark (1988). Preferred argument structure in an active language. *Lingua* 74: 1–25.

Erikson, Frederick (1992). They know all the lines: rhythmic organization and contextualization in a conversational listing routine. In Peter

Auer and Aldo di Luzo (eds.), *The Contextualization of Language*, pp. 365–97. Amsterdam: Benjamins.

Ford, Cecilia E. (1993). *Grammar in Interaction: Adverbial Clauses in American English Conversations*. Cambridge: Cambridge University Press.

Ford, Cecilia E., Fox, Barbara A. and Thompson, Sandra A. In press. Practices in the construction of turns: the "TCU" revisited. *Pragmatics*.

Fox, Barbara A. (1986). Local patterns and general principles in cognitive processes: anaphora in written and conversational English. *Text* 6: 25–51.

(1987). *Anaphora and the Structure of Discourse*. Cambridge: Cambridge University Press.

Givón, Talmy (1979). *Discourse and Syntax*. New York: Academic Press.

(1984). *Syntax*, Volume I. Amsterdam: John Benjamins.

(1990). *Syntax*, Volume II. Amsterdam: John Benjamins.

Goodwin, Charles (1979). The interactive construction of a sentence in natural conversation. In George Psathas, (ed.), *Everyday Language: Studies in Ethnomethodology*. New York: Irvington.

(1981). *Conversational Organization: Interaction Between Speakers and Hearers*. New York: Academic Press.

(1986a). Audience diversity, participation and interpretation. *Text* 6.3: 283–316.

(1986b). Between and within: alternative treatments of continuers and assessments. *Human Studies* 9: 205–17.

(1986c). Gesture as a resource for the organization of mutual orientation. *Semiotica* 62.1/2: 29–49.

(1987). Unilateral departure. In Graham Button and John R. Lee (eds.), *Talk and Social Organization*, pp. 206–16. Clevedon, England: Multilingual Matters.

Goodwin, Charles and Goodwin, Marjorie H. (1986). Gesture and coparticipation in the activity of searching for a word. *Semiotica* 62.1/2: 51–75.

(1987). Concurrent operations on talk: notes on the interactive organization of assessments. *IPRA Papers in Pragmatics* 1.1: 1–54.

(1992a). Context, activity and participation. In Peter Auer and Aldo di Luzo (eds.), *The Contextualization of Language*, pp. 77–99. Amsterdam: Benjamins.

(1992b). Assessments and the construction of context. In Alessandro Duranti and Charles Goodwin (eds.), *Rethinking Context: Language as an Interactive Phenomenon*, pp. 147–90. Cambridge: Cambridge University Press.

Goodwin, Marjorie H. (1980). Processes of mutual monitoring implicated in the production of description sequences. *Sociological Inquiry* 50: 303–17.

Halliday, M. A. K. (1985). Intonation and grammar in British English. The Hague: Mouton.

Heath, Christian (1992). Gesture's discreet tasks: multiple relevancies in visual conduct and in the contextualisation of language. In Peter Auer and Aldo di Luzo (eds.), *The Contextualization of Language*, pp. 101–27. Amsterdam: Benjamins.

Heritage, John C. (1984). *Garfinkel and Ethnomethodology*. Cambridge: Polity Press.

(1989). Current developments in conversation analysis. In D. Roger and P. Bull (eds.), *Conversation: an Interdisciplinary Perspective*. Clevedon, England: Multilingual Matters, Inc.

Hopper, Paul J. (1987). *Emergent Grammar*. Proceedings of the thirteenth annual meeting, Berkeley Linguistics Society, pp. 139–57. Berkeley: Berkeley Linguistics Society.

Hopper, Paul J. (1988). Emergent grammar and the a priori grammar postulate. In Deborah Tannen (ed.), *Linguistics in Context*. Norwood, NJ: Ablex.

Hopper, Paul J. and Sandra A. Thompson. (frth.) Language universals, discourse pragmatics, and semantics. In Philip W. Davis (ed.), *Language and its Cognitive Interpretation*.

Houtkoop, Hanneke, and Mazeland, Harrie. (1985). Turns and discourse units in everyday conversation. *Journal of Pragmatics 9*: 595–619.

Jefferson, Gail (1973). A case of precision timing in ordinary conversation: overlapped tag-positioned address terms in closing sequences. *Semiotica 9*: 47–96.

(1978). Sequential aspects of storytelling in conversation. In Jim Schenkein (ed.), *Studies in the Organization of Conversational Interaction*, pp. 219–248. New York: Academic Press.

(1983). Notes on some orderlinesses of overlap onset. In V. d''Urso and P. Leonardi (eds.), *Discourse Analysis and Natural Rhetoric*, pp. 11–38. Padua: Cleup.

(1984). On the organization of laughter in talk about troubles. In J. Maxwell Atkinson and John Heritage (eds.), *Structures of Social Action*. Studies in Emotion and Social Interaction, pp. 346–69. Cambridge: Cambridge University Press.

(1987). On exposed and embedded correction in conversation. In Graham Button and John R. Lee (eds.), *Talk and Social Organization*, pp. 86–100. Clevedon, England: Multilingual Matters.

(1989). On the sequential organization of troubles-talk in ordinary conversation. *Social Problems 35*: 418–41.

Kendon, Adam (1972). Some relationships between body motion and speech. In Siegman, A. and B. Pope (eds.), *Studies in Dyadic Communication*, pp. 177–210. Elmsford, NY: Pergamon Press.

(1980). Gesticulation and speech: two aspects of the process of utterance. In Key, Mary R. (ed.), *The Relationship of Verbal and Nonverbal Communication*, pp. 207–28. The Hague: Mouton.

Kingdon, R. (1958). *The Groundwork of English Intonation*. London: Longmans, Green, and Co.

Labov, William and D. Fanshel (1977). *Therapeutic Discourse*. New York: Academic Press.

Labov, William and David Fanshel (1977). *Therapeutic Discourse: Psychotherapy as Conversation*. New York: Academic Press.

Lerner, Gene H. (1987). Collaborative turn sequences: sentence construction and social action. Unpublished Ph.D. dissertation, University of California, Irvine.

(1989). Notes on overlap management in conversation: the case of delayed completion. *Western Journal of Speech Communication* 53: 167–77.

(1991). On the syntax of sentences-in-progress. *Language in Society* 20.3: 441–58.

In press. Finding "Face" in the preference structures of talk-in-interaction. *Social Psychology Quarterly*.

Levelt, Willem J. M. (1989). *Speaking; from Intention to Articulation*. Cambridge, MA: MIT Press.

Liberman, Mark and Sag, Ivan (1974). Prosodic form and discourse function. Papers from the Tenth Regional Meeting, Chicago Linguistic Society, 416–27. Chicago: Chicago Linguistic Society.

Liberman, Mark and Pierrehumbert, Janet (1984). Intonational invariance under changes in pitch range and length. In M. Aronoff and R.T. Oehrle (eds.), *Language Sound Structure*, pp. 157–233. Cambridge: MIT Press.

Local, John and Kelly, John (1986). Projection and "silences": notes on phonetic and conversational structure. *Human Studies* 9: 185–204.

McLemore, Cynthia (1991). The pragmatic interpretation of English intonation: sorority speech. Unpublished Ph.D. dissertation, University of Texas.

Milenkovic, Paul H. and Charles Read (1992). *CSpeech Version 4: User's Manual*. University of Wisconsin-Madison, Department of Electrical and Computer Engineering, Madison WI 53706.

Nespor, Marina and Irene Vogel (1986). *Prosodic Phonology*. Dordrecht: Foris Publications.

Oreström, Bengt (1983). Turn-taking in English conversation. Lund Studies in English 66. Lund: CWK Gleerup.

Pierrehumbert, Janet (1980). The phonology and phonetics of English intonation. MIT Ph.D. dissertation. Reprinted by Indiana University Linguistics Club, 1987.

Pierrehumbert, J. and Beckman, M. (1988). *Japanese Tone Structure*. Cambridge: MIT Press.

Pomerantz, Anita (1984). Pursuing a response. In J. Maxwell Atkinson and John Heritage (eds.), *Structures of Social Action*. Studies in Emotion and Social Interaction, pp. 152–63. Cambridge: Cambridge University Press.

Power, R. J. D. and Dal Martello, M. F. (1986). Some criticisms of Sacks, Schegloff and Jefferson on turn taking. *Semiotica* 58–1/2: 29-40.

Quirk, R., Svartvik, J., Duckworth, A. P., Rusiecki, J. P. I. and Colin, A. J. T. (1968). Studies in the correspondence of prosodic to grammatical features in English. In Quirk, R., *Essays on the English Language: Medieval and Modern*, pp. 120–35. London: Longman.

Read, Charles, Eugene H. Buder, and Raymond D. Kent (1992). Speech analysis systems: an evaluation. *Journal of Speech and Hearing Research* 39: 314–32.

Reichman, Rachel (1978). Conversational coherency. *Cognitive Science 2*: 283-327.

Sacks, Harvey (1974). An analysis of the course of a joke's telling in conversation. In Bauman, Richard and Joel Sherzer (eds.), *Explorations in the Ethnography of Speaking*, pp. 337–53. Cambridge: Cambridge University Press.

(1987). On the preference for agreement and contiguity in sequences in conversation. In Graham Button and John R. Lee (eds.), *Talk and Social Organization*, pp. 54–69. Clevedon, England: Multilingual Matters.

Sacks, Harvey and Schegloff, Emanuel, (1979). Two preferences in the organization of reference to persons in conversation and their interaction. In Psathas, George (ed.), *Everyday Language: Studies in Ethnomethodology*, pp. 15–21. New York: Irvington.

Sacks, Harvey, and Schegloff, Emanuel (1987). Notes on laughter in the pursuit of intimacy. In Graham Button and John R. Lee (eds.), *Talk and Social Organization*, pp. 152–205. Clevedon, England: Multilingual Matters.

Sacks, Harvey, Schegloff, Emanuel and Jefferson, Gail, (1974). A simplest systematics for the organization of turn-taking for conversation. *Language* 50.4: 696–735.

Sankoff, Gillian and Brown, Penelope (1976). The origins of syntax in discourse. *Language* 52: 651–66.

Schegloff, Emanuel A. (1979). The relevance of repair to syntax-for-conversation. In Givón, *Discourse and Syntax*, pp. 261–88.

(1980). Preliminaries to preliminaries: can I ask you a question? *Sociological Inquiry* 50: 104–52.

(1982). Discourse as an interactional achievement: some uses of "uh huh" and other things that come between sentences. In Deborah Tannen (ed.), *Analyzing Discourse: Text and Talk*, pp. 71–93. Georgetown: Georgetown University Press.

(1984). Iconic gestures: locational gestures and speech production. In J. Maxwell Atkinson and John Heritage (eds.), *Structures of Social Action*. Studies in Emotion and Social Interaction, pp. 266–96. Cambridge: Cambridge University Press.

(1986). The routine as achievement. *Human Studies* 9: 111–31.

(1987). Recycled turn beginnings: a precise repair mechanism in conversation's turn-taking organisation. In Graham Button and John R. Lee (eds.) *Talk and Social Organization*, pp. 70–85. Clevedon, England: Multilingual Matters.

(1988). Discourse as an interactional achievement II: an exercise in conversation analysis. In Deborah Tannen (ed.) *Linguistics in Context: Connecting Observation and Understanding*, pp. 135–58. Advances in Discourse Processes XXIX. Norwood, NJ: Ablex.

(1989). Reflections on language, development, and the interactional character of talk-in-interaction. In Marc H. Bornstein and Jerome S. Bruner (eds.) *Interaction in Human Development*, pp. 139–53. Hillsdale, NJ: Lawrence Erlbaum.

(1990). On the organization of sequences as a source of "coherence" in talk-in-interaction. In Bruce Dorval (ed.) *Conversational Organization and its Development*. Norwood, NJ: Ablex.

(1992). To Searle on conversation: a note in return. In John R. Searle et al. (On) *Searle on Conversation*, pp. 113–28. Amsterdam: John Benjamins.

Schegloff, E. A., Jefferson, Gail, and Sacks, Harvey (1977). The preference for self-correction in the organization of repair in conversation. *Language* 53: 361–82.

Schegloff, E. A. and Sacks, Harvey (1973). Opening up closings. *Semiotica* 7: 289-327. Reprinted in R. Turner, (ed.), *Ethnomethodology*, 1974, pp. 233–64. Harmondsworth: Penguin; and in John Baugh and Joel Sherzer (eds.) *Language in Use: Readings in Sociolinguistics*, 1984, pp. 69–97. Englewood Cliffs, NJ: Prentice-Hall.

Schiffrin, Deborah (1986). Functions of *and* in discourse. *Journal of Pragmatics* 10: 41–66.

(1987). *Discourse Markers*. Cambridge: Cambridge University Press.

Schuetze-Coburn, Stephan (1992). Prosodic phrase as a prototype. Proceedings of the IRCS workshop on prosody in natural speech, University of Pennsylvania, August, 1992. (Institute for Cognitive Research Report, pp. 92–137.)

(1993). Prosody, grammar, and discourse pragmatics: organizational principles of information flow in German conversational narratives. Ph.D. dissertation, UCLA.

Schuetze-Coburn, Stephan, Marian Shapley, and Elizabeth G. Weber (1991). Units of intonation in discourse: acoustic and auditory analyses in contrast. *Language and Speech* 34: 207–34.

Selkirk, Elizabeth (1984). *Phonology and Syntax: The Relation Between Sound and Structure*. Cambridge, MA: MIT Press.

Streeck, Jürgen (1988). The significance of gesture: how it is established. *Papers in Pragmatics* 2: 60–83.

Streeck, Jürgen and Hartge, Ulrike (1992). Previews: gestures at the transition place. In Peter Auer and Aldo di Luzo (eds.), *The Contextualization of Language*, pp. 135–57. Amsterdam: Benjamins.

Tannen, Deborah (1989). Interpreting interruption in conversation. Papers from the 25th annual regional meeting of the Chicago Linguistic Society, Part II: Parasession on Language in Context, 266–87. Chicago: Chicago Linguistic Society.

Wilson, Thomas P. and Zimmerman, Don H. (1986). The structure of silence between turns in two-party conversation. *Discourse Processes* 9: 375–90.

Wilson, Thomas P., Wiemann, John, and Zimmerman, Don H. (1984). Models of turn taking in conversational interaction. *Journal of Language and Social Psychology* 3: 159–83.

Resources and repair: a cross-linguistic study of syntax and repair[1]

BARBARA A. FOX, MAKOTO HAYASHI, AND
ROBERT JASPERSON

4.1 Introduction

The organization of repair in conversation has been the focus of
much work in conversation analysis and related fields over the last
twenty years (e.g., Hockett, 1967; Du Bois, 1974; Jefferson, 1974,
1987; Moerman, 1977; Schegloff, Sacks, and Jefferson, 1977;
Schegloff, 1979, 1987a; Goodwin, 1981; Levelt, 1982, 1983,
1989; Carbonell and Hayes, 1983; Hindle, 1983; Levelt and
Cutler, 1983; Reilly, 1987; van Wijk and Kempen, 1987; Good,
1990; Postma, Kolk, and Povel, 1990; Bredart, 1991; Blacker and
Mitton, 1991; Bear, Dowding, and Shriberg, 1992; Couper-
Kuhlen, 1992; Local, 1992; Shriberg, Bear, and Dowding, 1992;
Nakatani and Hirschberg, 1993). This work has uncovered the
mechanisms of self- and other-initiation of repair, self- and other-
achievement of repair, repair position, perception of repair, and so
on. But within this fairly extensive literature, the relationships
between repair and syntax have received relatively little attention
(the major exceptions being Schegloff, 1979; Goodwin, 1981;
Levelt, 1983; Geluykens, 1987; van Wijk and Kempen, 1987; Fox
and Jasperson, frth.). And the operation of repair in different languages, with different syntactic systems, has, to the best of our
knowledge, been the object of only a small body of research (see
Schegloff, 1987b).

This present study aims to begin to fill this gap by focusing on the
syntax of repair from a cross-linguistic perspective. Cross-linguistic
work on repair is especially compelling to us given our own, and
others", research on the relationships between same-turn (also

known as first-position) self-repair and syntax in English conversation (Schegloff, 1979, this volume; Fox and Jasperson, frth.).

As Schegloff (1979) makes clear, same-turn self-repair and syntax are interdependent and co-organizing: each requires the other as part of its operation. As Schegloff points out, repair cannot exist without syntax, since syntax organizes the linguistic elements through which talk is constructed, and without talk, there can be no repair. Similarly, syntax cannot exist without repair: it is always possible that at any point in the course of an utterance the speaker could not know how to continue the utterance, or might have selected an inappropriate lexical item, or might find that the utterance projected is eliciting pre-disagreement indicators from the recipient;[2] in such cases, speakers must have access to mechanisms by which they can stop the utterance under construction before it reaches completion and project a completion anew. Syntax, at least syntax-for-conversation, must thus allow for the operation of same-turn self-repair.

Even stronger evidence for the interdependence of same-turn self-repair (henceforth just: repair) and syntax has come from studies of syntactic organization and repair. For example, Fox and Jasperson (frth.) found that repair in English conversation is strongly organized according to syntactic constituents. In that study, we found that when English speakers recycle part of an utterance, they do not back up a random number of words, as one might in replaying a tape, or even back to a randomly selected syntactic constituent boundary; in all cases of recycling in our data, speakers returned either to the beginning of a word within the phrasal constituent under construction when repair was initiated or to the beginning of the clause, but not to a word in a prior phrasal constituent or clause.[3] For example, when repair was initiated during a constituent in an adverbial subordinate clause, speakers recycled either to the beginning of a word in that constituent (e.g., a noun phrase) or to the beginning of the adverbial subordinate clause, but *not* back to the beginning of the turn or to some arbitrary place within the adverbial subordinate clause. The following utterances illustrate some of these patterns (we have used an asterisk to indicate the site at which repair is initiated):

(1) ^J: But it- it does i- it does work out if you have just the common

dena-* denominator here

(2) ^M: Okay, well we could- do it from that angle then, because I don't-*

I don't really .hh encounter that concept problem

(3) ^K: Okay, let's see if- before I go and look at the solution if I can-

C: Mhm

K: follo-* if I can break it out here

In example (1), the speaker recycles just the noun under construction when repair was initiated; in example (2), the speaker recycles
back to the subject of the adverbial subordinate clause (and
not back to the main clause); and in example (3), the speaker
recycles back to the adverbial subordinate marker *if*.

We take these findings, and others like them, to be strongly indicative of the interdependence of repair and syntax. If speakers
recycled back some number of syllables or words, or some number
of units of time, or to a last pause, an interdependence of repair and
syntax would not be indicated. However, speakers do not seem to
orient to such possibilities.

Now, if it is the case that repair and syntax are interdependent,
then it ought to be true that repair will be organized according to
the syntactic organization of the language in question; in other
words, the organization of repair ought to be different for communities of speakers with different syntactic practices. The reason for
this can be stated in the following way. If repair represents a collection of strategies for responding to certain interactional pressures,
and if languages consist of different syntactic (or even phonological)
practices for managing those pressures, then their procedures for
repair will be spun from those practices, and repair will reflect the
organizations of those syntactic practices in general.

If these hypotheses are true, it ought to be possible to argue, at
least tentatively, in the following manner. If we find differences in
the organization of repair across languages, then we can suggest (if
not deduce) that these differences arise at least in part from the
different syntactic practices employed by the speakers of those
languages. Of course, we cannot rule out the possibility that
other factors may influence the organization of repair; for example,
it is possible that certain "styles" of repair are fashionable for a

given language/culture or that they work in that language/culture to create a certain construction of self (as perhaps tentative, submissive, unintelligent, etc.) and that these styles are more constrained than is required by the syntax of that language. It is also obviously plausible that other facets of a language – e.g., its phonology – would influence the operation of repair (cf. Schegloff, 1987b). Nonetheless, it is still possible that one could detect in the workings of repair the larger workings of general syntactic practices in a language. It is in fact this line of argumentation that we pursue in the present study.

This study seeks to explore the ways in which repair, whose operation is rooted in various interactional pressures, is managed in languages with vastly different syntactic practices to meet these pressures. To this end, we will discuss three ways in which the organization of repair differs across two languages, English and Japanese, and we will argue that these differences in repair organization – and possibly even differences in the mechanisms of turn-taking – correlate, at least in part, with larger differences in the syntactic practices employed by speakers of these two languages. We also examine the ways in which repair is used as a syntactic practice by speakers of both languages (see Ford and Mori, 1994, for a similar line of argumentation).

While such a study would, ideally, be done on a wide range of genetically and areally diverse languages, because it is extremely difficult to collect and analyze the appropriate data, we are able to report on repair in only two languages: English and Japanese. Even though the study is thus obviously limited in its data base, we believe our findings are sufficiently compelling to warrant the detailed discussion we provide here. This study is thus part of a growing enterprise which seeks to understand how interaction and grammar shape one another. Even though the findings are, of course, preliminary, it is our hope that it makes some small contribution to this increasingly fascinating endeavor. And perhaps this work will spur further studies on other languages.[4]

This chapter is organized as follows. Section 2 covers methodological issues of the study. Section 3 provides a brief introduction to the syntax of conversational Japanese and English, which will serve as background information for the subsequent discussions of Japanese and English repair. Section 4 discusses three differences in the organization of repair between Japanese and English which we argue are rooted in syntactic differences between the two languages. Section 5 examines in detail two cases, one from English and one from Japanese, in which repair is used to produce two different syntactic projections within a single turn, thereby providing a resource for speakers to expand the syntactic possibilities present for them at the moment of speaking. Section 6 presents a discussion of the significance of these findings for the study of repair, and for the study of syntax.

4.2 Methodological preliminaries

4.2.1 Definitions

A possible first understanding of repair might be that repair is the process by which speakers correct errors they have made in their immediately prior talk. But, as Schegloff, Jefferson, and Sacks (1977) note, repair is not limited to error-correction; there are many instances of what we would like to call repair in which no error is made (in fact the reason for the repair is not obvious):

(4) M: I don't kno:w but it's-* it's gonna cost quite a bit

And in some cases, the projected utterance under construction is aborted, and one with a new syntactic organization is started, so there is no direct replacement involved:

(5) H: And I haf-* (.) my class starts at two:.

These sorts of repair here, then, involve instances in which an emerging utterance is stopped in some way and is then aborted, recast, continued, or redone. Further examples illustrating the range of phenomena included in this category are given below:

(6) D: ((clears throa//t))

    J: I gave,* I gave up smoking cigarettes::.

(7) M: Called her 'n I t-* well actually I told her that my

       best friend had gotten the measles.

(8) B: She said they're usually harder <u>mark</u>ers 'n I said

wo::wuh huhh! .hhh I said there go, I said there's-*

there's <u>three</u> courses already that uh(hh)hh//ff

A: Yeh

B: I'm no(h)t gonna do well i(h)n,

(9) A: Like they- the biggest debate ih-* in our

department. in:,* at Trenton was that when we had

these faculty meetings.

(10) K: <u>Plus</u> once he got- (0.8) some* um (1.3) he got some

battery acid on: (0.2) on his trunk or <u>some</u>thing.

Also included in the formal notion of repair are cases involving utterances which contain occurrences of syllables such as *um* or *uh* and their equivalents in Japanese, but in which the syntax continues as projected:

(11) ^ K: .hh And I'm in the uh (0.2) school of law,

Similarly, there are cases in which the speaker does a cut-off at the end of a word, as if initiating repair, but then continues with the syntax as projected:

(12) ^ K: they've given me (1.5) the value of tangent in-

the sense that it's less than zero

While these classes of utterances are considered repair, they played no significant role in the present analysis.

In this study we restrict our attention to *same-turn self-repair*. We use the term same-turn self-repair to mean the following. By "self-repair" we mean repair which is produced by the speaker of the repairable (see Schegloff, Jefferson and Sacks, 1977), as in:

(13) H: .hh And t<u>s</u>he-* this girl's fixed up onna <u>da</u>-* a blind <u>da</u>:te.

In this utterance, H cuts off the subject pronoun *tshe* (the '-' indicates glottalized cut-off) and in a sense replaces that pronoun with a full noun phrase, *this girl*. This example is classified as self-repair because both the repairable – the pronoun – and the repair – the full noun phrase – are produced by the same speaker. A second instance of self-repair occurs in this utterance: the first try at *date* is cut off to introduce a modifier – *blind date*.

The term "same-turn repair" refers to repair which takes place within the same turn constructional unit as the repairable. In utterance (13), for example, the cut-off and replacement of the subject pronoun occur within the same clause as the pronoun.

Throughout the chapter, we use the term *repaired segment* to refer to the part of the utterance which is repaired; we use the term *repairing segment* to refer to the part of the utterance which accomplishes the repair.[5] In examples where we thought some visual cues would aid the reader in understanding the organization of the repair, we put the repaired segment within square brackets and the repairing segment in boldface.

We use the term Turn Constructional Unit (TCU) according to Sacks, Schegloff, and Jefferson (1974) and Ford and Thompson (this volume). According to Sacks, Schegloff, and Jefferson (1974), the turn-taking system of English conversation, and perhaps of conversation in all cultures/languages, initially allots one TCU to each current speaker. A TCU is thus a word, phrase, clause, or sentence which can constitute an entire turn (e.g. *yeah*, *in the cupboard*, *How are you?*). At the possible end of every TCU, speaker transition is possible (but not necessary). Speakers can, of course, make a bid for a multi-TCU turn, if, for example, they want to tell a story; such bids often take the form of what Sacks (1974) calls "story prefaces," of the sort "Did I tell you who I ran into yesterday?"

Throughout this chapter we use the term *syntactic practices* rather than more traditional terms, such as syntactic resources, syntactic constructions, and so on. We have done this for two reasons: first, since we view language as primarily for doing rather than for representing, we wanted to use a term that would remind us that syntax is an activity. Second, work on conversational data is sometimes dismissed as dealing with behavior (as in "performance") rather than with syntax per se (as in "competence"); such a distinction between syntactic behavior and syntax rests, we believe, on the assumption that syntax consists of a set of pre-stored (mental) constructions and that these representations may be implemented by speakers in more or less accurate ways during real-time speech. Because we do not wish to invoke this distinction and the view of language it presupposes in the present study (see Fox, 1994), we have avoided terms for syntax that hint at static pre-existing mental representations and have chosen instead a term that arises from a different metaphor of language.

4.2.2 Language sample

Although this study draws conclusions which may apply to all languages, it is in fact based on only two languages, Japanese and English. We chose these two languages for the following reasons. English is an obvious choice for work that requires conversational data, since a great deal of English conversation has been recorded and transcribed, and a great deal of research has been done on the interactional organization of English conversation. And, as many students of conversation know, it is much easier to work with conversational data from one's native language: English is the native language for two of us and a fluent second language for the third.

Japanese was also an obvious choice for us because there is a small but growing body of transcribed conversational data (to which one of us contributed substantially); Japanese is also the native language for one of us, and a fairly fluent second language for another.

The three of us thus have a fair amount of expertise, and data, in these two languages. We hope in the future to expand the research, and our research group, to include native speakers (and their data) of a wide range of typologically and areally diverse languages.

4.2.3 Data collection

Both the English data and the Japanese data were collected for the purposes of earlier projects (see Fox and Jasperson, frth; Hayashi, 1994).

For the English data, we culled 500 examples of repair from transcripts of naturally occurring conversations: the first 300 were from everyday conversations (both face-to-face and telephone conversations); the remaining 200 were culled from our own collection of English face-to-face tutoring sessions. We gathered instances of repair from the tutoring sessions in order to increase the sample size. The two sets of data were kept separate both in the collection stage and in the analysis stage of this project. Utterances appearing in the text below which are taken from the tutoring sessions are preceded by "^".

Since tutoring is a bit different from everyday conversation, a few words about the tutoring data are in order. In the summer of 1986 one of us (Fox) received a grant to study human tutoring dialogue, as part of an endeavor to build more robust computer tutoring systems. As part of this project, we hired graduate students from math, physics, chemistry and computer science to serve as tutors; students needing tutoring were attracted to the project through ads in the student newspaper. Tutor and student pairs then met in a small lab room for an hour, where the interaction was audio- and video-taped. The pair was given no instructions beforehand on how to proceed, and the whole interaction was guided by the genuine needs of the student (several had tests coming up, for example). The resulting conversations were thus spontaneous and natural, in the sense that they were not in any way planned or orchestrated in advance. However, they are on rather abstract topics, and they bear many marks of the asymmetrical roles of the tutor and student in the teaching/learning process (and tutor and student had never met before this session). For these reasons, to be cautious, we have kept the tutoring session data separate from the everyday conversation data. But in fact in the analysis we found no consistent differences in repair between the two data sources.

For the Japanese data, we found 225 instances of same-turn self-repair in the transcripts of naturally occurring Japanese conversations (both telephone and face-to-face). The conversations were audio- and video-taped by a variety of researchers for a range of purposes. The conversations were transcribed by the researchers, all native speakers of Japanese, who originally made the tapes. As was the case for the English data, all participants in the conversations were native speakers of the language under study.[6]

Because the collection of Japanese conversational data is a relatively new enterprise, we did not have available to us an extensive body of Japanese data – hence the fairly small number of instances of repair in Japanese. Comparability between the English and Japanese repair data is thus obviously an issue. Nonetheless, we feel that the pool of repairs in Japanese is large enough to allow us to draw certain general conclusions about repair in Japanese; of course, additional data will be important in advancing more specific claims.

4.2.4 Data coding

Instances of repair in both languages were coded for (1) the phrasal syntactic constituents, including clause, that were under construction when the repair was initiated (e.g., noun phrase and clause or verb phrase and clause); and (2) the syntactic organization of the repair (e.g. just the repairable was repeated, or the entire clause was redone). We used syntactic categories for the analysis, rather than, for example, interactional categories, to see if there were indeed syntactic patterns through which repair operates, or which emerge as constraining the operation of repair. Of course, in the analysis the interactional locus of each utterance was considered, so the analysis is by no means a purely syntactic exercise. But as syntax-linguists, we were interested in the possible syntactic configurations of repair.

Choosing syntactic categories for analyzing such data obviously poses several risks. First, it is not possible to know at the outset whether the phenomenon in question is organized according to syntactic categories. For example, Schegloff (1987a) demonstrates that one type of repair is governed by turn organization and *not* by sentence organization. So it was certainly possible that no description of repair could be made in syntactic terms. Second, it is possible that the categories we used, while widely accepted by linguists, would not be the *appropriate* syntactic categories; that is, it is possible that repair is indeed organized through syntactic categories – just not the syntactic categories typically recognized by linguists (Langacker, frth.).

Choosing syntactic categories that are appropriate for two typologically divergent languages is also complex. For example, in coding the English data it makes sense to distinguish subject and object noun phrases from prepositional phrases, since only the latter are marked with a separate linguistic element (the relevant elements are italicized):

(14) ^K: *I* have *a wai value* that I kno::w, (0.3) is uh, less than zero.

(15) M: ... on the back of his pickup truck with a, (0.4) *with a jack*

In (14), the noun phrases *I* and *a wai value* are not preceded by any markers indicating their grammatical roles in the sentence; in (15), on the other hand, the role of the noun phrase *a jack* is marked by *with*. So for English, it makes sense in some way to distinguish subject and object noun phrases (like *I* and *a wai value*) from prepositional phrases (like *with a jack*), although prepositional phrases involve noun phrases.

But for Japanese, this distinction would distort the facts of the language: in Japanese, referring nouns can be marked with a "case" particle, which follows the noun. Subject noun phrases, object noun phrases, and locative phrases are marked each with their own postpositional case particle (subject and object case particles are sometimes omitted in conversation):[7]

(16) H: teyuuka **YUUkosan** (.) **jishin ga**   OOkii kara::, ...

      I.mean   Yuko   self SUBJ   tall   because

      'I mean, because Yuko herself is tall,...'

(17) Y: ichioo   zen kokumin no (0.7) **joohoo**   **o**   nigitteru, ...

      by.and.large all citizen   GEN[8]   information OBJ   have

      'By and large, (they) have information about all the citizens'

(18) K: Takashimaya no   ano un nan- **chijoo**   **de**   matteta.

      Takashimaya GEN   um uh wha-   ground.floor LOC waiting-past

      '(I) was waiting um uh wha- on the ground floor of Takashimaya.'

Because of these facts, it is not clear that there is any reason to distinguish these phrases as noun phrases and postpositional phrases. So, for Japanese, all noun phrases were treated together. In general we tried to be as true to the nature of the language under study as we could, rather than trying to force an unnaturally parallel treatment of both languages.

Throughout the coding we tried to be conscious of the pitfalls of our syntactic analyses; the usefulness of these analyses can be seen in the fact that we did find extensive differences in the organization of repair across the two languages which we believe are real differences.

4.3 Syntax in Japanese and English

This section provides background information on the conversational syntax of Japanese and English; this information will be used in sections 4 and 5. It should be kept in mind that the syntax of conversational Japanese and English differs from the syntax of the written varieties of these languages, as well as from linguistic descriptions based on elicited sentences.

The descriptions offered here are not meant to be exhaustive of the phenomena examined but are rather meant as rough guides to later discussions.

4.3.1 Syntax in conversational Japanese

Japanese is often described as an SOV, or verb-final, language (where S stands for subject, O for direct object, and V for verb). In our conversational data, some utterances are verb-final, at least in the clauses that contain a verb:

(19) T: soo yatta   to   **omou**.

    so be-past quotative think

    '(I) think that (it was) so.'

(20) H: de: tashoo   **maketoku**.

    and more.or.less   discount

    'and (we) discount more or less.'

However, there are many utterances in which elements follow the verb (see Ono and Suzuki, 1992; Maynard, 1989; Clancy, 1982; Hinds, 1982; Ford and Mori, 1994; Simon, 1989). The following examples illustrate the use of lexical elements after the verb (the postverbal element is in boldface):

(21) H: tabun (.) ichiban ue de: **Yuukosan ga:**.

    probably most older be Yuko   SUBJ

    'Probably (she) is the oldest, Yuko

(22) H: YUUdachi   ga (.) kek- kuru mitai yo **ashita**.

    evening.shower SUBJ li-   come seem FP tomorrow

    'It seems li- like there might be an evening shower, tomorrow.'

Japanese also has a large class of what are called "final particles," whose specific functions include the marking of how a speaker knows what was just said (evidentiality), politeness, and so on:

Japanese conversational discourse is characterized by frequent final particles whose use is to appeal to the interpersonal feelings of the recipient of the message. (Maynard, 1989: 30)

These so-called final particles have been the subject of a great deal of research (e.g. see Maynard, 1989; Uyeno, 1971; Martin, 1975), because they seem to be an important part of the organization of conversational Japanese. An indication of their importance can be seen in the fact that Maynard (1989) found that 32 per cent of her Pause-bounded Phrasal Units (similar to Chafe's (1987) Intonation Units) were marked by final particles. Consider the following example:

(23) I: aa sugoi   **ne::**.

    oh amazing FP

    'Oh, (it is) amazing.'

So far we have suggested that the notion "verb-final" is a complex issue in Japanese. The distribution of S and O is also more complex than suggested by the order SOV. It is commonly known that S and O are often not expressed in conversational Japanese (Hinds, 1982; Kuno, 1978; Maynard, 1989). Consider the following examples (words which are not expressed in the Japanese are given in parentheses in the English translations):

(24) I: okaasan ni   na no, otoosan ni   na no::?

    mother resemblance be FP father resemblance be FP

    '(Does she) take after (her) mother or (her) father?'

(25) H: hajimete   mita kedo.

    for the first time saw but

    '(I) saw (her) for the first time.'

In (24), the subject is not expressed; in (25) neither the subject nor the object is expressed.

Even verbs can remain unexpressed. Consider the following example:

(26) H: Imanaka-san mo izure   sochira de?

      Imanaka   also some.day there   LOC

      'Ms. Imanaka, (are you getting married) there some day too?'

In this example, we have a subject noun phrase ("Ms. Imanaka"), a time adverbial ("some day"), a locative, and no expressed verb. Of course, the action performed by the subject is clear to the participants from the preceding context.

The result of these patterns is that clauses in conversational Japanese often show one or more nouns which are not S or O but are rather nouns describing locations, times, and other settings; these are then followed by a verb in some utterances, though not in all; final particles often follow the verb.

In some cases, only a verb is expressed:

(27) K: a soo soo   kiteta kiteta.

      oh yeah yeah came   came

      'Oh yeah, yeah, (a typhoon) was coming.'

(28) K: atsui yo ne: toka   yutte,

      hot FP FP quotative say

      '(she) said like, "(it'll be) hot, won't it?"'

The order of nouns that do occur in an utterance is flexible, responding to the interactional needs of the moment of utterance.

Prescriptive Japanese grammar says that referring nouns must be followed by case particles, or postpositions, which indicate the role of the noun in the clause (e.g. subject, direct object, locative). These particles function somewhat like case marking systems in languages like German and Russian (but see Shibatani, 1990, Ch. 11, for a discussion of the complexity of Japanese case particles). Examples exhibiting case particles are given above in (16) - (18). In casual conversation, however, case particles for subject and direct object can be omitted; examples illustrating this phenomenon are given below (nouns that could have been marked with a case particle appear in boldface):

(29) C: demo **kane**   motte nee mon **ano hito**.

      but   money have NEG FP that person

      'But (she) doesn't have money, that person.'

(30) Y: konna   jikan **koitsura**   <u>ZE</u>ttai **terebi** mitehen   wa ...

     like.this time   these.guys   ever   TV   watch.NEG FP

     'Around this time (of the day), these guys never watch TV...'

In English, complex clauses often consist of first a main clause and then a complement clause. A complement clause is a whole clause that occupies the slot for a direct object.[9] For example, in English one can say *I think this* or *I think you're beautiful* where *this* and *you're beautiful* both are the direct object of *think*, but *you're beautiful* is a whole clause and not just a noun. Examples follow (the complement clause is enclosed in curly braces):

(31) ^J: I don't think {I'll do this}

(32) ^J: So I'd recommend- {working through some of the mid-range ones}

Unlike English, Japanese places the main clause *after* the complement clause, which often results in a structure like this (where NP stands for Noun Phrase and C stands for complement marker): [NP V] C V. Consider the following example:

(33) K: datte   {gonen   mo   iru} to   omotte sa::

     because   five.years as.long.as stay quotative think   FP

        NP   V   C   V

     'Because (you) think that (you)'ll be (here) as long as five years'

The structure of this utterance is: NP V Complement-marker V FP, where the second verb is the verb *omou* "think"; notice that this word order is the mirror image of word order in English (where "think" comes before the verb of the complement clause, "stay").

Furthermore, markers of other kinds of relationships between two clauses – for example, subordinate clause markers (like *when* and *because* in English) – tend to occur at the end of clauses in Japanese while they occur at the beginning of clauses in English (see also Ford and Mori, 1994). Consider the following utterance:

(34) H: ano   chotto HONya   ni: ne yoritai   **kara::**

     um   just   bookstore LOC FP stop.by.want **because**

     'um because (I) just want to stop by the bookstore'

Notice that in this example the Japanese subordinate clause marker *kara* occurs at the end of the clause, while in the English translation *because* appears at the beginning. This is another instance of the general pattern across the two languages that items that tend to precede in English (e.g., *pre*positions, main clauses) tend to follow in Japanese (e.g., *post*positions, main clauses). Readers should keep in mind this apparent "mirror image" relationship between Japanese and English word order for the discussion in section 4.4.3.

Verbs in Japanese are marked for tense and various kinds of modes. In at least one case, a conjunction (*-te*, roughly equivalent to English *and*) can occur as an ending attached to a verb. Verbs in Japanese do not exhibit agreement with the subject (that is, there is no marking on the verb for the person or number of the subject).

For further information on Japanese syntax, interested readers should consult Kuno (1973), Martin (1975), Maynard (1989) and Shibatani (1990).

4.3.2 Syntax in conversational English

English is usually described as a rigid SVO language. While there is some word order variation in our conversational data, in fact most utterances do tend to be SV(O), with prepositional phrases coming after the direct object, if one is present. Subjects in our data are overwhelmingly pronominal:

(35) ^J: **We're not missing anything**

(36) ^J: **You've just dropped the minus sign essentially**

It is important to point out here that English is somewhat odd cross-linguistically in requiring the presence of a subject in all utterances; this constraint produces the "dummy" *it* constructions for which English is well known, in which a non-referring *it* occurs as the subject of an utterance ("*it* takes one to know one," "*it*'s raining," "*it* takes two to tango," etc.). In some cases, this "dummy" *it* projects a complex clause structure (as in "*it* seems to me that ..."). It is rare, even in fast conversation, for speakers to produce a main clause without explicit mention of the subject.

Subjects and objects are unmarked in English; other kinds of nominals are marked by prepositions. While subjects and objects tend to be relatively fixed in their order with regard to the verb (just before and just after the verb, respectively), prepositional phrases exhibit a greater range of positions in a clause/TCU. Consider the following (the prepositional phrases are in boldface):

(37) ^J: .hh **In this case** (0.7) you again want to go (.) one degree down in your

   denominator

(38) ^J: You're left **with the stuff** that you started with

In (37), the prepositional phrase occurs at the beginning of the TCU, while in (38) it occurs after the verb.

Verbs in English exhibit subject agreement: they are marked for the person and number of the subject. Verbs are also marked for tense/aspect.

Readers interested in further details of English conversational syntax should consult Chafe (1987), Givón (1993), Fox and Thompson (1990), Ford and Thompson (this volume), Ford (1993), Ono and Thompson (frth).

4.4 Organization of repair

In this section we present a discussion of three ways in which repair is organized differently across the two languages in question. We then argue that these differences in repair organization arise, at least in part, from more general syntactic differences exhibited across the two languages (the findings reported here were first noted in Hayashi, 1994).

We start with a discussion of the most straightforward case and work up to more complex instances.

4.4.1 Morphological repair

Our first type of difference comes from the realm of morphology,[10] which is typically included in the larger domain of syntax, especially in cross-linguistic studies.

We found in our Japanese data a kind of morphological repair which did not occur in the English data. Consider the following example (we have not attempted to translate the repair itself in this example into English):

(39) K: ja   nanji   goro ni   kurida[shi-*]soo?

      then what.time   about OBL   go.out

      'Then about what time (shall we) go out?'

In this example, the speaker K replaces only the inflectional ending of the verb with another. The citation form of the verb used by K is *kurida-su*, which has the "conclusive" ending *-su* (we are using terms from Shibatani, 1990, in this discussion of verb inflection in Japanese). The first form that K produces in this example (*kurida-shi*) has the "adverbial" ending *-shi*. The adverbial endings of Japanese verbs may or may not be followed by certain kinds of auxiliaries and/or particles, but in the context of this example, the ending *-shi* was very likely to be followed by some auxiliaries and/ or particles. However, K cuts off the verb and replaces *-shi* with the "cohortative" ending *-soo*. In other words, K has replaced one bound morpheme with another.

In our English data, we found no examples parallel to example (39) from Japanese. That is, we found no examples of the following invented sort, in which the past-tense morpheme *-ed* is replaced by the present tense morpheme *-s*.

(40) She look[ed]-*s at the table.

We would like to argue that this difference in repair can be attributed to the differences between English and Japanese verb morphology. While both languages do exhibit verb morphology, and, more specifically, they both exhibit suffixes (endings) rather than prefixes (beginnings), the nature of these endings is different across the two languages, both in sound structure and in meaning. And it is these differences which we believe produce the difference in repair.

To begin with, consider the sound structure of the Japanese verb endings in example (39). The endings *-shi* and *-soo* (as well as the citation form ending *-su*) are full syllables, each consisting of a consonant and a vowel. Now consider the sound structure of the English verb endings in example (40). Although *-ed* is spelled with two letters, in most cases it is actually pronounced as a single consonant sound (either [t] or [d]), and *-s* is clearly a single consonant.

Thus the English verb endings are not full syllables, and hence are unlikely to be pronounceable by themselves. (An exception to this is the suffix -ing).

Now consider the form-meaning relationships of verb endings in the two languages. Japanese is considered to be an agglutinating language, which means that in Japanese each morpheme has roughly a single grammatical meaning. For example, -shi is associated just with the grammatical meaning "adverbial" and not with person and number, or any other possible category (as mentioned earlier, person and number are not marked on verbs in Japanese). English, on the other hand, is considered to be a fusional language, which means that in English most bound verbal morphemes are associated with several grammatical meanings. For example, -s carries not only the meaning of present tense; it also signals that the subject is third person singular. Bound verbal morphemes are thus semantically complex in English in a way that they are not in Japanese.

There is one more difference related to this that is probably relevant. In Japanese, the verb endings (suffixes) are not agreement markers; that is, they do not signal anything about the subject of the utterance. They modify the verb in a more adverbial way than do agreement markers. In English, on the other hand, verb suffixes sometimes overtly indicate characteristics of the subject (person and number). Verb suffixes in English thus in a way refer back to something earlier in the utterance, namely the subject, while in Japanese, the verb endings have no explicit relationship to what has gone before (although they may signal possibilities to come, as with the "adverbial" ending).

These three differences between English and Japanese verb endings suggest to us that at a variety of levels verb endings in English are more tightly "bonded" to the verb than are verb endings in Japanese and hence are less available for individual replacement than are verb endings in Japanese.[11] In a sense then, it is possible that English verb suffixes are not available as interactional objects in the same way that Japanese verb suffixes are. Differences in repair strategies across the two languages may thus arise from differences in the organization of their verb morphology.

4.4.2 Procedures for delaying next noun due

The second type of difference in repair has to do with the general function of delaying the production of a next item due. In this study we focused on delays involved in the production of lexical parts of noun phrases – in particular, nouns.[12]

Both Japanese and English share a set of repair procedures involving the use of "fillers." This phenomenon is well-documented for English (cf. (11) above, and Schegloff, 1979), and many instances from both languages occurred in our corpora. The following is an example from the Japanese corpus.[13]

(41) I: jaa   honyasan no   mae   no   sa: .h ano: nanka: moyooshi: no: .hh hh

        then bookstore GEN front GEN FP   um   like   amusement GEN

      a- a- itsumo nanka (0.7) kitaroo toka ...

      uh- uh- always like   Kitaro etc.

However, we discovered that syntactic differences between the two languages may be implicated in a different set of repair procedures for delaying the production of a noun. Consider first the following examples from English:

(42) M: on the back of his pickup truck [with a,*] (0.4) with a jack.

(43) B: We're gonna take it [through the*] through the mill so to speak.

(44) ^K: .hh So I'm going to start just- very simply [with-*] with number one.

(45) B: are you going here [for an-*] for an Indian class by any chance

(46) ^A: What if you put (4.6) what if you put double quotes around (0.2) the:

        (0.2) the thing [with a-*] with: a space in it.

In these examples, the speakers have begun a prepositional phrase, initiated repair, and then recycled the preposition and a possible article before progressing with the rest of the phrase. In each of these cases, recycling constitutes a procedure for delaying the production of a next item due. This procedure could, for example, be part of a word search, a request for recipient-gaze, management of overlapping talk, and/or production of a dispreferred. In the case of English prepositional phrases, what is delayed is the production of a noun, as in (42)-(44),[14] or modified noun, as in (45) and (46); it is also possible that this procedure could be used to delay items such as modifiers, as well as verbs, verb particles, etc.[15]

Our data, however, led us to focus on cases involving the delay of nouns.

Japanese speakers, it turns out, do not use recycling to delay the production of nouns. The reason for this seems to be that while prepositions and articles in English precede their nouns, postpositions such as case particles in Japanese follow their nouns. It is clear that English speakers make use of the fact that prepositions and articles precede their nouns; prepositions and articles provide material to be recycled *before* the speaker must produce a noun. Japanese speakers, on the other hand, do not have available to them non-lexical material to recycle before a noun, since case particles *follow* their nouns (and Japanese has no articles).

Because of the syntactic organizations of the two languages, then, English speakers can make use of preposition and article recycling as part of a delay strategy, while Japanese speakers cannot. Our data indicate that Japanese speakers make use of other practices for delaying the production of a next item due.

One interesting strategy occurred in our data. Consider the following examples:

(47) M: .hh maa sonna::: **are ga::::** (1.5) u:: meedosan ga   iru yoona: ie

            well like   that SUBJ   uhm maid   SUBJ exist such family

     ya nai kara:,

     be not because

     '... because, like. we are not the sort of family to have **that**, uhm a maid,'

(48) Y: demo sono mae   ni   WA:: (0.6) ano::: (0.5) **are ga**   attan desu yo.

         but   it   before OBL TOP   um   that SUBJ exist be   FP

     ano:: (1.0) e::::to ne. warito ano (1.0) nante yuun desu ka (1.0)

     um   well   FP sort.of um   what say   be question

     onngaku BANgumi toka.

     music   program   etc.

     'But before it, there was um **that**, you know, um, like ... sort of, what should I say,

     music program and so on'

In cases such as these, speakers make use of a repair procedure which involves the following elements: a demonstrative pronoun (translated as "that" or "there") and case particle, followed by the delayed noun and optional case particle. The demonstrative pronoun serves as a place holder while the speaker looks for some lexically specific noun. Markers translated as *um, well, what should I say*, etc. appear before the delayed noun phrase, though these may be part of a distinct repair procedure operating on the delayed noun, as in (41).

This is a useful strategy for speakers of a language which does not systematically provide phrase-initial grammatical material. Once again we see how it is possible that the syntactic practices employed by speakers shape the organization of the repair strategies that are used.

4.4.3 The scope of recycling

The third type of difference also involves recycling. In this case the difference leads us to postulate the possibility of very basic differences in the turn-taking mechanisms of the two languages. Consider the following examples from our English data:

(49) B: in this building- we finally got [a-*] .hhh a roo:m today in-

in the leh- a lecture hall,

(50) K: Plus once [he got- (0.8) some*] um (1.3)

he got some battery acid on: (0.2) on his trunk

or something.

In (49), repair is initiated after a noun phrase (defined as a noun plus any modifier that might occur) has been started. In recycling, the speaker only repeats the part of the noun phrase that has been produced so far – the indefinite article. The speaker does not recycle "back to" anything earlier in the utterance.

In example (50), the speaker also initiates repair after starting a noun phrase; in this case, however, the speaker repeats the whole clause (excluding "plus once") rather than just the part of the noun phrase produced so far.

One way of stating the pattern in English is to say that the domain of recycling can either be the local constituent under construction at the time repair is initiated (e.g. noun phrase), or it can be the clause. This pattern holds for all constituents, including verbs and prepositional phrases.[16]

Additional examples of this pattern in English are given below.

(51) B: ((to J)) (I don't think- I bedju would // nex'time we-)

  D: Hey would you like [a Trent'n::,*] **a Trentn**

  telephone directory.

(52) ^ M: Okay, well we could- do it from that angle then, because [I don't-*]

  I don't really .hh encounter that concept problem (0.3) in any of the

  problems,

In comparison to this pattern, our Japanese data show only con-
stituent-internal recycling; that is, at least in our data, Japanese
speakers do not make use of clausal recycling. This means that if
a speaker initiates repair after starting a noun phrase, s/he will
recycle back to the beginning of that noun phrase but not further
back; repair initiated during the construction of the verb usually is
handled by recycling just the verb, not other elements that might
have preceded the verb (except in one case the direct object of the
verb, which makes a local constituent – a verb phrase). So one does
not find counterparts in the Japanese data to example (50). Below
we give examples of recycling in Japanese:

(53) M: tteyuuka koko denwa   [kaket-*] **kakete** kite   sa,

  I.mean   here telephone   ca-   call   come   FP

  'I mean, (they) ca- called us here,'

(54) T: ... mukoo   no   [sutahhu-*] **sutahhu** mo sa: yuushuu.

  the.other.party GEN   staff   staff   also FP   excellent

  '... their staff- staff is also excellent.'

(55) M: sorede sa,   ne   [atashi wa-*] **atashi wa**   sa,   sokode sa,   koitsura

  then   FP,   FP   I   TOP   I   TOP FP   then   FP   these.guys

  karakatte   yare toka   omotte   sa,

  tease   do   quotative think   FP

  'Then, I, I then thought, "let's tease these guys,"'

We thus seem to have a systematic difference in the possible
domains of recycling between the two languages. The reason for

this difference, we believe, lies in the different syntactic practices employed in managing local interactional needs.

The different syntactic practices which seem to be at the heart of this difference in repair are the following. As mentioned in section 3, all referring nouns in Japanese can be marked for case, and the order of nouns before the verb is flexible (perhaps because of the case-marking). In addition, subjects and objects in Japanese, particularly subjects, are often not explicitly realized (e.g., (25)). The verb in Japanese comes at or near the end of the clause.

The kind of clausal TCU structure these facts commonly lead to typically, although of course not always, starts with some kind of discourse marker (e.g., *ano*, *nanka*), followed by adverbials, or nouns indicating setting of some kind, followed by the verb, and possibly followed by so-called final particles. So what occurs early in the TCU is often only loosely associated structurally with what is to follow. Conversational utterances in Japanese thus seem not to show tight syntactic organization (for similar findings see Iwasaki and Tao, 1993; Iwasaki, 1993).

What do we mean by "tight syntactic organization"? In most current views of syntax, including "functional syntax" of most varieties, the relationships between a verb and its subject and object (if it co-occurs with an object) create the basic syntactic organization of a clause. For example, in most functionally oriented views of syntax, subjects and objects are said to be "core arguments" of a clause, of which the verb is the nucleus; other elements are thought to be "peripheral," bearing looser syntactic relationships to the basic clause made up of S, O, and V (e.g., Foley and van Valin, 1984). So a language, like Japanese, which tends to leave S, O and even V unexpressed, appears to have more loosely organized syntax than a language which requires the expression of those basic elements (like English).

Consider, for example, the following utterance (example (26) repeated here as (56)):

(56) H: Imanaka-san mo izure   sochira de?

     Imanaka   also some day there   LOC

    'Ms. Imanaka, (are you getting married) there some day too?'

In this example, we have an utterance that begins with a noun phrase (*Imanaka-san*), then exhibits an adverbial particle (*mo*), then a temporal phrase (*izure*), then a locative phrase (*sochira de*). There is no expressed verb and the elements that are expressed do not bear usual syntactic relationships to each other and they do not form a coherent syntactic structure, as this notion was described above.

English, on the other hand, requires the presence of an overt subject and is fairly rigidly SV(O). This leads to TCUs which may begin with a discourse marker (e.g., *well, so*) and then continue with a subject, then verb, then a direct object if one is appropriate, and then prepositional phrases if appropriate; adverbials typically occur after the verb. Conversational utterances in English thus show a higher degree of syntactic coherence.

From a syntactic perspective, then, we can say that in English the subject begins a tightly knit clause structure and hence syntactically is the "beginning" of the clause, while in Japanese there is no consistent element that serves as the beginning of a tightly knit syntactic unit – in fact, there is no such tightly knit unit. In Japanese, elements in an utterance seem to be more independent from one another than are elements in an English utterance; we believe that the difference in the organization of recycling across the two languages reflects this difference.

We would like to suggest that these syntactic facts affect repair because they affect a crucial aspect of the turn-taking mechanisms of these two languages, namely *projection*. Although a full exploration of the turn-taking system of Japanese conversation is beyond the scope of the present study (see Maynard, 1989, for a beginning), we would like to offer as a possible explanation that turn-taking is managed in a different way in Japanese than it is in English, to wit: the beginnings of TCUs in Japanese do not tend to have elements that *syntactically project* the possible organization of what is to follow. For example, from the presence of an adverbial or a location-indicating noun a recipient cannot necessarily predict what kind of syntactic element will come next. It seems, however, that the beginnings of TCUs in English do project possible organizations for what is to follow; for example, often in English as soon as one hears the subject, one knows (in a practical sense) that a verb is coming; and as soon as one hears the verb, one knows what is likely to come after the verb: certain kinds of verbs typically co-occur with direct objects while others typically co-occur with embedded clauses. That is, the beginning of the clause in English is rich with information about how the clause is likely to continue. The beginning of the clause in English projects its likely continuation. Consider the following utterances:

(57) ^J: And we should've actually noticed this sooner

(58) D: I belie:ve you could <u>really</u> live in this area inna tent.

In (57), after hearing this instance of *we,* we know that some kind of verb is coming up; after hearing this instance of *should"ve,* we know that a main verb is still coming; after we hear this instance of *noticed,* we know that a direct object is coming. In (58), after hearing *I* we know that some kind of verb is coming; after hearing *believe* we can guess that a complement clause is coming, which will probably start with a subject and have a verb in it. In both cases, the recipient can make reasonably good guesses about how the clause is likely to continue on the basis of the subject and the verb (in particular the verb). Notice that these projections can be made after only a few syllables of the TCU have been produced.

Compare these utterances with the following Japanese utterance:

(59) H: shoo de   onnanoko ga   cho- [ta-*] **chanto**   **tabe:kireru** ...

         small as.for girl   SUBJ ju-   ea-   completely eat.up.can

         'As for a small (ramen), a girl can juh- ea- eat (it) up completely ...'

The clause begins with a noun phrase, *shoo de,* "as for a small (ramen)". This noun phrase is not the subject of the clause or the object. It is not possible to predict what syntactic elements will come next, since the subject or the object could be left unexpressed; perhaps the recipient can anticipate that eventually a verb will be produced. After this first noun phrase, another noun is produced which turns out to be the subject of the clause. Notice that because Japanese uses *post*-nominal case markings, it is not possible to know for sure the case of a noun until the case marker is produced, although of course native Japanese speakers can make reasonable guesses about the syntactic and semantic role of a noun (but these tend to be based on semantic characteristics of referents – e.g., humanness – and not necessarily on the syntax of the utterance so far); so we are quite far into the clause before we hear what we know to be a subject. After hearing the subject we might expect an object, but an object need not occur if (a) it is not explicitly realized or (b) the verb is not transitive. And in example (59), the object is left unexpressed. After hearing a subject noun phrase, the recipient can predict that a verb may be produced before the TCU is complete. So the syntactic projections for this utterance may come relatively late in the utterance.

So we are suggesting that English speakers and recipients are able to use an "early projection" strategy because of the syntactic practices they employ. As Schegloff (1987a) says, of English conversation:

Turn beginnings are an important initial place, and an important initial resource, for the projection of the turn-shape or the turn-type of the turn that is being begun at that turn beginning. Such projection is a critical resource for the organisation of the turn-taking system for conversation. It is a critical resource for the organisation of a system that aims to achieve, and massively does achieve, the feature: one speaker speaks at a time in conversation...(p. 71)

Japanese speakers and recipients, on the other hand, engage in syntactic practices which do not make easy "early projection" strategies; from our data, we believe it is possible that Japanese speakers make use of "wait and see" strategies which are enabled by the syntactic practices available to them. At any rate, we are suggesting that syntactic projection can take place earlier in an utterance in English than in Japanese. Obviously, neither set of strategies is in any way better than the other; they simply provide different resources for accomplishing transition to a next speaker.

We are not suggesting that Japanese recipients are completely unable to make predictions about what the speaker might say next, just that projection may take place later in the utterance in Japanese than in English. Obviously, any native speaker of a language has countless experiences with how utterances tend to go in their language, and the meaning of what is being said helps recipients to make guesses about what the speaker is likely to say. We are instead suggesting that the syntactic practices of English make *early* projection of the upcoming syntax a more straightforward process than do the syntactic practices of Japanese; the syntactic practices of Japanese do not facilitate this process to the extent that the syntactic practices of English do.

Evidence outside of repair for this difference in projection between English and Japanese comes from Maynard's (1989) study of turn-taking in Japanese conversation. While her study did not examine repair strategies, it does provide some interesting indirect evidence for our claim.

Maynard found that Japanese speakers tend to produce what she calls Pause-bounded Phrasal Units (PPUs), which are bits of talk surrounded by pauses (she does not say how long the pauses are). The average length of these PPUs is 2.36 words – much shorter than the average length of similar units (what Chafe, 1987, calls Intonation Units) in English, which is about four words per Intonation Unit (see Chafe, 1994). We take this as a piece of indirect evidence that Japanese speakers tend to produce their turns in small constituents, where each constituent is syntactically independent from other constituents to a degree greater than one would find in Intonation Units in English. Intonation Units in English tend to be clauses, which, as we suggested earlier, show a high degree of syntactic coherence, while PPUs in Japanese tend not to be clauses (although the definition of "clause" is tricky for Japanese, for all the reasons we have touched on). Japanese recipients tend to produce back-channels (continuers) at the end of each PPU, leading to a style of interaction which has led scholars of Japanese to conclude that Japanese conversationalists are more "involved" than their American English-speaking counterparts (see also Clancy, Thompson, Suzuki, and Tao, frth.).[17] We would not argue against the view that high social involvement is one of the goals of this kind of interaction; but we would like to suggest that it could also have a function related to the nature of Japanese syntax and its effect on turn-taking. That is, if we are correct that the beginnings of TCUs in Japanese do not provide the recipient with much information about how the utterance is going to proceed, then it makes sense for speakers to produce relatively short PPUs whose interactional implications the recipient can acknowledge or question as the speaker works on a larger turn (exactly what happens with multi-TCU turns in English). This allows the recipient to acknowledge small pieces without having to know exactly where the speaker is going with the full turn (see Iwasaki and Tao, 1993, for similar findings).

Maynard also found that smooth speaker transition tends to occur significantly more often at a point of grammatical completion followed by a *pause* than at other possible points. We feel that this, too, is indirect evidence for our claim, in the following way.

We have claimed that English recipients are able to use the beginning of a TCU to project a possible course for that utterance, while Japanese recipients "wait and see" how the utterance develops. It is thus possible that English recipients are able to predict with such accuracy how the utterance-under-construction will come to an end that they are able to plan their own utterance to start up exactly at the moment the current utterance comes to a possible completion point (this is, in fact, the claim made by Sacks et al. (1974) with regard to turn-taking in English conversation), with no pause between the end of the current turn and the start-up of their own turn. In Japanese, on the other hand, since recipients are not able to make such detailed predictions about the course of the current utterance, they wait until they hear the last few syllables of the turn (which often contain such "ending signals" as final particles, or special completion-relevant verb forms) before starting their own utterance.

It is also possible that final particles evolved at least in part to help manage this facet of Japanese conversation, that is, to serve as an overt indication of a point of possible completion of a turn. In a language in which early syntactic projection is not facilitated by the syntax, it makes sense that speakers would tend to be end-oriented rather than beginning-oriented, and would provide overt ending cues.[18] We would argue that conversational English tends to be beginning-oriented, in contrast with conversational Japanese.

We have seen so far that the beginning of TCUs carries with it different interactional possibilities in English than in Japanese. In fact, it is possible that TCU beginning, or "turn beginning," is not an interactional object in Japanese the way it is in English. This fact suggests a possible motivation for English speakers' return to the subject in some cases of recycling, while Japanese speakers stay within local constituents for recycling: in English, the beginning of the clause is a coherent syntactic and interactional object from which a re-projection for the entire clause can be made; whereas in Japanese the beginning of the clause may not be syntactically knit to what follows in the clause, and would not be the site of re-projection. In Japanese, projection may be done much more bit-by-bit than it typically is in English, and the organization of recycling reflects this fact.

Of course, at this stage of our research these suggestions on the organization of turn-taking in Japanese are merely speculations; extensive conversation analysis needs to be undertaken in Japanese to determine their actual predictive power.

4.4.4 Summary

In this section we have provided evidence (a) that the organization of repair differs across the two languages we examined, and (b) that this difference arises, at least in part, from differences in the syntactic practices available to speakers of each language in managing the functions typically associated with repair. In a sense, then, we have been exploring the ways in which syntactic practices constrain the organization of repair. In the following section, we explore another facet of the complex relationship between syntax and repair in examining how repair expands the syntactic practices available to speakers of a language.

4.5 Repairing limited resources

So far we have taken the view that the syntactic practices of a language shape the organization of repair. In this section we provide evidence that the shaping is not unidirectional; repair also serves as a resource for expanding the range of syntactic practices engaged in by speakers of a language by enabling them to create two different syntactic projections within a single TCU that otherwise could not be "grammatically" united before reaching a Transition Relevance Place (TRP; see Sacks, Schegloff, and Jefferson, 1974). We will consider one instance of this reprojection from each language.

4.5.1 English

Consider the following passage, taken from a transcript of a conversation between two couples, at the home of one of the couples (B and T are visiting H and C). H has been relating her traumatic past experiences as a young white teacher in an inner city school. B, who at the time of the conversation is teaching English as a Second

Language at a nearby university, relates a similar story of "getting shit" from a student in his class. The utterance we will focus on in our discussion of repair is B's *look, challenge yourself by asking me* continue to ask me hard questions.*[19]

(60)

    B: It's a little bit diff'rince from Japa:n.=

         =Ha:hn.

    T: (H)e( ) ((continues into beginning of H's telling below))

         [

    H: A(H)A(h)ahaha // .hhe::: .hhe:=

    B: Hehehe

    H: =W'll my experience was a bit diff'rent from (0.3) probably (0.5) most (.) Ame:rican.=

         =PLUS I don't- (0.4) -I: >think they probably< show more respect to somebody

         who (.) loo:ked older::, a:cts older::, .hh and has a mor:e um traditional type

         classroom=>I was< very:: BLUNT- an' (0.3) yu'kno:w

    B: tch

              (0.3)

    B: I: get (.) shi:t from a German (0.3) student in my cla:ss: (0.4) becuz I look younger than

         he- I don't think he thinks I'm as old as .hh

    H: You a:re

    B: I am. But I know if lik- like I looked older had greying hai:r or something,

         (0.5) •I would//n' get it.

    H: ↑Doesn't that* bug you?=

    B: =↑NOT- It's NOT shi:t >it's more of a< .hh // He doesn't kno::w what's::: (0.2) ↓culturally

         oka:y.=

    H: He's not respectful.

    B: = >B'cuz< (.) German culture'z a little bit diff'rent.=

    C: =It's very rou:gh.

    H: It's very respe:ct oriented too:: isn't it?

         ·

         ·

    C: No but dyu dyu dyu fee:l dyu fee:l like he's atta:cking,? >when'e< asks

         questio:ns?

```
        (0.6)
   C:  Is tha:t what it is?
        (0.7)
   B:  At fir:st I did but then later I just said loo:k, (0.7) since y'r so g(oo)-  ↓'cuz he
       is the bes:t student in the cla:ss, ↓'cuz one reason is th't he speaks a//n
       IndoEuropean language?
   T:  Y'mean-
   T:  (not) right no:w?
   B:  ↑Ye:s right now!=A:nd (0.5) he um (4.0) he uh: (0.2) ↓He was getting bored
⇒     >so I said< ↑loo:k, challenge yourself by asking me (0.4) continue to ask me
⇒     hard questions.>But wh't< FIR:st .hhhhh he was like challenging me.
```

B's utterance *look, challenge yourself by asking me* continue to ask me hard questions* is created through the use of repair: B appears to reformulate his first try, *challenge yourself by asking me* to *continue to ask me hard questions*. But we have found in analyzing this sequence that the second try is not meant to replace or correct the first try. Rather, we would like to argue that both parts of B's utterance do important work in managing the interaction at that point, and that in fact B is making use of repair to accomplish several competing interactional goals before reaching a TRP.

Recall that, according to Sacks, Schegloff, and Jefferson (1974), the turn-taking system of English conversation, and perhaps of conversation in all cultures/languages, initially allots one TCU to each current speaker.

Earlier in the passage B tells a story that is offered as an appreciation of H's earlier story about her difficult experiences in the classroom. H says that her students would have shown more respect to someone who *looked older, acts older*, than to her. B's story, in appreciating H's, makes a similar point: he "gets shit" from a student, and if he *looked older, had greying hair or something* he wouldn't *get it* (see Fox and Jasperson, frth., for a detailed analysis of this segment).

But the assessment of the student's behavior cast by the term *shit* comes to be seen as problematic in the interaction, as is evidenced by the ensuing series of attempts by B (and others) to correct the situation. B's first attempt is done as an explicit denial of that word choice: *Not, it's NOT shit,* followed by an explanation which proposes that the student comes from a different culture and so does not understand what kind of behavior is *culturally okay* here (in a part of the US).

A next attempt at mitigating the negative assessment of the student's behavior occurs in a story told in response to a question from C, repeated here:

B: At fir̲:st I did but then la̲ter I just said lo̲o:k, (0.7) since y'r so g(oo)- ↓'cuz he

    is the bes:t student in the cla:ss, ↓'cuz one reason is th't he speaks a//n

    IndoEuropean la̲nguage?

Here the student is praised as *the best student in the class*, although some of the value of this assessment is rescinded by the reason for the student's skill – he speaks a language closely related to English, a fact more about where he grew up than about his intelligence or hard work.

There are then two more attempts. One accounts for the student's behavior as a result of his boredom. The next occurs at the location of the repair with which we are concerned here.

B: A:nd (0.5) he um (4.0) he uh: (0.2) ↓He was getting bored

⇒   >so I said< ↑loo:k, cha̲llenge yourself by a̲sking me (0.4) conti̲nue to ask me

⇒   hard questions.>But wh't< FIR:st .hhhhh he was like cha̲llenging me.

B's emerging turn, describing how B handled the student, has revealed one more opportunity to address the problematic assessment. The repair at this location permits the addition of material which recasts "getting shit" as being asked "hard questions." It is legitimate for students to ask hard questions, not give shit.

B initially gains the floor in this segment through being selected by C with the question *dyou feel like he's attacking?* B's response, *at first I did*, projects an extended turn: one TCU for what happened "at first" and a second for what happened "later." Notice that the second TCU is self-interrupted twice with non-final kinds of clauses (started with *'cuz*), which are warranted here by their embedded status. In fact, the second TCU that B starts, *later I just said look, since y'r so g(oo)-*, is never completed; instead, after getting the floor again by answering T's question *(not) right now?* B starts with a new formulation of the second TCU. After *he was getting bored*, he uses a rush through (Schegloff, 1982) to secure the complex TCU we are concerned with here: *so I said look, challenge yourself by asking me* * *continue to ask me hard questions.*

Now we can ask: why does B initially start with *challenge yourself by asking me...* He has characterized the student as "getting bored," and his intervention with the student is obviously intended at least as a remedy for the boredom. One way to remedy boredom, in a classroom, is for the student to be challenged more, either by more difficult material from the instructor, or by more interesting interaction between the student and instructor. B offers the latter here, by suggesting the student challenge himself in the interaction – by asking B... And here is where repair comes in to play. B has projected an utterance which will be possibly complete after the production of an object of the verb *ask*. But the formulation of the object now presents a problem: if B says "challenge yourself by asking me hard questions," he implies that the student should change his behavior from whatever he was doing before to asking hard questions. But then that suggests that the student was not asking hard questions before; what was the student doing, then, that was so aggravating that B characterized it as "getting shit"? It must be something worse than asking "hard questions," but since B has been very concerned with mitigating the force of *get shit*, he presumably does not want to suggest now that the student was doing something worse than asking hard questions (what could be worse student behavior than asking hard questions if not disruptive, obnoxious, shit-like, behavior?). So if B finishes this TCU with "hard questions," he will be heard, potentially, as reinforcing, rather than mitigating, his earlier negative assessment.

At this point, before the object of *ask* is produced, B initiates repair. He appears to restart this clause, this time with a non-change of state verb: *continue*. By using a non-change of state verb, B equates the student's past behavior (previously characterized as giving shit) with the desired future behavior (now characterized as asking "hard questions"). *Continue to ask me hard questions* thus addresses the problem of *shit*, in recharacterizing *shit* as "hard questions." The non-change of state verb does not, however, address the student's boredom: if the student continues with the same behavior, he will presumably continue to be bored.

It is for this reason that we believe B intends his recipient to hear the whole utterance, not just the repairing segment; the first formulation crucially addresses the issue of the student's boredom by suggesting a *change*, and the second formulation crucially addresses the prior negative assessment of the student's behavior by recharacterizing it as asking "hard questions." Both parts are thus needed in the interaction, and B must produce both parts without completing the first formulation and before reaching a TRP (at which point one of the other parties present could begin to speak). The precise placement of the repair initiation and the nature of the second formulation allow B to accomplish both of these goals. Repair thus allows B to create two different syntactic projections with different goals within a single TCU.

One could ask at this juncture why B didn"t use some kind of complex syntactic construction which would have allowed him to grammatically unite both parts. We suggest that no such construction presents itself in English. Consider the following possibilities:

(61) Look, challenge yourself by asking me hard questions, which is what you've been doing

(62) Look, challenge yourself by asking me hard questions, as you've been doing

(63) Look, challenge yourself and continue to ask me hard questions

(64) Look, continue to ask me hard questions and challenge yourself

(65) Look, challenge yourself by continuing to ask me hard questions

All of these would fail for B's purposes. All but (64) seem contradictory given the change of state implied by *challenge* and the non-change of state implied by *continue*; if the student is just doing what he was doing before, and he was bored before, then how is this a new challenge? (64) seems to suggest that the student should continue to ask hard questions and then do something else to challenge himself, but that something else is left unspecified, so this statement would not be much help as a suggestion to the student.

We believe these nicely integrated constructions fail exactly because they are too integrated: they do not capture the tension between continuing and changing that is beautifully managed by B's real utterance. By using repair, B allows the interpretation that the second try is in fact a *second* try, a redoing of the first and not necessarily a smooth continuation of the first. But because the recipient will not erase the first formulation from his/her memory, the first formulation also stands. Both parts are allowed to stand, and they are not required to exist in some consistent syntactico-semantic relation to each other.

As a syntactic device, then, repair provides B with a mechanism for creating what from a traditional perspective looks like a spliced utterance which could not otherwise be licensed by the syntax of English. Repair thus expands the syntactic possibilities present for B; in fact, we would claim that repair in general expands the syntactic possibilities present for speakers of any language. Below we discuss a similar example from Japanese.

4.5.2 Japanese

Consider the following passage from our Japanese corpus, where H and T are talking about the sister of their mutual friend Fukaya (the repair in question appears at line 7, marked by an arrow):

(66)

```
1. T: ikutsu   nandesu ka?      imootosan      tte.=
      how.old  be        question younger.sister quotative
      'How old is (this) younger sister?'

2. H: =imootosan::    wa     nijuu:::
       younger.sister TOP    twenty::
       'She is twenty::'

3. T: aa sonnani // ookii no          ka:.
      oh that.much  big   nominalizer  FP
      'Oh, that big. (I didn't know that she is as old as you just said)'
```

4. H: go?

    five

    '... five.'

5.   (0.5)

6. T: nijuu   <u>go</u>:?

    twenty five

    'Twenty five?'

⇒ 7. H: de   mata ne: (.) taikaku   mo Fukaya yori: dek-* (0.8) a<u>shi</u> wa   sukunakutomo

    and also FP   body   also Fukaya than bi-   leg TOP at.least

    Fukaya yori: nagai no. // hhh

    Fukaya than long   FP

    'And also, (her) body is bi-, at least (her) legs are longer than Fukaya's.'

8. T: a:::n a! // ookii ( ).

    hmm oh   big

    'Hmm. Oh (she is) big.'

1. T: How old is this younger sister?

2. H: She is twenty

3. T: Oh, that // big?

4. H: five

5.   (0.5)

6. T: Twenty five?

⇒ 7. H: And also, her body is also than Fukaya bi- at least her legs are longer than Fukaya's.//

    hhh

8. T: Hmm. Oh she is big.

In this fragment, H and T are discussing the sister of their mutual friend Fukaya. In line 1, T asks H how old this sister is. H replies with *nijuu go* "twenty five," and T expresses in line 3 her surprise at this age – twenty-five is unexpectedly older than she had thought. In fact, T seems to have thought that the sister was even under twenty years old, as can be seen by the fact that she starts responding right after H produces *nijuu* "twenty". What is important here is that T uses the word *ookii* to describe the unexpected age of Fukaya's sister. *Ookii* literally means "big," but it can also be used to refer to the age of young people (as can *big* in English).

Since T uses *ookii* in line 3 in response to H's description of the age of Fukaya's sister, *ookii* here is obviously not meant to refer to the physical size of Fukaya's sister. However, H's subsequent utterance in line 6, which actually introduces the topic of the sister's physical size, is produced in a way which displays its connection to the use of *ookii* in line 3. Notice that the particle *mo* "also" marks the subject *taikaku* "body" in line 7. *Mo* indicates addition to what has been expressed previously. Although the predicate of the sentence that contains *mo* in line 7 was cut off and abandoned in the middle, it appears that it was going to be *dekai* "big," which is a slang equivalent of *ookii*. From these facts it is clear that H's talk about the sister's physical size in line 7 is built in a way that anchors it in the prior use of *ookii* as its source.

H begins the utterance at line 7 by talking about the sister's *taikaku*, "body." But right before he completes the predicate adjective, at the end of which he would reach a TRP, he initiates repair and reformulates his statement about the physical size of the sister by specifying a part of her body ("legs"). What is the significance of this repair?

First of all, the repair may have been initiated just to correct an incorrect statement and thereby avoid a possible misunderstanding. The word *taikaku* here refers to the size of the sister's body (in both vertical and horizontal dimensions). After H produces *taikaku*, he uses the comparative *Fukaya yori* "than Fukaya." So it appears, when he starts to produce the adjective *dekai* "big," that he is saying that the sister is actually physically bigger than Fukaya (notice that in Japanese the comparative phrase occurs before the adjective, while in English the comparative phrase occurs after the adjective: *Fukaya yori dekai* "bigger **than Fukaya**").

de mata ne: taikaku   mo Fukaya yori: dek-*

and also FP body   also Fukaya than bi-*

'and also she is than Fukaya bi-' or 'and also she is bigger than Fukaya'

But later in the conversation H suggests that the sister is in fact shorter than Fukaya by two or three centimeters (line 14 in Appendix 1), and it can also be inferred, from another part of H's talk about her, that she is not wider than her brother, either (cf. the story H initiates at line 21). So the utterance he appears to be producing is factually incorrect: Fukaya's sister is not bigger than Fukaya. It is therefore possible that this repair is an instance of error correction; and as Schegloff, Jefferson, and Sacks (1977) point out, repair within the same TCU as the repairable (as in line 7) is the preferred locus of error correction.

Although this repair may indeed be a case of error correction, the repair accomplishes interactional goals beyond simple error correction. As we argued above, the repaired segment (*dek-*) functions as a warranted way of introducing the physical size of the sister, by linking it to the preceding topic, the sister's age.

That is, if H had started with the "corrected" statement about the length of the sister's legs, he would not have been able to use the predicative adjective *dekai* or *ookii*, because *ashi* "leg" requires a different predicate adjective (such as *nagai* "long," which in fact is chosen by H in the repairing segment).[20] And if *dekai* or *ookii* cannot be used, the introduction of physical size would not be warranted by the preceding utterance by T at line 3, in which she uses the word *ookii*, because it is this lexical item that H utilized to build his utterance in a way that creates coherence between the two topics. Moreover, "leg" is too specific a comment about physical size given that the level of generality in the preceding utterances was at the level of "age"; that is, it would probably be odd to go directly from talking about the sister's age to the length of her legs. From these observations we can conclude that the repairable (*dek-*) plays a significant role in creating coherence with the preceding utterances which warrants getting a mentionable mentioned at this moment in the interaction.

Also, H's formulation of the repairable in line 7 accomplishes another piece of interactional work – managing the talk in the turn so as to "get what needs to be said said before the end of the first unit's completion" (Schegloff, 1982:75). "What needs to be said" in our case is the somewhat unusual, and possibly funny, fact that the younger sister has longer legs than Fukaya.[21] Now, the turn at line 7 is not constructed in such a way that attempts to achieve a multi-unit turn (e.g. through the use of devices such as story-preface; see Schegloff, 1982), and thus there is a systematic basis for H to complete the talk about the "funny tellable" before he reaches a TRP, where the current non-speaker T may start up. In the present case, H accomplishes this interactional goal by exploiting the occasion of error-correction.

To see how this interactional work is achieved through the repair in line 7, let us reconsider possible reasons why repair may get initiated at this point in the turn's talk. We have suggested that one source of the problem with the repairable is the connotations that the word *taikaku* conveys. As mentioned above, it refers to both vertical and horizontal dimensions of the human body, and by using this word, the speaker could be heard as speaking of, for instance, how fat this sister is. We then argue that one plausible reason for initiating repair is to cancel this possible interpretation. This analysis is grounded in the fact that H is concerned only with the vertical dimension of the sister's body (height, length of legs) in the repairing segment as well as in his subsequent talk about this topic (see Appendix 1).[22]

Now, consider another aspect of the problem with the repairable. Notice that it contains the comparative phrase *Fukaya yori* "than Fukaya" in it. In Japanese, a comparative sentence and its non-comparative counterpart differ only in the presence of a comparative phrase, as in the following:

a.   taikaku   mo   **Fukaya yori** dekai

      body   also Fukaya   than   big

      'She is also bigger than Fukaya.'

b.   taikaku   mo   dekai

      body   also big

      'She is also big.'

Considering the fact that the sister is more than one hundred seventy centimeters tall (lines 9 - 11 in Appendix 1), which may be considered "big" by Japanese standards, the statement in (b) above may not be so problematic as (a), which is factually incorrect. In other words, it could be argued that it is the presence of the comparative phrase that makes the repairable in line 7 problematic.

One possible way of repairing this aspect of the problem of the repairable, then, could be to cancel the comparative sense conveyed by the inclusion of *Fukaya yori*, by saying something like the following, which does not have a comparative phrase in it (the replacement of *taikaku* with *se* "height" is intended to cancel the problematic connotation of the former discussed above):

taikaku	mo	Fukaya	yori	dek-*	**se**	**mo**	**sugoku**	**takain**	**da**	**yo**.
body	also	Fukaya	than	bi-	height	also	very	high	be	FP

[Translation of the bold-face part]: 'She is also very tall.'

Notice, however, that, instead of canceling the comparative sense, H in fact chooses to construct the repairing segment in such a way that retains the comparative phrase *Fukaya yori*. That is, his formulation of the repairing segment orients to elaborating on the comparative sense by mentioning the specific body part (*ashi* "legs") for which he is sure that the comparative sense he has introduced in the repaired segment holds. *Sukunakutomo* "at least" indicates this move of H's clearly. Why he chooses this move rather than canceling the comparative sense appears to stem from the funniness (at least to H) and the "tellability" of the fact that the sister has longer legs than Fukaya, for the telling of which, the presence of the comparative sense is crucial. A ground for arguing that not only we analysts but also H *himself* finds this fact funny and worth telling is found in H's subsequent attempts to elaborate on it and re-tell it in the form of a story whose punchline is to reveal this fact (see lines 21–27 in Appendix 1).

As we argued above, H's first attempt to launch into the telling of this "funny tellable" in line 7 is done without devices that warrant a multi-unit turn, and thus a systematic orientation to finishing the telling in a single TCU operates at this moment in the interaction. H then effectively exploits the occasion of error-correction to accomplish this task – since the repaired segment has already established coherence with the prior topic, H can use the opportunity of repair to get a mentionable mentioned in a way that anchors it in the prior usage of *Fukaya yori* as its source. At the same time, he brings in the specific part of the body (*ashi* "legs") and the predicate adjective (*nagai* "long"), which could not have been introduced in the repaired segment, and which are part of the essence of the funniness of the fact that H is to mention before relinquishing the floor.

The complex utterance at line 7 created by syntactic reprojection thus allows H to accomplish two goals before reaching a TRP: he can introduce a new topic in a way coherent with the preceding one; and he can get a mentionable mentioned before yielding the floor.

4.5.3 Summary

In this section we have argued that repair is not just constrained by the syntactic organization of a language, but in fact serves as a resource for expanding the syntactic possibilities present to a speaker at a given moment in an interaction. We believe this to be true for speakers of English and Japanese, and perhaps to speakers of all languages, making it possible for them to achieve multiple goals before reaching an interactionally vulnerable locus – a TRP. Speakers can thus use repair to create utterances whose interactive achievements would not be possible within the limits of "normal" syntax in a given language at a given moment in time.

This function of repair has, to the best of our knowledge, not been described before; it seems to us to be significant in at least two ways: first, it demonstrates the deep relationships between grammar and interaction; and second, it raises interesting questions concerning the domain and units of syntax (e.g. should a whole repair utterance be considered a single construction?).

4.6 Conclusions

In this study we have explored the ways in which repair is shaped by the syntactic practices of the speakers of a language, and, to a lesser extent, the ways in which repair shapes these practices. This mutual influence is already a recurrent theme in the research on interaction and grammar (e.g. see Goodwin, 1981; Fox, 1987; Ford, 1993; Ochs, 1988; Ochs and Schieffelin, 1989; Ono and Thompson, frth.; Geluykens, 1987; Schegloff, this volume; Ford and Thompson, this volume); the cross-linguistic methodology adopted here merely makes the influence more striking.

We were particularly excited by the possibility that the syntactic organization of different languages might affect their deep interactional workings, for example, the mechanisms by which speaker transition is accomplished in those languages. So although we started with the possibility that repair is influenced by the syntactic practices of speakers of a language, we may have found an even deeper connection between interaction and grammar: the heart of interactionality – multiple speaking parties – may be the locus of the workings of the grammar of a language. The importance of this possible relationship between interaction and grammar cannot be overstated – it lies at the center of our understanding of grammar and of interaction. It suggests that those of us interested in interaction must also turn our attention to the specifics of the languages whose conversations we analyze, and it suggests that those of us interested in grammar cannot avoid the interactional functions which those patterned practices we call "syntax" have evolved to serve. It clearly calls for empirical testing on a wide range of languages.

Moreover, this possible relationship between interaction and grammar calls into question our common understanding of syntax as a set of structures which can be deployed in a discourse (see also Hopper, 1987, 1988). If it is true, as we suspect, that interaction and syntax are not in fact separable but are rather different ways of looking at the same phenomenon, we may be better off thinking of syntax as a "hermeneutic for interpretation" (a term suggested to us by Stephen Tyler), and interaction as the occasion for that interpretation. This view of syntax recasts the academic fields of conversation analysis and syntactic analysis as essentially the same enterprise, with different foci of course, depending on the interests of the analyst. And it allows us to see how, for participants in a conversation, they might be one and the same.

Appendix 1

The following are the lines subsequent to lines 1 - 8 in 5.2.

9. H: hyaku   nanajuu:: ne::,
      one.hundred seventy   FP
      'One hundred and seventy-...'

10. T: e::   //II   na::::.
       oh   good FP
       'Oh, I envy her.'

11. H: ikuts(u)- (0.2) gurai   arun   (da   yo) tashika (0.3) imootosan.
       something   about exist be   FP   I'm.sure   younger.sister
       'She's about [one hundred seventy-] something in height, I'm sure, his younger sister.'
12.   (0.5)

13. T: sonnani toshi ga   chikaino ka//::.
       such   age   SUBJ close   question
       'I didn't know she was that close in age to him.'

14. H: u:n   DE:: shichoo mo   ni   san   senchi   shika tashika   chigawanai
       yeah and   height   also two three centimeter only   I'm.sure different:not
       ka   gura//i nanda yo.
       question about   be   FP

       'Yeah, and (her) height is also only two or three centimeters different from his.'

15. T: sugo::i   ookii   ne.=
       amazing big   FP
       'Amazing. She is tall.'

16. H: =de: (.) sooshitara sa::,=
       and   then   FP
       'And then,'

17. T: =u::n.

    uh.huh

    'Uh huh.'

18. H: ano e- e- (.) tto kore wa moo koo<u>koo</u>   no   toki no   hanashi ka   na

    uhm well   this TOP now high.school GEN time GEN story   question FP

    // daigaku no   koro no   hanashi ka   wasureta kedo // sa,

       college GEN time GEN story   question forgot   but   FP

    'Uhm, well, I forgot if this is an episode from our high school days or from our

    college days, but ... '

19. T: u::n.

    uh.huh

    'Uh huh'

20. T: un.

    uh. huh

    'Uh huh'

21. H: sono imootosan   ga   sa: Fukaya no   sa nanka sa ji- jiipan ka nanka

    that younger.sister SUBJ FP Fukaya GEN FP like   FP je- jeans or something

    // sa: .hhh koo nanka // koo:: hako- // machigaete ka nanka   SHIRANAI

       FP   uhm like   uhm put.on by.mistake or something know.not

    KEDO ha- haite   tara   sa:,

    but   pu- put.on when FP

    'That younger sister put on Fukaya's je- jeans or something- I don't know if

    um, well, (she did so) by mistake, but when she was pu- putting (them) on,'

22. T: u::n

    uh.huh

    'Uh huh'

23. T: II   na::

    good FP

    'I envy her'

24. T: atashi nanka zettai hakenai.   un.

    I   TOP ever wear.cannot. yeah

    'I can never wear. yeah'

25. H: nani yo kore toka   itte. konna   deteta // tok(h)a itte.

    what FP this quotative say this.much stick.out quotative say

    '"What is this!" she says. Her legs stuck out (of the jeans) this much'

26. T: ah hah hah hah

27. H: nande konna   mijikai zubon // haiten no toka   iwarete (   ) toka   sa:,

    why   like.this short pants   wear P quotative be.said   quotative FP

    'She says, "Why do you wear such short pants?"'

28. T: ie::::::::

    wow
    'Wow!'

Notes

1 We would like to thank Sandra Thompson and Emanuel Schegloff for
very helpful comments on earlier versions of this paper. We would also
like to thank John Du Bois, Charles and Marjorie Harness Goodwin,
and Emanuel Schegloff for the use of their transcripts. Thanks also to
Graeme Hirst, Ed Hovy, Willem Levelt, and Elizabeth Shriberg for
providing much needed assistance in finding literature on repair in
Psycholinguistics and Computational Linguistics. We are also grateful
for comments offered by an anonymous reviewer. Transcription conventions are described in the glossary.
2 We use the term recipient in this study to refer to the hearer of the
utterance, for whom the utterance was designed.
3 By recycling we mean the repeating, either with no apparent changes
or with some additions or deletions, of the repaired segment. Recycling
is thus a subtype of repair (see Schegloff, 1987a).

4 In an attempt to make this study accessible to a wide range of scholars in diverse disciplines, we have tried to write it as much as possible in non-technical language. In cases where we thought that technical terms from linguistics or conversation analysis would make the discussion clearer, we have defined those terms as early in the discussion as possible (in some instances this means the definition appears in a footnote). Given the rather technical nature of the subject matter, it would be impossible for us to eliminate all technical jargon from a discussion like the present one, but we have tried to keep it as readable as we could. Any failings in this area, as in any other, are our own. We ask the reader's patience with the definition of basic terms from their fields.

5 The terms "repaired segment" and "repairing segment" relate to the terms "repairable/trouble source" and "repair segment" of Schegloff, Jefferson, and Sacks (1977). A repaired segment contains the repairable or trouble source, and a repair-accomplishing repairing segment is just a repair segment.

6 We would like to thank Ryoko Suzuki and Tsuyoshi Ono for the use of their conversational data. The Japanese data used as the basis for this study represent a range of varieties, including Tokyo and Kansai.

7 Case marker and other abbreviations used in the glosses are:
   SUBJ = subject
   OBJ = direct object
   LOC = locative
   GEN = genitive
   TOP = topic
   OBL = oblique
   FP = final particle
   NEG = negative

8 The grammatical relationship "genitive" is roughly equivalent to certain uses in English of the preposition *of*, as in *The door **of the building***.

9 Complement clauses can also be subjects of clauses, but we will not focus on these here.

10 Morphology is the domain of morphemes, which are the smallest units of meaning in any language. Morphemes are typically either free, in which case they can usually occupy a variety of positions in an utterance, or they are bound, in which case they are attached to another kind of morpheme. For example, the morpheme *-s* in English is a bound morpheme – it cannot occur by itself and must be attached to either a noun (if it is the plural marker) or a verb (if it marks third person singular present tense). In this discussion we are focusing on bound morphemes.

11 Bybee (1985) provides confirming evidence for this in her cross-linguistic examination of where verb markers occur with regard to the verb stem. She found that the more relevant a verb marker was to the

meaning of a verb, the more likely it was to be (a) closer to the verb stem, and (b) phonologically fused with the verb stem.

12 The term "lexical part" is being used in contrast to grammatical morphemes such as articles and adpositions, and would include pre-nominal adjectives though we were not able to consider these. In some sense, lexical items are more contributionally consequential, semantically richer, and perhaps possibly less available (e.g., during word searches) than the more restricted class of grammatical morphemes.

13 We have tried to translate the repairs in the English free glosses; such translations are obviously only approximations to the original repair.

14 Example (43) may in fact involve a delay in the production of the whole idiomatic chunk, *take something through the mill*, as is evidenced by the utterance-final marker which references it, *so to speak*.

15 But see Fox and Jasperson (frth.) for important possible restrictions on the delay of just post-verbal items in English.

16 Verb phrases turn out to be an exception to this pattern (see Fox and Jasperson, in press, for a discussion of this fact).

17 In her comparative study of American English and Japanese conversation, Maynard found that Japanese speakers use roughly twice as many back-channels as do their English-speaking counterparts (Maynard, 1989).

18 Maynard's comments on this topic resonate with our own:

The fact that the Japanese language provides for devices such as final particles not only at the end of the sentence but also sentence-internally makes it possible to make [sic?] overtly the potential moments for back-channel expressions. (1989: 173)

19 Fox and Jasperson (frth.) discuss another repaired utterance from the same part of this conversation.

20 The utterance

Ashi mo Fukaya yori dekai
foot also Fukaya than big

has a different meaning than the one H wants to convey, since it means that the sister's feet are bigger than Fukaya's feet. This is because *ashi* can mean both "leg" and "foot," but when it is used with *dekai* "big," it almost always means "foot."

21 To elaborate on possible reasons why this fact is tellable, we may note at least the following: (1) culturally (at least for many young people) having short legs is considered embarrassing; (2) men are usually thought to be taller than women, and consequently to have longer legs; (3) since the society respects age differences (even age differences of only a few years), incidents showing that a younger person is in some ways superior to an older person can be worth telling. Thus, although Fukaya is male, older than his sister, and actually two or three centimeters taller than she, what gets told in the repairing seg-

ment reveals that he has shorter legs than she does, which is embarrassing to him and funny to other people.

22 This point was brought to our attention by Tomoyo Takagi.

References

Auer, Peter (1996). On the prosody and syntax of turn-continuations. In Elizabeth Couper-Kuhlen and Margaret Selting (eds.), *Prosody in Conversation*. Cambridge: Cambridge University Press.

Bear, J., Dowding, J., and Shriberg, E. (1992). Integrating multiple knowledge sources for detection and correction of repairs in human-computer dialog. In *Proceedings of the Association of Computational Linguistics*.

Blackmer, E. and Mitton, J. (1991). Theories of monitoring and the timing of repairs in spontaneous speech. *Cognition* 39: 173–94.

Brazil, David (1985). Phonology: intonation in discourse. In Teun A. van Dijk, (ed.), *Handbook of Discourse Analysis* volume 2: *Dimensions of Discourse*. London: Academic Press.

Bredart, S. (1991). Word interruption in self-repairing. *Journal of Psycholinguistic Research* 20: 123–38.

Bybee, J. (1985). *Morphology: A Study of the Relation Between Meaning and Form*. Amsterdam: John Benjamins.

Carbonell, J. and Hayes, P. (1983). Recovery strategies for parsing extra-grammatical language. *American Journal of Computational Linguistics* 9: 123–46.

Chafe, W. (1987). Cognitive constraints on information flow. In R. Tomlin (ed.) *Coherence and Grounding in Discourse*, pp. 21–51. Amsterdam: John Benjamins.

(1994). *Discourse, Consciousness, and Time*. Chicago: University of Chicago Press.

Clancy, P. (1982). Written and spoken style in Japanese narratives. In D. Tannen (eds.) *Spoken and Written Language*, pp. 55–76. Norwood, New Jersey: Ablex.

Clancy, P., Thompson, S., Suzuki, R., and Tao, H. (frth.). The conversational use of reactive tokens in English, Japanese, and Mandarin. *Journal of Pragmatics*.

Couper-Kuhlen, E. (1992). Contextualizing discourse: the prosody of interactive repair. In P. Auer and A. di Luzio (eds.) *The Contextualization of Language*, pp. 337–64. Amsterdam: John Benjamins.

Du Bois, J. (1974). Syntax in mid-sentence. In C. Fillmore, G. Lakoff, and R. Lakoff (eds.) *Berkeley Studies in Syntax and Semantics, I*. III, pp. 1–25. Berkeley: Department of Linguistics and Institute of Human Learning, University of California.

Foley, W. and van Valin, R. (1984). *Functional Syntax and Universal Grammar*. Cambridge: Cambridge University Press.

Ford, C. E. (1993). *Grammar in Interaction: Adverbial Clauses in American English Conversations.* Cambridge: Cambridge University Press.

Ford, C. E. and Mori, J. (1994). Causal markers in Japanese and English conversations: a cross-linguistic study of interactional grammar. *Pragmatics* 4: 31–61.

Ford, Cecilia E., Fox, Barbara A. and Thompson, Sandra A. In preparation. Practices in the construction of turns: the "TCU" revisited.

Fox, B. (1987). *Discourse Structure and Anaphora.* Cambridge: Cambridge University Press.

—— (1994). Contextualization, indexicality, and the distributed nature of grammar. *Language Sciences* 16: 1–37.

Fox, B. and Jasperson, R. (frth.). A syntactic exploration of repair in English conversation. In P. Davis (ed.) *Descriptive and Theoretical Modes in the Alternative Linguistics.* Amsterdam: John Benjamins.

Fox, B. and Thompson, S. (1990). A discourse explanation of the grammar of relative clauses in English conversation. *Language* 66: 297–316.

Geluykens, R. (1987). Tails (right dislocations) as a repair mechanism in English conversation. In J. Nuyts and G. de Schutter (eds.) *Getting One's Words into Line: On Word Order and Functional Grammar,* pp. 119–29. Dordrecht: Foris.

Givón, T. (1993). *English Grammar: A Function-based Introduction.* Amsterdam: John Benjamins.

Good, D. (1990). Repair and cooperation in conversation. In P. Luff, N. Gilbert, and D. Frohlich (eds.) *Computers and Conversation,* pp. 133–50. London: Academic Press.

Goodwin, C. (1981). *Conversational Organization.* New York: Academic Press.

Halliday, M.A.K. (1967). *Intonation and Grammar in British English.* The Hague: Mouton.

Hayashi, M. (1994). A comparative study of self-repair in English and Japanese conversation. In N. Akatsuka (ed.) *Japanese/Korean Linguistics, vol. IV*: 77–93. Stanford: CSLI.

Hindle, D. (1983). Deterministic parsing of syntactic non-fluencies. In *Proceedings of the Association of Computational Linguistics.*

Hinds, J. (1982). *Ellipsis in Japanese.* Carbondale and Edmonton, Canada: Linguistic Research, Inc.

Hockett, C. (1967). Where the tongue slips, there slip I. In *To honor Roman Jakobson,* pp. 910–36. The Hague: Mouton.

Hopper, P. (1987). Emergent grammar. *Proceedings of the Berkeley Linguistic Society* 13: 139–57.

—— (1988). Emergent grammar and the A Priori Grammar postulate. In D. Tannen (ed.) *Linguistics in Context,* pp. 117–34. Norwood, NJ: Ablex.

Houtkoop, Hanneke, and Mazeland, Harrie (1985). Turns and discourse units in everyday conversation. *Journal of Pragmatics* 9: 595–619.

Iwasaki, S. (1993). The structure of the intonation unit in Japanese. In S. Choi (ed.) *Japanese/Korean Linguistics, vol. III.* Stanford: CSLI.

Iwasaki, S. and Tao, H. (1993). A comparative study of the structure of the intonation unit in English, Japanese, and Mandarin Chinese. Paper presented at the LSA Annual Meeting.

Jefferson, G. (1974). Error correction as an interactional resource. *Language in Society* 2: 188–99.

(1987). On exposed and embedded correction in conversation. In G. Button and J. R. E. Lee (eds.) *Talk and Social Organization*, pp. 86-100. Clevedon: Multilingual Matters.

Kuno, S. (1973). *The Structure of the Japanese Language.* Cambridge, MA: MIT Press.

(1978). *Danwa no Bunpoo* [Grammar of discourse]. Tokyo: Taishukan.

Langacker, R. (frth.). Conceptual grouping and constituency in cognitive grammar. *Linguistics in the Morning Calm 3.*

Levelt, W. (1982). Zelfcorrecties in het spreekproces. *Mededelingen der Koninklijke Nederlandse Akademie van Wetenschappen* 45: pp. 215–28.

(1983). Monitoring and self-repair in speech. *Cognition* 14: 41–104.

(1989). *Speaking: From Intention to Articulation.* Cambridge, MA: MIT Press.

Levelt, W. and Cutler, A. (1983). Prosodic marking in speech repair. *Journal of Semantics* 2: 205–17.

Local, J. (1992). Continuing and restarting. In P. Auer and A. di Luzio (eds.) *The Contextualization of Language*, pp. 273–96. Amsterdam: John Benjamins.

Local, John, and Kelly, John (1986). Projection and "silences": notes on phonetic and conversational structure. *Human Studies 9*: 185–204.

Martin, S. (1975). *A Reference Grammar of Japanese.* New Haven, CT: Yale University Press.

Maynard, S.K. (1989). *Japanese Conversation: Self-contextualization Through Structure and Interactional Management.* Norwood, New Jersey: Ablex.

Moerman, M. (1977). The preference for self-correction in a Tai conversational corpus. *Language* 53: 872–82.

Nakatani, C. and Hirschberg, J. (1993). A speech-first model for repair detection and correction. *Proceedings of the ACL*, 1993.

Ochs, E. (1988). *Culture and Language Development.* Cambridge: Cambridge University Press.

Ochs, E. and Schieffelin, B. (1989). Language has a heart. *Text 9*: 7–25.

Ono, T. and Suzuki, R. (1992). Word order variability in Japanese conversation: motivations and grammaticization. *Text 12*: 429–45.

Ono, T. and Thompson, S. (frth.). What can conversation tell us about syntax? In P. Davis (ed.) *Descriptive and Theoretical Modes in the Alternative Linguistics.* Amsterdam: John Benjamins.

Postma, A., Kolk, H., and Povel, D.-J. (1990). On the relation among speech errors, disfluencies and self-repairs. *Language and Speech* 33: 19–29.

Power, R. J. D. and Dal Martello, M. F., (1986). Some criticisms of Sacks, Schegloff and Jefferson on turn-taking. *Semiotica* 58-1/2: 29–40.

Reilly, R. G. (ed.) (1987). *Communication Failure in Dialogue and Discourse*. Amsterdam: North-Holland.

Sacks, H. (1974). An analysis of the course of a joke's telling in conversation. In R. Bauman and J. Sherzer (eds.) *Explorations in the Ethnography of Speaking*, 1st edn., pp. 337–53. Cambridge: Cambridge University Press.

Sacks, H., Schegloff, E., and Jefferson, G. (1974). A simplest systematics for the organization of turn-taking in conversation. *Language* 50: 696–735.

Schegloff, E. (1979). The relevance of repair to syntax-for-conversation. In T. Givón (ed.) *Syntax and Semantics: Vol. 12*. New York: Academic Press.

(1982). Discourse as an interactional achievement: some uses of "uh huh" and other things that come between sentences. *Analyzing Discourse: Text and Talk*. In D. Tannen (ed.), pp. 71–93. Washington DC: Georgetown University Press.

(1987a). Recycled turn beginnings: A precise repair mechanism in conversation's turn-taking organisation. In G. Button and J.R.E. Lee (eds.) *Talk and Social Organization*, 70–85. Clevedon: Multilingual Matters.

(1987b). Between micro and macro: contexts and other connections. In J. Alexander, et al. (eds). *The Macro-micro Link*, pp. 207–34. Berkeley: University of California Press.

(1988). Discourse as an interactional achievement II. In D. Tannen (ed.) *Linguistics in Context: Connecting Observation and Understanding*, pp. 135–58. Norwood, New Jersey: Ablex.

Schegloff, E., Sacks, H., and Jefferson, G. (1977). The preference for self-correction in the organization of repair in conversation. *Language* 53: 361–82.

Shibatani, M. (1990). *The Languages of Japan*. Cambridge: Cambridge University Press.

Shriberg, E., Bear, J., and Dowding, J. (1992). Automatic detection and correction of repairs in human-computer dialog. In *Proceedings of the DARPA Speech and Natural Language Workshop*.

Simon, M.E. (1989). An analysis of the postposing construction in Japanese. Unpublished Ph.D. dissertation, University of Michigan.

Thompson, S. and Mulac, A. (1991). A quantitative perspective on the grammaticization of epistemic parentheticals in English. In E. Traugot and Heine, E. (eds.) *Approaches to Grammaticalization, vol. 2*, pp. 313–29. Amsterdam: John Benjamins.

Uyeno, T. (1971). A study of Japanese modality: A performative analysis of sentence final particles. Unpublished dissertation, University of Michigan.

van Wijk, C. and Kempen, G. (1987). A dual system for producing self-repairs in spontaneous speech: evidence from experimentally elicited corrections. *Cognitive Psychology* 19: 403–40.

5

On the "semi-permeable" character of grammatical units in conversation: conditional entry into the turn space of another speaker*

GENE H. LERNER

> In dialogue, the lines of the individual participants are grammatically disconnected; they are not integrated into one unified context. Indeed, how could they be?
> V. N. Volosinov, *Marxism and the Philosophy of Language*
> (p. 116).

Language structure has long been described in isolation from its natural home of talk-in-interaction. Some have even made this a research policy. On the other hand, a central concern of those disciplines that study speech has been to describe its function. For the most part grammar and particularly syntactic structure has been ceded to those who study language as a self-contained system. However, grammatical structure is not merely an artifact of linguistic inquiry that has isolated language form from its actualization as talk-in-interaction. Features of talk-in-interaction are structured by their producers, and an orientation to the structure of various features of talk-in-interaction can be seen in the ways participants treat various aspects of talk. Two prominent examples are the structuring of talk as turn-constructional units (Sacks, Schegloff, and Jefferson, 1974; Schegloff, this volume) – henceforth TCUs – and the further structuring of some turns at talk into "preferred" and "dispreferred" turn shapes (Sacks, 1987 [1973]; Pomerantz, 1984). Turns at talk are designed for (and as a part of) practical action in interaction. The structures of talk-in-interaction are social structures of practical actors, and the features of their talk then are features of practical action.

When one considers the grammatical structure of language as a set of social resources that is in the first instance situated in the hands of participants who can deploy and exploit (and play with) these used-in-common features of sociality, then the ground for grammatical description shifts from the structures of language to the structures of practice. This does not erase language structure from the description, but respecifies the features of language as features of talk in interaction. One question not addressed under the ordinary purview of grammar, but one that can be addressed by a sequentially informed "applied" linguistics concerns the *permeability* of grammatical units of turn construction.

Ordinarily, the transfer of speakership from one party to another becomes relevant at TCU possible completion, yet there are types of actions that can be accomplished by starting to speak elsewhere. Such an action may not so much interrupt the turn or the action(s) being accomplished in it, as forward the projected turn or its action project in some manner. In this chapter I take up some aspects of turn construction that provide the resources for such *conditional entry* into the turn of another speaker. What are the features of talk-in-interaction that provide enhanced resources for conditional entry? Here I emphasize the turn-constructional aspects of this organization, but I would like to stress at the outset that these considerations cannot be divorced either practically or analytically from the organization of the actions such grammatical resources sustain.

This chapter first briefly recapitulates and then extends previously published work on jointly constructed TCUs to set off a here newly reported line of work on the directional or progressive structure of language used as turns at talk. The first part of this report examines the moment of preliminary component completion of *compound TCUs* and shows how its sequential structure provides a place for anticipatory completion by another participant. The second part of this report describes additional directional aspects of turn construction that enhance the possibility of a recipient interposing talk before possible completion of a TCU. By examining the permeability of TCUs it becomes possible to, in effect, observe language users *in situ* as active analysts of language structure.

5.1 Compound turn-constructional units

In a previous report I identified an ordered two-component type of TCU – the compound TCU (Lerner, 1991). In brief, a compound TCU includes a preliminary component that projects roughly what it will take to bring that component to possible completion and projects a possible form for the final component of the TCU as well, and thereby a shape for the TCU as a whole. It is not until a recognizable final component is begun that the *place* of TCU possible completion becomes (roughly) projectable. It is the possible completion of the final component that constitutes a transition-relevance place. For example, it is not until the "then" component of a "when-then" or "if-then" TCU is begun (and this can be delayed by additional components after the first preliminary "when" or "if" component) that the TCU-in-progress heads toward unit completion. The preliminary component of a compound TCU is shown in boldface in excerpt (1).[1]

(1)   [Smith:Thanksgiving]

> Lynn: **When you don't get any appreciation back**
> **from the teachers,** well its like ferget it.

Many different aspects of talk in interaction can furnish participants with the features of a compound TCU-in-progress – i.e. project preliminary component completion and final component form – including syntactic features such as the TCU-initial subordinating conjunction in excerpt (1),[2] productional features such as contrastive stress, as well as other aspects of the sequential organization of conversation such as the "dispreferred" form disagreements can take (Ford, 1993; Lerner, 1991).

The features that constitute compound TCUs represent one specification of the turn taking features that comprise TCUs generally: recognizable possible completion and the projectability of possible completion. It is by reference to TCU possible completion that transition to a next speaker is ordinarily organized and understood. However, compound TCUs-in-progress furnish the sequential resources for the *anticipatory completion* of the TCU by another speaker. Turns produced in a compound turn-constructional form provide a *place* – a projectable place at preliminary component possible completion – and a *form* – the projected final component form – for another speaker to finish the current TCU. In each of the following excerpts the arrowed contribution is produced in the course of the ongoing TCU (and thereby in the course of an ongoing turn) as a recognizable continuation of that turn's talk from a possible completion of the preliminary component.

(2) [GTS]

Dan:	when the group reconvenes in two weeks=
-> Roger:	=they're gunna issue strait jackets

(3) [GL:FN]

Alan:	Did you use the button holer on that?
Beth:	Once you cut the button hole open
-> Alan:	you can't use the button holer.

(4) [HIC]

ot

David:	So if one person said he couldn't invest (.)
-> Kerry:	then I'd have to wait till

In each case, the arrowed utterance continues the projected compound TCU to a next possible completion place for the unit as a whole.[3] Furthermore, in some (though not all) sequential environments, the production of an anticipatory completion by another participant can initiate a small sequence – the collaborative turn sequence – in which the acceptance or rejection of the proffered completion becomes a specially relevant responsive action as in excerpt (5).

(5) [CDHQ:II]

1	Marty:	Now most machines don't record that slow. So I'd wanna-
2		when I make a tape,
3	Josh:	be able tuh speed it up.
->4	Marty:	Yeah.

Also notice that in (5) the compound structure is not furnished at the outset of the turn or turn-constructional unit in which it is produced, but in the course of the TCU. Here the compound structure is established by the parenthetical insert at line 2.

5.2 A place for speaker transition

While distinctly different in social and interactional terms from TCU possible completion as a place of transition relevance, preliminary component completion (using grammatical and prosodic features in a fashion similar to those used to produce and recognize TCU completion) also provides a place for another participant to begin speaking. Some preliminary components even seem to be more or less actively eliciting completion by another participant through the deployment of intonational resources or the relevance of an ongoing knowledge differential as found in e.g. a tutoring session. However, preliminary component completion provides an opportunity for another to begin speaking even when no form of elicitation is evident and the first speaker continues on without hesitation. Composing and positioning an utterance as a conditional entry into another's turn does not require an "invitation."

With anticipatory completion, onset occurs at a TCU-internal component completion, and therefore not at a place the turn itself could in most circumstances be finished. That is, a next speaker begins speaking before the projected completion of a TCU and thus within the projected turn space of the still current speaker.[4] The onset of an anticipatory completion in the course of a compound TCU-in-progress shows that the possible completion of the preliminary component can be an oriented-to feature of the turn. Anticipatory completions launched just at the completion of the preliminary component can begin, and go toward completion, without incurring overlapping talk. In contrast, anticipatory completions that begin earlier or later than preliminary component completion regularly initiate overlapping speech.

How do anticipatory completions that are initiated at preliminary component completion come to start in the clear while others ordinarily do not? Component completion furnishes a socially organized site for possible silence – the slight pause that can precede the final component. Speakers may permit a beat of silence before continuing on to the final (or at least next) component of a compound TCU as in excerpt (6).

(6) [HIC]

> Sparky: If dad and Sherrie got together,
> (.)
> they would have a quorum,

Pausing at preliminary component possible completion is ordinarily not indicative of trouble in the forward movement of the turn (Schegloff, 1979), as its occurrence can be understood if positioned elsewhere in a TCU. Here, it is merely pausing before continuing. Pausing is treated as a rest beat in the normal cadence of the ongoing utterance. Indeed, work on the intonation patterns of naturally occurring speech has shown that intonation units are regularly bounded by a slight pause or rest beat (Du Bois et al, 1993; Du Bois, personal communication). A rest beat does not always occur between adjacent intonation units, but such junctures provide a foreseeable environment for a beat of silence.[5]

Similarly, other productional features that can be indicative of completion, for example, a sound stretch, can be indicative of possible trouble if it occurs away from a possible completion place, whether preliminary component possible completion or TCU possible completion. On the other hand, the occurrence of a sound stretch in the vicinity of preliminary component possible completion or TCU possible completion can be part of the procedure for bringing a preliminary component or a TCU to completion. A stretch can adumbrate a possible halt in speaking. When it occurs adjacent to a possible syntactic completion, it certifies the possible completion; when it occurs elsewhere it can forecast possible trouble ahead. In other words, the syntactic environment of a stretch or a pause informs the action it performs.

The syntax-sensitive nature of intonational features of talk can illuminate the relationship of intonation contour (and especially terminal intonation contour) to syntax in another way, when we consider the relationship of preliminary component possible completion to TCU possible completion. The intonation contour of an utterance can certify various syntactic constituents as complete; however, it is the syntax (informed by its sequential location) that will show if the completion of an intonation unit is a preliminary component completion or a TCU completion.[6]

By placing an anticipatory completion at the completion of the preliminary component (or the completion of any extension of it), the utterance has a systematic chance of beginning in the clear, as David's contribution does in excerpt (7).

(7) [HIC]

    Sparky: An if you and Cheryl got together
    David: you don't have enough

David begins his utterance, which is tied syntactically to the compound TCU-in-progress as a continuation of it, at a possible completion of the preliminary component. No pause is marked on the transcript between the two utterances, but for David to have started in the clear Sparky must necessarily have stopped talking. In addition to this, Sparky also refrains from resuming his turn even though he has not yet completed the TCU he began. Notice that the TCU is in fact continuing toward completion, but out of the mouth of a different participant – i.e. David is producing a rendition of the final component. In this way, two participants collaborate in the production of a single TCU.[7] This results in an *intra-turn* change of speakers. The entitlement of a speaker to produce a complete TCU has been relaxed, but not abandoned (cf. Sacks and Schegloff, 1979). The achievement of one speaker talking at a time and the entitlement to produce at least one TCU to completion are intimately related, but they are not always co-occurring features as anticipatory completion demonstrates. Here participants manage to achieve one speaker talking at a time, and a rendition of the projected final component is produced – i.e. the TCU is brought to a next possible completion. Only the animator (Goffman, 1979) of the turn's talk has changed.

This exploitation of turn taking can be used to accomplish a number of distinct types of action (Lerner, 1987). An analysis of these action types is not developed in this chapter, but the following represent the range of actions that can be accomplished by anticipatory completion. Anticipatory completion can be used to demonstrate agreement, or pre-empt a disagreement-in-progress with a current speaker or it can be used to collaborate with a current speaker in explaining something to another participant. It can even be used to heckle a storyteller by, in effect, placing words in their mouth.

The earliest point one can begin at preliminary component completion, and thereby possibly project beginning in the clear, is by latching the anticipatory completion to the completion of the preliminary component as in excerpt (2) above. Onset of the final component by still-current speaker closes down the systematic possibility of a recipient beginning a preliminary completion in the clear. (Yet, as I will show below, this does not completely close down the possibility of anticipatory completion.)

If an additional preliminary component is produced by current speaker, then another chance will become available. In the next excerpt, Kerry misses his chance at the first juncture provided by an indirect quotation marker, but then tries again at the next projected juncture. This time he begins just at preliminary component completion. (Talk prior to this excerpt and the design of "let the:m make the dec:isions" itself reveal the utterance to be the first part of a contrast.)

(8) [HIC]

```
   1 Sparky:  It sounds like what you're saying
   2          is that (.) [let the:m make the dec:isions=
   3 Kerry:              [(if ya)
->4 Kerry:     =an let us know what it is
```

Of course a pause before the next component is not assured. The current speaker can simply continue through from the completion of the preliminary component to the next component without a pause.

In summary, when an anticipatory completion is initiated, it is ordinarily begun just after the preliminary component, at a place the final component could be due, and is designed as a syntactic continuation of the utterance part it follows at the point of onset, and in the absence of further talk by the prior speaker. This placement maintains contiguity of turn-constructional components (sustaining the progressivity of the turn's talk toward completion), while achieving speaker transition that regularly results in one and only one participant speaking at a time. However, anticipatory completions do start elsewhere in the course of the turn-in-progress, for example, after the onset of the final component.

5.3 Late-placed anticipatory completions

The onset of the final component by the current speaker does not close down the possibility of an interposing speaker beginning their own completion.[8] However, in this case the preliminary component completion and not the point of actual onset still can be seen to have been the target that was aimed for – and missed, thereby rendering the anticipatory completion as "late." This can be seen in the following excerpt.

(9) [US]

```
   Rich:   if they come en pick it up it'll co[st yah
   Mike:                                       [they charge yuh
```

Mike begins his anticipatory completion after Rich has already begun the projected final component, but the anticipatory completion is not designed as a continuation of the prior turn unit from the point of its onset. Instead, it is designed to connect to the completion of the preliminary component as its starting place, and thereby marks its own misplacement – i.e. its own lateness.

There is a sequential limit as to how late a completion can be, and still result in a collaboratively produced TCU. Once a speaker finishes a compound TCU, the production of what earlier might have been an anticipatory completion may now be hearable as (or turned into) instead a next turn repeat of a prior turn's (now ratified) completion. Whether an utterance is heard as continuing a syntactic unit, and thus as a contribution to the turn-in-progress it comprises, or as a repeat of a portion of a syntactic unit, and thus as a new turn repeating part of a prior turn (or for that matter as a new turn that stands in some relation to the prior other than as a repeat), hinges on the position of its onset in relation to other contributions.

There are constraints on the production of late anticipatory completions. These are (1) *component contiguity*, i.e. achieving (or at least demonstrating an orientation to) contiguous placement of the affiliating utterance with the preliminary component, and (2) *turn space occupancy*, i.e. starting and producing the affiliating utterance within the current turn space, where the boundary of the current turn space is constituted by the impending possible completion of the final component of the compound TCU-in-progress. (That is, recipients produce late anticipatory completions in a manner that is oriented to getting it said prior to when the current speaker's utterance – their TCU-in-progress – reaches the next transition-relevance place.)

No conflict arises in the achievement of these features when the anticipatory completion is initiated at the completion of the preliminary component and the current speaker does not resume speaking. Anticipatory completions that begin after the current speaker has begun a next increment of their TCU can nonetheless demonstrate component contiguity by locating – through syntactic design – the completion of the preliminary component as their proper starting place. And speakers can accomplish turn space occupancy for anticipatory completions through utterance compression, by quickening the pace of their talk, or actually compressing the words which make up the utterance, or both. In the following excerpt orientations to component contiguity and within-turn-space production are simultaneously displayed.

(10) [HIC]

```
    Sparky:   when it doesn' involve the basic agreement
              it is b[y    s t o c k ]
-->    Dad:              [it's by major]ity
```

Here the anticipatory completion ("it's by majority") is designed to be both contiguous with the preliminary component (even though its actual onset occurs later) and compressed. First, Dad begins with "it's," after Sparky has used the form, "it is." By producing a version of "it is," Dad positions his talk after completion of the preliminary component; by eliding it, Dad displays the compression appropriate for achieving within-turn-space production. Also, most of Dad's utterance ("its by majority") is done within Sparky's, "y stock." This attempt is not completely successful, since a small portion of Dad's utterance occurs after Sparky has reached a TCU possible completion. However, as with component contiguity, the speaker displays an orientation to the achievement of within-turn-space placement even when that feature is not completely achievable. The attempt displays an "intent" and thereby becomes a recognizable replacement for, or realization of, the attempted action.

Lexical compression can be taken further and still result in a recognizable anticipatory completion. In excerpt (11) Roger begins his anticipatory completion in the course of the second part of a contrast at the last possible place to produce it as an *anticipatory* completion (i.e., still be within the turn space).

(11) [GTS]

```
    Dan:      the guy who doesn't run the race  doesn't win=it
              (.) but he doesn['t  l o s e  it]
    Roger:                    [>but- lu:zit<]
```

In this instance contiguity and within-turn-space completion are both achieved since both the beginning and end of the anticipatory completion are produced. However, the middle of the unit is skipped. Not only does Roger use a faster pace and condense the utterance, but he abandons the part of the utterance on which the display of agreement literally hinges in favor of attempting to finish his utterance before Dan completes the contrast himself.[9]

The interactional significance of these practices must be seen against the backdrop of the ordinary course of overlap competition. In contrast to the practices of condensing and speeding up their talk in order to finish before the still-current speaker does, speakers in overlap regularly call on procedures that are oriented to *outlasting* the other speaker. Rather than speeding up an utterance, participants stretch and extend their talk in various ways (Jefferson and Schegloff, 1975; Schegloff, 1987).

Anticipatory completions are designed to occur as part of the current turn and not in opposition to it. Though the beginning and middle of the anticipatory completion may be sacrificed, the final part of the utterance cannot be abandoned in the same way, since stopping the utterance prior to a recognizable completion shows that the affiliating utterance has failed as an anticipatory completion (and the various kinds of interactional work that such completions can accomplish fail with it).

The intersecting organizations of actions into sequences-of-action, on the one hand, and talk into locally allocated turns-in-a-series, on the other, furnish one systematic basis for the compressed form of late anticipatory completions. The following instance demonstrates the "pressure" that speaker sequencing exerts on the placement of the initiation of an anticipatory completion.

(12) [US]

```
Rich:    if they come en pick it up it'll co[st yah]
Mike:                                        [t h e y][ charge yuh]=yeh
Carol:                                                 [y e a h    ]
```

At the moment Rich's entire compound TCU comes to possible completion, Mike has only produced a single word ("they"), which is not yet recognizable as the beginning of an anticipatory completion. At this point, another participant (Carol) produces a next turn that ratifies Rich's turn as completed, thereby placing the continuing anticipatory completion outside of the turn space. Mike has failed in a bid to provide a rendition of the TCU's final component. The "yeh," which occurs in the clear at the end of Mike's utterance, transforms the attempted completion into having been a receipt of the prior turn rather than a continuation of it. The interactional import of this is that the action Mike comes to have produced has been transformed from collaboratively answering a question that Carol has asked about getting a cat "fixed" to confirming Rich's answer, and doing this after Carol herself has done so.

5.4 Early-placed anticipatory completion

In this section I examine anticipatory completions in which initial onset occurs before the completion of the preliminary component. First, I examine the pre-beginning of one anticipatory completion, then I examine an excerpt in which the anticipatory completion itself actually begins prior to preliminary component completion.

In excerpt (13), Fran, a recipient of an at least somewhat tongue-in-cheek correction, produces an anticipatory completion just at completion of the preliminary component, but launches it with a "response cry" (Goffman, 1978) prior to component completion.

```
(13)  [CS:3]
   1  Fran:    BUT WHUT UH YUH GONNA DO, YUH JUST GONNA SPREAD
   2           THAT STUFF ON THE DRI:VEWAY?=
   3  Mike:    = >'s gonna load [up with it<
   4  Steve:                    [I'm not gonna spread it
   5           on the dri:[veway, I'm gonna dump't
 ->6  Fran:               [Aih!  you gonna dump it
   7           (0.4)
```

There are various actions that can occur in the moment before a participant produces the beginning of a TCU and thereby the beginning of a turn at talk. For example, participants produce such things as audible inhalations that foreshadow the onset of speech. This can be done in a manner that matches the pace of the end of the current turn so that the recipient culminates the inhalation and begins speaking just at possible completion. A turn at talk does not always begin after such inhalations, but they can be treated as indicating that a turn is on the way and as such are elements of a turn's pre-beginning. "Aih!" occupies this pre-beginning position in excerpt (13) and it is placed in the course of the ongoing utterance in a manner that shows Fran to be precisely targeting completion of Steve's preliminary component for the onset of her anticipatory completion. In this case, the stretch in "dri:veway" (indicated by the colon) puts Fran's token a bit before the final syllable of preliminary component completion and so puts the onset of her anticipatory completion a bit early also.

Similarly, the anticipatory completion in excerpt (14), or more precisely its initial onset, "we're s-" at line 8, can be characterized as

having begun "early." Though this utterance is begun in the course
of the preliminary component, it is syntactically tied to the completion of the preliminary component. The utterance, "we're s-,"
which is cut off, is designed to follow "agreement," though it was
begun before "agreement" has ended. (Note that in the first part of
the contrast concerning types of decision making (lines 1 to 2)
Sparky uses the term "agreement" and not "agreement contract"
to refer to the document they are discussing. In line 7 "contract"
seems to be added as a way to extend the preliminary component,
and thus manage the incipient overlap in an unmarked fashion.)

(14) [HIC]

```
 1  Sparky:  so what yer saying then is that when (.) when it doesn'
 2           invol:ve thee basic agreement, it is b:[y  s t o c k ]
 3  Dad:                                            [its by major]ity
 4  Sparky:  by majority according to stocks=
 5  Dad:     =(right)
 6  Sparky:  an when it do:es: ah involve the basic
 7           agree[m e n t ] cont[r a c t  i t s  b y:  u h m  ]
->8 Dad:          [we're s-]      [we're still letting us set aside]
 9           the agreement  contract (   )
10  Sparky:  its- its by ah unanimous decisi[on
11  Dad:                                     [right
```

Dad, having begun early and finding himself in overlap, recycles
(Schegloff, 1987) "we're s" at precisely the place the preliminary
component could be finished.[10] This suggests that the juncture was
taken to be an upcoming potential *within-turn* place to begin the
anticipatory completion. That is, the anticipatory completion is
built to display its placement at the completion of the preliminary
component of the projected compound TCU-in-progress, even
though it began early; and it is at just this preliminary completion
that the early, overlapping completion is recycled.

Both speakers are engaged in competition for the turn here. For
his part, Sparky adds the clearly awkward "contract" as an attempt
to outlast the overlapping utterance – i.e. to extend the current
preliminary component, rather than progressing with what is a
far from finished TCU. Both participants are oriented to what is
only a *preliminary* completion as a completion nonetheless – i.e. as
an organizationally relevant locus for overlap resolution. Also, here
we see an overlap management device – the recycled turn beginning
– that ordinarily operates at turn transition relevance places, also
available to the interposing speaker for use within a TCU. That is, a

practice ordinarily associated with the boundaries of a TCU, is also available for use at internal boundary points.

Taken together, these excerpts, then, evidence the orientation to the juncture at preliminary component completion as a projectable place for anticipatory completion onset, and as the location where the onset of anticipatory completion should properly occur. Exact placement is not required since fine tuning of placement can be accomplished *in situ* (cf. Goodwin, 1986).

5.5 A restricted opportunity to speak: what gets done at these junctures

Since the juncture between components of a compound TCU provides a projectable place for speaker onset, one would expect that it could be used to begin actions other than anticipatory completion of the projected final component. These other actions can also display an orientation to this internal juncture in a compound TCU-in-progress as a site for restricted or conditional access to the ongoing turn of another speaker. Further, the actions accomplished by entry can be built upon the intra-turn nature of that entry or alternatively display their misplacement.

Just as each next turn in a conversation is ordinarily designed to follow the just prior turn, so a recipient's utterance begun internal to a turn's talk (i.e. in the midst of the projected turn space of the current speaker) is shaped by, and understood by reference to, its placement. For example, acknowledgment tokens or "continuers" are often used in the course of an extended turn to show that the current turn-so-far, though at a possible completion of a turn-constructional unit, is understood not to be a transition-relevance place for the turn (Schegloff, 1982; Jefferson, 1984). Continuers can also be used in the same way at the completion of the preliminary component of a compound TCU, as in Ann's "Mm hm" at line 4 in excerpt (15). (It is important to note here that the tempo of Dad's talk is quite slow relative to Ann and that he often pauses. I mention this here in order to suggest that the slight pause at line 3 should not be seen as a marked pausal extension of the preliminary completion.)

(15) [Mother's Day]

```
 1   Dad:   s- so if if ah you were strong in yer fee̲li:ngs
 2          about (0.2) people
 3             (0.2)
->4  Ann:   Mm hm=
 5   Dad:   =your thet you li:ked (0.3) an it was in complḙtely (.) contras=to (0.4)
 6          what your mother (.) thought was right (0.8) completely (.) .hhh it would
 7          be extremely difficult for yer mother to=ah to to adapt to that (0.2) .h
 8          where she co̲uld adapt to=.h se̲e:ing yo̲u::
 9             (0.2)
10   Ann:   Mm hm
11   Dad:   but not (.) endorse what cher doing
12   Ann:   Yeh.
```

By producing an acknowledgment token at line 4, Ann both
acknowledges the turn-so-far and shows that she expects the turn
to continue. That is, she is treating it as a preliminary component of
a not-yet-completed turn and thereby demonstrating that her contribution is not to be taken as a full turn at talk that should itself be
attended by subsequent talk. (It is the work that this placement and
design accomplish that is ordinarily glossed and lost by the term
"back-channel.")

In addition to producing anticipatory completions and continuers, recipients of a compound TCU sometimes begin a new
turn at the completion of the preliminary component. Beginning a
new turn in this way can be compared to recognition point entry
(Jefferson, 1973, 1983a). In recognition point onset recipients use
the recognizability of the emergent action as a resource and warrant
for beginning a new turn. One feature of many recognition point
entries is that they are done not merely as responses to a forecasted
complete TCU, but are used in circumstances where it would be
felicitous to pre-empt the current speaker's utterance before completion – i.e. to forestall the action that is currently underway and
recognizable as part of the TCU's projectability.

The projectability of a TCU-internal preliminary component
completion furnished by a compound TCU provides an additional
syntactic resource for recognitional entry. In excerpt (16) Cathy
pre-empts her mother's warning to show that she has already
"learned her lesson." (Here "that" at line 3 and "it" at lines 4
and 5 refer to an ankle bracelet Cathy has just received as a birth-
day gift.)

(16) [BIRTHDAY]

```
  1  Mom:    now when you take yer stockins off, er things
  2          like that (0.4) kinna ease um down cause
  3          if that's caught on i[t
->4  Cathy:              [I know I broke [ my other one just like it
  5  Mom:                               [y'll bust it
```

One option here would be for Cathy to produce an anticipatory completion to co-opt the consequence of not heeding the warning, thus demonstrating that she has already learned her lesson. But in this case Cathy uses preliminary component completion to begin an early next turn response. Even though her utterance is designed as a new turn and not as an anticipatory completion, its placement contributes to a demonstration that she has already learned her lesson and does not need to be reminded by her mother. That is, it is placed and designed to pre-empt the relevance of the projected final component of Mom's turn (i.e. the consequence of not taking off her stockings carefully), and not merely as an early response to it.

Anticipatory completions continue the current TCU, while continuers encourage continuation by other. Recognitional entry can be used to interdict the completion of a turn, thereby forestalling the turn's project. In each of these three cases the mode of utterance initiation presses the speaker's claim that they are entering the turn space of another to accomplish work that cannot wait for completion; indeed it is by reference to their early placement – early, vis-à-vis TCU completion – that the action import of these utterances is recognizable.

On the other hand, next speakers sometimes begin in the course of a TCU in a fashion that shows itself to be unresponsive to the current TCU, e.g., by responding to an earlier increment of talk by the current speaker and beginning the response at other than a place of transition relevance. Preliminary component completion can be used as a resource for this. In excerpt (17) speaker B is responding to something said in an earlier increment of A's turn, but the onset of her turn is hearable as sensitive to the projected completion of the preliminary component ("if you're going out").

(17) [JJ:Invitation]

```
  1  A:   I was just gonna say come out
  2       and come over here and talk this evening.
  3       But if you're going out [ you can't very well do that.
->4  B:                          [Talk you mean get drunk, don't you.
  5  A:   what?
```

Speaker B's turn begins with a turn initial repeat of a word used in an earlier TCU by speaker A. This explicitly shows that her utterance is not to be heard (as it otherwise ordinarily would be) as coming next after the talk it directly follows, but is responsive to something else – the reported invitation.

Notice that this is quite different from the way the "late" anticipatory completions discussed earlier are tied to the completion of the preliminary component of a compound TCU. Here in excerpt (17), an element is placed at the beginning of the TCU to show its "misplacement"; while in the case of anticipatory completion, it is precisely the fact that the utterance is not specially designed either constructionally or intonationally to have a marked turn beginning that allows its structural connection to preliminary component completion to be registered.

In summary, preliminary component completion might be thought of more generally as a TCU-internal place for recipient entry, where a variety – a *restricted* variety – of utterance forms may begin. In the first part of this chapter I have been examining the character of compound TCU permeability that this grammatically formed place provides. As I have shown, compound TCUs project the form of the final component and indicate a place for recipient entry. In the next section I examine one two-part action format that can projectably furnish recipient with the form of the second part, but does not always furnish a preliminary component completion. This can provide enhanced resources for producing a completion, but it does not also provide a distinct TCU-internal completion place to begin.

5.6 Two-part formats without preliminary completion places

There are certain actions in conversation that regularly go together and have a sequential ordering between them, yet are not produced in a compound turn-constructional form, and thus do not provide a distinct syntactic place for anticipatory completion. For example, complaints can take the form: disparaging reference + complainable action, as in excerpts (18) and (19).

(18) [US]

    Vic: He's a bitch he didn' pud in duh light own dih sekkin flaw,

(19) [US]

-> Joe: The son of a bitch comes back the nex' <u>da</u>:y. En nevuh usetuh tear the
           furniture but aftuh I let im alone f'bout one da:y man he tore up
           <u>e</u>vrything.
    Carol: Ih hnh He got back, re<u>ve:n</u>ge.

Not only do disparaging references accompany complaints, but
they regularly precede the complainable action. So, in (18) Vic
first uses a disparaging reference "He's a bitch" then follows this
with a complaint "he didn't put in a light on the second floor." In
(19) Joe first refers to someone as "the son of a bitch" then issues
the complaint "he tore up <u>e</u>vrything."

This constitutes a two-part format, in which the action-type of
the second part can be projectable from the first. Yet, in contrast to
excerpts (18) and (19), the two parts of the format may be combined in a single grammatical unit, such that the first part does not
project that is ordinarily followed by a beat of silence a preliminary
component completion. Nevertheless, this format does provide a
resource for TCU completion by an interposing speaker as in
excerpts (20) and (21).

(20) [JS]

```
1  Joe:     oh hundreds of automobiles parked around there en people walkin
2           across the bridge you know? en all a' these go:dam people onna
3           freeway [were stoppin-
->4 Edith:           [were rubbernecking
```

(21) [US]

```
1  Joe:     B't he wannid duh dawg tuh bite iz wife.
2           (0.4)
3           So he come[s home one night'n the sonofa]bitch [bit him.
->4 Carol:            [heh-heh-heh-heh-heh-heh-heh]      [bit hi:m
```

(Note that in (21) Joe is reporting someone else's complainable
matter, and so here the two-part format is preserved in the form
of the report of the complainable action.) The "disparaging reference + complainable action" two-part format provides an additional resource for projecting the form of TCU completion and
this is used to finish the TCU-in-progress. Yet, notice that in each
case the interposing speaker's completion comes quite near the end
of the TCU. This TCU position alone can contribute resources for
completion.

5.7 Terminal item completion

The final word or two – the terminal item of a TCU – can be co-
produced by a recipient, as in (22), or actually co-opted by an
interposing speaker, as in (23). (I cannot here provide an explication of the differences between choral co-production of a completion and co-optation of another's completion, but I would at least
like to register that these can be quite distinct forms of action by the
entering speaker.)

(22) [Family Tree:4]

```
  1 T:      Greg can be Santa Claus.
  2 M:      Yeah, he's got the [beard!
->3 C:                         [beard!
```

(23) [CDHQ: Hurricane I:5]

```
  1 Tiny:    Chief Jerruso and Vic are on their way to Haynes Boulevand now, and
  2          they say you better have yer transperta:tion=
->3 Charlie: =ready,=
  4 Tiny:    =alerted 'hh
```

So, the beginning edge of the turn transition space (what Schegloff,
this volume, calls the "pre-completion" position in a TCU) can also
be used for completion of the current turn by a recipient. Here
possible completion of the ongoing TCU is both projectable and
imminent. It is the turn-taking mandated orientation to the imminent possible closure of the turn and with it the opening up at the
point of pre-completion of the relevance of transition (and not any
particular turn-constructional format) that furnishes an opportunity
for completion. Terminal item completion begins in the same place
in current turn (its pre-completion) as the pre-beginning of a next
turn could begin, and therefore, in one sense, might be thought of as
an alternative to it. Correspondingly, Jefferson (1983a), looking at
overlap onset, finds that the beginning of the terminal item of a
TCU (i.e. at pre-completion) is one systematic place for another
speaker to begin a next turn.

5.8 Unprojected opportunities for completion

Up to this point in the discussion I have only considered opportunities for completion that are foreseeable in the course of a turn-in-
progress. The discussion of TCU permeability will now turn to a
characterization of several features of TCU production that furnish

unprojected opportunities to enter another's turn. That is, I examine features of TCU production that are ordinarily not available to recipients until (or just before) their occurrence, but nonetheless afford them entry into the turn, and thereby the opportunity to complete the TCU-in-progress.

The temporal character of talk provides the possibility that it can be directional. The organization of talk-in-interaction into turns realizes that directionality as a directionality toward possible completion (Schegloff, this volume) that can be found (at least in part), and projected, in the directional structure of TCUs – i.e. it can be found and projected in the *progressivity* of the turn's talk toward (next) possible completion. (The compound TCU form is one realization of that directional structure.) However, the progressivity of a turn's talk is an emergent, productional and social-interactional achievement, and therefore is not guaranteed. There are systematic and local bases for the occasional halting of a turn's progressivity prior to TCU possible completion. These unprojected "disruptions" to progressivity can occasion practices aimed at continuing the turn toward possible completion, both by current speaker and by recipients. Unprojected disruptions to a TCU-in-progress afford an opportunity for recipient entry into the stalled turn and can provide a warrant for TCU completion.

Unprojected opportunities for entry are occasioned by any conversational practice that disrupts the progressivity of talk within a turn (Jefferson, 1983a; Schegloff, 1979). For the present discussion, progressivity can be thought of as constituted by the co-occurrence of two features of talk that concern the adjacent placement of words. First, after a turn at talk is launched, talk ought to continue – and show itself to be continuing beat by beat – at least until a recognizable TCU completion is reached (at which time the relevance of utterance progressivity can end). The adjacent placement of words both achieves the pace of the talk and, through the pace of the local preceding talk, provides a metric for what constitutes continued adjacency. Second, after a turn at talk is gained, each next word ought to be a successive word. That is, a turn's talk should show continued *syntactic* progress, word by word, toward a completion.

The first feature represents serial adjacency, while the second can be characterized as sequential adjacency. Serial adjacency proposes that talk ought to be continuous to a next transition-relevance place, while sequential adjacency proposes that the words that are produced reveal reflexively that they represent progress for the turn-so-far toward a (next) possible completion. (Schegloff (1979) further extends progressivity to a consideration of "sound progressivity.")

Progressivity ordinarily requires the concurrent fulfillment of both types of adjacency. However, they are separable features, at least insofar as the undoing of one does not necessarily imply the breakdown of the other; a serially adjacent word can be delayed (e.g., by pausing or laughing), a sequentially adjacent word can be delayed (e.g., by word repetition) or both can occur. In either case, the impedance of progressivity provides an opportunity – a restricted opportunity – for another speaker to talk prior to the next (now delayed) word. I will refer to entry by a recipient to complete a TCU-in-progress at such unprojected openings as "opportunistic completion."

5.8.1 Laugh tokens

In the case of TCU-internal laughter, it is possible to distinguish between in-speech laughter that only minimally retards the progressivity of the TCU and laugh tokens placed within the TCU, but between the words that comprise the unit, that retard the serial adjacency of the words. The former furnishes a social-sequential basis for entry (i.e. affiliation with the laugher), but no place to begin without incurring overlap, while the latter can provide a place for a recipient to begin, as well. I will first look at between-word laughter, then in-speech laughter.

Between-word laughter. Laughter by current speaker can constitute an opening for opportunistic completion. Laughing can impede the progressivity of an utterance-in-progress. The serial adjacency (and thereby the pace) of the utterance-in-progress is disrupted even though there is a continued stream of sound bursts. However, sequential adjacency is not actually disrupted.[11] Rather the adjacent placement of successive words is held in abeyance by the laugh tokens since a next word has not yet occurred after a last word.

In excerpt (24), there is a strongly projected utterance completion since the utterance-in-progress is somewhat idiomatic. Though "through circumstances" strongly projects "beyond their control" it is important to remember that no preliminary component completion is forecast here – i.e. there is no foreseeable place for another speaker to co-opt the completion.[12] In (24) a break in the utterance's progressivity occurs. Here the laugh token (really a gasping in-breathing laugh token) occurs within the TCU and forestalls its completion. This *TCU-internal* laughter can be contrasted to the *in-speech* laughter that occurs earlier in Roger's turn (e.g. "c(h)ircumsta(hh)nces") that does not retard the progressivity of the talk in the same fashion. The in-breath laugh at line 3 ("·hmhh") gives Dan a place to initiate an opportunistic completion.

(24) [GTS]

```
 1  Roger:   by the time they're eighteen they're back wa(h)lki(h)ng
 2           (0.6) ·hhhehh through c(h)ircumsta(hh)nces
->3           ·hmhh [hheh
 4  Dan:           [beyond their contro[l
 5  Roger:                             [uh(hh) ye(h)s
```

Jefferson, Sacks, and Schegloff (1973) have suggested that laughers can and regularly do terminate their laughter at the onset of speech. Thus a speaker can initiate a completion in the course of a laugh and nevertheless have a good chance that it will run off in the clear.

In-speech laugh tokens. Jefferson (1979) has shown that in-speech (and therefore TCU-internal) laughter makes recipient laughter specially relevant as a demonstration of understanding or affiliation. There are, of course, ways of asserting or showing understanding or affiliation through talk, but ordinarily these must wait until transition to a next turn becomes relevant at TCU possible completion. (But see M. H. Goodwin, 1980, and C. Goodwin and M. H. Goodwin, 1987.) In the case of laughter – since it is not turn organized[13] – a recipient need not delay affiliation until next turn. Opportunistic completion furnishes another way to respond without delay after the onset of in-speech laughter. Producing an opportunistic completion renders an version of the upcoming portion of the utterance, thus demonstrating understanding of it or affiliation with it or both. Excerpt (25) provides an instance of this usage.

(25) [GTS:4]

```
     Jim:      that's why her an misses McGee
               getta l(h)o(hh)n(h)[g  s(h)o  we(hh)ll   ]
--> Ken:                          [>getta=long< so well] ye(h)h
```

In this excerpt the in-speech laughter by Jim provides an occasion
for recipient affiliation. Ken's opportunistic completion provides a
way to achieve agreement with the proffered opinion in the course
of its production.

5.8.2 Intra-turn silence

A range of conversational practices result in or contain speaker
silence as a feature. Pausing speech (in any of a variety of ways)
in the course of a TCU retards the forward movement of the turn's
talk toward next possible completion. This type of silence belongs
to current speaker – i.e. it is treated as a pause *within* a turn (Sacks,
Schegloff, and Jefferson, 1974; Schegloff, 1979). In the following
excerpts the progressivity is halted by the current speaker pausing,
and this intra-turn silence provides a recipient with an opportunity
to complete the TCU.

(26) [GTS]

```
     Jim:      Did they do that old trick with the basketball where they putta
               (0.4)
     Ken:      string around it
```

(27) [GTS]

```
     Dan:      Well I do know last week thet=uh Al was certainly very
               (0.5)
     Roger:    pissed off
```

The silences in (26) and (27), on their occurrence, provide recipients
of the turn the chance to initiate talk without being implicated in
overlap. However, the character of the utterance is somewhat constrained, insofar as designing an utterance as a new turn may be
seen as pre-empting another speaker's not-yet-completed turn.
However, not every new contribution of talk begun in such a
place will constitute an interruption of the current speaker's turn.
It will not if, for example, the new talk is hearable as furthering the
action partially constituted by the pause, as in the case of searching
for a specific or a delicate word (as in (26) and (27) respectively).
Here, recipient contributions, whether furnishing a single word,

completing the TCU, or beginning a new turn that, for example, provides a clue, can be seen to be in the service of the further progress of the halted turn; i.e. they further the project of the turn-in-progress.

I am not suggesting that every intra-turn silence is equally available for opportunistic completion. The circumstances, sequential position, method of "braking" (so to speak) and the position of the silence in the turn and within the TCU matter here. For example, Goodwin (1980) describes the use of pauses as a device for achieving mutual gaze at turn-beginnings. He writes, "By producing a pause near the beginning of his sentence, a speaker is able to delay its onward progression until the gaze of a recipient has been obtained." Clearly, this use of intra-turn silence near turn beginning (to repair possibly problematic recipiency) will not provide the prospective recipient with much material on which to build a completion. In Schegloff's (this volume) terms, "post-beginning" is not a position for completion, while, for example, pre-completion is (as terminal item completion demonstrates).[14]

Word searches. Word searches (Sacks, 1992; Goodwin and Goodwin, 1986) are specifically designed for conditional entry by recipients. Though word searches can expand into long sequences, roughly they minimally provide conditional access to the current turn for other participants to aid in the search by suggesting candidate words and a slot for the original speaker to accept or reject proffered candidates. In a word search, progressivity toward TCU completion has been halted, but the search is organized to show that an ongoing attempt is being made to continue the TCU. The halt in TCU progressivity does provide the possibility for another participant to produce an opportunistic completion for the TCU, but ordinarily only the searched-for next word is actually produced as in excerpt (28).

(28) [GL:DS]

```
L:      he said, the thing thet- thet- sad about the uhm black uhm
        (0.3)
P:      muslims,
L:      muslims, he said is thet they don't realize ...
```

However, notice that L's first utterance in (28) is designed so that P does, in fact, produce a "completion," the completion of a preliminary component in a compound structure of the type called a pseudo-cleft construction.[15] In fact, many turn units that end up containing word searches are designed in such a way that the search is placed near the end of the unit, thereby providing a place for candidates which will concomitantly be terminal item completions as in excerpt (29).

(29) [Adato:II]

> Jay: Well, I- I pretty much had in mi:nd the:::,
> G: the human race.

One finer distinction can be drawn here concerning the placement of contributions by recipients to a word search. Repair organization seems to divide the opportunity to contribute to the search into "immediate" and "delayed" contributions. Many word search candidates are held off or delayed, giving the current speaker an opportunity to self-repair (Schegloff, Jefferson, and Sacks, 1977) and when a candidate is finally produced it is regularly designed as a confirmable – "try-marked" (Sacks and Schegloff, 1979) – guess as in excerpt (30).

(30) [GTS]

> Roger: He just had to take that attitude
>   because everybody says why be y'know-
>   (2.0)
> Louise: Big man?
> Roger: well uh- I don't know how to phrase it
>   lemme think about it awhile.

In contrast, recipient contributions initiated at the beginning of a search – i.e. immediately after the onset of the search – are ordinarily not produced as guesses. As in excerpt (31), the searched for word is produced by speaker L right at the outset of the search and is designed as an assertedly correct continuation and not as a try-marked candidate. Here V is addressing a third participant (i.e. V is not addressing L).

(31)   [GL:DS]

> V: oh, it was funny we were up at Elsinore when they were having an
>   airplane, uh=
> L: =contest

The point here is that, while delayed candidates may also be done as assertedly correct, the early phase of the search seems to be left to the speaker, except when a co-participant can assert some special access to the trouble source. For example, early opportunistic completion of a word search is a device that can be used to initiate or sustain a special alignment with a speaker, one of story consociate-ship or association co-membership rather than recipientship (Lerner, 1992, 1993).

Word cut-offs. Word searches are designed to allow entry into the turn by recipients, but specifically limit that entry to the search for the item due next. Other practices for self-initiation of repair also disrupt the progressivity of a TCU and allow for opportunistic completion, but are not designed to elicit entry.

In a discussion of "conversational disruption markers" Jefferson (1974) describes a two-part format which she calls "the error cor-rection format." This format is used to begin one type of self-initiated self repair (Schegloff, Jefferson, and Sacks, 1977). Here a speaker abruptly cuts off a word before it has been fully articulated and then produces another word that is recognizable as a replace-ment for the cut-off word. Speakers use this procedure to replace a word that is currently being uttered or to recast a turn-in-progress or to launch a variety of other types of self-repair. The cut-off can show recipients that the unfinished word, or some (as yet) unspeci-fiable unit containing this word, may be being withdrawn (see Fox et al., this volume). Recipients can make use of this social-sequential fact by offering a replacement themselves. That is, the production of the first part of the format (cut-off) provides an opportunity for a recipient to offer up a replacement as a next action.

The continued progress of the turn is delayed by the initiation of repair. Error correction or other forms of self-initiated same-turn repair disrupt the progressivity of the utterance-in-progress. There is, however, a continued orientation to progressivity (Schegloff, 1979). Though the "error correction" format requires a suspension of sequential adjacency, it is built to minimize the disruption of serial adjacency.

While this device constitutes a recognizable self-repair, and does not in itself relinquish the ongoing turn, it nevertheless provides an unprojected opportunity for the production of talk by others. In the following instance, the cutoff ("across ah-") marks a break in adja-cency that provides an occasion for opportunistic completion.

(32) [GTS]

> Al: We get a thrill outta goin a hundred an fifty miles an hour
>   across ah- (·) in a [quater
> Roger: [across the intese(h)cti(h)on

In excerpt (32) Roger initiates opportunistic completion somewhat after Al has resumed a reprojected turn. Nonetheless, Roger locates his utterance as a continuation of the TCU to coincide with an earlier constituent boundary that the incipient replacement by Al shows to be the point the replacement begins from. (When the opportunity to enter the turn is taken by the recipient, and the prior speaker then also continues trying to produce the utterance-in-progress, it results in the "progressional overlap" that Jefferson, 1983a has described.)

"No-trouble" silences. Intra-turn pauses are regularly associated with "trouble" in the talk and with repair, but repair import is not a prerequisite for the production of an opportunistic completion. In excerpt (33) there is a pause of more than one second after the third part of what has been pre-formulated as a four part list.

(33) [HIC]

> Sparky: now dad wants to ah wants to have ah four officers
>   for the coming year, president, (0.5) vice president
>   secretry=treasurer (1.1) an [dah agent
> Dad: [agent

Here the pauses in the talk are "filled" with writing by the still current speaker. Pauses result since the writing of the list takes longer than the saying of the list. Pausing in the course of the list is organized by reference to writing and provides time to catch up. The speaker silence does not indicate trouble in producing the next item. However, the pause furnished by the writing activity provides an opportunity to produce the final list member.[16] The progressivity of the utterance itself (or more specifically its serial adjacency) is halted even though the disruption is "incarnately" accounted for in the scene. Various conversational practices can result in – and furnish a context for understanding – a pause in a TCU, yet the mere presence of a pause seems to provide a chance for a recipient to interpose an opportunistic completion. On the other hand, some self-initiation of repair can halt the progressivity of a TCU without necessarily resulting in a pause in the talk. (For example, cutting off a word and then producing another word as a replacement need not result in speaker silence.)

5.8.3 Word repetition

Though there are exceptions (such as intensification), word repetition ordinarily disrupts one aspect of turn progressivity: sequential adjacency is abandoned, while serial adjacency may be sustained. When words are repeated the sheer serial production of one word followed by a next may not be undone. No pause need occur in the talk; however, the adjacent placement of grammatically complementary words (that constitutes the sequential progressivity of the turn's talk) is halted by the repetition of the just prior word(s) as in excerpt (34).

(34) [GTS]

```
Ken:    There's kids in electric shop who get the biggest kick
        outta sticking a sticking a bobby [ pin-
Jim:                                      [their finger in.
```

Here, the serially adjacent next words by Ken after "outta sticking a" are recognizable as the repetition of words already spoken and not possible sequentially adjacent words. In addition, the repetition foreshows, in its course, where the sequential adjacency of the syntactic unit can be resumed, and the TCU may again begin progressing toward completion. This provides an enhanced opening for opportunistic completion. Moreover, once the progressivity of a TCU has been halted – even if it is subsequently re-established after a repeat as in (34) or after a cut-off as in (32) – the chance of interposing a completion continues as a possibility into the resumed TCU. However, there is one complication here. If more than one word is repeated, it cannot be determined (in real time) during the repeat of the first word whether the speaker is repeating, for example, two words, or whether they are recasting or reprojecting the TCU by repeating the first word and then changing the second word.

5.9 Extending opportunities for entry

Projected and unprojected opportunities for entry into another's turn space are not mutually exclusive. Retarding the progressivity of a TCU can occur in conjunction with preliminary component possible completion – as an extension of it – as in excerpts (35) to (37) below.

(35) [GTS] *Quote + laugh*

Roger: they rationalized it. they say heh heh heh
Louise: it wasn't there it was a(h)ll in hi(h)s imagination.

(36) [GL:DF] *Quote + pause*

Joan: she wz wi:se she'd pick up the pho:ne en say,
(0.4)
Linda: I'm comin over,

(37) [GTS] *List + pause*

Roger: Think about it you gotta be strong.
That's- that's three bottles a' champagne,
three: exerting rides, and uh
(0.5)
Al: three [exerting women
Dan: [six exerting rides

In each of these cases the disruption provides an extension for a preliminary component completion as indicated.

In addition, word cut-offs and repetition, and within-turn laughter and silence can occur in combination to produce and then extend an unprojected opportunity for entry as in excerpts (38) and (39). (Of course, the combination of these practices is partially ordered, insofar as, for example, a pause cannot be extended by a cut-off.)

(38) [GTS] *Cut-off + pause*

Louise: my father's six foot two feet he's large
an' he's a very s- (1.0)
Ken: st(hh)able person

(39) [GTS] *Cut-off + pause + repeat*

Ken: Like he c'd he c'n draw uh uh room
that's- that's round, and he c'd make it square,
and it's still- (0.2) still [the same kind-
Jim: [looks like a round room ehhhehhh

These instances show that the onset or initiation of a break in progressivity of a TCU can sometimes be distinct from its extension. The way in which the progressive movement of the talk is halted can indicate what sort of procedure is underway: a cut-off demonstrates retraction or consideration of retraction and adumbrates replacement of some type, while a sound stretch (or pre-pausal token such as "uhm") shows a concern not with current or prior words, but with the item due next (Schegloff, 1979). Either of these may or may not result in a pause. Further, a pause can occur without any pre-pausal indications and it may or may not occur in circumstances that indicate trouble in the talk. Yet, each of these halts the forward movement of the TCU (and the turn), and therein provides a chance for opportunistic completion. And this opportunity can be constructionally invoked by tying an opportunistic completion to the prior locus of retardation even if progressivity is re-established by current speaker. Further, the action accomplished by the interposed talk hinges on the context of its occurrence.

Recipients treat the progressivity of an utterance in a way that suggests that the orientation to minimizing gaps in the talk is not only an aspect of the production of turn transition at transition-relevance places, but reaches into turns as well. One cannot stop talking and maintain silence indefinitely in the course of a turn or otherwise retard the turn's progressivity indefinitely. *A speaker is entitled to produce a complete turn, but he or she is also obliged to continue the turn's talk to that completion.* Moreover, a speaker is obligated to continue the forward movement of the utterance-in-progress – i.e., its progress toward completion. The possibility of opportunistic completion provides a systematic "motivation" or basis for speakers to produce their turn without extended pauses and as fluently as possible. Opportunistic completion furnishes recipients with one device for enforcing this obligation, since the recipient of a halted turn-in-progress can bring the current turn-constructional unit to completion once the turn's progressivity has been disrupted. On the other hand, speakers of TCUs-in-progress also have practices available to them to maintain or re-etablish their speakership of the turn once another speaker attempts completion. One type of current speaker's device that has been identified is delayed completion (Lerner, 1989).

5.10 Concluding remarks

One aim of this chapter has been to show that the juncture between the preliminary and final components of a compound TCU is a grammatically specifiable locus for anticipatory completion. One import of this characterization is that it represents a formal speci-fication of the place a small sequence of action begins – the collaborative turn sequence – and further provides a specification of the form of its initiation – anticipatory completion.

This juncture amounts to a completion opportunity place, since (1) it is a systematically locatable possible intra-turn/intra-TCU component completion point, and (2) anticipatory completions are *designed* to begin here even when next speaker actually begins speaking elsewhere in the ongoing compound TCU. Moreover, I have shown how one material feature of speech production (a beat of silence at preliminary component completion) is a systematic possibility. This allows for the possible achievement of speaker transfer without overlap in the talk.

Moreover, I have shown that an "orientation to completion" extends beyond TCU completion to TCU-internal preliminary component completions, with some of the practices associated with the former available to participants at the latter location. Further, I have shown that this completion opportunity place is located at the point of completion of the preliminary component, but is operative (i.e. it can be invoked by a recipient through utterance tying) well into a current speaker's final component-in-progress. The opportunity to complete another's TCU, then, can be characterized as both bounded and flexible, with those completions begun after onset of a current speaker's next or final component nonetheless attending preliminary component completion as the proper locus of anticipatory completion onset.

In summary, this chapter has described some of the turn-constructional resources for initiating intra-turn talk by recipients of the current turn, and it has examined some of the forms this entry can take.[17] An orientation to grammatical structure – or perhaps a more felicitous term might be "grammatical *practice*" – in the form of compound TCUs, projectable TCU completion, and TCU progressivity provides recipients with resources for recognitional, pre-transitional (i.e. terminal item) and progressional completion of the TCU-in-progress, respectively.[18] As such, these grammatical practices in the emergent construction of turns at talk can furnish semi-permeable points of reference for organizing bits of sequential and interactional business.

Notes

* Elinor Ochs, Sandy Thompson, Tom Wilson and especially Manny Schegloff contributed to the development of this chapter. The work of Harvey Sacks has informed my analysis, both in its broadest strokes and in its finest detail.

1 It must be remembered that a transcript presents the talk in a manner that is unavailable to participants. Speakers issue their talk in real time and each increment of it can continue, modify, or abandon a previously projected turn-constructional form. So, for example, at a possible completion of a preliminary component, a speaker may extend that component or produce another recognizably preliminary component, as well as begin the projected final component or re-project the turn altogether. Please consult the glossary in the Appendix to this volume for an explanation of the transcript symbols that were used to prepare the data excerpts in this chapter.

2 In the case of excerpt (1), participants must suspend analysis of "when" until at least the next word to be able to determine what sort of unit type is underway, since it can also turn out to have been the beginning of a question.

3 In excerpt (4) the anticipatory completion is left incomplete. A fuller excerpt shows that Kerry has not simply stopped prematurely. Rather, he drops out after David begins a delayed completion of his own prior utterance.

[HIC]

```
David:    So if one person said he couldn't invest (.)
Kerry:    then I'd have to wait [till
David:                          [he'd have ta wait till January
Kerry:    Ri:ght
```

The concern of this report is with the structure of the juncture between the preliminary component and the projected final component as a place for speaker transition. Here transition occurs without overlap as in excerpts (2) and (3) and then continues the TCU *toward* a possible completion place. A characterization of the type of overlapping talk that occurs later in the turn has been described elsewhere (Lerner, 1989).

4 I believe this feature of anticipatory completion has led some researchers (e.g. Duncan and Fiske, 1977) to include it in their list of "back channel" responses. This designation obscures the range of interactional work anticipatory completion can accomplish and lumps it together with such distinct practices as the use of continuers (Schegloff, 1982). Though some forms of anticipatory completion can be specifically designed to accomplish adjunct speakership, positioning the anticipatory completion to begin at preliminary component

completion is ordinarily a move to speak in the "forefront" of the turn and not in its background.

5 Similarly, a slight pause can occur between TCUs in what turns out to be a multiple TCU turn. This beat of silence (typically left unmarked on transcripts, since it seems to be unmarked for participants) is consistent with Sacks, Schegloff and Jefferson's (1974) proposal that opportunities for self-selection by next speaker come *before* current speaker's option to continue. Wilson and Zimmerman (1986) provide some additional evidence for this position as a socially organized site for a beat of silence. Of course, in anticipation of another participant possibly self-selecting to speak next, a current speaker can reduce or eliminate this beat of silence by rushing-through the transition space (Schegloff, 1982, 1987).

Also, in a discussion of overlap onset, Jefferson (1983a) reports that of all the transition-place points, "unmarked next position" onset seems to be the most frequently used. In describing this position she states, "A recipient/next speaker ... *permits just a bit of space between the end of the prior utterance and the start of his own*" (emphasis in original). Here Jefferson is describing onset of overlap, with both current speaker continuing and next speaker beginning, one beat after possible completion of a TCU. This can also be seen to operate at preliminary component completion.

[Gerald]

```
   1  R:    if you don't put things
->2         on yer calender (.) [(f o r g e t  i t)]
   3  D:                        [yer outta luck.] Yeah(p). Fo:get it.
```

Here D begins in overlap with R. Since D begins simultaneously with R's continuation after a rest beat, it is not by reference to that continuation that he starts to speak. D's completion is responsive to R's preliminary component completion.

6 This distinction can be seen in an excerpt from Ford and Thompson (this volume, note 12) that they offer as a puzzling instance of two intonation units with final (i.e. downward) intonation contour, yet which do not coincide with syntactic completions as is otherwise massively the case in their data. These intonation units occur at lines 1 and 6.

[Ford & Thompson, this volume]

```
   1  V:    so the doctor said.
   2         that they would
   3         (0.3)
   4         If he:
   5         (0.5)
   6         didn't wanna keep being active and do sports 'n things.
   7         right now at his age and with the bad condition of his knee,
   8         they normally put in a plastic knee.
```

Strikingly, both of these intonation units constitute preliminary components of a compound TCU type that I have described elsewhere (Lerner, 1991). They are preliminary components from [quote marker + quote] and [if x + then y] compound TCUs, respectively. The downward intonation contours can thus be understood as coinciding with (and certifying) preliminary component completion.

7   Note that unlike most of the previous cases, this anticipatory completion is produced not by the addressed recipient, but by a co-aligning speaker. Both the position of the interposing speaker (as addressed recipient or other participant), and the "target" of the anticipatory completion itself (erstwhile current speaker or their addressed recipient) are constitutive of the type of action accomplished. These two features of anticipatory completion furnish four "directional" combinations, all of which can be found in empirical materials. However, only two seem to be structurally preferred or unmarked.

8   In contrast, in another TCU-internal environment, that of "post-conjunctional silence," Jefferson (1983b) found that others do not start speaking once the current speaker restarts. And that the converse – if another speaker begins speaking, the erstwhile current speaker regularly does not restart – also seems to be the case for post-conjunctional silence. Jefferson proposes that this is one specification of "First starter gets the turn" (Sacks, Schegloff, and Jefferson, 1974), but applied to the not-currently-speaking occupant of the turn space. However, neither of these findings hold for preliminary component possible completion. That is, even if current speaker begins the next component of a compound TCU, an interposing speaker may still render a completion as in excerpt (9) and even if an interposing speaker begins in the clear at preliminary component possible completion, the erstwhile current speaker may very well interject their own completion as the excerpt in note 3 demonstrates. I believe the difference here lies in part in the form of the contribution of the interposing speaker and the different types of actions they can accomplish. Jefferson examined cases in which the interposing speaker begins a new turn, while I am describing cases in which a rendition of the foreshown final component of the TCU-in-progress is produced.

9   This sort of compression may be taken further, though the compression itself makes this difficult if not impossible to establish. In the following excerpt, Mike, at line 7, begins in the course of a compound TCU, but not until the last possible place to begin still within the current turn space.

[CS:5]

```
1  Mike:    Are you actually gonna use a whole, leave a whole mound of horseshit in
2           the middle of Dean's dri:veway?
3           (0.9)
4  Steve:   Its fer:tilizer
5  Mike:    hh hahhah: I(h)m so(h)rr(h)y,
6  Fran:    when it comes intuh Encino it becomes fert[ i l i z e r  ]
->7 Mike:                                              [>fertilizer<]
```

Here most of the "then" part of a [when X + then Y] format may have
been skipped. Mike may be producing a very late anticipatory completion in which component contiguity is abandoned in favor of producing what could still be recognizable as an anticipatory completion
prior to the completion of current speaker's final component. The
faster tempo of line 7 (">fertilizer<") does show he is hurrying to
completion. On the other hand, another systematic form of next
speaker completion is "terminal item" completion in which only the
final word or two of a TCU is produced. See, for examples, excerpts
(22) and (23). These need not occur in compound TCUs. It may be that
Mike has abandoned a demonstration of contiguity with the preliminary component, but in doing so he ends up producing a terminal item
completion.

10   Recycling the beginning of the anticipatory completion is only one
      option here. Speakers, finding themselves in overlap after having
      started an early anticipatory completion, can continue to completion
      as Kerry does in the following excerpt. Here the compound turn-con-
      structional format is furnished by the production of a parenthetical
      insert ("if we're gunna do it on that").

[HIC]

```
Dad:     but I would like to change that twenny five percent
         if we're gunna do it on th[at to twenny
Kerry:                             [to fifteen
```

As Jefferson (1986) has noted, "merely continuing" provides one standard practice for dealing with overlapping talk.

11   One could argue the opposite: that laugh tokens constitute on-time
      next increments to the TCU preserving serial adjacency, but they
      delay arrival of next elements that "count" syntactically, thus disrupt-
      ing sequential adjacency. However, it is my view that laughter is not
      treated as an element of TCU production, though it is an element of the
      turn – or in Schegloff's (this volume) terms, the laughter does not
      belong to the TCU, though it belongs to the turn. It is only when an
      element can be entertained as possibly the sequentially next word that
      the possibility of a delay in sequential adjacency can be assessed.

12   In this regard, this instance is similar to the two-part complaint format
      described earlier that provides enhanced resources for completion, but
      does not foreshow a preliminary component completion that could
      further enhance the possibility of pre-empting the current speaker.

13   However, initial investigation suggests that there are circumstances where isolated laugh tokens are used as interjections to construct short responsive turns. Nevertheless, most laughing that occurs in talk is not bound by an orientation to "one at a time" and in fact Jefferson (1979) shows that there seems to be an orientation to not laughing alone, but laughing together. In that sense, initial laugh tokens can be seen as an "invitation" to others to also laugh.

14   Schegloff (this volume) provides another example of post-beginning silence. In describing a speaker's rush-through at a transition-relevance place, he writes, "it is common for the speaker to allow the break which might otherwise have occurred at possible completion to develop just after the start of the new TCU, at a place of ... 'maximum grammatical control'."

15   I am indebted to Manny Schegloff for pointing this out to me.

16   It is worth noting that the participant who adds "agent" had been mentioned as the author of the yet-to-be enumerated list of officers, and in addition has been, wants to continue to be, and as it turns out does continue to hold the position of, "agent."

17   This chapter has focused on various forms of restricted or conditional entry into the turn space of another speaker. However, there are other social-organizational bases for jointly participating in the production of a single TCU. Certain courses of action shape what counts as a contribution to the talk, in terms local to that course of action. So, for some activities, a TCU can sometimes constitute a shared environment or shared opportunity for participant contributions. For example, when elementary school students in a cooperative work group are jointly engaged in defining a word or answering a story question, they can accomplish this task by contributing candidate definitions or answers-to-the-question designed as complete TCUs. However, students can also accomplish these tasks by transforming them into shared tasks of utterance completion (Lerner, 1995), as they are doing in the following excerpt.

[CIRC:Dugg]

```
        A:      Doctor Moore wouldn't tell mister (Auldin) becau::se.
                (.)
-->     B:      uhm,
                (0.2)
-->     A:      because .hh doctor Moore wanted to keep it a secret,
-->     B:      because doctor Moore wanted to keep him working for him
        A:      ((A begins writing the group's answer))
```

(In a related vein, Ochs, Schieffelin, and Platt (1979) have examined major arguments and their predications in the propositions of language-learning children that are produced across utterances.) These courses of action, and they are not found only in classroom interaction, provide a shared opportunity to produce the anticipated completion. In these instances it is not so much the case that one speaker is entering the turn space of another speaker, but rather that there is a shared entitlement to speak (cf. Lerner, 1993).

18 This closely complements Jefferson's (1983a) description of overlap onset loci, since overlap in each of these locations (e.g. excerpts (13), (22) and (32) respectively) can result from recipient attempts at completion, if current speaker also continues speaking.

References

Du Bois, J., Schuetze-Coburn, S., Paolino, D., and Cumming, S. (1993). Outline of discourse transcription. In J. Edwards and M. Lampert (eds.) *Talking Data: Transcription and Coding Methods for Language Research*, pp. 45–89. Hillsdale, NJ: Lawrence Erlbaum.

Duncan, S., Jr., and Fiske, D. W. (1977). *Face-to-Face Interaction: Research, Methods, and Theory*. New York: Wiley.

Ford, C. (1993). *Grammar in Interaction: Adverbial Clauses in American English Conversations*. Cambridge: Cambridge University Press.

Goffman, E. (1978). Response Cries. *Language* 54: 787-815.

(1979). Footing. *Semiotica* 25: 1–29.

Goodwin, C. (1980). Restarts, pauses, and the achievement of a state of mutual gaze at turn-beginning. *Sociological Inquiry* 50(3/4): 277–302.

Goodwin, C. (1986). Between and within: alternative sequential treatments of continuers and assessments. *Human Studies*, 9, 205-17.

Goodwin, M. H. (1980). Processes of mutual monitoring implicated in the production of description sequences. *Sociological Inquiry* 50: 303–17.

Goodwin, M. H. and Goodwin, C. (1986). Gesture and coparticipation in the activity of searching for a word. *Semiotica* 62(1/2): 51–75.

Goodwin, C. and Goodwin, M. H. (1987). Concurrent operations on talk: notes on the interactive organization of assessments. *IPrA Papers in Pragmatics* 1, no.1: 1–52.

Jefferson, G. (1973). A case of precision timing in ordinary conversation: overlapped tag-positioned address terms in closing sequences. *Semiotica* 9(1) 47–96.

(1974). Error correction as an interactional resource. *Language in Society*, 3(2): 181–99.

(1979). A technique for inviting laughter and its subsequent acceptance/declination. In G. Psathas (ed.) *Everyday Language: Studies in Ethnomethodology*, pp. 79–96.) New York, NY: Irvington Publishers.

(1983a). Notes on some orderlinesses of overlap onset. *Tilburg Papers in Language and Literature* 28(1): 1–28.

(1983b). On a failed hypothesis: "Conjunctionals" as overlap-vulnerable. *Tilburg Papers in Language and Literature* 28(2): 1–33.

(1984). Notes on a systematic deployment of the acknowledgement tokens "yeah" and "mm hm". *Papers in Linguistics* 17(2): 197–216.

(1986). Notes on "latency" in overlap onset. *Human Studies* 9: 153–83.

Jefferson, G., Sacks, H. and Schegloff, E.A. (1973). Preliminary notes on the sequential organization of laughter. *Pragmatics Microfiche*. Cambridge: Cambridge University Department of Linguistics.

Jefferson, G. and Schegloff, E. A. (1975). Sketch: some orderly aspects of overlap in natural conversation. Unpublished paper.

Lerner, G. H. (1987). *Collaborative Turn Sequences: Sentence Construction and Social Action*. Unpublished doctoral dissertation. University of California, Irvine.

(1989). Notes on overlap management in conversation: the case of delayed completion. *Western Journal of Speech Communication* 53(2): 167–77.

(1991). On the syntax of sentences-in-progress. *Language In Society* 20(3): 441–58.

(1992). Assisted storytelling: deploying shared knowledge as a practical matter. *Qualitative Sociology* 15(3): 247–71.

(1993). Collectivities in action: establishing the relevance of conjoined participation in conversation. *Text* 13(2): 213–45.

(1995). Turn design and the organization of participation in instructional activities. *Discourse Processes* 19(1): 111–31.

Ochs, E., Schieffelin, B., and Platt, M. (1979). Propositions across utterances and speakers. In E. Ochs and B. Schieffelin (eds.) *Developmental Pragmatics*, pp. 251–68. New York: Academic Press.

Pomerantz, A. (1984). Agreeing and disagreeing with assessments: some features of preferred/dispreferred turn shapes. In J. M. Atkinson and J. Heritage (eds.) *Structures of Social Action: Studies in Conversation Analysis*, pp. 57–101. Cambridge: Cambridge University Press.

Sacks, H. (1987). On the preferences for agreement and contiguity in sequences in conversation. In G. Button and J. R. E. Lee (eds.) *Talk and Social Organisation*, pp. 54–69. Clevedon, England: Multilingual Matters.

(1992). *Lectures on Conversation*. 2 volumes. Edited by G. Jefferson, with Introductions by E. A. Schegloff. Oxford: Blackwell.

Sacks, H. and Schegloff, E. A. (1979). Two preferences in the organization of reference to persons in conversation and their interaction. In G. Psathas (ed.) *Everyday Language: Studies in Ethnomethodology*, pp. 15–21. New York, NY: Irvington Publishers.

Sacks, H., Schegloff, E. A., and Jefferson, G. (1974). A simplest systematics for the organization of turn-taking for conversation. *Language* 50: 696–735.

Schegloff, E. A. (1979). The relevance of repair for syntax-for-conversation. In T. Givón (ed.) *Syntax and Semantics 12: Discourse and Syntax*, pp. 261–88. New York: Academic Press.

(1982). Discourse as an interactional achievement: some uses of "uh huh" and other things that come between sentences. In D. Tannen (ed.) *Georgetown University Roundtable on Languages and Linguistics*, pp. 71–93. Washington DC: Georgetown University Press.

(1987). Recycled turn beginnings: a precise repair mechanism in conversation's turn-taking organization. In G. Button and J. R. E. Lee (eds.) *Talk and Social Organisation*, pp. 70–85. Clevedon, England: Multilingual Matters, Ltd.

Schegloff, E. A., Jefferson, G., and Sacks, H. (1977). The preference for self-correction in the organization of repair in conversation. *Language* 53(2): 361–82.

Wilson, T. P. and Zimmerman, D. H. (1986). The structure of silence between turns in two-party conversation. *Discourse Processes* 9: 375–90.

On repeats and responses in Finnish conversations*

MARJA-LEENA SORJONEN

6.1 Introduction

Every language has conventionalized means for providing responses in talk-in-interaction. One set of these devices are particles, such as *niin* and *joo* in Finnish or *yes* in English. They are one-word linguistic expressions that have a potential for forming an utterance by themselves.[1] These expressions are inherently indexical in their nature (on indexicality see, e.g. Silverstein, 1976; Heritage, 1984a; Ochs, 1988 and 1990). They point to their prior utterance which is prototypically produced by another speaker. By reference to that prior utterance, they offer an analysis of it. This analysis is being embedded in the action that they constitute. Furthermore, they are fitted to the trajectory of the larger activity and they participate in the progression of it. The response tokens, like other actions, are "'reflexive" in maintaining or altering the sense of the activities and unfolding circumstances in which they occur" (Heritage, 1984a: 140). Their meaning is particularized by reference to the specific contexts of their use in which they are deployed in highly systematic ways for achieving particular interactional ends.

The purpose of this paper is to shed light on the meaning of response tokens by presenting initial observations on the particles *niin* and *joo* as constituting social actions in Finnish conversations. *Niin* and *joo* are among the most common response tokens in Finnish conversations. They have entered the field of Finnish discourse practices from different directions. *Joo* is a loan word from Swedish (Suomen sanojen alkuperä, s.v. *joo*) which has acquired its distinctive conventions of use in Finnish. The meaning of the particle is described in the etymological dictionary of Finnish as equivalent

to the German particle *ja(wohl)*. *Niin*, by contrast, is an original
Finno-Ugric word which etymologically belongs to the paradigm
for the demonstrative *se* "it; that" as its instructive case form in
plural. *Se* is the most common device in anaphora: "it freely links
with anything that was previously stated, especially with something
that is prominent and relevant in what was just said" (Larjavaara,
1990: 326–27).[2] The instructive case found in *niin* indexes, for
example, manner of action.[3] However the status of *niin* as a case-
marked, inflected element has faded early on, and it has been understood as a particle (Hakulinen, 1961: 74, 330). *Niin* functions, for
example, as an adverb of manner and as a degree word.[4] It is, however, also capable of forming an utterance and turn at talk of its own
in several different contexts. In such cases its distribution partially
overlaps with the distribution of *joo*. For example, both of them are
used as affirmative answers to a subset of yes-no interrogatives and
as continuers displaying an understanding that coparticipant has not
finished her or his talk yet (cf. Schegloff, 1982). Only one aspect of
the usages of *niin* and *joo* will be discussed here:[5] the use of these
particles to provide a response to a repeat. The sequence type to be
discussed can be schematized initially as follows:

1 A   Turn at talk
2 B   Repeat of 1
3 A   (a) *niin*
        (b) *joo*[6]

The response tokens will be discussed as a response to a nonclausal repeat, that is, the repeat contains constituents other than
the finite verb. Furthermore, in the cases to be discussed this constituent is the only element in the repeat turn.[7] In most of the cases,
the repeat is partial, that is, the repeated utterance contains more
than the constituent that gets repeated.

In addition to the particles, the paper contributes also to our
understanding of types of actions done through repeats and their
sequential and activity contexts. Utterances which repeat the entire
utterance by the coparticipant or its part have been discussed in the
linguistic literature by reference to issues such as sentence structure,
ellipsis and question types (see, e.g., Bolinger, 1957; Quirk et al.
1972; Halliday and Hasan, 1976; Chisholm (ed.), 1984; Ueki,
1989). This literature offers a noteworthy contribution to linguistic

studies by recognizing the existence of types of utterances that may take the form other than a clause and that through such form presuppose in a particular way what the coparticipant has just said. The literature also makes reference to functions that repeats may carry. For example, the reference grammar of English by Quirk et al. (1972: 408–11) states that all "echo utterances" are, depending on their intonation, either interrogative or exclamatory in function; "echo questions" carry a rising tone, whereas "echo exclamations" are done with a rising-falling (or high falling) tone. A further functional characterization is presented by appealing to the kind of response that is made relevant by a repeat. Thus a "recapitulatory echo question" repeats the prior utterance or its part in order to have its content confirmed (e.g. *The Browns are emigrating. – Emigrating?*), whereas an "explicatory echo question" is always a WH-question and serves as a request for clarification (e.g. *Take a look at this! – Take a look at WHAT?*). The basic function of "echo exclamations" is to express astonishment. In their discussion on ellipsis in English, Halliday and Hasan (1976: 214–15) offer repeats among the examples of "question rejoinders" which have the function of "querying a preceding statement or command, or eliciting supplementary information about it." Such a rejoinder can, for example, presuppose the entire prior utterance and seek confirmation of it as a whole (e.g. *Peter's here. – He is?*), or identify one item to be confirmed (e.g. *John's coming to dinner. – John?*). Finally, Bolinger's study on interrogative structures in American English introduces (1957: 8) a distinction between "echo" and "reflex" questions to capture the type of prior utterance repeated: in echo questions the coparticipant's repeated utterance is a question; in reflex questions the speaker repeats, as a question, a part or all of the preceding non-question.

These studies draw attention to the structural relationship between the repeat and its prior utterance and to prosody as an index for utterance function. The discussion, however, stays on a rather general level as to the more specific composition of repeats, their interactional environment and the types of verbal actions done through them. Interactional studies have specified the types of verbal action accomplished by repeats and the association between these actions and their sequential and activity context (see e.g. Jefferson, 1972, 1981; Goldberg, 1975; Ochs [Keenan], 1977; Schegloff et al. 1977; Goodwin, 1983; Heritage, 1984b; Button and Casey, 1985; Norrick,

1987; Schegloff, 1987, 1994; Tannen, 1987a,b). So for example, Jefferson (1972) discusses repeats as a way of initiating a side-sequence within an on-going activity in order to, for example, focus on a problem with the prior utterance. Similarly, Schegloff et al. (1977: 367–68) present two types of partial repeat among the devices through which a recipient of some talk can, in a next turn, initiate a repair on some trouble in hearing or understanding that talk (a partial repeat plus a question word, e.g. .hhh Well I'"m working through the Amfat Corporation. – The who?, and a partial repeat, e.g. Well Monday, lemme think, Monday, Wednesday, an" Fridays I'"m home by one ten. – One ten?). Jefferson (1981: 62–66) and Heritage (1984b: 339–44) discuss "pro-repeats" as "newsmarks", that is, as utterances that express ritualized disbelief and treat the prior talk by coparticipant as news rather than mere informing (e.g. They charge too much Guy, – Oh do they?). Goldberg (1975: 276–77) mentions repetitions as a way of receiving instructions. Schegloff (1994: 17–18) brings together much of the prior work on repeats by laying out three types of sequential position that a repeat can at least occupy, and actions associated with repeats in those positions: a repeat may be used to initiate a sequence, most commonly a repair sequence; it can be deployed as a response in a second position in a sequence, for example, as an answer to a question; or it can occupy a third position, where it may receive a response, for example, an answer to a question.

Interactional studies demonstrate the constitutive role that sequential and activity context play in the production and interpretation of linguistic forms such as repeats, and a range of actions a form can be used to accomplish. However repeats of the type discussed in this paper, i.e. nonclausal repeats, have not been a focus of detailed studies. Furthermore, responses to repeats form an even more uncharted area of research. In what follows, the work accomplished by the particles niin and joo as response to a repeat will be demonstrated through analyses of the particular sequential and activity contexts of their occurrence. The term "sequence" is used here mainly to refer to sequences such as adjacency pair and its parts (see Schegloff, 1990, on adjacency pairs as a basic sequence type), whereas the term "activity" is deployed to capture a course of action which is topically coherent and/or goal-coherent and which may be achieved across a sequence or series of sequences (cf. Heritage and Sorjonen,

1994: 4–5). It will be suggested that the two response tokens are typically associated with different kinds of contexts. Two important issues in these contexts are the participants' epistemological stances toward some state of affairs and the completeness vs. incompleteness of the on-going sequence and/or activity. The data for the present study are drawn from a corpus of recordings and transcripts of thirty-six telephone calls;[8] one example (example (4)) comes from a face-to-face conversation. I will first discuss instances in which the repeat is responded to by the particle *niin*. I will start with a single case analysis through which I will lay out some important aspects of the types of contexts that are the focus of this paper.

6.2 *Niin*: doing a confirmation

6.2.1 *Single case analysis*

A central task for a recipient of an utterance is to understand the type of action done in and through that utterance. An utterance gets recognized as a repeat on the basis of its structural relationship to its prior utterance. This dependence relation indexes that the specifics of the prior utterance and the action(s) accomplished by it contribute in a crucial way to the interpretation of the repeat.[9] By doing a repeat a speaker foregrounds an element in the prior utterance for some interactional end. But given that a repeat, as mentioned above, can be used to accomplish multiple different tasks the question for the recipient of the repeat in example (1) is: what is the other participant doing by responding to her utterance at lines 2-3 by repeating a part of it and doing only so in her turn at talk? Let us start the analysis of the example from the first utterance in the dependence chain, that is, from the utterance that is the target of the repeat (lines 2–3).[10]

(1) [Invitation:5]

```
1  S:    Hy[vä juttu.            ]
         good  thing
         Goo:d.                  ]
         [                       ]
2  T:    [>.h ↑Arto   ei  pääse ]   tule-e.  Se on vähä
         [    1nameM NEG be able to come-ILL it is a little
         [>.h ↑Arto can't make it. That's a bit of a
```

```
3          tyhmä-ä<.
           stupid-PAR
           nuisance.


4          (0.3)


5   S: --> Arto.


6   T: ==> Nii<


7          (0.4)


8   S:     [(Kui nii,)          ]
           [ how so             ]
           [(Why,)              ]
           [                    ]
9   T:     [Si-l    on esi:tys ]   #sillo#.  °.hh[h°
           [it-ADE is performance then           [
           [He's perfo:rming   #then#.          °.hh[h°
                                                     [
10  S:                                    [He-
                                          [name (=Helsinki)
                                          [He-


11         Turu-s    vai Helsingi-s°sä°.
           name-INE  or  name-INE
           In Turku or in Helsin°ki°.

12            (.)


13  T:     Turu-ssa.
           name-INE
           In Turku.


14  S:     £(Ei   ku   se on-ki)=
             NEG PRT it is-CLI
           £(No it's)=


15  T:     =Tam[peree-lla eh heh heh .hh]
              name-ADE                  ]
           =In Tampere eh heh heh .hh   ]
```

```
S:        [Tamperee-lla eh heh heh ] .hhh °Voi: juku.°

          [name-ADE              ]       oh boy


          [In Tampere eh heh heh ] .hhh °Oh: boy.°


17   T:   °Joo:.°

          °Yea:h.°


18   S:   m: Mut Sini   tulee.

             but 1nameF comes

          m: But Sini is coming.
```

The segment in (1) comes from a call which Tiina (T) has made to invite Susanna (S), a friend of a friend, to a housewarming party; Susanna has accepted the invitation shortly before the segment at hand. The turn at lines 2–3 initiates a sequence, i.e. it is a first pair part of an adjacency pair, and offers a new topical line into the talk through its two utterances (on the difference between sequence and topic, see Schegloff, 1990). The type of utterances and their temporal order make the turn heard to accomplish particular kind of actions.

The first utterance at line 2 offers a report of a prospective non-occurrence. This utterance may potentially be heard as a complaint: one common type of action that such negative formulations do, through attributing a failure, is a complaint (Schegloff, 1988: 121). The second utterance contributes to that hearing by evaluating, through the descriptor *tyhmää<* lit. "stupid; nuisance" the reported state of affairs as undesirable. The turn makes relevant certain types of next action. As a complaint it invites, for example, some kind of agreement or alignment by the recipient (cf. Schegloff, 1988: 122; Pomerantz, 1984b). As a report it sequentially implicates, for example, a registering of its informativeness or a claim of prior knowledge (Heritage, 1984b: 300–07; Schegloff 1988: 122). We can also observe that as a report the turn is hearably incomplete: more could be told about the reported state of affairs, for example, the reason why the third person, Arto, is not able to attend the party. In this sense the turn may also be heard as an invitation to the recipient to forward the telling by explicitly requesting for an account (cf. Button and Casey, 1985). Thus the type of action accomplished by the turn provides a multiplicity of possibilities for the response.

The temporality of talk is an important resource for interactants in producing and understanding meaning in talk-in-interaction: whatever it is that follows a turn is heard as against its sequential implications. In (1), the turn at lines 2–3 is followed by a silence (line 4). As against the normal temporal progression of actions, the response to the complaint/report/topic offer is heard missing. A delay of this type, that is, after a possibly completed turn that has made relevant some action by the recipient, typically indexes some trouble on the part of the recipient with respect to the prior talk (Pomerantz, 1984a,b).

It is at this point that the repeat is produced. The composition of the turn, its prosodic architecture and the choice of the repeated element are crucial for the ways in which utterances done as a repeat may be understood. The fact that the speaker does not proceed into further talk rules out the possibility that in this sequential environment the repeat would have been used as a receipt that registers the prior talk: the way for the speaker to indicate that kind of function would be to go on into further talk after the repeat that would, for example, assess the report or request for further information. In the case at hand, the repeat has a falling final contour which is associated not only with statements but also frequently with questions in Finnish (Hirvonen, 1970; Iivonen, 1978). By doing a repeat only the speaker is heard doing an action that invites a response from the other party; more specifically, she is heard doing an inquiry of some sort.

The position and type of the repeated element in its original turn narrows down the set of possible functions of the repeat further. As mentioned above, one possible next action made relevant by the turn at lines 2–3 is an inquiry that would address the incompleteness of the report. However the way to indicate that kind of orientation would be to repeat the predicate verb, for example *Ei pääse vai* "cannot make it *vai*" or *Ei vai.* "no *vai.*"[11] In the case at hand, the repeated element, *Arto*, is the subject of the first utterance. We can now notice that the turn at lines 2–3 was initiated in overlap and the repeated element was the one to begin the overlap. This makes it plausible that *Arto* was obscured by the overlap – the repeat could have been done in order to solve a problem in hearing it. A further, more remote possibility might be that the repeat targets the possible implications of the report for the recipient. Arto, the protagonist of the report, is the husband of Sini, a mutual friend who, as it has turned out earlier in the call, is a link between the participants. The husband's inability to attend the party might imply that his wife would not come either which would leave Susanna without any friends at the party. The repeat may be targetted to clarify this issue by drawing attention to the fact that only one member of the couple was mentioned. The composition of the repeat turn displays that the action done by the recipient is none of the responses implicated by the report in lines 2–3. Rather, the repeat is heard initiating a repair on some trouble with the prior talk (Schegloff et al. 1977). Minimally, it invites the recipient to offer a confirmation as the response.

In (1), the recipient responds to the repeat by the particle *niin*. Through this response, she registers the repeat as an inquiry of a type "request for confirmation" and aligns with its sequential implications by doing a confirmation. What is it that gets confirmed then? We have already touched upon two possible issues that the repeat may be raising (cf. also Comrie, 1984: 37): (1) a question concerning the expressions used in which case the confirmation would orient to the repeat as an attempt to solve a problem in hearing: "*Arto* - is that the name you mentioned?"; (2) a question concerning the validity of the report: "You said that it is *Arto* who cannot make it. Is that so?" But even though the repeat in the latter case would, by virtue of its form, seem to invite a simple confirmation as its response, it would interactionally ask for an elaboration, for example, an account for what was stated. *Niin* as a response does not orient to possible ambiguities in the interpretation of the repeat: in (1), it provides both a response to a hearing problem and to a question about the validity of the statement. However both of these two ways of understanding the force of the repeat still treat it as a display of some trouble.

What would then be the implications of a confirmation for the subsequent talk if it were the only action by the speaker? By confirming but doing nothing else the speaker is heard suggesting that the state of talk before the repeat prevails and that a response to the utterance that was the target of the repeat is now due. In example (1), the confirmation is followed by a silence (line 7). The participants begin simultaneously turns (lines 8 and 9 respectively) that are congruent with each other: the repeat speaker requests for an account and the report initiator provides one. These actions orient to one feature in the prior report: its incompleteness. Thus the recipient of that report produces now an action that was among the actions that were sequentially implicated by the report. The report initiator, on the other hand, volunteers an elaboration implicated by the report.

But what is then the silence at line 7 doing? Against it, the account given by the confirmation speaker at line 9 may well be responsive to the absence of talk by the repeat speaker: it can be heard responding to an inference from the silence that more than a confirmation was needed as a response. Similarly, the repeat speaker's request at line 8 can be oriented to the silence in which case, by implication, it may display that more than a confirmation was looked for by the repeat. The participants may thus have oriented to the repeat in two different ways initially: its speaker as a request for confirmation and elaboration; its recipient as a request for confirmation.[12] Thus, the subsequent development of the talk after the repeat has specified the interpretation of the repeat. Simultaneously it has recast the sufficiency of *niin* as a response.

The aspects of the sequential and activity context in example (1) characterize environments for the particle *niin* as a response to a repeat also more generally. *Niin* is associated with contexts in which a repeat is produced as a response to a turn that either initiates a sequence as in example (1) above, i.e. is a first pair part in an adjacency pair, and/or where the larger activity is otherwise, e.g. in terms of the topic and/or its goal, continuation relevant. In such context, the repeat is hearable as an inquiry that minimally invites a confirmation as the response. *Niin* registers the repeat as a request for confirmation and aligns with it by providing a confirmation. It thereby formulates the prior turn and itself as a unit of action, as an adjacency pair. *Niin* by itself does not serve to disambiguate between different possible ways of understanding the more specific function of the repeat. It provides the response, a confirmation, that the repeat through its form projects. In so doing it accomplishes an epistemological task of claiming to remove an uncertainty conveyed by the repeat. By providing a confirmation *niin* possibly closes down the sequence initiated by the repeat and suggests a continuation of the on-going larger sequence and/or activity.

6.2.2 Trajectory of talk after a confirmation: same-speaker continuations

We have seen in the previous section how subsequent talk can select from among the actions that the repeat and the particle *niin* can accomplish. The trajectory of talk after *niin* in general gives us resources for understanding what is being done through the repeat and the particle. There are two important dimensions with respect to the subsequent talk: (1) which of the two participants produces the next bit of talk and (2) what is being done through the talk. Let us first look at instances in which the speaker of *niin* proceeds into further talk in the same turn.

When the speaker continues her or his turn after *niin*, the continuation displays an orientation that more than a one-word confirmation was needed as a response to the repeat, that is, the focus of the talk is kept on the same issue raised by the repeat. More specifically, the continuation provides an elaboration which treats the repeat as an indication of some trouble other than a hearing problem. In example (2) the *niin* speaker proceeds to clarify his prior talk that was the target of the repeat.

(2) [Hunting:11-13]

```
1 M:    =↑No: joku-ha      ampu:    e  tytö-n   #ö::#
        PRT somebody-CLI shoot(PST) um girl-ACC er::
        =↑Well: somebody you know sho:t um a girl #er:#


2       metso-na        vai#::y  mi-nä    se am#pu.
        wood grouse-ESS or       what-ESS it shoot(PST)
        as a wood grouse or#::er what was it (he)/(she) shot.


3 K:    Ällä.
        don't
        No kidding.

               [
4 M:           [.hh Joo joo:.
               [.hh Yeah yea:h.


5       (0.4)
```

```
 6 M:      Kuustoist-vuotias kimma.
           sixteen-year(ADJ) gal
           A sixteen year old gal.


 7         (0.7)



 8 K:      Kuol-i-k   se,
           die-PST-Q  it
           Did she die,


 9 M:      Kuol-i.
           die-PST
           She did.


10         (.)


11 M:      Suoraan        #naama-an#.
           straight(ADV)  face-ILL
           Straight #in the face.#


12         (1.0)


13 K: -->  ↑Suoraan       naa:ma-a[n.
           straight(ADV)  face-ILL
           ↑Straight in the fa:ce.

                                   [
14 M: ==>                          [#N̲ii:: siis p̲ää#-hä,hh
                                   [ PRT   PRT  head-ILL
                                   [#N̲ii:: in other words in the h̲ead,hh



15 K:      N'    ampu        si-tä.
           they  shoot(PST)  it-PAR
           They sh̲ot at her.
```

```
16 M:      J_o:,

           Y_ea:,
```

```
17 K:      M_etso-na.

           wood grouse-ESS

           As a w_ood grouse.
```

Just before the segment, Martti (M) has launched a report on a news story about a hunting accident as advice to Kari (K) who is going to hunt the following weekend. As an elaboration of his answer to Kari's question about the consequences of the accident, Martti identifies the part of the body hit by the bullet (line 11). This elaboration is, after a full second silence, responded to by the recipient with a repeat at line 13 which, through its prosody (high initial pitch and vowel lengthening), indexes surprise and puzzlement. The teller first responds to the repeat by the response token *Nii: :* and then proceeds to continue his response with *siis pää̲hä̲,hh* "in other words in the head" (line 14).

Niin confirms the repeat. The continuation offers a reformulation (expressed by the connector *siis* "in other words/that is to say") of the description that was the target of the repeat. The reformulation is provided as the intended meaning of the prior description. What the speaker is in effect doing is to correct the other participant's understanding of the sense in which the repeated lexeme had been used by its original speaker. In so doing he challenges the disbelief he had heard the repeat to index and thereby transforms *niin* from a confirmation targetted to a display of disbelief into one that confirms that the repeated element was what was said by the speaker in the original utterance. The occurrence of *Nii̲::* before the reformulation, as against, for example, a disconfirmation or a turn without any response token, makes the provided description *pää̲hän* "in the head" heard as a reformulation but not as a replacement of the earlier description: the intended meaning is treated as a meaning which would naturally be understood as the meaning of *naamaan* "in the face" in this connection. In this case, the *niin* carried act of confirming and the epistemological claim made in and through it bears crucially on the way in which the subsequent utterance (*siis pää#hä̲,hh* "in other words in the head") by the speaker is understood. This subsequent utterance, on the other hand, specifies the way in which the repeat was heard and simultaneously recasts the function of *niin*. It shows that the repeat was heard to index a particular problematic understanding of what the speaker had said.

In some cases, the type of the larger on-going activity unambiguously invites more than a confirmation as a response, and the recipient of the repeat displays an orientation to that kind of implication. However a confirmation is still provided and it is provided by *niin*. The order of the actions is invariant: the confirmation is done before the talk that responds to the interactional import of the repeat. Example (3) is a case in point.[13]

(3) [Bus:14-15]

```
 1 V:    fKyl-hä        sä  tiedä-t (.) mikä on bussi
         certainly-CLI you know-2      what is bussi
         fYou certainly know (.) what the bus is


 2              [tamperee-[ks.
                [Tampere dialect-TRA
                [in Tampere dialect.
                [          [

 3 M:           [Moro.    [Jo(h)o hoh .ih .hih [.hhh
                [Hi:.     [Yh(h)eah hah .eh heh [.hhh
                                               [

 4 V:                                          [Tiedä-t sä   mikä
                                               [know-2  you what
                                               [Do you know what the


 5       on bus[si tamperee-ks.]
         is bus     Tampere dialect-TRA
         bus is in Tampere dialect.
               [                ]
 6 M:          [fEi::.         ]
               [ NEG           ]
               [fNye::.        ]


 7 V:    [Nysse.]
         [      ]
 8 M:    [(Qi-) ]
         ?would it be
```

```
 9 M:    Mikä.

         what(NOM)

         What.


10 V:    [Ny:sse.]

         [         ]

11 M:    [Onni-  ]

         ?onnikka ((another word meaning 'bus'))


12 M: --> >Nysse<,


13 V: ==> Nii:. Kato    [ne-hän    sano-o   että<]  (.) pysäki-llä

         PRT   look(IMP) they-CLI say-SG3 that        bus stop-ADE

         Nii:. See they say you know that< (.) when standing at

                         [                    ]

14 M:                    [°Ai  jaa:.°         ]

                         [ PRT PRT            ]

                         [°Oh I see:.°        ]


15 V: ==> seiso-e-ssa-an      @No  nys-se tulee@.

         stand-INF-INE-POS3  PRT  now-it comes

         a bus stop @No nysse tulee@.


16 M:    Aa   hah [hah hah haa .ha          [.ih .ih .ih


17 V:             [eh heh heh .hhh £Niih, ja [tie-t  sä   mikä

                                             PRT   and know-2 you what

                  [eh heh heh .hhh £Yes, and do you know what


18       on kuljettajaf    tamperee-ksi,

         is ((bus)) driver Tampere dialect-TRA

         the driverf is in Tampere dialect,
```

The activity exhibited in example (3) is telling a joke. The joke is one of a series of jokes about the ways in which the inhabitants of the city of Tampere speak.[14] In this example, the repeat is done at a place in

which the telling has reached a culmination: the joke teller has
provided the recipient the crucial piece in the puzzle and the next
step within the mainline of the joke is to deliver the joke itself. At
that point, the recipient repeats the crucial element *Nysse* at line 12.
The repeat is done in a puzzled tone: it is done a little louder and
faster than the surrounding talk. This kind of prosody, the fact that
the word repeated has been produced in overlap and may thereby
have not been heard properly (see lines 10–11) and a possible stran-
geness of the word, may contribute to a hearing that the repeat at
least in part would orient to get a correct hearing of the word confirmed. But having been done within a particular type of activity,
telling a joke, the repeat can simultaneously be heard as a "go-
ahead" (Schegloff, 1990), as an invitation to deliver the joke: [15]
the conventional distribution of the tasks among participants in
joke telling is one in which the participant constituted initially as
the joke teller also delivers the joke (on telling a joke see, e.g., Sacks,
1974, 1978 and 1992).

However the joke is delivered only after the prosodically self-
standing response token *niin*. The response token orients to a
"request for confirmation" function of the repeat. It confirms the
repeat and in so doing re-establishes the repeated element as a part
of its speaker's own prior utterance. So even though in this particular case, by virtue of the type of the larger on-going activity, the
interactional import of the repeat is hearably other than that of
requesting for confirmation, the recipient of the repeat shows an
orientation to this epistemological aspect of the repeat.

In sum, the speaker of a confirmation can proceed into further
talk after the confirmation. This continuation is marked as a specification or clarification by connectives in the database. In highly
conventionalized activities such as telling a joke an elaboration
which delivers the joke is a canonical sequential implication of
the prior talk. In less ritualized cases, the repeat may or may not
be heard as an invitation to an elaboration. In these cases, a production of an elaboration displays an orientation to the repeat as an
indication of disbelief or noncomprehension and as an action that
made relevant more than a confirmation as its response. The confirmation and the subsequent elaboration are congruent with each
other: the elaboration maintains the epistemic stance displayed by
niin toward the issue raised by the repeat.

We now turn to cases in which it is the recipient, the repeat speaker, who produces the next bit of talk.

6.2.3 Trajectory of talk after a confirmation: delivery of the pending next action by recipient

As mentioned earlier, if the utterance responded to by a repeat is built out so as to make relevant some particular type of next action by the recipient, then, if the repeat is received by a confirmation only, a systematic possibility for the subsequent talk is that the recipient would produce the pending next action. Examples (4) and (5) exhibit a situation in which the recipient goes on to produce the pending second pair part after the confirmation.

(4) [Alko5; face-to-face]

```
          [new topic begins:]


 1  A:    Mutta kuule     mi̱-tä-s       se   muuten     se-ki

          but    hear(IMP) which-PAR-CLI it  by the way it-CLI

          But listen what does


 2        Akapeettus tarkottaa.

          name         means

          Agapetus mean by the way.


 3  B: --> Akapeettus.


 4  A: --> Ni̱i:.


 5  B: ==> E-n    mä muu-ta    t(h)iä mut se on pakinoitsija.

          NEG-1 I  else-PAR know   but it is columnist

          I don't know except that he's a columnist.


 6  A:    .h Nii nii  [          mut]ta se Akapeettus tarkottaa

             PRT PRT  [          but     it name         means

          .h Yeah yeah [          bu]t Agapetus means

                      [               ]

 7  B:               [((coughs))  ]
```

```
 8  A:    [ (ka-)     ]
          [?probably]

          [          ]
 9  C:    [Siis      ] se nimi.
          [PRT       ] it name
          [You mean the name.


10  A:    Nii nii se  (sana) Akapeettus ni   se
          PRT PRT it  word   name        PRT it
          Yeah yeah the (word) Agapetus it


11        tarkottaa tuota,
          means     PRT
          means you know,


12        (0.4)


13  B:    No si-tä minä e-n   tiä mi-tä     se (.) mi-tä
          PRT it-PAR I   NEG-1 know which-PAR it     which-PAR
          Well that I don't know what it (.) what


14        se sitte tarkotta-s.
          it then  mean-CON
          it would mean then.


15  C:    E-n   mä vaan tiä  mi-tä    (se [on). ]
          NEG-1 I  only know which-PAR it  is
          I don't know (what it is.)      [      ]
16  A:                                    [Se on] kyllä
                                          [it is] surely
                                          [It's surely


17        hevose-n  nimi ---
          horse-GEN name
          a name of a horse ---
```

(5) [Chapel:4-5]

```
1   R:      No  näh-dä-än::  öö  .mthh  >övövövö<

            PRT see-PAS-4   er

            Well let's mee:t er .mthh >uvuvuvu<


2           (1.0)


3   T:      ↑Näh-dä-än to-ssa:  pää-rakennukse-n  siinä (.)

            see-PAS-4 that-INE main-building-GEN there+IN

            ↑Let's meet there: in the main building's there (.)


4           kahvila-n °puole-lla°.=

            cafe-GEN   side-ADE

            in the cafe °section.°=


5   R: -->  =#e# Pää[-raken]nukse-n kahvila-n puole-lla.=

            er main-building-GEN  cafe-GEN  side-ADE

            =er In the cafe section of the main building.=

                       [       ]
6   T:                 [hh     ]


7   T: -->  =Nii.=


8   R: ==>  =Selvä.=

            clear

            =Alright.=


9   T:      =Siin  [alhaa-l]la,  [.hh                      ]

            there+IN down-ADE   [                          ]

            =Downstairs there,   [.hh                      ]

                   [       ]  [                         ]
10  R:             [Joo:.  ]  [>Mä ajattel-i    ensi] (te-hä)

                   [PRT    ]  [ I  think-PST(1) first do-INF

                   [Joo:.  ]  [>I thought I'd first (do


11          jotai)        kaupungi-lla mutta tuota .hh

            something(PAR) town-ADE     but    PRT  .hh

            something) downtown but well .hh
```

```
12         [( )    ]

           [      ]

13  T:     [↑No me ] voi-da-an sit  men-nä
           [ PRT we] can-PAS-4 then go-INF
           [↑Well we can go then


14         sii[t         jonnekki    kive-m#p]a-a#,=
           there+IN+FROM somewhere+TO nice-COM-ILL
           from there to some nicer one,=
           [                              ]
15  R:     [No nii just.                  ]
           [PRT PRT PRT                   ]
           [Yeah that's right.            ]
```

In (4), a response to a question is given (line 5); in (5) a suggestion is accepted (line 8). These second pair parts are preceded by a repeat which is responded to by the response token *niin*. The types of utterances that are targetted by the repeat here have a certain kind of impact on the way in which the repeat can be heard and on the way in which the target of the confirmation can be understood. If understood as an inquiry, the repeat raises a trouble in hearing the prior utterance; the issue of truth value does not arise with respect to questions and suggestions. Alternatively, it can also implicate a trouble in identifying the referent of the expression repeated or its sense. On the other hand, the repeat may be heard, under certain conditions, as a registration of the prior turn.

However the fact that the speaker in (4) does not continue with, for example, the projected second pair part, makes the repeat into an inquiry and a response by the recipient becomes relevant. In (5), the recipient orients to the repeat as an inquiry by latching a response to it (indicated by =-signs at the end of line 5 and at the beginning of line 7; notice also that Tiina orients to the repeat as an inquiry by specifying the location under discussion at line 9). In both cases, the response to the repeat is *niin*.

Here, it seems so initially, both of the parties show an orientation to the repeat primarily as a request for confirmation: the recipient of the repeat by doing a confirmation and the repeat speaker by doing the second pair part (line 5 in (4); line 8 in (5)). However in both of the instances the subsequent talk provides retrospectively a different understanding of the initial state of affairs. In (4), the utterance at line 5 provides a response which is not an answer to the question. It should be mentioned that to provide a confirmation only might be strategic in this case: it turns out later (lines 16-17) that the question was a test question, that is, the questioner knew the answer.[16] In (5), the subsequent talk (lines 10-11) reveals that the recipient of the suggestion had possibly another kind of plan in her mind. In these two cases, the repeat can thus be seen as an indication that a dispreferred response was on the way. The recipient, however, oriented to it as a request for confirmation by responding with the particle *niin*. By doing a confirmation only the speaker suggested that the still pending next action, the second pair part, is now due, and the recipient went on to provide one.

6.2.4 Trajectory of talk after a confirmation: elaborations by recipient

A further pattern of subsequent talk in the database is one in which the recipient of the response token *niin* produces a turn that requests an elaboration. Thus in these cases the recipient further delays a response implicated by the turn that was the target of the repeat. In the following example, the recipient responds to *niin* with a request for an account.

(6) [Amigo:1-2]

```
1  S:    Haloo,

          PRT

          Hello?


2  J:    mt No tääl on se Jaa:na se Savioja-n   Jaana.

          PRT here is it 1nameF it surname-GEN 1nameF

          .tch Well this'z Jaa:na the Savioja's Jaana.


3  S:    Ai  seh Sano    pian    mu-lt (   ) jäähtyy,

          PRT it say(IMP) quickly I-ABL       gets cold

          Oh that one Say it quickly my (  ) gets cold.


4       (0.5)
```

```
5 J:     mJoo mä puhu-n kauheen pian.=Kuule    mä e-n   ees

         PRT I   speak-1 terribly soon  hear(IMP) I NEG-1 even

         Yeah I'll talk terribly soon.=Listen I didn't even


6        tien-ny et   m:     o- on-k-s  tää  ees oikee

         know-PPC that ?which ?be be-Q-CLI this even right

         know w- whether this is even the right


7   -->  Laarssoni.=mt Kuule    sellas-t.=Mitä sä   tee-t

         surname        hear(IMP) such-PAR  what you do-2

         Larsson.=.tch Listen to this.=What are you gonna do


8   -->  huomen-illa-lla?

         tomorrow-evening-ADE

         tomorrow evening?


9        (0.5)


10 J:    mt

         .tch


11       (0.4)


12 S: -->  hHuomennah,

           Tomorrow,


13 J: -->  Nii. Illa-lla.

           PRT  evening-ADE

           Nii. In the evening.


14       (0.4)


15 S: ==>  °mi:[:. (1.0) m::: (0.5) Miten nii,]

             [                 how   so  ]

           °mi:[:. (1.0) m::: (0.5) Why:,     ]

             [                              ]
```

```
16 J:        [.hhh hhh .hhh hhh .hhh hh    ] .hhh Ku    me

             [                             ]      since we

             [.hhh hhh .hhh hhh .hhh hh    ] .hhh Since we were


17           aatel-t-i-i      et ---

             think-PAS-PST-4 that

             thinking about ---
```

In (6) above a pre-invitation (see, e.g., Schegloff, 1990) at lines 7-8 gets responded to by a modified partial repeat of its last constituent (*hHuomennah,* "tomorrow," line 12). This repeat is first responded to by *niin* whereafter the speaker proceeds to a continuation (line 13). The continuation *Illalla.* "in the evening" addresses the modification in the repeat by adding what was left out of the original NP in the repeat. It thereby sustains the state of talk – a second pair part to the pre-invitation should now be produced – instead of, for example, explicating the projected invitation. After a substantial delay (line 14 and a display of "thinking aloud" at line 15: °*m::.* *(1.0) m:::(0.5)),)* the recipient responds by a request for an account (*Miten nii,* "why", line 15) for making the pre-invitation. What she is doing is what Schegloff (1990) has termed a "pre-second": a request for information she considers as crucial before delivering the second pair part.

In example (7), the confirmation is followed by a candidate understanding by the recipient at line 7, seeking to clarify a place reference. After a response to it, a second pair part is delivered (line 10).

(7) [Chapel:4-6]

```
1   T:      =>Joo. .hh ↑Hei:: itse asia' me-hä voi-ta-s

            PRT      PRT    in fact   we-CLI can-PAS-CON(4)

            =>Yeah. .hh ↑Hey:: in fact we could you know


2           men-nä tonne     .hh tonne    #m# me voi-ta-s

            go-INF there+TO       there+TO  m  we can-PAS-CON(4)

            go to .hh to #m# we could


3           tava-ta  Kappeli-ssa<.

            meet-INF name of a building, a restaurant and a cafe-INE

            meet at Kappeli.
```

```
4        (0.8)


5   R:  --> Kap:pelis[sa.

                 [

6   T:  -->        [ENii:f,


7   R:  ==> Eli Es:pa-n  siellä puis[to-ssa ja] >siellä .hh=
            PRT name-GEN there  park-INE   and there
            In other words there in the Es:pa park and >there .hh=

                                [      ]
8   T:                          [Joo:, ]


9   T:     =Joo.=[Siel  kahvila-ssa.]
            PRT  [there cafe-INE    ]
           =Joo.=[In the cafe.      ]
            [                       ]
10  R:      [ Joo Voi ku  kiva.]
            [ PRT PRT PRT nice ]
            [ Joo How nice.    ]
```

In both (6) and (7) the recipient of *niin* thus produced a turn that took up an issue that needed to be clarified in coparticipant's turn that was the target of the repeat – the recipient displayed orientation to some problem in that turn. The target of the clarification was different in these two cases. In example (6), the recipient sought clarification of the background motivation for the other's prior turn, i.e. for the pre-invitation, whereas in example (7) the recipient, by doing a candidate understanding, displayed uncertainty of the reference of the key term in the prior suggestion.

A slightly different case is such as (8) below in which the turn that provided a confirmation only results in a challenge to the truthfulness and seriousness of the turn that the repeat targetted. However in (8) the challenge is not so much serious, rather it is a display of ritualized disbelief (cf. Heritage, 1984b: 339). The segment is part of a larger stretch of talk which Eeva (E) has initiated in order to convey to her brother Seppo (S) a report by their mother about a letter sent to Seppo by the tax office.

(8) [Taxes:5-6]

```
 1 S:     No  mitä-s          siel[lä muka.           ]
          PRT what(PAR)-CLI there   PRT(HEARSAY)   ]
          Well what do you say there is then.

                               [                      ]
 2 E:                          [.hh Sinä oo-t saa]-nu  t-
                                   you  be-2 get-PPC  ?back
                               [.hh You've gotten b-

 3        semmose-n tuhat      kaks-sata-a        takas.
          like-GEN  thousand   two-hundred(PAR)   back
          about one thousand two hundred back.


 4        (0.8)


 5 S: --> #Taka:si#,=
          #Ba:ck#,


 6 E: --> =Nii:.


 7        (1.1)


 8 S: ==> ö Nyt kyllä   nyt valehtele-t [jotta     vipa:t]taa.
            now surely  now lie-2        so that swings
          uh Now surely now you're lying in your throa:t.

                                        [               ]
 9 E:                                   [↑No  ei::.    ]
                                        [PRT NEG(3)    ]
                                        [↑Well no::.   ]


10 E:     E(h)i-n valehtele niin se äiti    sano. .h
          NEG-1   lie        so  it mother say(PST)
          I'm no:t lyi:ng that's what mother said. .h


11        (0.8)
```

```
12 S:    Ihan-ko oike[e.

         quite-Q right

         Is it really so.

                        [

13 E:              [↑No  iha    oikeesti ↓mutta sitte se

                   [PRT  quite  right     but   then   it

                   [↑Well it's really so ↓but then she


14       käsk-i   sano-o  että .hhh ei    nyt pie sitte pan-na

         tell-PST say-INF that       NEG(3) now must then put-INF

         told me to tell you that .hhh you shouldn't now


15       haise-ma-an   kaikki-a siellä Helsingi-ssä. .hh=

         smell-INF-ILL all-PAR  there  Helsinki-INE

         throw away all of them there in Helsinki. .hh=
```

The delivery of the information about the contents of the letter at
lines 2-3 is, after a substantial silence, received by Seppo with a
repeat of the last element of Eeva's turn (line 5: *Taka:si.*). This
repeat shows what is of relevance for him in the report. The silence
at line 4 as well as the high initial pitch and vowel lengthening in the
repeat index surprise. Again, the repeat is received by the response
token *niin*. It displays in and through its prosody (a strong stress) an
alignment with the action accomplished by the repeat and assigns a
particular meaning for the act of confirming: what was delivered as
a piece of news was noteworthy. Furthermore, the confirmation is
done with a tone of voice which indexes that the news is good. The
turn makes relevant a further receipt of the news by the recipient,
for example, an evaluation of its quality on a scale good-bad. After
a substantial silence (line 7) the recipient takes a turn (line 8)
through which he displays a ritualized disbelief toward the informing. This kind of display of disbelief is used as a "newsmark"
(Jefferson, 1981: 62-66; Heritage, 1984b: 339-44), that is, it receives
the prior turn as news rather than mere informing and expresses
Seppo's treatment of the news as extraordinary (see also another,
a milder version of display of ritualized disbelief at line 12).

In all of the instances discussed above, the recipient of the repeat
treated the repeat as a request for confirmation. The repeat speaker,
however, displayed subsequently that there was a further trouble

with respect to the prior talk through doing a request for elaboration in (6), a request for confirmation for an offered understanding in (7), and a display of ritualized disbelief in (8).

6.3 *Joo*: doing a reconfirmation

6.3.1 Basic environment

We have seen in the previous section that the particle *niin* as a response to a repeat is associated with contexts in which a larger sequence and/or activity has still some way to go in order to reach a possible completion. The repeat is understood as a display of uncertainty, that is, as a display of disbelief, surprise, noncomprehension of or nonalignment with the prior utterance. *Niin* registers and aligns with these implications by providing a confirmation. It treats the repeat and itself as an adjacency pair. After the confirmation, a continuation of the larger on-going sequence or activity emerges or a new sequence that delays further a resumption of the larger activity is initiated.

The particle *joo* as a response to a repeat is associated with different kinds of sequential positions and activities. It typically occurs in an environment in which the repeat is hearable as a registration of prior talk, for example, instructions (see Goldberg, 1975 on transfer of instructions in English interactions). Examples (9) and (10) exhibit that kind of a case.

(9) [Request:7]

```
1 P:    (Se-) Oota-s        ny  mikä se ala-nu[mero ol-i.
        it    wait(IMP)-CLI now what it sub-number be-PST
        (It-) Wait now what was the extension again.
                                        [
2 M:                                    [°#öö#°
                                        [°#er#°


3 M:    Se< ol-i:: (0.2) öömh .mh kaks kolme yhdeksän neljä.=
        it  be-PST               two  three nine     four
        It< wa::s (0.2) uh:m .mh two three nine four.=
```

```
4         =Siis se [on tää viis seitsemän viis. ]
          PRT  it  is this five  seven  five ]
          =So it's this five seven five.       ]

                    [                          ]
5 P: -->            [   °#Kaks kolme yhdeksän ne]ljä#,°
                    [   °#Two three nine        fo]ur#,°


6 M: ==> Joo:.h=


7 P:      =Viis seit[semän vi[is.
          =Five sev[en      fi[ve.

                    [         [
8 M:                [°.hhh° [°Nii tää   sama ku mu-lla.°=
                    [       [ PRT this same as I-ADE

                    [°.hhh° [°Nii this same as I have.°=


9 P:      =#Joo[:.

               [
10 M:          [.hhh[h

                    [
11 P:               [#↑Joo:.#


12 M:     Joo hän  asuu  Karkkila-ssa,hhh ja   häne-n
          PRT s/he lives name-INE         and  s/he-GEN
          Yeah she lives in Karjaa,hhh and her


13        numero-nsa   sinne    on ---
          number-POS3  there+TO is
          number there is ---
```

Example (9) above instantiates an activity in which one participant provides the other a telephone number. Just before the segment, Meeri (M) has given Paavo (P) a third party's extension number which has partially been obscured by overlap. She then begins to supply that person's home number at which point Paavo asks the question in line 1 which still targets the extension number. Meeri provides the extension (line 3) and then rushes to volunteer the initial part of the number (line 4). Her turn gets overlapped by Paavo who repeats the extension in *sotto voce* (line 5). This repeat is hearably a receipt of the information. Its *sotto voce* delivery indexes a possible simultaneous activity of writing down the number – an activity which can only be conveyed to the recipient verbally. At the same time, however, it provides the recipient a possibility to see that the number was received correctly. The repeat is received by the response token *Joo: .h* by the recipient (line 6).

Example (9) shows us basic differences between the response tokens *niin* and *joo* as responses to a repeat. Whereas *niin* comes as a response to a repeat that targets a sequentially initiative utterance, *joo* occurs after a repeat which possibly closes down an activity. *Joo* treats the repeat as an action which primarily registers the prior turn by reconfirming the correctness of the information in the repeat. It does not orient to the repeat as an action which would raise some trouble with the prior talk and would require subsequent further treatment. In some cases, the response token is not really produced as a response to a request by the other party, rather, it is volunteered. However by doing a repeat only the speaker provides an opportunity space for the other participant to do a reconfirmation and in that sense invites an action by the other.

The use of the response tokens is not a matter of an automatic alignment but selection. This can be in example (9) above in which a subsequent repeat is responded to by [*niin* + elaboration] instead of *joo* at line 8. In this case, *niin* offers a confirmation and the elaboration reformulates the number by reference to the speaker's own phone number. The reformulation displays an understanding that a clarification was relevant with respect to the part of the number that had just been provided. The clarification is very likely directed to the overlapping of the first saying of the number at line 4. A further possible reason for it is the order in which the parts of the telephone number have been supplied. The request for the number at line 1 concerned the extension part of the number. As a response to it, the recipient first offered the extension at line 3 and then volunteered also the initial part of the number. The parts of the number were thus delivered in an order which is reverse as compared to the one in which they should be used, and they were repeated in the order of the delivery by the recipient. The reformulation at line 8 might be oriented to make it sure that the action-

relevant order of the parts is understood correctly.[17] Even though
the repeat at line 7 is not built up so as to request for an elaboration, not even to request for a confirmation, the recipient treats the
situation as one that makes relevant a clarification. Her clarification
is addressed to the repeat and the response token chosen is *niin*.

In example (10), from the same call as example (9), the response
token speaker displays, through her subsequent talk, an orientation
to the fact that the repeat has been dealt with and is not continuation relevant.

(10) [Request:2-3]

```
1 P:    Hän    ol-i    anta-nu  tämmöse-n     nime-n   ku

        she/he be-PST give-PPC this kind-ACC name-ACC as

        She had given a name like


2       Ii:ris,hh Rau:tto,hh tai Rau:kko-ko se on.=

        1nameF     surname   or surname-Q  it is

        Ii:ris,hh Ra:utto,hh or is it Rau:kko.=


3 M:    =Raukko,hhh


4 P: --> Raukko,


5 M: ==> Joo:.=.hhh Hän     on mei-llä< tämmöse-nä<

        PRT          she/he is we-ADE   this kind-ESS

        Joo:.=.hhh She is with us< as a kind'v<


6       tunti-opettaja-na.hh

        hour-teacher-ESS

        temporary teacher.hh


7       (.)


8  P:   Ai  jaa[:.

        PRT PRT

        I see:.
```

```
                          [
 9  M:          [.hh öö (.) oikee (.) vauhdikas ja  hyvä,hhh

                [          very      brisk     and good

                [.hh uh (.) a very (.) brisk and good,hh


10              (.) nainen.hh .h[h
                (.) woman.hh   .h[h

                               [
11  P:                         [On hy[vä.
                               [is good
                               [Sh's good.

                                     [
12  M:                               [myös. Joo:.
                                     [too   PRT
                                     [too. Joo:.
```

Paavo has called Meeri to ask her to come and give a talk in a course he is organizing. In the absence of a response, which foreshadows a dispreferred response, a rejection of the request, he turns in lines 1-2 to report that a third person had been recommended to him. This report suggests that Meeri knows the person, and by virtue of that it can be heard as a request for her opinion. The mentioning of the third party, however, is built into a display of uncertainty as to how to spell the name: it invites a response from the other party, a turn design which enables the speaker to avoid making a direct request for opinion. Meeri responds to the "display of uncertainty" aspect of the turn by providing the correct version of the name (line 3) but does not go on to respond to the relevance of the prior turn. The turn is received by a repeat (line 4). That repeat can be heard as a receipt of the prior answer and also as a display that the speaker got the name right. By doing the repeat but not proceeding to elaborate on the issue which was the point of the utterance at lines 1-2, Paavo sustains the local focus of the talk, getting the name right. This repeat is responded to by the response token *Joo:.* at line 5. Through it, Meeri reconfirms the prior repeat. She subsequently (from line 5 onwards) moves to respond to the relevance of the turn at lines 1-2, that is, to give information about the person in question. In this case, the repeat at line 4 is done as a part of an activity which is embedded within a larger activity and it makes the closure of that embedded activity relevant. The response token *joo* treats the repeat as something to be reconfirmed but at the same time registers and aligns with its closure-implicativeness. By moving to the larger activity projected by the report at lines 1-2, the speaker shows a further orientation to the closing of the embedded activity.

In some occasions, the recipients do not orient to a repeat as an action that would need a reconfirmation, as in examples (11)-(12). Example (11) comes from the same call as (9) and (10) above.

(11) [Request:5-6]

```
1 M:    No  sit  mei-1  on nyt  toinen-ki   tämmöne
        PRT then we-ADE is now another-CLI this kind
        Well then we have another one of these


2       tunti-opettaja joka on: on (.) kirjotta-nu  tämmöse-n<
        hour-teacher   who is  is      write-PPC    this kind-ACC
        temporary teachers who has: has (.) written kind of< book


3       kirja-n-ki   ku Sana-t  ja  puhe. Joka on mietti-ny just
        book-ACC-CLI as word-PL and talk  who is think-PPC just
        like this called Words and Talk. Who has really thought


4       paljo tollas-i-a     esittämise-n    ja  .hhhhhh hhhh
                                                  ----(1.6)---
        a lot that kind-PL-PAR presentation-GEN and
        a lot about things like presentation and .hhhhhh hhhh


5       sellase-n     ongelm-i-a      #mm::# ja< ol-lu
        that kind-GEN problem-PL-PAR         and be-PPC
        that kind of problems #mm::# and< she has been


6       mietti-mä-s     tä-tä    uut-ta
        think-INF-INE this-PAR new-PAR
        planning this new
```

```
7        aikuis-koulutus-ta-kin.hh

         adult-education-PAR-CLI

         adult education as well.hh


8        (0.8)


9 P:     A[i jaa:.            ]

         PRT PRT              ]

         I see:.              ]

         [                    ]

10 M:    [Jonka    nimi on]  Tuulikki Saa:rinen.hhh

         [who(GEN) name is]  1nameF    surname

         [Whose name is   ]  Tuulikki Saa:rinen.hhh


11       .hh[hh

            [

12 P: -->    [°Tuulikki Saa[rine hh°          ]

                          [                   ]

13 M: ==>                 [Hän  pitää mei-lle] tämmös-t

                          [s/he holds we-ALL ] this kind-PAR

                          [She gives us this kind of


14       puhe< ilmaisu-n       kurs:si-a-kin

         talk  expression-GEN course-PAR-CLI

         verbal< expression cou:rse as well


15       kevät-lukukaude-ll[a hh .hhhhh         ]

         spring-semester-ADE                    ]

         in the spring term hh .hhhhh           ]

                          [                     ]

16 P:                     [No< liit- ei-k-s  ] se liitty-s

                          [PRT con-  NEG-Q-CLI] it connect-CON

                          [Well< would it con- now wouldn't it


17       nyt sitten siihen julkise-en puhumise-en-ki.

         now then   it+TO  public-ILL speaking-ILL-CLI

         connect with the public speaking as well then.
```

In (11), a speaker mentions a name of a third person (line 10) as a part of a recommendation for a job. The recipient repeats the name in *sotto voce*. His turn gets terminally overlapped (Jefferson, 1983) by the other participant who goes on to continue the recommendation (line 13). In this case, a speaker did not orient to a repeat as an action that would need a separate reconfirmation. However she implicates the correctness of the received information by not taking it up. It should be noticed that particular interactional ends may be achieved by not offering a reconfirmation in this case. The prior talk indexes that a dispreferred action, that is, a rejection of the recommendation, may be underway: the prior possibly complete recommendation is met first with a silence (line 8) and then with a mild newsmark by the recipient (9). A rejection might open up an undesirable possibility that the recipient would try to convince the speaker herself to take the job. Against these possibilities the speaker may be heard rushing to strengthen the recommendation. However even though there may be particular local reasons for the non-occurence of a reconfirmation here, the crucial point is that a response is not heard missing as it would be in the case if the repeat were understood as a request for confirmation.

Example (12), from the same call as example (1), provides an instance in which the way in which a speaker responds to a repeat displays an orientation to the boundaries of a response and its stepwise production.

(12) [Invitation:6]

```
1 T:     =mt Ja tota .hhhh °tota° puhelin   on viis kahdeksan
             and PRT        PRT   telephone is five eight
         =.tch And uh: .hhhh °uh:° the phone is five eight


2        ↑kolme,hh
         ↑three,hh


3        (1.4)


4 S: 1-> <Viis kaheksan ↑kolme,>°
         <Five eight ↑three,>°
```

```
5        (.)


6 T:    °Neljä yheksän yheksän kaheksan, hhh°
        °Four nine nine eight, hhh°


7 S:    2->°Neljä yheksän yheksän kaheksan.°
        °Four nine nine eight.°


8 T:    ==> °mJoo.°


9        (1.4)


10 ?:    °.mhh°


11       (0.8)


12 ?:    .mhh


13 S:    3-> °Kolme neljä yheksän yheksän kaheksan.°
         °Three four nine nine eight.°


14 T:    ==> Jọo:. Ja ↑sit  me ol-la-an ajatel-tu et    ol-is   kiva
             PRT    and then we be-PAS-4 think-PPC that be-CON nice
             Jọo:. And ↑then we've been thinking that it'd be nice


15          jos kaikki to-is     jotai        ruoka-a ---
            if  all    bring-CON something(PAR) food-PAR
            if everybody'd bring some food ---
```

In this case a telephone number is broken into two units by a speaker. When the first half of the number is supplied, the recipient receives it by a repeat (line 4), after which the speaker goes on to provide the second half. The second half is again repeated by the recipient (line 7). This repeat, by contrast, is received by *joo* (line 8). In these cases, at a point in which the response is still incomplete, the recipient of the repeat does not provide an explicit reconfirmation but goes on to complete the response. However, by implication, the receipt of the information is understood to be reconfirmed simultaneously. When the response has come to a possible completion place and the last piece of information has been repeated by the recipient, an overt reconfirmation is offered and an orientation to the closure of the activity is displayed.

In sum, the particle *joo* is typically associated with sequences in which the utterance that is the target of the repeat provides some information the recipient has requested and this exchange of information is the main business of the activity. The recipient repeats the information provided. Often the manner of the delivery of the repeat, such as its production with *sotto voce*, indexes that the action is backgrounded by the speaker. The repeats that are responded to by *joo* in the data at hand do not raise a problem with the prior talk, nor do they index surprise or disbelief. By responding to a repeat by *joo* a speaker reconfirms the correctness of the repeat as a receipt of its prior talk. *Joo* registers and aligns to the epistemic stance indexed by the repeat: it agrees with the display of certainty suggested by the repeat. The repeats responded to by *joo* do not necessarily sequentially implicate an explicit reconfirmation, and a speaker can leave the reconfirmation to be inferred from the fact that she or he proceeds to a next bit of talk.

The environments for the response token *joo* are closure relevant. The target utterance of the repeat is a second pair which as such may be closing implicative. The repeat receives the second pair part and it is also closure relevant. *Joo* registers and aligns with the closing implicativeness of the prior talk. The type of the subsequent talk indicates further the closing implicativeness of *joo*: the activity and topic is shifted either by the *joo* speaker or by the other participant.

6.3.2 Some strategic usages of joo

The features associated with *joo* in its basic environments can be deployed for achieving particular interactional ends. The use of *joo* may suggest a closure relevance of an issue raised by the repeat in cases in which the repeat is hearably continuation relevant, as in (13).

(13) [Dog:1-2]

```
1 T:     .ehh No   mitä-s        Iita-lle    ((huokaa:)) kuuluu.hh=
                   PRT what(PAR)-CLI 1nameF-ALL   sighs     is heard
         .ehh Well how ((sighing:)) are things with Iita.hh=


2 A:     =No   mi:tä-s       Ii:da-lle tässä tul-i-n     joku aika
                PRT what(PAR)-CLI 1nameF-ALL here come-PST-1 some time
         =Well no:thing special with Ii:da I just came home


3        sitten kotia   ja   .nhhh on niin ihana  vaikka   täällä
         ago    home+TO and        is so   lovely although here
         some time ago and .nhhh it's so lovely although it's


4        on kyllä     ku o-is    pommi     heite-tty.h .hh[hh
         is certainly as be-CON bomb(ACC) throw-PPPC
         you know like a bomb had been thrown here.h .hh[hh
                                                         [
5 T:                                                     [Kuka-s
                                                         [who-CLI
                                                         [Well who


6        siellä on käy-ny [terrori-teko-j-a  teke-mä-ssä.]
         there  is go-PPC terror-act-PL-PAR do-INF-INE   ]
         has been there doing terrorist actions.        ]
                          [                             ]
7 A:                      [.h .h .h .h                  ]

8        No  @mitä-s      luul-isi-t [ol-is-ko-han]
             PRT what(PAR)-CLI think-CON-2 be-CON-Q-CLI]
         Well @what would you think  [could it perhaps be]
                                     [                  ]
9 T:                                 [he hih             ]


10 A:    KOIRA KARVANEN,h[h@ .hh
         dog   hairy
         THE DOG HAIRY,h[h@ .hh
                        [
```

```
11 T:            [he Nii::n .ihhh fVoi: sentä mie täälä

                 [  PRT          PRT PRT  I    here

                 [he Nii::n .ihhh fO:h go:d I'm here


12         tö-i-ssä    oo    #ja  m [mm#

           work-PL-INE be(1)  and

           at work uu #and m          [mm#

                                      [

13 A: -->                             [↑↑Tö-i-s:sä.

                                      [  work-PL-INE

                                      [↑↑At wo:rk.


14 T: ==> >Joo: k'le tänään tulee tommone<  super-pitkä päivä

          PRT  hear today  comes that kind super-long  day

          >Joo: listen it's gonna be a< super long day


15         ku ensi mä ol-i-n    siel  seminaari-s ja  sit  tul-i-n<

           as first I be-PST-1 there seminar-INE and then come-PST-1

           as I attended first the seminar and then I came<


16         tän:ne  ja ((rykäisee:))    khym .mt ↑mä oo-n i:tke-ny

           here+TO and clears throat             I  be-1 cry-PPC

           he:re and ((clears throat)) grhm .tch ↑I have cri:ed


17         ku  Niagara-n    pu[tous tänää kuule  ] ku   .hhhh

           like Niagara-GEN fall  today hear(IMP)] since ،

           like the Niagara fal[ls today you know] since .hhhh

                               [                 ]

18 A:                          [No::h,           ]

                               [PRT              ]

                               [Ye::s?           ]


19 T:      Riitta tänää vika päivä-ä tö-i-s:sä  ja ---

           1nameF today last day-PAR work-PL-INE and

           Riitta had her last day at wo:rk today and ---
```

In (13), Tarja (T), the caller, begins to give a report of her day at line 11. She marks the first piece of the report as not-main-news by using the verb final word order (see Vilkuna, 1989: 121–31) and proceeds to project continuation with the connective *ja* "and" whereafter she goes into word search (line 12). At that point the recipient responds by repeating the last element in the report so far (line 13). The repeat is done with a very high initial pitch, stress and sound lengthening which index surprise. It topicalizes the element repeated and invites an elaboration of it. This repeat gets a *joo* response by the recipient, followed by an elaboration (line 14). *Joo* confirms the repeat and the subsequent utterance (*k'le tänään tulee tommone< superpitkä päivä* "listen it's gonna be a< super long day today") provides a specifying confirmation for what was implicated by the repeat and the two subsequent utterances elaborate on the issue further. After the mentioning of her arrival to the workplace (*ja sit tulin tän:ne* "and then I came he:re", lines 15–16) the speaker projects, by the connective *ja* "and", a new unit to come. This new unit is, after a hitch, started with a rise in the pitch which indexes a shift in the talk. The utterance so started eventuates into a beginning of a troubles telling: it describes a strong emotion (↑*mä oon i̯: tkeny ku Ni̯agaran pu̯tous tänää kuule* "I have cri̯:ed like the Ni̯agara fa̲lls today you know", lines 16–17). An extensive report of the situation ensues.

Here, the troubles telling might be understood as the point of the telling initiated at line 11. The recipient, however, responded to the first piece of the telling by her repeat. The teller took up the repeat by talking to its possible implications but subsequently shifted the line of the talk. The later talk revealed that the issue raised by the repeat was not oriented to as one to be developed into the main topic by the teller. Even though the repeat was responded to and its implications were taken up subsequently the issue raised by the repeat was treated as a side issue by the teller. In this connection, the use of the response token *joo,* instead of *niin*, might be heard projecting a closure of the issue raised by the repeat.

The closing implicativeness of *joo* may be deployed to avoid taking up trouble-implicativeness in the repeat, as in example (14).

(14) [Hiking:8-9]


```
1 P:    Monen aikaa te      oo-tte täällä,hh
        what  time  you(PL) be-2PL  here
        What time will you be here,hh


2       (0.8)


3 R:    No jos mä se-n   Jukka-n      sillon (.) käy-n (.) sielt
        PRT if I  it-ACC 1nameM-ACC  then        go-1      there+FROM
        Well if I pick up Jukka then (.) take (.) from there


4       (.) yhe-n    aikoihin koukkaa-n ja  sitten mä käy-n
            one-GEN around   snatch-1  and then   I  go-1
        (.) around one snatch him and then I go to


5       Käpylä-s hake-e     se-n   yhe     (.) El Aa puhelime-n ja,
        name-INE fetch-ILL  it-ACC one(ACC)    L.A.  phone-ACC and
        Käpylä to get the (.) S.W. ((=short wave)) phone and,


6       (1.6) kompassi-n,  .hh ((yskäisee:)) khyh (1.0) niin tota
              compass-ACC                              so   PRT
        (1.6) the compass,  .hh ((clears throat)) khrm (1.0) so well


7       (.) mä usko-n     et  mä oo-n siel   k-  ol-la-an joskus
            I  believe-1 that I  be-1 there  ?two be-PAS-4 sometime
        (.) I believe that I'll be there t- we'll be there sometime


8       voi-ta-is          jo        kahde-n aikaan mutta .hh sit
        can-PAS-CON(4) already two-GEN time    but        then
        we could be there at two already but .hh then


9       vo-is      suoritta-a ne    kauppaostokse-t,
        can-CON do-INF      they shopping-PL(ACC),
        one could do the shopping,
```

```
10 P:    Mmː: Mmː:,


11 R:    Kun   ei  su-st   tiedä koska sä  pääse-t.
         since NEG you-ELA know  when  you get off-2
         Since we don't know when you can leave.


12 P:    No< puol neljä-ltä näil näkymin
         PRT half four-ABL  with these views
         Well< at half past three the way it looks now


13       kyllä      ((haukottelee:)) [.hhhh        ]
         certainly ((yawns:))        [.hhhh        ]
                                      [             ]
14 R: -->                            [Puol neljä,]
                                      [half   four ]
                                      [Half past three,


15 P: ==> ((haukotellen:)) Joo:,
          ((yawning:))     Joo:,


16       (0.8)


17 R:    Just(s),
         PRT
         Right,


18       (2.6)


19 P:    ((haukottelee:)) °hhöh[hmm°  ]
         ((yawns:))       °hhöh[hmm°  ]
                               [       ]
20 R:                          [↑Tota,]
                               [ PRT  ]
                               [↑Well,]
```

```
21 P:   Mä sa-i-n:  #yy# iso-n   kasa-n   lavoja duuni-s(t)

        I  get-PST-1      big-ACC pile-ACC wood   work-ELA (slang)

        I got #er# a big pile of wood from work


22      tota noin ni  eilen      et,h jos tei-ll     jää

        PRT  PRT  PRT yesterday so   if  you(PL)-ALL remains

        uh well yesterday so,h if you've got


23      vapaa-ta aika-a    ni   te-hän      voi-tte tossa

        free-PAR time-PAR PRT you(PL)-CLI can-2PL  there+IN

        spare time you can you know


24      alka-a     pilkko-ma-an nii-tä.

        begin-INF chop-INF-ILL they-PAR

        begin to chop them there.


25      (0.3)


26 P:   ((fake laughter:)) @#ha:h hah hah#@ eh hmh hmh heh heh .hhh


27 R:   °Joo.°


28      (1.0)


29 R:   Ol-i-k    su-l     m(h)uu-ta.

        be-PST-Q you-ADE else-PAR

        Did you have anything e(h)lse:.
```

In (14), Reijo has called Pekka to make final arrangements for a weekend hike. An issue which he has taken up recurrently during the call is the time of the departure and the time for picking up Pekka, though no time has been fixed yet. In the segment above Pekka himself takes up the time for the pick up (line 1). As a response to the inquiry, Reijo mentions a tentative time (line 8: *kahden aikaan* "at two (p.m.)") and later states the uncertainty factor and the problem, Pekka's work schedule that day (line 11).

This turn can be heard as a complaint and as a request for the other party to provide an exact time. Pekka responds to the turn (lines 12–13) by stating a time which is considerably later than the one provided by the other party and only approximate.

The response is received by a modified repeat of the time reference: *Puol neljä,* "half past three" (line 14). Both its parts are stressed and it carries a level terminal contour which formulates the utterance as a display of disbelief and as such something to be responded to. The recipient responds to the repeat by the response token *Joo:* , (line 15). *Joo* treats the issue raised by the repeat as a fact, as something that is unproblematic and needs no further discussion but only a reconfirmation; the manner of delivery – the token is done by yawning – indexes a further stance towards the issue: "doing being bored" and/or "doing being indifferent". Through *joo* the speaker formulates the issue of time as dealt with and closure-relevant. After a substantial silence which indexes a trouble on the part of the recipient, the recipient responds by a closing-implicative response token *Just(s)* (line 17) which conveys an understanding that the other party has nothing more to say about this issue. It should be noticed that even though the *joo* speaker takes up the possible inconvenience of his time schedule for the others at lines 21–24, he still treats the time he had set up as fixed.

Thus, the association of *joo* with closure relevant sequential environments and its epistemic task in those environments may be deployed to achieve particular interactional ends in contexts in which the prior repeat has hearably raised a trouble. In these contexts, the use of *joo* can be heard indexing that a speaker avoids taking up the implications of the repeat turn, for example, its trouble implicativeness or its topicalizing force.

6.4 Conclusion

We started this paper with a distributional observation concerning the particles *niin* and *joo*: they occur as responses to nonclausal repeats. The formulation of this context was thus formal, and unanalyzed: "repeat" is a term that refers to a formal relationship. However analyses of particular instances have revealed that the kinds of repeats *niin* and *joo* are associated with differ in terms of their sequential and activity context and hence also in terms of the actions they themselves are used to accomplish. This difference in context means also difference in the use and meaning of the response the repeat gets, that is, difference between *niin* and *joo* respectively. Contexts for *niin* are characterized by the following intertwined poles: (1) the repeat to which *niin* offers a response is done within a larger sequence and/or activity which has not yet reached its possible completion; (2) *niin* treats the repeat as an expression of some form of uncertainty and claims to remove it. *Joo*, on the contrary, is associated with the following kinds of contexts and actions: (1) the repeat to which it responds forms a possible closure of a sequence and activity; (2) it reconfirms the repeat as a non-problematic registration of prior talk.

In the type of context discussed in this paper, that is, after a nonclausal partial repeat, the epistemological strength of *joo* and *niin* can be compared from two different angles. *Joo* does not orient to the local current state of talk constituted by [repeat + response token] as one that would contain doubt and in that sense it could be treated as epistemically stronger than *niin*. On the other hand, by orienting to the repeat as a display of doubt and claiming to remove that doubt *niin* is specifically a tool for accomplishing epistemic work. In doing such epistemic work *niin* as a response token can be seen to voice its semantic link to its prior history as a member of a demonstrative paradigm and to its use as an anaphoric device. Indeed, its history can be understood as a semantic motivation for its use as a particular kind of response token.

Our general knowledge of the use of such linguistic forms as *niin* and *joo*, and their relatives in different languages, as tools for displaying (e.g. epistemic) stance as well as accomplishing social actions simultaneously is, at best, fragmentary at the moment. Not so uncommonly these one-word responses, if discussed at all, are treated as an undifferentiated class of minimal answers or responses. Consequently, we do not yet have any developed metalanguage for talking about the kinds of more specific work this kind of linguistic forms do. However response forms such as *niin* and *joo* are integral in forming particular coherent activities and they help to specify some parameters of what a given activity might be. Their analysis indicates that social activity is not only a context for linguistic forms; it is also integral to the meaning and organization of linguistic forms. Response forms such as *niin* and *joo* form a part of activity grammar, that is, they belong to semiotic tools through which members of a speech community collaboratively and in a systematic fashion go about constituting activities in and through which they manage their relationships and practical tasks in the everyday life.

Notes

*   I am grateful to Auli Hakulinen, John Heritage, Anssi Peräkylä, Manny Schegloff, and two anonymous referees for their helpful comments at various stages in the development of this paper. I am especially grateful to John Heritage and Manny Schegloff for their detailed discussions on earlier drafts. All shortcomings are, of course, mine.

1   This type of expressions has traditionally been referred to as "interjections" in parts-of-speech classifications, see, e.g., Schachter, 1985: 58.

2   Finnish has a three-part demonstrative paradigm. In addition to *se*, the paradigm contains the proximal demonstrative *tämä* and the distal demonstrative *tuo*:

  Singular, nominative: *tämä* –   *tuo*   *se*
                          this   *that*   *it/that*
                          ‖   ‖   ‖
  Plural, nominative: *nämä* – *nuo* – *ne*

3   The following are examples of the instructive case:
  Puhu   *hitaa-mm-i-n!*
  Speak(IMP) slow-COM-PL-INS
  Speak more slowly!

  Lapse-t juokse-vat palja-i-n   *jalo-i-n.*
  child-PL run-PL3   bare-PL-INS   foot-PL-INS
  The children are running barefoot.

4   Examples of *niin* as an adverb of manner and as a degree word:
  Tee   *niin.*
  do(IMP)   so
  Do so.

  Kipu on niin hirveä.
  pain is so   terrible
  The pain is so terrible

5   The discussion presented in this paper is part of a larger on-going project on response tokens in Finnish conversations (Sorjonen, in preparation).

6   *Niin* and *joo* do not exhaust the types of responses to a repeat in this environment. A repeat can also be responded to by the response token *mm*, by a repeat or by an utterance that does not contain any confirmation or reconfirmation device in it. A discussion of these cases has to be left for another occasion.

7   Cases in which the repeat would be, for example, prefaced by a particle, will not be discussed here. In the database, the most frequent preface to repeats is the particle *ai* which expresses a change in the current state of knowledge of its speaker (cf. Heritage, 1984b). A repeat prefaced by *ai* is in many cases followed by further talk by the same speaker. When the repeated element is the finite verb, the repeat contains either the bound interrogative morpheme *-kO* or the utterance-final particle *vai* which turns the utterance into a question. In both of the cases only the particle *joo* can be used as an affirmative answer to the repeat. *Niin* as an affirmation is ungrammatical which reflects its historical roots as a nominal element. These issues will be discussed in Sorjonen (in preparation).

8   Most of the telephone calls are among peers, but some business calls are also included in the database. The length of the calls varies, as well as the social characteristics of speakers in terms of such conventional parameters as age, sex, socio-economic status, education, occupation and the regional dialect spoken.

9   Every utterance in talk-in-interaction is, of course constructed with respect to its prior talk and gets partially its meaning from it. What is emphasized here is that to describe an utterance as a repeat is to recognize that it is structurally built up as a second, as an utterance that for its understanding is crucially dependent on its prior utterance.

10 For the transcription symbols, see the glossary for this volume. Notice the following symbols that are additional to the symbols in the glossary. Talk surrounded by #-signs is said with a creaky voice (see line 9); the £-sign indicates smile voice (see line 14); the @-sign indicates animated voice (example (3), line 15). For a key to the glossing conventions, see the appendix to this paper.

11 *Vai* is a question particle that shows up in queries that are built to be dependent on their prior talk.

12 It should be noticed that the subsequent talk reveals further aspects of the sequence under discussion. At line 16, when the talk about the reason for the prospective absence of Arto at the party has come to a possible completion place, the recipient of the original report produces an assessment (°*Voi: juku.*° "oh: boy") which indexes alignment with the stance taken by the teller in her report in lines 2-3. Furthermore, at line 18, she brings up the issue of Arto's wife's presence at the party; a possible implication of the report thus turned out to be an issue for the recipient.

13 The talk surrounded by @-signs in line 15 is said with animated voice.

14 At line 3 Martti is still laughing at the prior joke. The joke in (3) is based on sound assimilation observed in Tampere dialect. In formal spoken Finnish and some other varieties of Finnish, the utterance used to explain the term *"nysse"* at line 15 (*No nysse tulee*) would be *no nyt se tulee* "well now it comes." In Tampere dialect, the final *t* in *nyt* "now" has assimilated to the initial *s* in *se* "it": *no nys se tulee*. The utterance is re-analyzed in the joke so that *nys se* has understood as one word with the meaning "bus": *no nysse tulee* "well the bus is coming."

15 The choice of repeat as the go-ahead may have a specific importance here: a preliminary study suggests that a basic device for doing a go-ahead in Finnish is the particle *no*. The choice of repeat here may orient to display both a trouble with the prior talk and a go-ahead to the teller.

16 Agapetus (*Akapeettus* in the transcript) was a Finnish writer of humorist columns and he was well known at the time of the recording in 1958. It can be inferred from lines 16-17 that A has confused two Greek names: Agapetus and Pegasos.

17 From the ethnographic information we can infer that Paavo knows that "575" is the beginning part of all the numbers within that section of the institution in which Meeri works. Furthermore, he has implied that he knows the beginning of the number by requesting only for the extension number at line 1. However, Meeri might still be in doubt whether Paavo recorded the number correctly.

References

Atkinson, Maxwell J. and Heritage, John (eds.) (1984). *Structures of Social Action*. Cambridge: Cambridge University Press.

Bolinger, Dwight (1957). *Interrogative Structures in American English. Publication of the American Dialect Society, Number 28*. Alabama: University of Alabama Press.

Button, Graham and Casey, Neil (1985). Topic nomination and topic pursue. *Human Studies* 8: 3–55.

Chisholm, William S. Jr. (ed.) (1984). *Interrogativity*. Typological Studies in Language, volume 4. Amsterdam: John Benjamins.

Comrie, Bernard (1984). Interrogativity in Russian. In W. S. Chisholm Jr. (ed). *Interrogativity*, pp. 7–46.

Goldberg, Jo Ann (1975). A system for the transfer of instructions in natural settings. *Semiotica* 14: 269–96.

Goodwin, Marjorie Harness (1983). Aggravated correction and disagreement in children's conversations. *Journal of Pragmatics* 7: 657–77.

Hakulinen, Lauri (1961). *The structure and development of Finnish language*. Indiana University Publications, Uralic and Altaic series, vol. 3. Bloomington: Indiana University.

Halliday, M. A. K. and Hasan, Ruqayia (1976). *Cohesion in English.* London: Longman.

Heritage, John (1984a). *Garfinkel and Ethnomethodology.* Cambridge: Polity Press.

— (1984b). A change-of-state token and aspects of its sequential placement. In J. M. Atkinson and J. Heritage (eds.) *Structures of Social Action,* pp. 299–345.

Heritage, John and Sorjonen, Marja-Leena (1994). Constituting and maintaining activities across sequences: *and*-prefacing as a feature of question design. *Language in Society,* 23: 1–29.

Hirvonen, Pekka (1970). *Finnish and English Communicative Intonation. Publications of the Phonetics Department of the University of Turku, No. 8.* Turku: University of Turku.

Iivonen, Antti (1978). Is there interrogative intonation in Finnish? In E. Garding, G. Bruce and R. Bannert (eds.) Nordic prosody. Papers from a Symposium. *Travaux de l'"Institut de Linguistique de Lund, XIII.* pp. 43–53. Lund: Lund University.

Jefferson, Gail (1972). Side sequences. In David Sudnow (ed.) *Studies in Social Interaction,* pp. 294–338. New York: Free Press.

— (1981). *The Abominable "ne?": a Working Paper Exploring the Phenomenon of Post-Response Pursuit of Response.* University of Manchester, Department of Sociology, Occasional Paper No. 6.

— (1983). Two explorations of the organisation of overlapping talk in conversation. *Tilburg Papers in Language and Literature* 28. Tilburg: Tilburg University.

Keenan, Elinor Ochs (1977). Making it last: repetition in children's discourse. In S. Ervin-Tripp and C. Mitchell-Kernan (eds.) *Child discourse,* pp. 125–38. New York: Academic Press.

Labov, William (1972). The study of language in its social context. In P. P. Giglioli (ed.) *Language and Social Context,* pp. 283–307. Penguin Books.

Labov, William and Fanshel, David (1977). *Therapeutic Discourse.* New York: Academic Press.

Larjavaara, Matti (1990). *Suomen deiksis* [Deixis in Finnish]. Helsinki: Finnish Literature Society.

Ochs, Elinor (1988). *Culture and Language Development.* Cambridge: Cambridge University Press.

— (1990). Indexicality and socialization. In G. Herdt, R. Shweder, and J. Stigler (eds.) *Cultural Psychology: Essays on Comparative Human Development,* pp. 287–308. Cambridge: Cambridge University Press.

Norrick, Neal R. (1987). Functions of repetition in conversation. *Text* 7: 245–64.

Pomerantz, Anita (1980). Telling my side: "limited access" as a "fishing device." *Sociological Inquiry,* 50, 3/4: 186–98.

(1984a). Pursuing a response. In J. M. Atkinson and J. Heritage (eds.) *Structures of Social Action*, pp. 152–63.

(1984b). Agreeing and disagreeing with assessments: some features of preferred/dispreferred turn shapes. In J. M. Atkinson and J. Heritage (eds.) *Structures of Social Action*, pp. 57–101.

Quirk, Randolph, Greenbaum, Sidney, Leech, Geoffrey and Svartvik, Jan (1972). *A Grammar of Contemporary English*. London: Longman.

Sacks, Harvey (1974). An analysis of the course of a joke's telling in conversation. In R. Bauman and J. Sherzer (eds.) *Explorations in the Ethnography of Speaking*, pp. 337–53. Cambridge: Cambridge University Press.

(1978). Some technical considerations of a dirty joke. In J.N. Schenkein (ed.) *Studies in the Organisation of Conversational Interaction*, pp. 249–70. New York: Academic Press.

(1992). *Lectures on Conversation*. Volumes I-II. Edited by Gail Jefferson and with an introduction by Emanuel A. Schegloff. Cambridge, Mass.: Basil Blackwell.

Schachter, Paul (1985). Parts-of-speech systems. In T. Shopen (ed.) *Language Typology and Syntactic Description, Volume I, Clause Structure*, pp. 3–61. Cambridge: Cambridge University Press.

Schegloff, Emanuel A. (1982). Discourse as an interactional achievement: some uses of "uh huh" and other things that come between sentences. In D. Tannen (ed.) *Analyzing Discourse: Text and Talk*. Georgetown University Roundtable on Languages and Linguistics, pp. 71–93. Washington, DC: Georgetown University Press.

(1987). Some sources of misunderstanding in talk-in-interaction. *Linguistics*, 25: 201–18.

(1988). Goffman and the analysis of conversation. In P. Drew and A. Wootton (eds.) *Erving Goffman: Exploring the Interaction Order*, pp. 89–135. Boston: Northeastern University Press.

(1990). On the organization of sequences as a source of "coherence" in talk-in-interaction. In B. Dorval (ed.) *Conversational Organization and its Development*, pp. 51–77. Advances in Discourse Processes, volume 38. Norwood, NJ: Ablex.

(1994). *Confirming Allusions*. Mimeo, UCLA.

Schegloff, Emanuel A., Jefferson, Gail and Sacks, Harvey (1977): The preference for self-correction in the organization of repair in conversation. *Language*, 53: 361–82.

Schegloff, Emanuel A. and Sacks, Harvey (1973). Opening up closings. *Semiotica*, 7: 289–327.

Silverstein, Michael (1976). Shifters, linguistic categories and cultural description. In K. Basso and H. A. Selby (eds.) *Meaning in Anthropology*, pp. 2–55. Albuquerque: University of New Mexico Press.

Sorjonen, Marja-Leena (in preparation) On discourse particles in Finnish. Ph.D. dissertation, Department of TESL and Applied Linguistics, University of California at Los Angeles.

Suomen sanojen alkuperä. Etymologinen sanakirja [The origin of Finnish words. Etymological dictionary of Finnish] (1992). Volume 1. Helsinki: Finnish Literature Society.

Tannen, Deborah (1987a). Repetition in conversation: toward a poetics of talk. *Language*, 63: 574–605.

—— (1987b). Repetition in conversation as spontaneous formulaicity. *Text*, 7: 215–43.

Ueki, Michiko (1989). Echo questions in German and Japanese. *Text*, 9, 3: 307–20.

Vilkuna, Maria (1989). *Free Word Order in Finnish: Its Syntax and Discourse Functions*. Helsinki: Finnish Literature Society.

Appendix

The morphemes have been separated from each other with a dash (-). Elements that are not separable but are contained in a lexeme and carry important semantic information are indicated by adding a plus sign (+) and a capitalized glossing (e.g. *kotia* home+TO). The following forms have been treated as unmarked forms, not indicated in the glossing:

> nominative case
> singular
> 3rd person singular (except when there are special
> reasons for indicating it)
> active voice
> present tense
> 2nd person singular imperative

Different infinitives and participial forms have not been specified.

Abbreviations being used in glossing are:
1   1st person ending
2   2nd person ending
3   3rd person ending
4   passive person ending

Case ending abbreviations:

Case	Abbreviation	Approximate meaning
ablative	ABL	"from"
accusative	ACC	object
adessive	ADE	"at, on"
allative	ALL	"to"
essive	ESS	"as"
genitive	GEN	possession
elative	ELA	"out of"
illative	ILL	"into"

inessive	INE	"in"
instructive	INS	(various)
nominative	NOM	subject
partitive	PAR	partitiveness
translative	TRA	"to", "becoming"

Other abbreviations:

ADJ	adjective
ADV	adverb
CAU	causative
CLI	clitic
COM	comparative
CON	conditional
IMP	imperative
INF	infinitive
NEG	negation
PAS	passive
PC	participle
PL	plural
POS	possessive suffix
PPC	past participle
PPPC	passive past participle
PRT	particle
PST	past tense
Q	interrogative
SG	singular
1nameF	1st name, female
1nameM	1st name, male

7

"When I come down I'm in the domain state": grammar and graphic representation in the interpretive activity of physicists[1]

ELINOR OCHS, PATRICK GONZALES, AND SALLY JACOBY

"I" is not the name of a person, nor "here" of a place, and "this" is not a name. But they are connected with names. Names are explained by means of them. It is also true that it is characteristic of physics not to use these words.

L. Wittgenstein, *Philosophical Investigations* (1958: 123)

7.1 Linguistic resources for practicing science

This paper explores how scientists build meaning through routine interpretive activity involving talk, gesture, and graphic representation. In the course of making sense of their own and others' scientific research, scientists sometimes combine these semiotic resources in ways that seem to blur the distinction between scientist and the physical world under scrutiny. We shall argue in this paper that in scientific interaction, (1) grammar works together with graphic representation and gesture to construct a referential identity which is both animate and inanimate, subject and object, and that (2) the construction of this indeterminate referential identity plays an important role in scientists' efforts to achieve mutual understanding and arrive at a working consensus.

Our study is intended to be of cross-disciplinary interest. The analysis is motivated by cultural, philosophical, sociological, and historical research on scientific practice (e.g., Bloor, 1976; Lynch, 1985, 1993; Shapin and Schaffer, 1985; Pickering, 1992; Biagioli, 1993); anthropological and linguistic approaches to lexical and grammatical structure (e.g., Duranti, 1990; Hanks, 1990, 1992; Silverstein, 1993); interactional studies of conversational discourse (e.g., Schegloff, 1991; Goodwin, 1994); and psychological paradigms that take activity as a locus of human cognition (e.g.,

Voloshinov, 1973; Vygotsky, 1978; Leontyev, 1981; Bakhtin, 1993). Each of these enterprises imposes somewhat different methodological criteria for the interpretation of data. In our study, we attempt to synthesize these methodologies as a way of approaching and understanding grammar as constitutive of and constituted by the activities of working scientists. As such, we utilize detailed transcripts annotated with cultural glosses and provide ethnographic background that contextualize and render the interactions more meaningful to readers outside the field of physics.[2]

For nearly as long as science has been recognized as a profession, the character of scientific discourse and interpretive activity has been a topic of intense scholarly interest. Considerable attention has focused on the discursive representation of the triadic relationship between scientist, scientific findings, and members of the scientific community, especially in terms of the political, religious, and other socio-cultural forces that may structure this relationship and its representation over historical time (e.g., Kuhn, 1962; Fleck, 1979/1935; Shapin and Schaffer, 1985; Biagioli, 1990a, 1990b, 1992). An over-arching concern throughout studies of scientific discourse has been the manner in which scientists verbally portray their own or other scientists' subjective involvement in the world of physical events. A number of scholars have argued that the stances of relative involvement or detachment in scientific discourse are culturally constructed and historically situated, with detachment being the preferred stance in Western science (e.g., Latour and Woolgar, 1979; Gilbert and Mulkay, 1984; Shapin and Schaffer, 1985; Latour, 1987; Bazerman, 1988; Lynch, 1988; Traweek, 1988, 1992; Biagioli, 1993; Collins and Yearling, 1992; Gooding, 1992; Knorr-Cetina, 1992). Arguing against the view that scientific discourse represents "matters of fact," these scholars assert that scientists employ linguistic and other symbolic resources (such as illustrations and graphic displays) both to construct worldly entities, processes, states, relations, and outcomes as "matters of fact" and to mitigate their own role in producing these phenomena.[3]

Of particular relevance to these studies has been the observation that the discursive practices of scientists vary across informal scientific discussions and formal, especially written, scientific texts. According to these observations, whereas in more public and formal discourse, mention of scientists' involvement in research activities is minimal or nil, in everyday informal scientific discourse in laboratory interactions and in informal accounts of those interactions, scientists often refer to themselves as agents in the production of scientific knowledge (see especially Latour and Woolgar, 1979; Gilbert and Mulkay, 1984; Latour, 1987; Gooding, 1992). These studies suggest that the more impersonal style characteristic of public scientific texts helps render scientific accounts as objective and factual. On the other hand, they assert, the more personal style characteristic of informal laboratory talk renders scientific accounts as subjective, context-sensitive, and as somewhat like narratives of personal experience wherein particular protagonists (i.e., scientists) think, feel, and act to overcome obstacles and resolve problems.

This broadly dichotomous treatment of discourse repertoires in scientific communication, which threads through constructivist studies of scientific practice and knowledge, tends to be semantically conservative. It suggests that scientists have only one referential practice for expressing subjective involvement, namely, reference to discrete persons (scientists) acting in relation to some other discrete phenomena (physical or natural entities) in the world. Indeed, this sense of discreteness is implied in all discussions of scientists as agents who construct physical/natural entities and events, because agents are, by definition, separate forces affecting objects in the world.

But what about other practices for indexing subjective involvement, in particular ones in which scientists use referring expressions to identify with the objects they study? We propose that scientists express their subjective involvement not only by foregrounding their role as practitioners of scientific activity, they also express involvement more extremely by taking the perspective of (empathizing with) some object being analyzed and by involving themselves in graphic (re)enactments of physical events. Examples of these forms of reference can be seen in Segments (1a) and (1b) below:[4]

(1a) RO LAB (11-14)

```
Ron:      .hhh But as you go belo:w the first order (0.5)

          transition you're [still in the domain structure 'n

                            [((leans upper body to right))

          you're trying to get [ou:t of it.

                                [((sweeps right arm to left))
```

(1b) ROLAB (1-3)

```
Ron:    Well you also said [(the) same thing must happen here.
                           [(( moves to board; points to diagram))
            [When [I come down [I'm in  [the domain state.
        [(( points to right part of diagram))
                [(( moves finger to left))[
                            [(( moves finger to right))
                                 [(( moves finger to left))
```

We suggest that in using such forms of reference with predicates that describe entities as changing location/state or as attempting to do so, scientists are not referring exclusively to themselves as scientists nor exclusively to the object of scientific concern but rather to a conflation of both, and, in so doing, structure their relation to – that is, their subjective involvement in – aspects of the physical world in ways not explored in previous studies of scientific discourse. The present discussion will explore this referential possibility in scientific discourse through an examination of referential encoding in the laboratory deliberations among physicists. Specifically, we consider what a group of physicists might be communicating when they use a particular set of linguistic resources, namely, constructions consisting of *personal pronominal subjects* (especially "I" and "you") and *predicates of motion/change of state* (e.g., "go," "break up").

Our study is practice-centered, interaction-centered, and activity-centered in the sense that it views scientists' language behavior as (1) a set of historically rooted practices having the potential to alter social order and cultural structures of knowledge and belief (Bourdieu, 1977; Hanks, 1990, 1992); as (2) a form of social interaction (Bakhtin, 1981; Goodwin and Goodwin, 1992; Schegloff, 1972, 1991) having the potential to recontextualize past and to precontextualize future interactions;[5] and as (3) a form of social activity having the potential to recontextualize past activities and to precontextualize future ones.[6] Indeed, social activities are jointly achieved through interaction and rely on tools, including symbolic tools like language, to coordinate participants' actions and accomplish goals (Vygotsky, 1978; Leontyev, 1981; Engeström, 1987, 1990).[7] We thus consider how grammatical constructions and other symbolic tools, such as graphic representations, mediate between and symbolically bring together not only scientists in joint activity but also scientists and the objects they study. We examine scientists' talk and their (re)construction of graphic representations as finely integrated practices and draw on both these types of inter-actionally produced symbolic practices in our exploration of how meaning may be assigned to utterances.[8]

7.2 Ethnographic context

Located within an American university, the physics laboratory that is the field site of our ethnographic and linguistic study carries out research within the area of solid state physics. The laboratory undertakes research comprising theoretical, experimental, and theoretical-experimental collaborative work on condensed matter phenomena, including spin glasses and random magnets. The group is, in this sense, unusual in that (1) its members are both theoreticians and experimentalists, (2) the principal investigator (PI) is a theoretician mentoring experimentalist graduate students and (3) holds a high-level full-time administrative position within the university. In general, the research pursued by this laboratory represents a move throughout the field of solid state physics in recent decades to study disordered systems (Fleury, 1981; Ford, 1982; Hurd, 1982).

Our study involved six months of participant field observations, concurrent and subsequent interviews with each regular member, and audio- and videorecordings of members of the physics group interacting in various work settings, including the experimental laboratories, small group meetings, and the weekly group meetings. Approximately sixty hours of interaction were recorded and tran-scribed according to the conventions of conversation analysis (see note 4), and particular segments of interaction have been further transcribed to include eye gaze, hand, head, and body movements, as well as gestures to the graphic displays produced or shown in the course of these interactions.

In addition, copies of versions of overhead transparencies ("viewgraphs") and most of the printed materials which members brought to the meetings were collected. We also have a corpus of electronic messages sent between a member of this group and a colleague in Europe concerning a particular coauthored research project which was often discussed in the group meetings. An archive of the members' research papers, published articles, and dissertations arising out of their research activities was also assembled. Finally, several tutorial sessions, during which members of the physics group explained the concepts and principles behind their research, were audiotaped for future reference, and background articles on relevant topics, which they recommended, were consulted.

The analysis presented here draws from videorecordings of the group meetings in which members present experimental or theoretical findings to the PI ("Ron" in our transcripts). During these presentations, the presenter, the PI, and, on occasion, other members of the group discuss and evaluate the experimental findings or theoretical calculations in light of their current understanding of physical phenomena and in comparison with the work of other physicists, try to arrive at a working consensus, and plan the next steps of a particular project. At times, members may move to the blackboard or the overhead projector to present, suggest, or otherwise probe physical phenomena (Ochs, Jacoby, and Gonzales, 1994). They also often come to the meetings with various types of printed materials, including published articles, computer printouts of experimental data, facsimile transmissions, and other sorts of correspondence.

To provide background to the interactions analyzed in this chapter, we briefly summarize the research topic under discussion.[9] The analytic thrust of this laboratory is the physics of atomic spins (magnetic moments) in a crystalline lattice. One project focuses on how atoms in a disordered alloy system interact with one another as a result of internal physical processes which have been affected by magnetic fields and temperature changes. This project relies, in part, on experiments carried out by Miguel, one of the advanced graduate students. For several months, he designed and conducted a series of experiments to test a computer-simulated model published by Grest et al. (1986). Figure 7.1 is our own schematic representation of the main argument of this model.[10]

Grest et al.'s (1986) theoretical argument is that, depending on the combination of temperature and strength of magnetic field, atomic spins in a diluted antiferromagnet will exhibit different kinds of order.[11] At a given magnetic field at high temperatures,

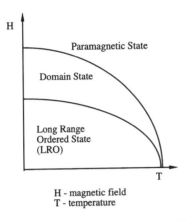

Figure 7.1 Phase transitions in a diluted antiferromagnet (based on Grest et al., 1986)

atomic spins in a diluted antiferromagnetic system are uncorrelated, i.e., in a randomly disordered ("paramagnetic") state. As the magnetic field decreases and/or the temperature lowers, the system undergoes a phase transition and moves into a partially ordered ("domain") state.[12] At a certain point, at even lower fields and lower temperatures, the system undergoes another phase transition and moves into a "long range ordered" state.[13] The paramagnetic, domain, and long range ordered states are separated in Figure 7.1 by "phase transition" lines. Figure 7.2 schematically represents these three different phases of atomic order. We have adopted the physicists" convention of using arrows to represent atomic spins.

This introduction to the ethnographic setting and content of one of the group's projects is sufficient, we feel, for readers to get a sense of the local work culture of the physicists and the ideas which inform their conversations, excerpts of which appear throughout this chapter.

7.3 Grammatical realizations of subjective involvement

In the interactions we have analyzed, members of the physics group use a number of referential practices for grammatically encoding their subjective involvement in scientific practice. Among these practices are the two discursive practices which have received the bulk of attention in rhetorical, sociological, and anthropological

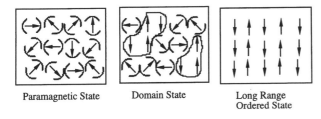

| Paramagnetic State | Domain State | Long Range Ordered State |

Figure 7.2 Long range ordered, domain, and paramagnetic states in a diluted antiferromagnetic system

studies of scientific life (e.g., Latour and Woolgar, 1979; Gilbert and Mulkay, 1984; Bazerman, 1988; Traweek 1988, 1992; McCloskey, 1990). In the first kind of grammatical realization, said to be typical of private, informal scientific discourse, scientists construct a "physicist-centered" account of scientific phenomena by referring to themselves as the thematic agents and experiencers of these phenomena. In the second kind of grammatical realization, said to be typical of public, formal scientific discourse, scientists make no explicit reference to themselves as physicists but rather construct a "physics-centered" account of scientific phenomena, i.e., an account which foregrounds the physical constructs of research interest and masks human involvement in the manipulation of nature. (We use the term "physics" here in one of the senses in which it is routinely used by members of this group: to refer to properties and processes of the physical world.) "Physics-centered" discourse is often characterized by using agentless passive structures or syntactically active structures in which the thematic subject of an utterance is a physical entity or process.[14]

7.3.1 Physicist-centered grammar: physicist as thematic focus

Segments (2) and (3) below illustrate utterances in which the grammatically encoded thematic focus is on the physicist as active participant in the making of science and scientific discovery, whether as agent or experiencer.

Physicist as agent. Segment (2) illustrates physicists referring to themselves as agents in relation to physical phenomena, acting upon physical entities through manipulations of experimental conditions:

(2) RO LAB (1-3)

```
Miguel: Yeah: not only that u- [we did experiments
                                [((points to diagram))

        [where we (.) we uh:(0.2)   [we (.) brought the
        [((Ron backs away from board))  [((moves left hand to diagram))

        system: uh: [(0.8) [here
                    [((hand to chin))
                           [((points to diagram))

Ron:    Mm hm

Miguel: [And then we uhm (0.2) °or was it there?,°
        [((moves hand lower on diagram then moves left hand to chin))

        (0.2) [uh: that's right.
              [((moves left hand to board))

        [Here.  [Then we lowered the field, (0.2)
        [((points to diagram))
                [((lowers hand on diagram; looks at Ron))

        [raised the field,
        [((raises hand on diagram))
```

Physicist as experiencer. Segment (3) illustrates physicists referring to themselves as experiencers, perceiving, understanding, or reacting to physical phenomena and measurements:

(3) RO LAB (1-3)

```
Ron:    Is there a po:ssibility that he hasn't
        [seen anything real?,
        [((points to equation on board))

        (0.5)

Ron:    [>(I) mean< is there a
        [((points to lower part of diagram, upper, lower again))

        possibil[ity
Miguel:         [I- i- it is possible and there [i-
                [((vertical headshakes))        [((horizontal
                                                    headshakes))

        [(0.2) [I'm ama:zed by his measurements because when=
        [((Ron moves from board to other side of table))
```

(3) RO LAB (1-3) continued

```
Ron:              [(The-)
Miguel: =you quench: (.) from five to two tesla (.) a magnet a
        superconducting magnet [.hhh e:: [(.)
                               [((mild vertical headshakes))
                                          [((moves head forward))
Ron:     °That's what I'm wondering.°
```

7.3.2 Physics-centered grammar: physics as thematic focus

Segments (4) through (6) illustrate physicists foregrounding inanimate physical entities as the thematic focus and grammatical subject of clauses. In such utterances, the physical entities are assigned two related semantic roles through predicates which refer either to a motion/change of state event or to a cognitive experience.

Physics + motion/change of state. Segment (4) illustrates how physicists grammatically construct physical entities (e.g., an atomic system) as moving through space and/or undergoing changes of state:

(4) RO LAB (1-3)

```
Miguel: So: (.) what I was saying is the following [At h- high
                                                   [((gestures
                                                     high on board))
        fields (i-) or high temperatures, [the system is in
                                           [((looks at Ron))
        the paramagnetic reg[ime.
                            [((looks at board))
        [(.)
        [((Miguel puts hand on board))
Miguel: Then (.) it crosses [to a: domain state.
                            [((looks at Ron))
        [.hhh (.) [ A::nd (.) there's also
        [((looks at board))
                  [((puts hand on board))
        a: long range (.) ordered state [at
                                        [((looks at Ron))
        [low fields and low [temperatures
        [((hand traces diagram))  [((drops hand to side))
```

Physics as experiencer. Although we do not normally think of inanimate entities as capable of cognition, Segments (5) and (6) illustrate how physicists also grammatically construct physical entities as experiencers, by selecting predicates of sentience and understanding:

(5) RO LAB (1-3)

```
Ron:      [If this were a first order [pha:se transition, (0.2)
          [((moves to board; points to diagram))
                                    [((looks at Miguel))

Miguel: Mm hm?

Ron:      [Then   that means   [that- that- this system has no
          [((looks at board))   [((Miguel looks at board))

          knowledge of [tha:t system.
                       [((looks at Miguel))
```

(6) RO LAB (11-14)

```
Miguel: Let me uh: tell you why I'm raising the question. .hh uh-
          [this is a modest field.
          [((points & circles pen towards table))
          (0.5)

Miguel: Ts! So the [region, .hhh [where the system is
                   [((places fingers on narrow area of diagram))
                                [((moves hand down diagram))

          experiencing random fields is very narrow in

          temperatures.And if you [coo:l extremely fast (1.2)
                                  [((stretches out right arm))

          the system may [never have the time to experience
                         [((rapid horizontal headshakes))

          those random fields and therefore you

          [have a long range ((losing breath)) ordered state at
          [((places both arms palms up at side of body))

          the low temperatures (.) in low fields.
```

7.3.3 Commonality of physicist-centered and physics-centered discourse practices

Although much has been made of the different rhetorical effects created by that discourse practice which draws attention to the scientist (physicist) as the thematic focus of an utterance and the other discourse practice which draws attention to the object of inquiry (a physical entity or system) as a thematic focus, these two discourse practices actually share a common perspective. In particular, *both practices presuppose scientist and objects of inquiry as separate and distinct entities.* This is perhaps more easily seen in physicist-centered discourse, in which the physicist is encoded as a distinct agent (e.g., "when you cut the field") or experiencer (e.g., "we observe the drop at high fields") separate from the object of inquiry.[15] But it is important to note that physics-centered discourse presupposes the same separateness and distinction between physicist and the object of inquiry precisely because the physicist is nowhere to be seen. Moreover, while frequently not referentially present in physics-centered discourse, the physicist is implied as a distinct referent in constructions such as agentless passive clauses (e.g., "it still (is) the case that they [the measurements] were obtained at different temperatures").

7.3.4 Physicist and physics as blended thematic foci: the problem of indeterminacy

Do these two discourse practices exhaust the possibilities for grammatically structuring the relationship between physicist and physics? As we indicated briefly at the outset, we think not because we have noticed that, in addition to the varied grammatical realizations of physicist and physics as distinct entities, our data are full of utterances which encode an *indeterminate* referent, as in "as you go below the first order transition you're still in the domain structure and you're trying to get out of it" (1a) and "when I come down I'm in the domain state" (1b). That is, the referent constructed in these utterances appears to be neither exclusively the physicist nor the object of inquiry but rather a blended identity that blurs the distinction between the two. Such utterances cannot, of course, be literally understood as indexing events in which physicists participate. Nevertheless, they appear to be completely unproblematic for the physicist interlocutors. Indeed, no one ever stops an interaction to ask, "What do you mean "*I'm* in the domain state"?" or "How could *you* possibly "go below in temperature"?" Moreover, they are also ubiquitous in our data.

Several co-occurring linguistic properties of these indeterminate utterances work together to convey a sense of indeterminacy. First, their verb forms tend to be realized in the simple present or present progressive, which depict events as generic, enduring, or iterative rather than as specific, unique, and punctual. Second, the pronominal subjects, generally "I" and "you," do not appear to be restricted to either the speaker or addressee, but rather to a class of referents who may participate in these generic, enduring, or iterative events (e.g., "As you [or any entity] go below the first order transition"). Third, while the pronominal subject of these utterances presupposes an animate referent, the predicate appears to refer to a physical event or state attributable to an inanimate referent (i.e., the physical object under consideration), as represented below:

Personal Pronoun$_{animate}$ | | **Predicate**$_{inanimate}$

These utterances thus seem to have a semantically schizoid, illogical character which blurs the boundaries between the animate subject (physicist) and the inanimate object (physical entity/system).

Segment (7) presents a typical sequence in which all three types of thematic foci – physicist-centered, physics-centered, and indeterminate – alternate in rapid succession. The segment begins with Ron and Miguel at the blackboard, with Ron articulating a problem he is having in understanding the results of Miguel's recent experiments. The ensuing discussion[16] centers on (1) differences between Miguel's results and those of the computer-simulated model proposed by Grest et al. (1986); (2) differences between Miguel's experiments and those found by another experimental group (headed by Kleeman); and (3) differences in Miguel's measurements obtained from two different experimental procedures (zero field cooled vs. field cooled). [17]

Throughout this interaction, Ron and Miguel point, gesture, and add to a freehand abstracted sketch of the Grest et al. phase transition model on the blackboard (see Figure 7.1). The progressively

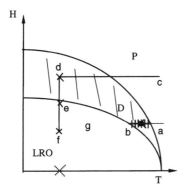

Figure 7.3 Key to nonverbal gesturing within blackboard sketch

annotated graphic display is thus constituted as a highly intertextual representation through which the participants can move fluidly from a discussion of one set of results to another (Ochs, Jacoby, and Gonzales, 1994). Figure 7.3 represents the graphic display. We use lowercase letters to identify places which the participants point to or touch in the course of their conversation.

Here, then, is the sequence between Ron and Miguel:

(7) RO LAB (1-3)

```
 1   Ron:   When I approach a phase transition
 2          line [in different
 3                 [((looks at board; points to 'X' between a and b))
 4          [directions.  That I understand.
 5          [((looks at Miguel))
 6          (.)
 7   Ron:   [But what I [(.) tryin to- what I can't
 8          [((looks at board; points to e))
 9          [((Miguel looks down; moves away from board))
10                     [((Miguel looks at board))
11          figure out is if this is truly
12          [a phase transition line
13          [((looks at Miguel))
14          (0.2) [why [don't I [go: [(0.2) to the
15                [((looks at board))   [
16                     [((moves finger to d))
17                          [((moves finger to f and holds))
```

(7) RO LAB (1-3) continued

```
1 8                                    [((looks at Miguel))
1 9         long range ordered phase in the Kleeman experiment.
2 0         (1.0)
2 1   Ron: [Cause you're telling me [that [I
2 2         [((looks at board))           [((points to d))
2 3                                          [((moves finger to f))
2 4         go [here [and there's still a decay (present).
2 5            [((looks at Miguel))
2 6                  [((Miguel looks down; turns body away from board))
2 7         .hh [But you're telling me that [if I
2 8             [((looks at board))          [((points to a))
2 9         [come in [this way [(0.5) and [go he:re there's
3 0         [((moves finger to b))[         [
3 1                  [((looks at Miguel))   [
3 2                        [((Miguel looks at board))
3 3                                     [((moves finger to g))
3 4         no decay.
3 5         (1.0)
3 6   Ron: [Nothing happens.
3 7         [((slight shrug))
3 8         (0.2)
3 9 Miguel: [Yeah well eh: I [I don't know.  [I: (.) nu-
4 0         [((moves to board)) [            [
4 1         [((Ron steps back from board))   [
4 2                          [((picks up chalk))[
4 3                                          [((looks at Ron))
4 4         (if from) I'm going to throw ideas in the pot.
4 5         Uh [HEre (.) (when) you reach this point
4 6            [((points to c))
4 7         [here   (0.5)    [u- prior to cutting the field we
4 8         [((marks 'X' at d)) [((with other hand, points to d))
4 9         are in (the) domain state.
5 0   Ron: Yes
5 1 Miguel: [And [as- when you cut the field [(0.8) you
5 2         [((points to d))                [((points again))
5 3            [((moves finger to f and lowers hand))
```

```
54              uh reach the [long range order state.
55                         [(((looks at Ron))
56              (.)
57   Miguel:  [So maybe the domains need to grow.
58              [(((raises both hands into air with upward motion))
59              (.)
60   Miguel:  [Although that's not what we observe
61              [(((looks up))
62              really experimentally.
63   Ron:     Well you also said [(the) same thing must happen here.
64                              [(((moves to board; points to b))
65              [When [I come down [I'm in [the domain state.
66              [(((points to a))      [        [
67                   [(((moves finger to b))   [
68                            [(((moves finger to a))
69                                  [(((moves finger to b))
70   Miguel: Yeah.
```

Table 7.1 shows more clearly how, within this single strip of inter-action, interlocutors switch among physicist-centered, physics-cen-tered, and indeterminate perspectives within and across turns. The table follows the segment in time and is to be read from left to right, returning to the next leftmost utterance as one gradually moves down the table.

The compact character of this constant perspective-switching seems to preclude topic as influencing the use of indeterminate constructions. What does seem influential, however, is that indeter-minate constructions seem to be a referential resource especially suited to the activity of thinking through research problems together. Indeed, it does seem, in our data, that in contrast to phy-sics- and physicist-centered constructions, indeterminate construc-tions tend not to appear outside of this activity. More specifically, these constructions primarily appear *after* graduate students or post-doctoral fellows have initially presented research findings to the PI, and that the PI is the main producer of these constructions as he struggles to understand and evaluate the findings of the junior members. Nevertheless, other members produce these constructions as well when they participate in the ongoing discussion. When the PI uses these constructions, he typically uses the first person singular

Table 7.1 Switching among alternative perspectives in unfolding interaction
(from segment 7)

PHYSICIST FOCUS	PHYSICS FOCUS	INDETERMINATE FOCUS
Ron:		When I approach a phase transition line in different directions.
That I understand. But what I tryin to-		
what I can't figure out is	if this is truly a phase transition line	why don't I go to the long range ordered phase in the Kleeman experiment.
Cause you're telling me that		I go here
	and there's still a decay (present).	
But you're telling me that		if I come in this way and go he:re
	there's no decay.	
	Nothing happens.	

Table 7.1 (continued)

Miguel: Yeah well eh I I don't know. I nu- (if from)		
I'm going to throw ideas in the pot.		Uh here (when) you reach this point here
u- prior to cutting the field		we are in (the) domain state.
Ron: Yes		
Miguel: And as- when you cut the field		you uh reach the long range order state.
	So maybe the domains need to grow.	
Although that's not what we observe really experimentally.		
Ron: Well you also said	(the) same thing must happen here.	When I come down I'm in the domain state.

pronoun "I," as in "when I come down I'm in the domain state," or "why don't I go to the long range ordered state in the Kleeman experiment." When graduate student and post-doctoral presenters use indeterminate constructions, they tend to use either the second person pronoun "you" or the first person plural pronoun "we," as in "uh here when you reach this point we are in the domain state."

7.4 Two interpretive strategies

In trying to understand these physicists' use of indeterminate constructions, we consider two main interpretive strategies. As will be shown, we ultimately align with the second strategy because it widens the basis for assigning meaning beyond the utterance to include the referential gestural practices which accompany the linguistic stream and which are integral to the activity in scientific practice of collaboratively interpreting graphic representations.

7.4.1 Interpretive strategy 1: pronominal referent = physicist

One strategy for understanding indeterminate utterances is to posit that they have an underlying logical form containing a causal predicate. Thus, (8a) might be interpreted as having the underlying logical form of (8b):

(8a) I'm in the domain state.

(8b) I cause some physical entity to be in the domain state.

With Strategy 1, the pronominal form refers exclusively to the *physicist* who functions in the semantic role of *agent*, i.e., as a physicist carrying out an experimental protocol. Such an interpretation treats the construction as a physicist-centered locution and preserves the rhetorical and philosophical distinction between scientist as subject and the physical world as the object of inquiry: it is understood that the scientist is a separate entity who causes some change in the physical world.

Support for this interpretive strategy comes from similar constructions in English, such as "I remodeled my house," the interpretation of which may depend on interlocutors supplying background knowledge so as to evaluate whether or not the referent of the pronoun has actually physically carried out the action. Thus, while "I remodeled my house" could mean that the speaker physically carried out the remodeling, it can also mean that the speaker caused someone else to remodel his/her house. An interlocutor would need to supply cultural and personal knowledge to interpret such utterances, including knowledge of the speaker's right, ability, and/or predilection to be the referent which causes some other entity to participate in the event.[18]

However, positing an underlying causal predicate is problematic for at least two reasons:

(1) As we have shown, physicists explicitly express causality through both transitive physicist-centered constructions such as "And then I lower the temperature" and indeterminate constructions such as "If I go below in temperature" in alternation within the same activity. Is there a cognitive advantage perhaps? We think not because the positing of an underlying form would require the comprehender to supply abstract causal predicates to understand them, whereas transitive forms do not.

(2) Indeterminate constructions pragmatically imply that the subject pronoun referent is more directly involved in the change of location or state of a physical entity than the subject pronoun referent in an underlying causal proposition. For example, the pronominal referent of "I" in "If I go below in temperature" seems involved to a greater degree in the change of state between temperatures than does the pronominal referent of "I" in "I cause some physical entity to go below in temperature." Thus, indeterminate constructions create a zone of *ambiguity* which allows the interpretation that the referent could actually be doing the activity described.

7.4.2 Interpretive strategy 2: pronominal referent = blended identity

A more satisfying way to understand the meaning of indeterminate constructions, then, is to posit a more extreme form of subjectivity in which the distinction between the scientist as subject and the physical world as object is blurred. In this interpretation, the pronominal referent (the referent of "I" in, for instance, "When I come down I'm in the domain state") is a blended identity composed of both the animate physicist and the inanimate physical entity undergoing some change of state. Whereas Strategy 1 attempts to resolve the apparent semantic contradiction (of an animate subject linked to a predicate which presupposes an inanimate subject), Strategy 2 accepts the schizoid character of such constructions as a linguistic resource used non-problematically by scientists in their everyday interpretive work. Strategy 2 thus acknowledges that referential ambiguity is a necessary poetics of mundane scientific problem-solving in that by using indeterminate constructions as a linguistic heuristic, scientists constitute an empathy with entities they are struggling to understand. Such a referential poetics allows interlocutors to symbolically participate in events from the perspective of entities in worlds no physicist could otherwise experience. Moreover, scientists take such "interpretive journeys" (Ochs, Jacoby, and Gonzales, 1994) in two intertwined constructed realms: (1) the world of physical events, and (2) the world of visual representations of those events.

The constructed world of physical events. When physicists use indeterminate constructions, they may be symbolically repositioning themselves in an imagined realm of physical events (Bühler, 1990/1934; Hanks, 1990, 1992). In so doing, they evoke a referent of "I" which is subjectively involved in the world of physical events. Rather than causing events, as Strategy 1 would have it, the referent of "I" in Strategy 2 is experiencing physical events from the perspective of physical entities. Thus, for example, the pronominal referent of "I" in "I'm in the domain state" (1b) is understood to be directly experiencing the domain state. In example (1a), the pronominal referent of "you" is understood to be "go[ing] belo:w the first order transition . . . still in the domain structure 'n' . . . trying to get out of it." In other instances of indeterminate constructions, the pronominal referents "go into the long range ordered phase," "break[ing] up into domains," and "go below in temperature."

In the poetics of interpretive Strategy 2, therefore, the referent indexed by the pronoun "I" or "you"[19] travels through temperature and magnetization conditions, crosses phase transition boundaries, and experiences the effects of these changes. But who or what is participating in these physical events? Strategy 2 suggests that it is both physicists and the inanimate physical matter which they study (e.g., sub-atomic particles, random magnets). Indeterminate constructions are thus a resource which enables physicists to routinely manifest an extreme form of subjectivity by stepping into the universe of physical processes to take the perspective of physical constructs (i.e., to symbolically live their experiences). Like actors playing characters or reporters quoting others, however, while both voices are heard, the voice of the physicist is backgrounded, and that of the physical construct is foregrounded (Voloshinov, 1973; Bakhtin, 1981, 1993).

Referential displacement of this sort seems especially suited to the scientists' efforts to think through physical problems. Indeed, as noted earlier, indeterminate constructions frequently appear when one physicist (especially Ron, the laboratory director) is trying to retrace and interpret what may have transpired in the course of experiments carried out by another physicist in the laboratory. Support for this interpretive strategy also comes from mythic accounts of scientists' flashes of insight concerning physical phenomena in the universe. It is reported, for example, that when Einstein was sixteen, ten years before formulating the theory of relativity, he "tried to imagine what he would observe if he were to travel through the ether with the same velocity as a beam of light" (Whitrow, 1972: 105). Similarly, Jonas Salk recalls that early in his life he developed a technique in which he would picture himself "as a virus, or as a cancer cell, for example, and try to sense what it would be like to be either in order to better understand the viruses" (Salk, 1983: 7). Further, members of the laboratory team acknowledge using language to identify with the objects they are trying to understand. An especially revealing statement came from an interview with Ron, the most prolific user of indeterminate constructions, when he was asked what he thought these kinds of utterances meant:

(9) Interview with Ron (8-2-91)

Sally: Elinor is very interested in all the phrases like . . . "When I cross over that line"[20] . . . This is her favorite line in the

whole corpus . . . "When I cross over that line" . . . Who's
I? ((*lines omitted*))

Ron: This comment that Elinor picked up is <u>certainly</u> true . . .
that we personalize inanimate objects. That's a <u>very</u> common physical phenomenon ((*laughter*)) or, I should say, a
phenomenon among physicists.

Two things especially strike us about Ron's response. The first is
that he volunteers an interpretation of indeterminate constructions
as utterances in which "we [physicists] personalize inanimate
objects." This comment emphasizes more the propensity of physicists to animate or anthropomorphize physical objects rather than
to take on their identities.[21] The second striking aspect of Ron's
comment which reflects a Strategy 2 interpretation is his displayed
awareness of his own blurring of identities (of physicist and physical entities) in the phrase "physical phenomenon." After laughing,
he disambiguates this phrase (through self-repair) by reformulating
it as "a phenomenon among physicists."

The constructed worlds of visual representations. While indeterminate utterances may help to displace physicists into constructed
worlds of physical events, they do so as part of embodied interpretive practices. To understand such constructions, it is therefore crucial to pursue an analysis that integrates the language, gestural
practices, and visual arrays which comprise physicists' interpretive
activities.[22] For example, in Segment (7), when Ron says, "I
approach a phase transition line in different directions" (lines 1–4)
and "come in this way and go here" (line 29), the meaning of
"line," "this way," and "here" are interpretable not only as places
on the blackboard in the meeting room but also as symbolic places
on the graph, which conventionally represent states and events in
the physical world.[23]

Graphic displays thus provide physicists with a cognitive and
spatial domain to inhabit and wander in. They also transport physical phenomena into the perceptual presence of physicists[24] and
serve as a locus in which physicist and physical phenomenon can
be brought into physical and symbolic contact with one another
(Ochs, Jacoby, and Gonzales, 1994).[25] This intertextual and multi-
modal process is depicted in Figure 7.4. As can be seen in this series

[If I . . .
[((*points to a*))

. . . [come in <u>this</u> way (0.5) and . . .
 [((*moves finger to b*))

... [go he:re ...
    [((*moves finger to g*))

Figure 7.4 "If I come in this way (0.5) and go he:re"

of video stills, when Ron says, "If I come in this way," he points his
finger first to the rightmost limit of Miguel's measurements at the
upper phase transition line (point [a] in Figure 7.3), then to the
leftmost limit of Miguel's measurements at the lower phase transition line (point [b]), and then looks at Miguel who has turned his
face and body away from the blackboard. After Ron's slight pause
pulls Miguel's gaze back to the board (Goodwin, 1980), Ron adds,
"and go here," simultaneously moving his finger further left into the
long range ordered portion of the graph (at point [g]).

The meaning of "If I come in this way" is thus built simultaneously from (1) the sensori-motor action involving Ron's fingers
and hand on the blackboard and within the graphically defined
space, and (2) from the symbolic meanings which have already
been assigned to the marks, lines, and areas of the conventionalized
graphic representation in this and previous interactions. Moreover,
indexical gestures are so much a part of the physicists' discourse
practices, it appears that physicists come to their understandings

and interpretations of physics partly through such sensori-motor and symbolic re-enactments of physical events and that the collaborative thinking-through process requires that this sensori-motor involvement be witnessed and evaluated by others present.[26]

This characterization of the role of sensori-motor re-enactments is not mere musing on our part. Segment (10), taken from the same meeting as Segment (7), suggests that the physicists themselves are aware of how important sensori-motor re-enactments within graphic spaces are to collaborative interpretive activity:

(10) RO LAB (1-3)

```
 1   Ron:      ((resting head on right hand)) Now let's just s- (.) take your
 2             finger and start abo:ve the the:: upper transition line.
 3   Miguel:   Yes. ((turns toward board))
 4   Ron:      You're going to say I'm in the paramagnetic state
 5   Miguel:   [Mm hm? ((turns to Ron))
 6             [((vertical headshakes))
 7   Ron:      Just draw your line. ((Miguel turns to board))
 8   Miguel:   [O[kay.
 9             [((moves finger from a to b; hand to chalk ledge))
10   Ron:        [Okay.
11   Miguel:   (       )
12   Ron:      I've reached that point. ((Miguel looks at Ron)) And by the
13             fact that- (.) the time scale appears to set in right at-
14             right when I cross that line,
15   Miguel:   [Mm hm
16             [((vertical headshakes))
17   Ron:      You're gonna tell me that the random field
18   Miguel:   M[m
19   Ron:       [then uh:: (0.2) has caused a domain (.) structure (0.5)
20             whi:ch uh itself is [growing in time in some way,
21                                 [((opens right hand; horizontal headshakes)
22   Miguel:   Mm hm?,
23   Ron:      Because of presumably there's [a nucleation and uh it has
24                                           [((makes squeeze motion
25                                                    with fingers))
26             to reach an [equilibrium (.) [on the domain side.
27                         [((hand to head))  [
```

```
28   Miguel:                              [(Yes it does.)

29                                        [((vertical headshakes))

30               [Yeah.

31               [((vertical headshakes))

32   Ron:        [Which you may never get to.

33               [((hand opens to side; hand to head))

34               (0.5)

35   Miguel:     [Mm hm

36               [((vertical headshakes))

37   Ron:        A*nd I'm [purposely putting words in your mouth.

38                        [((waves right hand toward Miguel; hand to head))

39   Miguel:     [Y:es.

40               [((vertical headshakes))

41   Ron:        AND now I [continue down in temperature.

42                         [((moves index finger through air, right to left))

43   Miguel:     [Mm hm.

44               [((vertical headshakes))

45   Ron:        .hhh [Those domains have some physical: (.) si:ze by

46                    [((opens hand, moves it right))

47               now.  [They're grow[ing?,    ]

48                     [((moves open hand right))

49   Miguel:                        [Correct.]   That's right.

50                                  [((vertical headshakes))

51   Ron:        [When I cross the [lower line,

52               [((points to board; lowers head))

53                                 [((Miguel turns to board))

54   Miguel:     [Yes:

55               [((turns to Ron))

56   Ron:        you're gonna tell me [that I jump then, (0.2) to a state

57                                     [((snaps fingers))

58               where [I- m- I have large correlated regions, but the

59                     [((opens hand; horizontal headshakes; head tilts right))

60               [domains have   [no necessary relationship to

61               [((head straight)) [((moves hand left))

62               (.) [the domains in the crossed hatch region.

63                   [((points to board; hand to head))
```

There are several observations to be made concerning Segment (10) with regard to the relationship between the thinking-through process, gestural practices in a graphic space, and the frequent occurrence of indeterminate constructions. One is that, in line 1, Ron interrupts what appears to be the beginning of a hypothetical reasoning sequence ("Now let's just s-") to direct Miguel to place his finger on the line in the graph. When Miguel subsequently contributes a verbal compliance ("Yes"– line 3) to this directive and a continuer ("Mm hm"– line 5) to Ron's resumed reasoning-through process without placing his finger on the graph (lines 3-6), Ron redoes a directive to "Just draw your line" (line 7). Only when Miguel gesturally complies with this second directive (line 9) does Ron fully resume his reasoning-through process. A second observation is that the gesturing is topicalized as a heuristic procedure in the talk itself and is not merely an accompaniment to the deliberation between the participants about physics. A third observation is that in the early part of the segment (lines 12–14), Ron uses "I" in indeterminate constructions even though it is Miguel who has gestured to the board. Since Ron is sitting at the table, at some distance from the blackboard, his directives to Miguel are, in some sense, a way of constituting Miguel as an extension of Ron's own body into the graphic space.[27]

Finally, we note that the occurrence of indeterminate constructions are generally concentrated in two places in Segment (10): in the opening of the segment (lines 1–15) and towards the end of the segment (lines 41–63). Between these two parts of the segment, Ron switches to "physics-centered" constructions as he hypothesizes what might be occurring physically in the domain state phase given the argument he is following. It seems that the indeterminate constructions in this interaction come into the talk in those parts of the narrative about the experiment in which the system is moving from the paramagnetic state to the domain state and from the domain state to the long range ordered state, precisely at the phase transition boundaries represented on the graph by the large curved lines (see Figure 7.3). Ron's stopping and then resuming his use of indeterminate constructions, coupled with Miguel's gestures, thus lends an enhanced dynamism to the physical processes narrated through the talk and represented by the static graph.[28]

Similarly, let us return to Ron's utterance "When I come down I'm in the domain state" (Segment 7, lines 65-69):

```
Ron:     [When [I come down [I'm in [the domain state.

         [((points to a))      [         [

           [((moves finger to b))   [

                   [((moves finger to a))

                     [((moves finger to b))
```

The presence of the blackboard sketch provides a locus for Ron to perspectivize simultaneously not only what happens when a magnetic system "come[s] down [in temperature]," but also what happens when Ron, as a physicist in the here-and-now interaction, iconically "come[s] down [in temperature]" along a particular trajectory within the graph. Ron's movement is iconic with the graph in that when he "come[s] down [in temperature]," he moves his finger inside the graph from right to left along a horizontal line representing change in temperature. Note that within the conventions of the blackboard sketch (see Figure 7.3), the horizontal axis represents temperature and, thus, a movement leftward represents a decrease in temperature. Ron can therefore linguistically say he is coming "down" yet gesturally move his finger with respect to *how the graph represents a decrease in temperature* (i.e., horizontally, right to left). Ron can also iconically locate himself "in the domain state" by moving his finger back and forth within the area of the graph designated as the "domain state."

Segments (7) and (10) suggest that indeterminate constructions draw interlocutors into an intersection of multiple worlds, including the world of here-and-now interaction, the world of graphic space, and the world of physical events symbolically represented by the graphic display.[29] It is as if interlocutors are able to situate themselves simultaneously on three referential planes through their talk and interaction yet never experience referential confusion as a result of this multi-leveled distribution of attention: physicists (1) attend to people and objects (especially graphic displays) in their meeting room, (2) carry out symbolic gestural motions within graphic representations, and, facilitated by these graphic representations and their own gestural enactments, (3) imagine themselves as physical systems in different physical states. All these practices (and more) not only contribute to the meanings of the personal pronouns in indeterminate constructions, they also help to constitute the social, cognitive, and linguistic activity of interpreting procedures and findings in scientific discourse.[30]

It is important to point out that while the presence of a visually accessible representation appears to promote the use of indeterminate constructions, such constructions are also used when physicists are not actually gesturing within a graphic representation. We have already noted that one physicist may be speaking while another is doing the gesturing (see discussion of Segment (10)). Secondly, there may be an interactional history of gesturing and orienting to a graphic representation, which gives meaning to indeterminate constructions. This is especially relevant to our data in which discussions of the same topic can continue for more than an hour, with participants occasionally moving to the blackboard, then returning to the table to continue deliberating, using indeterminate constructions without further gesturing to the graph. Finally, a graphic representation may be nowhere in sight but may exist as a virtual reality by dint of its being part of the background knowledge base of the participants. Once knowledge of the model is part of their cognitive apparatus, physicists may speak of upper and lower phase transition lines, for example, without having to draw or hold in their hand a graphic representation of a phase transition model.

While these other scenarios are possible and do occur in our data, we cannot stress strongly enough that the pervasive context for the emergence of indeterminate constructions is participants' orientation to a visibly available graphic representation. Overwhelmingly, interlocutors are looking at, gesturing towards, and/or touching locations within these graphic spaces as they say utterances such as "And now I continue down in temperature," "If I come in this way (0.5) and go he:re there's no decay," or "Why don't I go: to the long range ordered phase in the Kleeman experiment." Indeed, the interlocutors appear to have difficulty sustaining interpretive activity without either jumping up from the meeting table to sketch out what they mean through diagrams and graphs on the board or leaning over printed materials on the table to relate their argument to graphically defined spaces. It may be that this frequent gestural referencing of graphic spaces may serve to reinvoke the mediating role of the graphic display in the participants' creation of meaning.[31]

7.5 Conclusion

This paper brings scientific practice to bear on the understanding of referential meaning in the interactions of physicists. It also examines how referential practice organizes scientists' subjective involvement in simultaneously relevant worlds. Our study has focused on a type of indeterminate utterance: one that combines a personal animate pronominal subject (e.g., "I") with an inanimate physical event predicate (e.g., "am in the domain state"). Such constructions appear syntactically cohesive but are semantically disjunctive in that an entity which is "in the domain state," "breaking up into domains," or "going to the long range ordered state" is not usually considered capable of being encoded as an "I" or "you" who is conscious, reflective, and able to give verbalized descriptions of its physical state.

We have considered two interpretive strategies which might be employed to resolve the semantic incongruity of these indeterminate constructions. The first, which we found to be lacking, attempts to resolve the semantic incongruity by positing an unrealized causative predicate. This strategy allows the personal pronoun to be understood as literally referring to the physicist as agent (e.g., "I'm in the domain state" -> "I cause a physical entity to be in the domain state"). The other, more satisfying strategy attempts to resolve the semantic incongruity by first positing a referential displacement of the identity of the physicist onto the identity of the physical entity or event. Such a displacement allows the personal pronoun to be understood as figuratively referring to the physical entity as if the physical entity were imbued with the capability of conscious self-description (e.g., "I'm in the domain state" -> "I, as physicist assuming the perspective of the physical entity, am in the domain state").

This second figurative strategy was modified further by bringing into the discussion the gestural practices and graphic representations because they are also part of physicists' activity of thinking through physics problems together. In this modified strategy, indeterminate constructions can be understood as literal predications about physicists in the here-and-now world of the interaction who gesturally locate themselves in the world of graphic representation. At the same time, because the world of graphic representations indexes a world of physical events, these same utterances can be understood as referring to physical entities experiencing the physical events represented by the graph. That graphic representations mediate between scientists and the physical entities they are struggling to understand is old hat to scholars of scientific practice. What is not old hat or obvious, however, is that *graphic representations can referentially constitute scientists and physical entities as simultaneous, co-existing participants in events.*

This analysis of indeterminate constructions contributes to the discussion of subject/object relations in science by illuminating how words, gestures, and graphic representations structure multiple relations between scientists and their objects of inquiry. It hopefully puts to rest the reductive notion, often voiced in studies of science, that scientists have but two discursive alternatives through which they communicate their subjective involvement: either topicalizing themselves as agents or actors who cause physical events, or suppressing their role in favor of topicalizing scientific instruments, systems, results, and other non-human constructs. We hope to have demonstrated that scientists routinely blur the boundaries between themselves as subjects and physical systems as objects by using a type of indeterminate construction which blends properties of both animate and inanimate, subject and object. Indeed, referential indeterminacy created through gesture, graphic representation, and talk appears to be a valuable discursive and psychological resource as scientists work through their interpretations and come to consensus regarding research findings.

Our analysis of referential meaning in the discourse of physicists also suggests that linguistic structures and the shapes of utterances cannot be adequately described without widening the scope of inquiry to include the participants' interaction. Indeed, what we mean by "grammar" may require a reconceptualization. Specifically, we are proposing that grammar cannot be merely a finite set of computational rules or operations in the brain, nor is it to be found only in the verbal sound stream of talk. Instead, "grammar" must also encompass the possibility that grammatical structures and their meanings are constituted through interlocutors' larger activities, tool use, and gestural practices.[32] Benveniste (1971: 220), arguing for a semiotic approach that collapses the distinction between *langue* and *parole*, suggests that grammatical forms such as pronouns and verbs are "an inextricable part of the individual instance of discourse: [they are] always and necessarily actualized by the act of discourse and in dependence on that act." Arguing for a social interactional approach to language, Sacks (1992: 31) similarly observes that "Grammar, of course, is the model of closely ordered, routinely observable social activities" (Lecture 4, Fall 1964 – Spring 1965, p. 31). It behooves us, therefore, to approach grammar as the interactional achievement of participants who creatively adapt language to their larger communicative needs.

Notes

1   We are grateful to Asif Agha, Mario Biagioli, Alessandro Duranti, Charles Goodwin, Marjorie Harness Goodwin, William Hanks, John Heritage, Greg Kenning, Marcos Lederman, Jay Lemke, Emanuel Schegloff, Jonathan Selinger, Michael Silverstein, Marja-Leena Sorjonen, Carolyn Taylor, Sandra Thompson, and two anonymous reviewers for their helpful comments at various stages in the development of this paper. This study is part of a larger project, "The Socialization of Scientific Discourse," directed by Elinor Ochs and funded by the Spencer Foundation (Grant no. M900824, 1990-1993). Additional funding has been provided by a UCLA Faculty Senate Grant. Earlier versions of this paper were presented at the Interaction and Grammar Workshop at UCLA (May, 1992) and at the International Conference on Discourse and the Professions, Uppsala, Sweden (August, 1992).
2   The reader is directed to Schieffelin (1979) for an explication of this endeavor.
3   It should be noted that there is considerable discussion of the philosophical underpinnings and socio-historical accuracy of constructivist studies of scientific discourse. For example, see the debates in Pickering (1992) and Schaffer (1991).
4   Segments of our recorded data are transcribed according to the conventions of conversation analysis (e.g., Atkinson and Heritage, 1984: ix-xvi). Detailed explanations of these notation conventions are included in a glossary at the end of this volume. There is, however, one additional convention used in this chapter:
    bolded text   indicates the phenomenon of focus
5   This point rests on the essential notion of "conditional relevance" (Sacks, Schegloff, and Jefferson, 1974) which argues that because certain types of utterances warrant other types of utterances as relevant next conversational moves, interaction is orderly and conventional.

6   An activity, in this sense, for example, could be "presenting narratives of experiments." But this activity can be undertaken as a reevaluation of past experimental activity, for instance, or as a precontextualization of projected new experiments.

7   Activity theorists are primarily concerned with the impact of tool-mediated, joint activity on thinking. In this perspective, scientists' thinking develops as an outcome of tool-mediated interactions with people and inanimate objects (including abstractions).

8   Goodwin 1994, 1995 and Goodwin and Goodwin (forthcoming a, forthcoming b) demonstrate the highly coordinated character of gestural and vocal symbolic practices in a variety of work settings, including the operations room of an airport, geochemical laboratories, archaelogical digs, and courtrooms. See also Lynch and Woolgar's recent (1990) collection which examines the interface of talk and figurative representation in constituting scientific "reality."

9   In the discussion of laboratory research that follows, we use descriptive terms and arguments drawn from the interviews, tutorial sessions, and informal conversations we have had with the laboratory members. We are aware that such descriptions may minimize the subjective involvement of the physicists in their own research and interpretive processes. We also realize that we are summarizing as "matters of fact" concepts which the physicists are well aware have not yet achieved "canonical" status within the field and which may eventually be shown to be "wrong."

10   Figure 7.1, and Figure 7.2 which follows, are diagrams which we are introducing into this discussion for the purpose of making it easier for our readers to understand the basic concepts informing the talk and interaction of the physicists we studied. We are aware, therefore, that these figures have the status of "working conceptual hallucinations" (Gilbert and Mulkay, 1984) typical of illustrations in introductory science textbooks and popular science journals. We have constructed these figures based on our reading of several theoretical and experimental articles and on our consultations with members of Ron's lab.

11   An antiferromagnet is a magnet in which the neighboring atomic spins are all antiparallel. An example of an antiferromagnet is FeF_2. A diluted antiferromagnet is a "dirty" antiferromagnet in which a large percentage of the atoms of one of the elements has been replaced by atoms of a third element. For example, $FeZnF_2$ is a diluted antiferromagnet in which zinc atoms have replaced a large percentage of the iron atoms.

12   According to Grest et al. (1986), a domain would be a pocket of atomic spin order within an otherwise disordered crystalline lattice. A domain state, therefore, would be a dynamic state in which previously randomly ordered domains grow in size as a function of time in a crystalline lattice. Until long range order is achieved (see

note 13), there would be order within each domain, but from one domain to the next there would be disorder.

13 According to Grest et al. (1986), in a long range ordered state the atomic spins throughout the crystalline lattice would be arranged in an orderly manner, and would remain so forever unless acted upon by other forces.

14 But see Traweek (1992) for an impassioned plea not to draw a sharp line between these two value-loaded discursive alternatives but to allow scientist-centered accounts to be as credible as science-centered accounts.

15 We don''t mean to give the impression that agent and experiencer exhaust the semantic possibilities which scientists have for referring to themselves. Scientists may be represented/constructed grammatically as interlocutors (e.g., "I **would have said** that y:er in the domain state"), possessors (e.g., "**you have** a number for the magnetization"), patients (e.g., "what I''ve been trying to do is to-**f:force you** into a (.) a position"), recipients (e.g., "Let me **tell you** how I'm picturing things."), recipient/benefactors (e.g., "I have this preprint **for you**"), and other semantic roles.

16 The discussion illustrates the observations of sociologists and ethnographers (e.g., Lynch, 1985; Latour, 1987) concerning the ways scientists deal with "trouble" by deciding if it is (a) inconsequential to the meaning of the results, (b) an artifact of the procedure (which renders the results meaningless), or (c) an original discovery.

17 In the zero field cooled procedure, a heated sample of prepared matter is cooled in a zero magnetic field. A field is then applied at a low temperature, and the magnetization is measured as the temperature is raised in incremental steps. In the field cooled procedure, a heated sample is slowly cooled in a magnetic field. The magnetization is measured while cooling is under way.

18 Hanks (1990, 1992) discusses similar utterances in Mayan and the set of assumptions about a candidate referent's status which are needed to interpret them. For example, Mayans need to know that the utterance "In this ditch I'm making, two rows will it take" means that the speaker is controlling the ditch-making but others are doing the physical work. Hanks speaks of the situation as follows: "DP's first person singular reference to what **he** was doing, when actually he was sitting watching us work, was a clear instantiation of his rank as the head, not only of the current undertaking, but of the household in which we all resided and the *solar* [homestead] in which we were working. Regardless of who wields the hoe, it is DP who is making a ditch to plant peppers" (Hanks, 1990: 124–5).

19 In indeterminate constructions, the pronoun "you" could refer specifically to the addressee in the interaction or to a generalized, unspecified referent (the impersonal "you").

20 The phrase "that line" refers to a phase transition line.

21 Anthropomorphization of physical objects in scientific discourse can be accomplished through a wide variety of physics-centered constructions, in which a physical system is imbued with intentions, knowledge of other systems, and the ability to experience random magnetic fields. As Lemke (1990) notes, such "humanized" scientific discourse appears to facilitate scientific problem-solving in classroom settings.

22 Bühler (1990/1934: 18–19) notes:

It goes without saying that linguistics cannot get along without observation... Of course, only what is *audible* in the concrete speech event can be fixed on records, and this first only weighs heavily in the methodological discussion. For there is more to the full speech event – we could just as well call it the "significant" or "meaningful" speech event – than just what is audible. But how is the rest of what belongs to the speech event also registered and made accessible to exact observation? However the matter is twisted and turned, the observer who is researching language must (whether from within or without, as the usual distinction has it) undersand what is registered with his eyes and ears...

Since the introduction of video technology, there has been a growing interest in the relationship between gesture, tools, and talk in discourse, in everyday as well as worksite settings (see, e.g., Goodwin, 1984, 1994, 1995; Heath, 1984; Schegloff, 1984; Egbert, 1991; Goodwin and Goodwin, 1992, forthcoming a, forthcoming b; Whalen, 1995).

23 Given that a graphic representation such as the blackboard sketch relevant to segment (7) (see Figure 7.1) can also be highly intertextual (Ochs, Jacoby, and Gonzales, 1994), deictic references such as "here" and "this way" may index multiple symbolic spaces in distinct graphic "texts." A graph may thus be an example of what Bühler (1990/1934: 156) calls "a systematized play of fiction supported by a thousand conventions."

24 Sociologists, anthropologists, and historians of science (e.g., Fleck, 1979/1935; Lynch, 1985; Latour and Woolgar, 1979; Latour, 1987) have noted that figures and graphs are "inscriptions" which make visibly present physical phenomena that cannot otherwise be directly seen by the naked eye, and thus they play a role in enhancing the reality status of physical constructs. But see also Gilbert and Mulkay (1984) who point out that scientists are well aware of the fictional status of many of the inscription devices they employ.

25 We are not saying that graphic displays *necessarily* lead to such symbolic contact. As can be seen in segment (7), physicists may use a graph to represent their actions as experimentalists ("When you cut the field") or they may treat the graph as an object to be known, understood, or otherwise experienced. Our point is that the graph affords physicists the *possibility* of symbolically engaging in physical events.

26 This practice recalls discussions of "witnessing" in the early periods of modern science (see, for instance, Shapin and Schaffer, 1985;

Bazerman, 1988), when scientists wishing to prove the factual status of their findings invited ratified colleagues to witness experiments with their own eyes. When colleagues could not be present to witness first-hand, they were invited to "virtually" witness the experiment by reading detailed accounts which included detailed drawings of instruments and other relevant objects. Our point here is that when the physicists in Ron's lab depict physical events verbally and gesturally within a graph, those co-present "virtually" witness experimental findings and theoretical physical events which took place (or could take place) at some other time or location.

27 This observation is very similar to the observations made by Hanks (1990) concerning referential practices in a ditch-digging worksite in the Mayan community he studied. See note 18 for a fuller description of the interaction he analyzed.

28 It also appears that the semantic incongruity of indeterminate constructions is effective because it is offset by a spate of semantically unproblematic "physics-centered" utterances. Thus, periodically switching from one type of utterance to the other reinforces and regrounds the interpretive possibility that the physical constructs could also be the referent of the animate pronoun.

29 Silverstein (personal communication) has suggested that the intersection of worlds is even more complex when we take into consideration that indeterminate constructions are often couched within metapragmatic predicates, such as "what I can't figure out is" and "cause you're telling me that," which we have categorized in Table 7.1 as a physicist-centered discourse practice. In addition, multiple worlds and multiple time frames are indexed and overlaid through the use of the simple present tense in indeterminate utterances such as "why don't I go to the long range ordered phase in the Kleeman experiment" (Segment 7, lines 14–19).

30 In advocating Strategy 2, we have pursued a perspective that is integral to the work of scholars in a number of related disciplines who explore linguistic structures as rooted in social practices and activities, including, among others, Sacks, Schegloff, and Jefferson's (1974) consideration of the interrelationship of syntax and turn-taking, Sacks and Schegloff's (1979) discussion of linguistic resources for person reference in talk-in-interaction, Duranti's (1990) study of agency in Samoan interaction, Hanks' (1990, 1992) work on Mayan deixis as a referential practice, Goodwin's (1994) treatment of the collaborative construction of categorization in professional interaction, Schieffelin's (1992) work on the impact of evidentials in constructing literacy practices and cultural change among the Kaluli, Sorjonen and Heritage's (1992) study of *And*-prefaces as agenda markers in interaction, Silverstein's (1993) work on shifters and creative presupposition, and Haviland's (in press) analysis of transposition in Tzotzil and Guugu Yimidhirr speech events.

31 Participants' frequent return to graphic displays as a way of grounding and regrounding subsequent talk about physical entities and processes may be similar to their use of and shifting to "physics-centered" constructions which, we suggested earlier, may serve to ground and reground the referential meaning of indeterminate constructions.

32 While we are calling for a wider scope of inquiry into language, we are by no means suggesting that grammatical categories have no sociological or psychological reality. Indeed, we take issue with Lee (1991: 224), who has called for "dissolving the conceptually un-analysed notion of "language" and language form" and for "seeking to locate structures . . . without preconceived notions of what these structures look like." The study of anything, including the ethnomethodological study of social order, is never free of "preconceived notions" and is inescapably constrained to some extent by its own vernacular and ideology (cf. Fleck, 1979/1935), and may even be enriched by constructs developed elsewhere. More importantly, the findings of conversation analysis (e.g., the work on collaborative completion, appendors, and repair initiation) provide ample evidence that interlocutors (and even sociologists) are oriented to and cognitively monitor many of the linguistic structures which linguists have named and analyzed.

References

Atkinson, M. and Heritage, J. (eds.) (1984). *Structures of Social Action: Studies in Conversation Analysis.* Cambridge: Cambridge University Press.

Bakhtin, M. (1981). *The Dialogic Imagination: Four Essays.* M. Holquist (ed.) C. Emerson and M. Holquist (trans.) Austin: University of Texas Press.

(1993). *Toward a Philosophy of the Act.* Austin: University of Texas Press.

Bazerman, C. (1988). *Shaping Written Knowledge: The Genre and Activity of the Experimental Article in Science.* Madison: University of Wisconsin Press.

Benveniste, E. (1971). *Problems in General Linguistics.* M. E. Meek (trans.) Coral Gables: University of Miami Press.

Biagioli, M. (1990a). The anthropology of incommensurability. *Studies in the History and Philosophy of Science,* 21 (2): 183–209.

(1990b). Galileo the emblem maker. *ISIS,* 81, 230–58.

(1992). Scientific revolution, social bricolage, and etiquette. In R. Porter and M. Teich (eds.) *The Scientific Revolution in National Context,* pp. 11–54. Cambridge: Cambridge University Press.

(1993). *Galileo Courtier: The Practice of Science in the Culture of Absolutism.* Chicago: University of Chicago Press.

Bloor, D. (1976). *Knowledge and Social Imagery*. London: Routledge and Kegan Paul.

Bourdieu, P. (1977). *Outline of a Theory of Practice*. R. Nice (trans.) Cambridge: Cambridge University Press.

Bühler, K. (1990/1934). *Theory of Language: The Representational Function of Language*. D. F. Goodwin (trans.) [originally published as *Sprachtheorie: Die Darstellungsfunktion der Sprache*] Philadelphia: John Benjamins.

Collins, H. M. and Yearling, S. (1992). Epistemological chicken. In A. Pickering (ed.) *Science as Practice and Culture*, pp. 301–26. Chicago: University of Chicago Press.

Duranti, A. (1990). Politics and grammar: agency in Samoan political discourse. *American Ethnologist*, 17 (4): 646-66.

Egbert, M. M. (1991). Scientists" orientation to an experimental apparatus in their interaction in a chemistry lab. *Issues in Applied Linguistics*, 2: 269–300.

Engeström, Y. (1987). *Learning by Expanding: An Activity-Theoretical Approach to Developmental Research*. Helsinki: Orienta-Konsultit Oy.

  (1990). Activity theory and individual and social transformation. Paper presented at the 2nd International Congress for Research on Activity Theory. Lahti, Finland.

Fleck, L. (1979/1935). *Genesis and Development of a Scientific Fact*. T. J. Trenn and R. K. Merton (eds.) F. Bradley and T. J. Trenn (trans.) [originally published as *Entstehung und Entwicklung einer wissenschaftlichen Tatsache: Einführung in die Lehre vom Denkstil und Denkkollektiv*]. Chicago: University of Chicago Press.

Fleury, P. A. (1981). Phase transitions, critical phenomena, and instabilities. *Science* 211 (4478): 125–31.

Ford, P. J. (1982). Spin glasses. *Contemporary Physics*, 23 (2): 141–68.

Gilbert, G. N. and Mulkay, M. (1984). *Opening Pandora's Box: A Sociological Analysis of Scientists' Discourse*. Cambridge: Cambridge University Press.

Gooding, D. (1992). Putting agency back into experiment. In A. Pickering (ed.) *Science as Practice and Culture*, pp. 65–112. Chicago: University of Chicago Press.

Goodwin, C. (1980). Restarts, pauses, and the achievement of mutual gaze at turn-beginning. *Sociological Inquiry*, 50: 272–302.

  (1984). Notes on story structure and the organization of participation. In M. Atkinson and J. Heritage (eds.) *Structures of Social Action: Studies in Conversation Analysis*, pp. 225–46. Cambridge: Cambridge University Press.

  (1994). Professional vision. *American Anthropologist*, 96: 606-33.

  (1995). Seeing in depth. *Social Studies of Science*, 25: 237–74.

Goodwin, C. and Goodwin, M. H. (1992). Context, activity and participation. In P. Auer and A. di Luzio (eds.) *The Contextualization of Language*, pp. 77–99. Amsterdam: John Benjamins.
(frth. a). Formulating planes: seeing as a situated activity. In D. Middleton and Y. Engeström (eds.) *Cognition and Communication at Work*. Cambridge: Cambridge University Press.
(frth. b). Crafting vision: perception as professional practice. In B-L. Gunnarsson, P. Linell, and B. Nordberg (eds.) *The Construction of Professional Discourse*. London: Longman.
Grest, G. S., Soukoulis, C. M., and Levin, K. (1986). Comparative Monte Carlo and mean-field studies of random-field Ising systems. *Physical Review B*, 33 (11): 7659–74.
Hanks, W. F. (1990). *Referential Practice: Language and Lived Space among the Maya*. Chicago: University of Chicago Press.
(1992). The indexical ground of reference. In A. Duranti and C. Goodwin (eds.) *Rethinking Context: Language as an Interactive Phenomenon*, pp. 43–76. Cambridge: Cambridge University Press.
Haviland, J. (frth.). Projections, transpositions and relativity. In J. J. Gumperz and S. C. Levinson (eds.) *Rethinking Linguistic Relativity*. Cambridge: Cambridge University Press.
Heath, C. (1984). Talk and recipiency: sequential organization in speech and body movement. In M. Atkinson and J. Heritage (eds.) *Structures of Social Action: Studies in Conversation Analysis*, pp. 247–66. Cambridge: Cambridge University Press.
Hurd, C. M. (1982). Varieties of magnetic order in solids. *Contemporary Physics*, 23 (5): 469–93.
Knorr-Cetina, K. (1992). The couch, the cathedral, and the laboratory: on the relationship between experiment and laboratory in science. In A. Pickering (ed.) *Science as Practice and Culture*, pp. 113–38. Chicago: University of Chicago Press.
Kuhn, T. S. (1962). *The Structure of Scientific Revolutions*. Chicago: University of Chicago Press.
Latour, B. (1987). *Science in Action*. Cambridge, MA: Harvard University Press.
Latour, B. and Woolgar, S. (1979). *Laboratory Life: The Social Construction of Scientific Facts*. London: Sage.
Lee, J. (1991). Language and culture: the linguistic analysis of culture. In G. Button (ed.) *Ethnomethodology and the Human Sciences*, pp. 196–226. Cambridge: Cambridge University Press.
Lemke, J. L. (1990). *Talking Science: Language Learning and Values*. Norwood, NJ: Ablex.
Leontyev, A. N. (1981). The problem of activity in psychology. In J. V. Wertsch (ed.) *The Concept of Activity in Soviet Psychology*, pp. 37–71. Armonk, NY: M. E. Sharpe.
Lynch, M. (1985). *Art and Artefact in Laboratory Science*. London: Routledge and Kegan Paul.

(1988). The externalized retina: selection and mathematization in the visual documentation of objects in the life sciences. *Human Studies*, 11: 201–34.

(1993). *Scientific Practice and Ordinary Action: Ethnomethodology and Social Studies of Science*. Cambridge: Cambridge University Press.

Lynch, M. and Woolgar, S. (eds.) (1990). *Representation in Scientific Practice*. Cambridge, MA: MIT Press.

McCloskey, D. N. (1990). *If You"re so Smart: The Narrative of Economic Expertise*. Chicago: University of Chicago Press.

Ochs, E., Jacoby, S., and Gonzales, P. (1994). Interpretive journeys: how scientists talk and travel through graphic space. *Configurations*, 2: 151–71.

Pickering, A. (ed.) (1992). *Science as Practice and Culture*. Chicago: University of Chicago Press.

Sacks, H. (1992). *Lectures on Conversation*, vol. 1. Oxford: Blackwell.

Sacks, H. and Schegloff, E. A. (1979). Two preferences in the organization of reference to persons and their interaction. In G. Psathas (ed.) *Everyday Language: Studies in Ethnomethodology*, pp. 15–21. New York: Irvington Publishers.

Sacks, H., Schegloff, E. A., and Jefferson, G. (1974). A simplest systematics for the organization of turn-taking for conversation. *Language*, 50: 696–735.

Salk, J. (1983). *Anatomy of Reality: Merging of Intuition and Reason*. New York: Columbia University Press

Schaffer, S. (1991). The eighteenth brumaire of Bruno Latour. *Studies in the History and Philosophy of Science*, 22 (1): 174–92.

Schegloff, E. A. (1972). Sequencing in conversational openings. In J. J. Gumperz and D. Hymes (eds.) *Directions in Sociolinguistics: The Ethnography of Communication*, pp. 346–80. New York: Holt, Rinehart and Winston.

(1984). On some gestures' relation to talk. In M. Atkinson and J. Heritage (eds.) *Structures of Social Action: Studies in Conversation Analysis*, pp. 266–96. Cambridge: Cambridge University Press.

(1991). Reflections on talk and social structure. In D. Boden and D. Zimmerman (eds.) *Talk and Social Structure*, pp. 44–70. Cambridge: Polity Press.

Schieffelin, B. B. (1979). Getting it together: an ethnographic approach to the study of the development of communicative competence. In E. Ochs and B. B. Schieffelin (eds.) *Developmental Pragmatics*, pp. 73–110. New York: Academic Press.

(1992). New worlds, new words: literacy and language choice among the Kaluli of Papua New Guinea. Paper presented at the annual meeting of the American Association for Applied Linguistics. Seattle, WA.

Shapin, S. and Schaffer, S. (1985). *Leviathan and the Air Pump: Hobbes, Boyle and the Experimental Life*. Princeton: Princeton University Press.

Silverstein, M. (1993). Metapragmatic discourse and metapragmatic function. In J. Lucy (ed.) *Reflexive Language: Reported Speech and Metapragmatics*, pp. 33–58. Cambridge: Cambridge University Press.

Sorjonen, M-L and Heritage, J. (1992). Constituting and maintaining activities across sequences: and-prefacing as a feature of question design. Paper presented at the International Conference on Discourse and the Professions, Uppsala, Sweden.

Traweek, S. (1988). *Beamtimes and Lifetimes: The World of High Energy Physicists*. Cambridge, MA: Harvard University Press.

(1992). Border crossings: narrative strategies in science studies and among physicists in Tsukuba Science City, Japan. In A. Pickering (ed.) *Science as Practice and Culture*, pp. 429–65. Chicago: University of Chicago Press.

Voloshinov, V. N. (1973). *Marxism and the Philosophy of Language*. L. Matejka and I. R. Titunik (trans.) New York: Seminar Press.

Vygotsky, L. S. (1978). *Mind in Society: The Development of Higher Psychological Processes*. Cambridge, MA: Harvard University Press.

Whalen, J. (1995). A technology of order production: computer-aided dispatch in public safety communications. In P. ten Have and G. Psathas (eds.) *Situated Order: Studies in the Social Organization of Talk and Embodied Activities*, pp. 187–230. Washington, DC: University Press of America.

Whitrow, G. J. (1972). *The Nature of Time*. New York: Holt, Rinehart and Winston.

Wittgenstein, L. (1958). *Philosophical Investigations* (2nd ed.). G. E. M. Anscombe and R. Rhees (eds.) G. E. M. Anscombe (trans.) Oxford: Blackwell.

8

Transparent vision*

CHARLES GOODWIN

8.1 Transparent vision[1]

When linguists use the term *grammar* they typically restrict the scope of that term to *sentential grammar*, e.g. rules, structures and procedures implicated in the production of well formed sentences and their subcomponents. In this paper the scope of the term grammar will not be limited to phenomena within the stream of speech, but will also encompass structures providing for the organization of the endogenous activity systems within which strips of talk are embedded. The following (which is analyzed in detail in Goodwin and Goodwin, 1987a, 1992) provides an example of what is meant by an interactionally situated grammar for the production of relevant activities. Here Nancy evaluates an asparagus pie Jeff made as "s : : : *so* : *goo* :d." Before she has spoken the word "*goo*:d" Tasha begins an equivalent assessment of her own: "I love it."

Nancy: *Jeff* made en asparagus pie

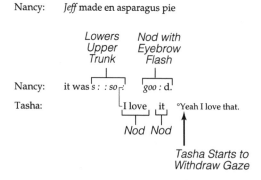

Figure 8.1 Concurrent assessments

The sequential organization of the talk that occurs here provides a very strong display of agreement. By starting to speak *before* Nancy says "*goo* : d" Tasha demonstrates that she is so in tune with Nancy that she is willing to commit herself to a position about the pie without having yet heard Nancy's. She does not however say exactly the same thing as Nancy. By using present tense to talk about asparagus pie as a food category, rather than matching Nancy's past tense reference to a specific pie, Tasha makes visible her different access to what is being assessed, e.g. the fact that each party is viewing the phenomenon being assessed from a different position is made visible in the structure of their talk. Moreover, what emerges from their overlapping talk is not merely two matching propositions about the pie, but a collaborative display of mutual appreciation that extends beyond the talk itself to encompass the participant's affect as a socially organized, collaboratively sustained phenomenon. As the assessment adjective is spoken both parties are gazing toward each other while nodding in appreciation, while simultaneously Nancy heightens the affective stance she is taking toward the pie with both an eyebrow flash and intonational enhancement of "*goo*:d." How can the participants disengage from such a state of heightened mutual orientation without downgrading their mutual assessment? A moment later Tasha modifies the participation framework made visible by the mutual alignment of their bodies by withdrawing her gaze from Nancy, while simultaneously showing continuing appreciation of what Nancy said by repeating her assessment.

Rather than looking at the talk, intonation, and body movement that occurs in this example as different channels of behavior to be analyzed separately, it seems more profitable to conceptualize what is happening as a single, *interactive activity* of assessment that the participants collaboratively recognize, bring to a climax or peak, and then withdraw from. This activity knits an array of heterogeneous phenomena – syntactic position, intonation, body movement, displays of agreement, differential access to a world beyond the activity, etc. – into a coherent course of collaborative action.

While investigation of how such multi-party interactive activities are organized encompasses a range of phenomena other than the grammar of sentences, it is quite consistent with Wittgenstein's

(1958) notion of grammar as analysis of the patterns of organization that provide for the orderliness and intelligibility of the
diverse language games within which talk and human action are
embedded. Moreover, such analysis can shed light on a range of
phenomena relevant to the deployment of syntax and other phenomena within sentences that are obscured when sentences are
analyzed as isolated, self-sufficient entities. For example how is
it possible for participants to *systematically* accomplish the coordinated action visible in the present data? Looking again at
Nancy's utterance it can be observed that the assessment adjective
which is overlapped by recipient's concurrent assessment is
preceded by an intensifier: "*so*":

Nancy: *Jeff* made en asparagus pie
           it was ⎡s : : *so*ᵣ:⎤   *goo* : d.
Tasha: ⎣ I love it.   °Yeah I love that.

Figure 8.2 Intensifier precedes assessment adjective

Moreover this intensifier is spoken with enhanced intonation
(indicated by the italics and colons in the transcript). Speaker's
involvement in her display of heightened appreciation thus begins
before the assessment adjective itself is actually spoken. This raises
the possibility that the recipient might use the intensifier to *project*
what is to be said next: an assessment adjective such as "good," and
indeed the end of the intensifier is the place where the recipient
begins to produce her own concurrent assessment. Syntactic structure places constraints on what can occur next in a strip of talk.
This provides an unfolding horizon of future possibilities that the
recipient can use as a resource for the organization of her own
action. Thus, by applying her knowledge of the syntax of English
to the talk so far produced, the recipient can anticipate in some
detail what that talk might become as it unfolds through time.
Visible structure in the stream of speech interacts with grammatical
knowledge to provide resources for the accomplishment of coordinated social action.

Several features of this process that are relevant to the analysis to
be developed in the present paper will be briefly noted. The mutual
concurrent assessment provides an elementary example of human
social organization, e.g. a form of action constituted through the
differentiated but collaborative work of multiple participants. A key

issue posed for the systematic production of such action, for participants as well as analysts, is how the separate parties know, and know together, what is going on such that each is able to produce at the appropriate moment specific forms of action that are linked in fine detail to relevant actions of her coparticipant. Thus for participants engaged in the production of joint collaborative action intersubjectivity emerges as a practical problem, and moreover one that must be resolved within tight time constraints (in these data within the scope of a very short utterance).

To maintain a developing sense of what it is that's happening, how each of them is positioned in that process, and what forms of action can count as relevant next moves in the activity of the moment it would appear that participants simultaneously attend to a range of different types of organization. First, *sequential organization*, a grammar for the production of talk-in-interaction that has been the object of sustained investigation by conversation analysts (Sacks, 1992; Sacks, Schegloff, and Jefferson, 1974; Schegloff and Sacks, 1973). For example adjacency pairs such as question–answer, greeting–return greeting, etc., provide structures that link the differentiated actions of separate parties into patterns of collaborative action that cannot be decomposed into their separate components without losing essential features of their organization, e.g. the status of an utterance as an *answer* cannot be determined by looking at it in isolation, but only by noting its sequential placement after some prior *question* (or other first pair part). The emphasis by conversation analysts on the systematic organization of sequences encompassing multiple actions and participants constitutes a strong alternative to speech act theory with its focus on the analysis of individual sentences and utterances in isolation (Levinson, 1983). Moreover, by virtue of properties such as *conditional relevance* (Schegloff, 1968) each next move in such a sequence provides a framework of intelligibility for the production and interpretation of subsequent action, constituting what Heritage (1984b) has called an architecture for intersubjectivity.

Second, as was seen in the asparagus pie data, participants attend to *sentential grammar* as a resource for the organization and production of collaborative action within interaction. Indeed as analysis of phenomena such as how a later speaker extends the sentence of an earlier speaker by adding new, syntactically appropriate units to that talk (Lerner, 1987, 1993; Sacks, 1992), or subsequent speakers reuse and transform elements of earlier talk in order to build an apt counter to that very same talk (Goodwin and Goodwin, 1987b), or of how single propositions are constructed across the utterances of different speakers (Ochs, Schieffelin, and Platt, 1979) demonstrates, sentential syntax constitutes a pervasive resource for tying the actions of one party to those of another, e.g. it should occupy a central place not only in linguistics but also in the analysis of social organization by sociologists and anthropologists (see Sacks, 1963 for an early statement of this argument). Similarly the indexical properties of language (Hanks, 1990) link elements of talk to features of the context that an utterance both emerges from and further helps to constitute (Goodwin and Duranti, 1992). A substantial part of the present paper will be devoted to the analysis of prospective indexicals.

Third, the production of talk and other forms of action is situated within *participation frameworks* of various types. Like sentential grammar and grammar for interaction these frameworks provide for the appropriate ordering of relevant elements, for example participant categories such as speaker and hearer. Some demonstration that participants actually attend to the distinction between well formed and inappropriate participation arrangements is provided by the fact that they not only recognize unacceptable combinations, but take active steps to remedy such situations. Thus a speaker who discovers that she is addressing a hearer who is not displaying orientation to her, will frequently mark the talk in progress at that point as defective (by for example abandoning her current sentence and beginning a new one) while taking active steps to secure a hearer (the phrasal breaks produced by her current unit of talk act as requests for the gaze of a hearer). Similarly addressing an utterance to structurally different kinds of hearers can lead to changes in both the length and the meaning of a speaker's emerging sentence so that its appropriateness to its recipient of the moment can be maintained and demonstrated (Goodwin, 1981). Particular kinds of talk, e.g. stories, laughter, opposition sequences, etc., invoke specific participation frameworks. A speaker can quickly and powerfully change the social organization of the moment by shifting to a different kind of talk with a new participation framework and thus reorganizing how those present are aligned to each other (Goodwin, 1990: chapter 10).

The organization of participation can be analyzed in at least two rather different ways. The first, which uses the work of Goffman (e.g. 1979) as a point of departure focuses on the description and analysis of typologies of participant categories (see in particular Levinson, 1987 and Hanks, 1990 for a critique and attempt to develop a more parsimonious grammar of participant categories). However it is also possible to analyze participation as a temporally unfolding, interactively sustained embodied course of activity. In the asparagus pie data while Nancy and Tasha constituted each other as speakers and addressees through not only talk but also mutual gaze (e.g. enacted the prototypical participant categories noted by Goffman and others as central to the production of a state of a talk), they also used temporally unfolding changes in visible participation to organize their movement toward, and then withdrawal from, the state of heightened mutual orientation at the climax of the assessment activity. More generally, while it is easiest for the analyst to display congruence in assessments on the printed page by noting similarities in their propositional content (as was done here), quite frequently it is phenomena such as intricate matching of intonation which creates the most powerful demonstration of not simply cognitive agreement but shared affect and coparticipation in a common framework of action. From such a perspective participation is not simply the instantiation of a particular analytic category for classifying participants, but an embodied activity, one that provides for the collaborative constitution of a shared stance lodged within vivid, unfolding, interactively organized experience. As the work of Jefferson (1979, 1984) showing how laughter is interactively organized syllable by syllable and Ochs and Schieffelin (1989) on affect in language demonstrate, such pheno-mena are not instances of disorganized "flooding out" but structured activities amenable to grammatical analysis.

In brief, the tasks of achieving joint action pose as a practical problem for participants the issue of mutual intelligibility. In order to provide organization for, and make inferences about, the unfolding structure of the activity they are engaged in participants attend to a range of phenomena including sentential grammar, sequential organization and participation frameworks. All of these phenomena are constituted through the embodied actions of the participants.

Key components of many activities involve orientation toward, and operations upon, a relevant environment. Such classifications are elements of language, and the issue of how language structures perception of the phenomenal environment of the group using it has been one of the enduring concerns of anthropological linguistics. Typically, following Whorf's (1956) analysis of how the grammar of Hopi differs from that of English in the way that it structures events, investigation of this issue has focused on comparisons between the semantic and syntactic organization of different languages. By way of contrast the present paper will examine how language structures perception within the context of situated activity by focusing on the organization of talk-in-interaction used to perform work tasks in a specific setting. Grammar occupies a central place in this process, as will be demonstrated by analysis of how prospective indexicals and ascriptive sentences are deployed to make sense out of relevant events in the group's working environment. However, when such structuring of perception is analyzed within situated interaction it will be seen that an equally important role is played by processes of organization constituted through language that were completely ignored by Whorf, e.g. the power of language to invoke temporally unfolding participation frameworks through which the actions and perception of multiple participants can be calibrated into a visibly displayed common stance toward the events being scrutinized.

8.2 The operations room

The setting that provides the data for the present analysis is the **operations** room that controls ground operations for a large airline at one of its hub airports.[2] The operations room is responsible for coordinating ground operations for the airline, for example making sure that baggage is transferred from incoming to outgoing flights, obtaining information about potential delays, keeping statistics on flights, etc. The operations room is not the tower, which is run by the airport itself and controls planes on runways and in the air. However, like the tower the operations room functions as a *center of coordination*.[3] A single task or activity, e.g. adapting to a delayed

Figure 8.3 The operations room

flight carrying passengers for subsequent outgoing flights, will require simultaneous but separate work by a number of different airline work crews (passenger service, ramp service, etc.). Workers in the Ops Room are faced with the tasks of determining what has to be done, contacting the different crews responsible for doing it, and co-ordinating and checking on the progress of those activities.

Though all Ops Workers have experience in at least some of the work crews being coordinated, they do not themselves go out to the ramps and gates where planes are actually parked, serviced, loaded and boarded. Instead they work together in a single interior room. However, in that room they require simultaneous perceptual access to events at many different locations. The Ops Room is thus equipped with many different tools – telephones, radios of various types, computers tied into the airline's nation-wide network, etc. – designed to extend the perception of workers within it to the distant settings that are relevant to their work. Of particular importance to the present analysis is an array of monitors at the front of the room which are connected to television cameras outside each gate:

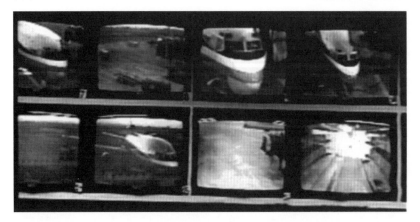

Figure 8.4 Gate monitors in front of the operations room

By glancing at these screens Ops Workers can look into a distant environment that they are charged with monitoring.

The Ops Room was arranged as shown in Figure 8.5 and contained a number of different stations. In order to encompass everyone in the room we videotaped with two cameras, one covering the left side of the room and one the right. Workers seated in the center of the room were visible on both cameras. A third camera was used to make closeups of the screens and other materials being worked with.

The diverse, heterogeneous, collection of tools found in the Ops Room at any single moment in time constitute a material sedimentation of solutions found in the past to the repetitive tasks and problems that constitute Ops work. The tension between the repetitive, habitual character of the work done in the Ops Room, and the novel character of each next emergency as an event requiring a fresh improvisation, a new mix and articulation of the resources provided by the room, cannot be overemphasized. A tool, such as a television link to a distant setting, bridges (without fully resolving) the contradiction between the need for a single operations center whose workers are copresent to each other, and their simultaneous need for immediate access to diverse locations.

The monitors that allow Ops workers actually to gaze at the gates and places they are working with do not however provide transparent access to these settings. Instead, the ability to see events on these screens that can be used to help accomplish work in progress

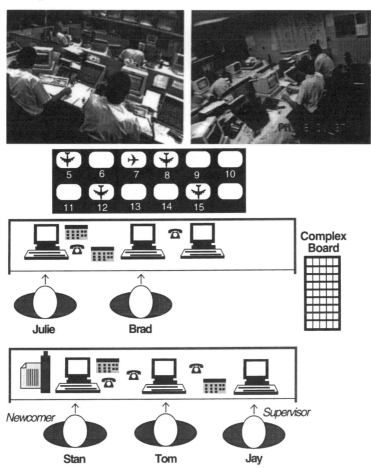

Figure 8.5 Participants and tools in the operations room

constitutes one type of endogenous craft knowledge situated within the larger complex of activities that make up Ops work.

8.3 Seeable trouble

The events which will now be examined provide us with an opportunity to investigate in more detail how talk in interaction and the proper seeing of work relevant phenomena mutually inform each other. The workers in this Ops room have just moved into a new terminal. In the old terminal passengers walked out onto the runway and boarded their flights by climbing up a set of movable stairs that was brought to the side of each plane. In the new terminal passengers never step outside but instead exit and enter through a *jet bridge*, a flexible tunnel that runs from the terminal to the door of the aircraft. These Ops workers have only had a few weeks of experience working with the jet bridges in their new environment. In the following Brad gets a radio call about a problem with the jet bridge at gate A12. To separate the radio conversation from other talk in the Ops Room boxes are drawn around talk within it and

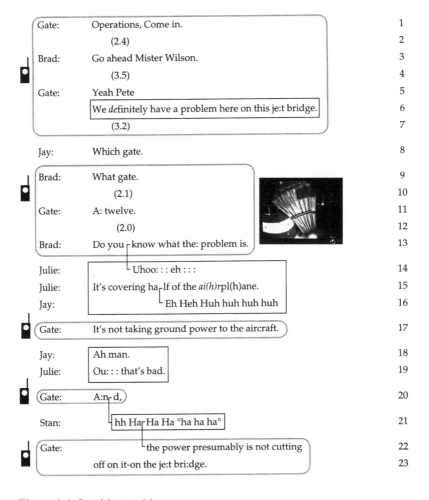

Gate:	Operations, Come in.	1
	(2.4)	2
Brad:	Go ahead Mister Wilson.	3
	(3.5)	4
Gate:	Yeah Pete	5
	We *def*initely have a problem here on this je:t bridge.	6
	(3.2)	7
Jay:	Which gate.	8
Brad:	What gate.	9
	(2.1)	10
Gate:	A: twelve.	11
	(2.0)	12
Brad:	Do you ⌈know what the: problem is.	13
Julie:	⌊Uhoo: : : eh : : :	14
Julie:	It's covering ha⌈lf of the *ai(h)r*pl(h)ane.	15
Jay:	⌊Eh Heh Huh huh huh huh	16
Gate:	It's not taking ground power to the aircraft.	17
Jay:	Ah man.	18
Julie:	Ou: : : that's bad.	19
Gate:	A:n⌈d,	20
Stan:	⌊hh Ha⌈Ha Ha °ha ha ha°	21
Gate:	⌊the power presumably is not cutting	22
	off on it-on the je:t bri:dge.	23

Figure 8.6 Seeable trouble

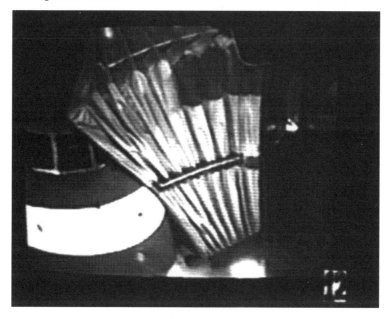

Figure 8.7 The canopy of the jet bridge

marked with walkie-talkie icons. For clarity square cornered boxes
are drawn around the report of trouble and the reaction of those in
the room to it. Upon seeing the image on the A12 gate monitor the
room erupts into laughter (lines 14-16, 21). Figure 8.7 shows what
they were looking at.

Those in the Ops Room treat the problem visible on the A12 gate
monitor as absolutely transparent. They break into spontaneous
laughter as soon as they see the position of the canopy (and indeed
the ethnographers at the back of the room, myself included, silently
joined into the laughter engendered by the scene); Julie in line 16
describes what is wrong with the jet bridge in the image visible on
the monitor: "It's covering half of the *ai(h)rp*l(h)ane;" and then in
line 20 explicitly evaluates the situation: "Ou::: that's bad." Shortly
after the data shown here a newcomer asks "What is the problem
with it." The supervisor replies by telling him to "Look at the: uh
canopy," i.e. all that one has to do to find the problem is look at the
image on the screen.

Such transparent vision is subsequently shown to be deeply problematic. Six minutes later, after a talk with the ramp crew that

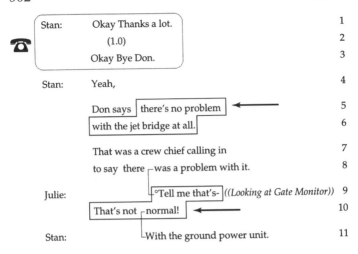

Figure 8.8 No problem

reported the problem, Stan turns to the rest of the Ops Room and reports (line 5-6) that there is no problem whatsoever with the jet bridge itself. Instead, consistent with Gate's original report (cf. lines 17, 22-23) the problem is confined to the Ground Power Unit.

Julie's incredulous "That's not normal!" goes to the heart of the anthropological concept of culture, i.e. the specification of what counts as normal within the lifeworld of a particular group. Indeed in these data we are able to catch a glimpse of the social and historical processes through which a community accumulates experience of the habitual scenes that constitute their working environment, and articulates for each other how these scenes should be properly interpreted. Through their work this night they come to see more clearly what constitutes the "normal appearance" of one of the objects that will figure repetitively in their work, the representation of a jet bridge on their gate monitors.

The way in which the room's initial view of the scene is subsequently made problematic illustrates quite vividly how such transparent vision is very much a crafted object. I now want to investigate in more detail the procedures used by those in the room to build this transparency. What subsequently happens to this image has the advantage of foreclosing arguments that would account for the laughter, and the trouble seen on the screen, by some notion of correspondence between perception and external event, i.e. the participants are just laughing at something that is in fact deviant. By using as a point of departure an object that was subsequently found to be "erroneous" I do not in any way want to suggest that interactive and social factors account for error while "true" vision transcends social biases (e.g. violate Bloor's (1976) principle of symmetry), but instead want to demonstrate just the opposite, that any such transparency of vision is something that is artfully crafted within an endogenous community of competent practitioners. Indeed, as these very data demonstrate, by continuing to massage and further transform the work relevant object visible in the screen through interaction with each other and their tools the Ops workers themselves eventually come to a quite different sense of it, i.e. their subsequent vision is as thoroughly social as the initial seeing that they eventually reject. In so far as the object being worked with does not exist as an independent entity somewhere "on the screen" or "at the gate" but is instead constituted through their interaction with that screen and each other in ways that are shaped by the tasks at hand, that object has both a distributed and a dynamic existence.[4]

8.4 Instructions for seeing

Though only one person in the Ops Room, Brad, actually talks to the man at the gate who is reporting the trouble at the jet bridge, all those in the Ops Room are situated within an interactively rich, tool saturated "backstage" from which they can attend to, and indeed collaborate in the production of, Brad's call. From this position they can use the talk in the call to interpret the images visible on the screens of the gate monitors, and reciprocally use those images to interpret the talk. How does that talk organize their interpretation of the screens in front of them such that they can independently and spontaneously find the "trouble" with the canopy? To begin to answer this question let's look more closely at how Gate's initial report of the trouble is structured as a discursive object which sets its recipients particular kinds of cognitive and perceptual tasks:

| Gate: | Yeah Pete | 5 |
| | We *defi*nitely have a problem here on this je:t bridge. | 6 |

Figure 8.9 A prospective indexical

The term "problem" is an instance of what I will call a *prospective indexical*. The sense of what constitutes the "problem" is not yet available to recipients but is instead something that has to be discovered subsequently as the interaction proceeds. Recipients are set the task of attending to subsequent events in order to find what particulars constitute "the problem" on this specific occasion. One prototypical environment for the occurrence of prospective indexicals is story prefaces, e.g. "terrible" or "wonderful" in utterances such as the following:

Teller: The most *wonderful/terrible thing* happened to me today.

Recipient: What happened.

Teller: ((*Produces story*))

Recipient: ((*Responds to story*))

Sacks (1974) notes how the characterization of the upcoming story provided by the prospective indexical within a story preface gives its recipients
(1) A framework for interpretation;
(2) A place to apply that framework: the talk following the preface sequence; and
(3) A motivation to engage in such analysis. Recipient is expected to respond to the story in an appropriate fashion when it reaches its projected climax or termination. The prospective indexical both helps recipient locate when that point has occurred (i.e. find that something "funny" or "terrible" has happened) and proposes the type of response that is relevant (i.e. laughter is an appropriate response to a story characterized as "funny" but not to one foreshadowed as "terrible").
The occurrence of a prospective indexical thus invokes a distributed, multi-party process. The cognitive operations relevant to the ongoing constitution of the event in process are by no means confined to speaker alone. Hearers must engage in an active, somewhat problematic process of interpretation in order to uncover the specification of the indexical that will enable them

to build appropriate subsequent action at a particular place.[5] Moreover this analysis is not static, complete as soon as the prospective indexical is heard, but is instead a dynamic process that extends through time as subsequent talk and the interpretative framework provided by the prospective indexical mutually elaborate each other. Moreover the nature of the collaborative work being done with a prospective indexical is shaped by the environment within which it occurs, e.g. the larger tasks of the story telling shape the particular ways in which both hearers and speakers use and find the appropriate sense of prospective indexicals that occur within story prefaces.

The sequential environment within which the term "problem" occurs in these data has essential similarities to that of the story telling sequences analyzed by Sacks. Thus an initial report that trouble exists ("We definitely have a problem here on this je:t bridge" line 5) is followed by recipient's request for elaboration ("You know what the: problem is" line 14), which leads to teller's description of the problem ("It's not taking ground power to the aircraft", etc., lines 18, 21, 23–24). The prospective indexical "problem" has its sense specified and filled in as the sequence between Brad and Gate unfolds.[6]

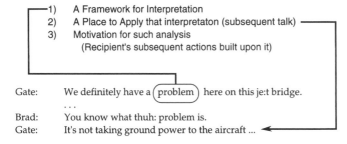

Story Preface *(Sacks 1974)*

1) A Framework for Interpretation
2) A Place to Apply that interpretaton (subsequent talk)
3) Motivation for such analysis
   (Recipient's subsequent actions built upon it)

Gate: We definitely have a (problem) here on this je:t bridge.
      . . .
Brad: You know what thuh: problem is.
Gate: It's not taking ground power to the aircraft ...

Figure 8.10 Structuring interpretation within sequences of collaborative action

The environment used by these participants to uncover the sense of "problem" that is relevant to their work does however include more than this sequence. First, Gate's initial report describes a place other than subsequent talk where the problem can be found: "on this je:t bridge." Second, unlike parties who have no access to a nonpresent event except through a speaker's talk,

workers in the Ops Room can use their video monitors to look at
the gate themselves. Third, the explicit work that the Ops Room is
charged with accomplishing is precisely resolving "problems" such
as this.   Resolution of that problem, which has not yet been
specified, may well involve work by others than Brad. Even parties
who will not produce a response to Gate's talk (i.e. everyone other
than Brad) have a motivation not only to listen to what he says,
but actively try to disentangle for themselves a relevant sense of
what the "problem" is. By comparison with the prototypical telling sequence analyzed by Sacks, the work activity of the Ops
room provides its inhabitants both an expanded motivational framework for trying to resolve as quickly as possible the prospective
indexicals used by outsiders to call them to work, and an
expanded perceptual environment for operating upon such indexicals. The gate monitors have been brought into the room at considerable expense precisely to help Ops workers formulate as
quickly as possible their own sense of the "troubles" and other
relevant activities occurring at distant locations.

The indexicality of the term "problem" is thus more complicated
than was originally indicated. It is not only the case that the sense of
"problem" appropriate to this particular occasion has to be determined through subsequent interaction. More crucially the resources
that will be used to make that determination are themselves indexical in the sense that different settings, sequence types, activity structures, etc. will provide participants in those events with different
ways of carrying out the discursive tasks posed by the occurrence of
a prospective indexical and different shapes for what a solution to
those tasks will consist of (cf. Heritage 1984b: 150). Moreover
these differences are not accidental or optional; someone in the
Ops room who ignores the gate monitors when they are relevant
to a task she is engaged in will be held accountable for incompetent
work.

The way in which distributed work groups can encompass asymmetrical perceptual environments is particularly relevant here. Gate
monitors are found only in the Ops room. They do not exist in
caller's environment. Let us assume for the moment that Gate is
not taking into account the way in which inhabitants of the Ops
room will use the gate monitors to make sense out of his talk. In
such a case recipients bring to bear on his talk resources that the

speaker is completely unaware of. In the data being examined here they do in fact come to a very different understanding of the problem than the one he reports, e.g. the canopy over the cockpit windows visible on the gate monitor rather than the ground power unit. Workers in the Ops room thus understand the problem he reports in ways that fall outside of his perceptual horizon. Rather than simply seeking to recover mental states of the speaker, his recipients use the tools provided by their environment to come to their own understanding of his talk.

Linguists have treated the relationship between speaker and hearer as profoundly asymmetrical, with a very active speaker complemented by a very passive hearer. Thus, according to Saussure (1959: 13)

> everything that goes from the associative center of the speaker to the ear of the listener is active, and everything that goes from the ear of the listener to his associative center is passive.

In the present data making sense out of the talk in progress is very much a distributed, collaborative process, one that encompasses not only the speaker's original talk but also very active operations on that talk by its hearers. Indeed the Ops room, as a cultural community encompassing competent members, systematic tasks, and relevant tools, has been built precisely to make such operations possible on calls reporting the troubles that it is designed to deal with.

Members of the Ops room use the gate monitors to elaborate and make sense out of what they hear. However, that talk simultaneously provides a set of instructions, an interpretative framework, for looking at those monitors that will heavily influence what will be seen in their images, e.g. they are primed to search for a "problem":

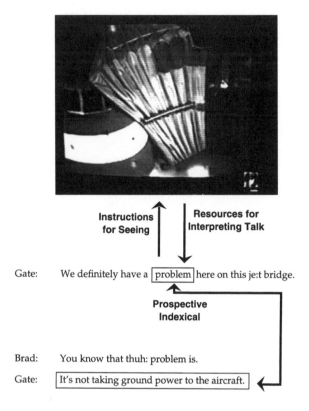

Gate: We definitely have a | problem | here on this je:t bridge.

**Prospective
Indexical**

Brad: You know that thuh: problem is.

Gate: | It's not taking ground power to the aircraft. |

Figure 8.11 Mutual shaping of the prospective indexical and the event it interprets

A two-way bridge has been built between (1) the tools being used, the images on the monitors that allow those in the Ops Room to gaze into the area that has become the current object of their concern, and (2) the language through which that object, the "problem" becomes visible to them and is articulated. Objects on both sides of the bridge change once it is built. As the images visible on the screen are used to elaborate the prospective indexical it achieves a more definite sense and begins to be shaped into a more definite and coherent object, while simultaneously what is seen in those images is structured by the talk which has generated the task of looking in the first place, i.e. a search for trouble.[7]

In looking at their monitors workers in the Ops Room are not acting as neutral, disinterested observers. The phenomenology of their perception is not lodged within an isolated consciousness, but instead emerges from a set of historically constituted discursive practices that are shaped by (1) the tasks they are engaged in, tasks which provide the charter for their community, the *raison d'être* for the existence of the Ops Room, i.e. finding the problem that it is their job to resolve;[8] and (2) the structure of language as deployed within human interaction, e.g. the cognitive, perceptual and interactive processes unleashed by the occurrence of a work relevant prospective indexical in talk.

The sense that a visible problem can clearly be found somewhere in the array of images on the gate monitors is intensified by other features of the talk. Gate opens his report, not with "I" (e.g. "I've got a problem here"), a description that would not suggest that the addressee as well as speaker might have access to the problem, but instead with "We," a term that presupposes not individual but organizational responsibility for finding a solution to the problem. Those in the Ops Room are, from the very beginning of his sentence, aligned to the trouble he is reporting, not as spectators, but as part of the work crew responsible for solving it. This is followed by a very strong evidential: "*definitely.*" Such a formulation leaves no room for doubt about the existence of consequential trouble.[9] The gates are to be inspected, not to see if there might be trouble, but to find the problem that is unambiguously there. Thus as Ops Workers move their gaze to the monitors they are primed to search for events of a particular type.

8.5 Extracting the image

Initially the inhabitants of the Ops Room are unable to find the trouble on their gate monitors. Just after the completion of Gate's talk Julie scans the monitor array but then immediately turns back to some papers she is working on. Neither she, nor anyone else in the room, displays any recognition of what might be the problem. It might be argued that this is quite simply explained by the fact that there is indeed no problem with any of the jet bridges visible on the monitors. However, in view of the way in which the whole room breaks into spontaneous laughter at what they see on these screens only a few seconds later, laughter which is initiated by Julie, the very party who has just found nothing interesting in the array, such an explanation adds very little to our understanding of what is happening here.

The monitor array contains views of eleven different gates. Finding the particular event of interest within such a complex visual field, especially when scenes encompassing complex webs of technology and activity have been reduced to comparatively small, flat, two-dimensional surfaces, can be a daunting task. In his analysis of the prospective work being done by story prefaces Sacks (1974) noted the importance of having a particular place to apply an interpretative template. In the present data, though Gate provides a clear prospective indexical, one that is enhanced by a strong evidential, his description of the place where the trouble exists ("a problem here on this je:t bridge") makes use of indexicals (e.g. "here", "this") that assume, quite wrongly, that his addressees already have access to that place. Each monitor is labeled with a gate number. In line 8 Jay prompts Brad to ask for the number of the gate where the trouble is to be found. The answer to Brad's request "A: twelve" specifies a particular place within the gate array upon which to focus the search for trouble.[10]

Julie attends to Brad's request as an action that will provide precisely this kind of information. In the slot where Gate's answer will occur, but before he has actually started to speak, she returns her gaze to the monitor array. Shortly after hearing the gate number Brad and Julie shift their gaze to the left side of the array where the monitor for gate 12 is positioned. Only when Brad has found gate 12 in the monitor array does he ask Gate if he knows what the problem is. Gate's description of the problem is thus not produced until Brad is in a position to scan independently the image of that scene that is available to those in the Ops room.

8.6 Formulating the problem

Almost immediately after finding the relevant place in the array (i.e. just after her head stops moving), and before Gate has had an opportunity to describe the problem, Julie produces the following reaction to what she sees there:

15   Julie: Uhoo: : : eh : : :

16   It's covering half of the ai(h)rpl(h)ane.

This is the place where the trouble with the jet bridge suddenly becomes transparently visible to those in the Ops room. Moreover it is the talk that touches off the laughter which quickly fills the room. It is therefore relevant to look in more detail at how it does this work.

Julie's action is organized in terms of a format that is used quite extensively to package experience in talk:

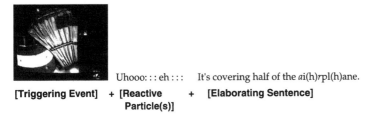

Uhooo: : : eh : : :   It's covering half of the *a*i(h)rpl(h)ane.

[Triggering Event]   + [Reactive   +   [Elaborating Sentence]
Particle(s)]

Figure 8.12 A format for reacting

Here are some more examples. For clarity the triggering event is not included. However the relevant existence of such an event can be clearly seen in the backwards referencing pro term that begins each sentence:

	Particle(s)	Sentence
Clacia:	Oo my God	He wz such a pain,
Nancy:	Ga : h	that's goo:d
Clacia:	Oh : Go:d	that'd be fantastic
Debbie:	Oh : :	She was so nice
Paul:	Oh :	It was beautiful.
Dianne:	Oh : : God	It wz r'lly funny.

Ignoring for the moment the particles and focusing on the sentences in this data set it can be observed that they all have a common underlying form:

Pro Term + Copula + (Intensifier) + Assessment Adjective

Sentences with this structure provide prototypical examples of what Lyons (1972: 471) has identified as *ascriptive sentences* which "are used characteristically... to ascribe to the referent of the subject-expression a certain property." Julie's utterance is slightly more complicated in that it contains not just a single assessment adjective but a more elaborate description. However, like the assessments her description includes an evaluation of the entity being commented upon (for example the laughter that occurs within it as well as other features of its intonation which are difficult to reproduce on the printed page). The structure of ascriptive sentences provides an economical but very powerful way of formulating for others how entities of many different kinds – objects, scenes, events, other people, etc. – should be interpreted. Thus the semantic structure of the second part of the sentence explicitly characterizes that entity in a specific way, one that proposes how it is to be perceived and understood (e.g. the choice of any term not only excludes but contrasts with other possible formulations). Moreover in many cases this semantic description is overlaid with an evaluative and frequently an affective dimension. Unlike "neutral" "scientific" descriptions which attempt to efface the persona of the author and achieve a disembodied objectivity, statements built with these affective and evaluative components depict an actor who commits herself to a position about the entity being commented upon.[11] Describing something as "beautiful," "ugly," "a pain," "funny" etc. requires an actor who experiences and evaluates what is being talked about, and in so doing visibly takes up a stance toward it. Consistent with Goffman's (1979) analysis of *footing*, the structures used to build these formulations provide laminated views of the entities they constitute, encompassing a referent, i.e. some entity that is being described, a semantic formulation of that entity, and the displayed alignment of an actor toward these events, quite frequently an alignment that is heavily charged affectively. Of particular importance to the general power of this structure is the pro term which begins the sentence. That term can make reference to, and thus incorporate into the talk of the moment with its attendant process of shaping, constituting and evaluating phenomena, an extraordinary range of different kinds of entities, people, actions, events, long strips of other talk,[12] etc. In the present data Julie uses the pro term that begins her sentence to incorporate into the world of her utterance the image on the screen, formulates what that image contains by using the syntactic and semantic components of her linguistic system, comments on the import of an event constituted in this way through her intonation and by embedding laughter in the midst of her description, and in so doing actively takes up a stance toward these events, a position about what the image reveals and how it should be treated (i.e. what can be seen there is something to be laughed at). Finally by laughing at what she sees here she marks it as outside the bounds of what is acceptable for an event of this type and thus attends to, and helps formulate (for example through her description of what is wrong in the image), what counts as "normal" in the working environment of this community.

8.7 Response cries

Initially, the particles in this data collection might seem far less interesting than the ascriptive sentences that follow them. Thus quite frequently the talk before the ascriptive sentence consists of a single nonlexical sound (Julie's "Uhoo: : : eh : : : " for example). What lexical components are found are drawn from a very narrow subset of the lexicon, essentially expletives. The effect of all this is that the prefaces are not only brief, but also quite simple in structure. The semantic resources used in the sentences that follow them to shape and characterize the referent being commented upon are completely absent. Indeed these particles are instances of what Goffman (1981) has analyzed as *response cries*, bits of speech that "externalize a presumed inner state" (Goffman, 1981: 89, see also 116).

I want to explore the possibility that instead of constituting actions that are best investigated within an analytic framework that focuses exclusively on the individual and her psychology, the response cries that occur in these data are also organized as social phenomena that provide very powerful resources for shaping the perception and action of others. We can begin by noting that participants themselves frequently portray response cries in a way that is entirely consistent with Goffman's characterization of them. Particularly clear examples are found in reported speech. Rather than describing a character *speaking* a response cry, storytellers frequently report them *thinking* it. In both of the following examples (**A** and **B**) the response cry "Oh Christ" is preceded by the mental verb (Quirk, Greenbaum, and Svartik, 1985) "thought":[13]

Example A

Tasha: She said <u>oh</u> yeah.

*hhh <u>Ka</u>ren usetuh date a guy named Prosser Mellon.

(^{Is that}) the same bank that Ron works for.
(_{He's at})

→   en I thought <u>Oh</u> : : <u>Chri</u>st.

<u>Pro</u>sser Mellon yer kindding.

Example B

Tasha: A:n I <u>ha</u>d- (0.3) said

Dju wanna go up t'the club- (0.2)

there's a <u>lu</u>au up there

en I said, (0.2) yeah okay en,

(seh) we'll go up fer, drinks'n'<u>di</u>nner

En I said well I'm sorry

I have a date at nine o'clo:ck (0.7)

→   An 'e thought oh Chri:st

y'know yer really n(h)<u>eat</u>!

These response cries should not however be analyzed in isolation. Both of them, as well as all of the other examples we have been looking at, occur in a particular environment: after some triggering event but before the sentence that comments on that event:

[Triggering Event] +[Response Cry]+[Elaborating Sentence]

The way in which the response cry is built to display a particular type of reaction to that event is well illustrated by the frequent occurrence within them of the particle "oh" which Heritage (1984a) analyzes as a change of state token. Moreover, in that response cries lack the syntactic anaphoric machinery of the sentences that follow them, the way in which they indicate what they are responding to is through adjacent positioning and immediate juxtaposition. The occurrence of the response cry thus locates (or at least notes the existence of) some other event and formulates it in a particular way, i.e. as something that has the power to elicit the strong reaction visible in the cry. In brief, the format being investigated here depicts a small activity structure, the unfolding of a single coherent course of action: an event, followed by the reaction to it of someone who has experienced that event, followed by a sentence that explicates the reaction that prefaced it.

Though lacking the descriptive power of the sentences that follow them, response cries have resources of their own for shaping, characterizing, and formulating events. Of particular importance to this process is the sudden, immediate and spontaneous character of the actor's reaction to the triggering event. Goffman argues that response cries reveal "something that has escaped control" (Goffman 1981: 98), "a flooding up of previously contained feeling, a bursting of normal restraints." This spontaneity is frequently enhanced by affective loading of various types (for example through intonation). The power and spontaneity of responses with such characteristics portray the reaction they make visible as in some sense "natural" and unpremeditated, i.e. the triggering event is so obvious and powerful that it leads to an involuntary flooding out that can only later be explained through an explicit statement. Nuckolls (1991) notes that

High degree of speaker involvement ... has been cited as evidence of an inability to speak analytically and impersonally, and also of a prevailing attitude which reacts to, rather than "knows" the world.

In opposition to such a view, we find here that it is precisely the reaction, the response cry with its affective loading, that establishes the unproblematic existence of an event, and sets parameters for how it should be known (e.g. both as something whose existence is unproblematic, obvious and taken for granted, and as something to be analyzed and responded to in a specific way).

8.8 Perception, intersubjectivity, and participation

From this perspective the spontaneity of Julie's "Uhoo: : : eh : : : " and the affective loading it carries which hints at the laughter that is about to emerge constitute very powerful structures for shaping how others in the room will make sense out of what is visible on the monitor screen. If the "problem" which the affect in her intonation now locates as found is so clear and vivid that she floods out as soon as she sees it, any one else who is competent to evaluate such a scene should also be able to find it. Moreover they can display when they have found it by providing a reciprocal display of their own, for example by laughing. Indeed, as Sacks (1974) notes, laughing as soon as a punchline in a story can be recognized frequently becomes a test; parties who are noticeably slow to laugh show themselves to not have gotten the point of the joke, to be dense, etc. Julie's response cry, precisely because of the way in which it presupposes the clear visibility of the trouble and loads that proposal with strong spontaneous affect displays, can exert powerful pressure on others in the room to also find the trouble as quickly as possible. Before Julie has finished her sentence Jay is also laughing:

90.10.26 9:01pm

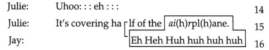

Julie:	Uhoo: : : eh : : :	14
Julie:	It's covering ha ⌈lf of the │ *ai*(h)*r*pl(h)ane. │	15
Jay:	⌊Eh Heh Huh huh huh huh│	16

Figure 8.13 Collaborative laughter

In view of the way in which Julie's first laugh token occurs only after Jay has started to laugh one might be tempted to say that Julie is responding to Jay's laughter. The situation is however more complicated than this. With her earlier response cry in line 14 Julie proposed a way of both seeing the image on the screen, and of aligning to it, that Jay's subsequent laughter may itself be responsive to. Having seeded the ground for such alignment possibilities she now escalates her own participation once someone else joins her (c.f. M. H. Goodwin's 1980 analysis of mutual monitoring). Consistent with Jefferson's (1979, 1984b, 1987) work on laughter what one finds here is an intricate, step wise building up of a collaborative laughing together.

Once this laughter becomes a socially distributed speech activity the social status of the events it is formulating is radically transformed. The mutual laughter displays a multi-party consensus about how the image on the screen should be interpreted. In that independent observers can come to the same conclusion about the sense and import of what they see there the factual status of that interpretation, the sense that it "really" exists "out there" instead of being a single individual's idiosyncratic misapprehension, is massively enhanced. In laying the foundations of modern science Robert Boyle "insisted that witnessing was to be a collective act. In natural philosophy, as in criminal law, the reliability of testimony depended upon its multiplicity" (Shapin and Schaffer, 1985: 56). According to Boyle (Shapin and Schaffer, 1985: 56):

For though the testimony of a single witness shall not suffice to prove the accused party guilty of murder; yet the testimony of two witnesses, though but of equal credit... shall ordinarily suffice to prove a man guilty; because it is thought reasonable to suppose, that, though each testimony single be but probable, yet a concurrence of such probabilities (which ought in reason to be attributed to the truth of what they jointly tend to prove) may well amount to a moral certainty.

As concerned as Boyle and his colleagues with the discursive structures through which "truth" can be enforced within a community are the eleven-year-old African American girls involved in a He-Said-She-Said dispute described by M. H. Goodwin (1990: 202):

Ruby: It's between Kerry, and you, (1.0)

> See *two* (0.5) two against one. (0.7)
> Who wins? The one is two.=Right? (0.5)

And that's Joycie and Kerry. (0.5)

> They both say that you said it.
> And you say that you didn't say it
> Who you got the *proof*

that you *didn't* say it

Figure 8.14 Multi-party consensus

When Jay and Julie laugh together at the image in front of them a multi-party consensus about how that image should be perceived and interpreted is publicly displayed to the others in the room. The power of this consensus resides not only, or even primarily, in the proposition explicitly stated (e.g. "It's covering half of the airplane"), but rather in the interactive organization of the participation framework through which this shared vision is constituted. Of particular importance to the cognitive organization of this process are its affective components which constitute the vision as something so solid and obvious that actors encountering it will spontaneously burst into laughter (and indeed others in the room do now begin to laugh). It is here that transparent vision, i.e. the ability to spontaneously find an event of a particular type in the pixels on the screen, is constituted. This transparency emerges as the product of interactive process, within which scenes and the proper alignment of actors to them are built through discourse.

8.9 Conclusion

What can be seen on the monitor screen is situated within a dense web of discursive practices, beginning with the organization of the Ops room itself as an entity charged with certain kinds of work, and proceeding to the prospective indexicals that announce the problem and structure initial vision of the screen, the participation frameworks that build socially distributed, shared perception and cognition, etc. The products of this work build events that are situated, context dependent (the gate monitors used in this particular work setting can shape perception of the talk being heard as much as the talk-in-interaction informs perception of the screen), and intensely local. However in building these local events participants make use of far more general interactive procedures (story formats, prospective indexicals, affect displays, etc.) that operate in other settings as well (cf. Schegloff, 1972). The study of discourse is not a minor subfield of the human sciences, but rather a key locus for the analysis of the discursive practices, cognitive operations and social phenomena through which human beings constitute together the endogenous worlds that they inhabit.

From such a perspective it is possible to view perception, not as something located within the psychology of the individual, or within a Cartesian mind isolated from the world that it inhabits, but instead as a thoroughly social phenomenon intrinsically tied to action in the world. In these data something in the working environment of this community, a representation of events at a distant work site on a television screen, is understood and shaped into a work-relevant perceptual event, by using a second representational system: language as deployed and constituted through talk in interaction.

The ability of language to shape a group's perceptions of the world it inhabits is central to the Sapir-Whorf hypothesis. Sapir and Whorf focused their inquiry on one order of linguistic phenomena: language-specific grammatical and semantic systems, and indeed in these data the grammar of the talk in progress, for example the structure of prospective indexicals, is essential to the organization of the interactive work that participants in this setting are pursuing. However the organization of language at the level of discourse as a systematic phenomenon in its own terms seems to

have been completely invisible to Whorf. Nonetheless when we look
at what Whorf considered to be the central issue for the questions
he was addressing we find that it is the process of reaching agreement:

...the background phenomena with which [linguistics] deals are involved in
all our foreground activities of talking and of reaching agreement, in all
reasoning and arguing of cases, in all law, arbitration, conciliation, con-
tracts, treaties, public opinion, weighing of scientific theories, formulation
of scientific results. Whenever agreement or assent is arrived at in human
affairs, and whether or not mathematics or other specialized symbolisms
are made part of the procedure, THIS AGREEMENT IS REACHED
BY LINGUISTIC PROCESSES, OR ELSE IT IS NOT REACHED.
(Whorf 1968: 44.

The processes that Whorf describes, agreement being the prototypical case, not only have discourse level components, but are, it can
be argued, intrinsically processes constituted through discourse (e.g.
arguing of cases, law, conciliation, what is now known about the
organization of scientific practices, etc.). Agreement is not something *known* in an individual brain[14] but something *done* in collaboration with others. It is not a static state of knowledge but instead
an interactive process that stretches across differentiated   parties
within a distributed field of action. The very existence of an agreement requires the coparticipation of others. As such its natural
home is human discourse. From such a perspective the processes
of discourse through which human beings accomplish common,
situated understanding with each other, are central to the analysis
of the questions raised by Whorf.

More generally to investigate the interactive organization of
knowledge we need access not only to the cognitive artifacts sedi-
mented within Saussure's *langue* but a much larger field of action
encompassing the activities that constitute the life world of endogenous communities, the tools used to carry out those activities, the
actual bodies of participants positioned so as to afford particular
kinds of access to each other and the events they are collaboratively
engaged in. Within such a framework participants use talk to not
only state propositions but also comment affectively on their alignment to those propositions, while pursuing further delineation of
the truthfulness of these statements through a discursive process of

interaction, situated within settings inhabited not only by other human beings but also artifacts implicated in the cognitive activities in progress. Despite this wider frame of reference the detailed organization of language and grammar, as articulated through talk-in-interaction, lies at the heart of this process, providing primary structures for interpretation and the organization of action, indeed a syntax for building not only sentences but social action and intersubjectivity.

Notes

*   I am deeply indebted to Steve Clayman, Françoise Brun-Cottan, Kathy Forbes, Candy Goodwin, Tim Halowski, Susan Newman, Elinor Ochs, Emanuel Schegloff, Lucy Suchman and Randy Trigg for comments on an earlier version of this analysis.

An earlier version of this paper was presented at the 90th annual meeting of the American Anthropological Association, Chicago, November 20–24, 1991, and at the Annual Meeting of The American Association for Applied Linguistics, Seattle, February 29, 1992, and at the Interaction and Grammar Workshop, UCLA, May 1, 1992.

1   The system developed by Gail Jefferson (Sacks, Schegloff, and Jefferson, 1974: 731–33) is used to transcribe talk. Relevant transcript symbols are described in the glossary. In addition subsections of a larger transcript have sometimes been highlighted by drawing boxes around the appropriate text.

2   The present analysis emerges from the Workplace Project initiated by Lucy Suchman at Xerox's Palo Alto Research Center. The project investigated how work was organized in multi-activity settings at a medium sized airport.

3   See Suchman (1992) for more detailed analysis of centers of coordination as situated, interactively constituted phenomena.

4   For more extensive analysis of how this object changes over time see Goodwin and Goodwin (in press).

5   See Goodwin (1986) for analysis of how a story with two competing characterizations of the events about to be told in two separate prefaces leads to conflicting interpretations of both the events in the story, and the structure of the story, e.g. when its climax can be seen to occur such that it is appropriate for recipients to start responding to it.

6   See Ochs, Taylor et al. (1989, 1992) for other analysis of how interactive narrative structures are relevant to the organization of scientific discourse.

7   Such interpretive structures provide powerful tools with strong political consequences in situations of contested vision. See Goodwin (1994) for analysis of how language was used by lawyers for the police who

beat Rodney King to shape the jury's perception of events visible on the tape of the beating.

8 Such a position is of course quite consistent with Heidegger's arguments that the primacy traditionally given disinterested knowledge must be overturned and replaced by an emphasis on actual work in socially constructed, contingent environments. Ops Workers' knowledge of what their screens have to offer them arises from situated, active, practical manipulation of "tools that already have a meaning in a world that is organized in terms of purposes" (Dreyfus, 1991: 47).

9 As an epistemic upgrade the phrase "We definitely have ..." might suggest prior interaction about this matter, e.g. that Gate has been assigned to check out a possible problem (I am indebted to Emanuel Schegloff for bringing this to my attention). While a preliminary search of our recordings has failed to locate such an exchange, this does constitute one possible way that this talk might be heard.

10 The request to specify the gate is relevant to more than finding a particular scene on the gate monitors. For example, if the Ops room is to dispatch a repair crew they have to know where to send that crew. Whalen (1995) describes in detail how workers in a 911 operations room "take control" of the reports of people who call them, intercepting what callers might take to be the interesting aspects of what they have to say, in order to collect as quickly as possible the information required by the report forms that structure work in the 911 center.

11 For analysis of the interactive organization of affect see Goodwin and Goodwin 1987a; Ochs, 1986, and Schieffelin, 1983, 1986, 1990.

12 One of the characteristic environments for such utterances is after stories and other extended descriptions where they are used to help formulate the gist of the preceding talk.

13 By using such mental verbs in these narratives the speaker is able to report both (1) a specific event, and (2) the unspoken assessment of that event by a relevant actor, e.g. to construct a multi-layered description that encompasses both a report of something that was said, and other participants' analysis of, and stance toward, that reported speech. See Capps and Ochs (1995) for extensive analysis of how mental verbs "illustrate the grammatical face of consciousness" by enabling a speaker constructing a narrative not only to report past thoughts, but also to focus on absorption in the activity of thinking and feeling as a process in its own right.

14 Even if others happen to know the same things, e.g. Saussure's notion of a shared storehouse which seems to form the basis for Whorf's notion (1968:45) of agreement being "codified in the patterns of our language."

References

Bloor, D. (1976). *Knowledge and Social Imagery.* London: Routledge and Kegan Paul.

Capps, Lisa and Ochs, Elinor (1995). *Constructing Panic: The Discourse of Agoraphobia.* Cambridge MA: Harvard University Press.

Dreyfus, Hubert L. (1991). *Being-in-the-World: A Commentary on Heidegger's Being and Time, Division I,* Cambridge, MA: MIT Press.

Goffman, Erving (1979). Footing. *Semiotica* 25: 1–29 (reprinted in Erving Goffman's *Forms of Talk,* 1981, pp. 124–59. 1981, Philadelphia: University of Pennsylvania Press.

(1981). *Forms of Talk,* Philadelphia: University of Pennsylvania Press.

Goodwin, Charles (1981). *Conversational Organization: Interaction Between Speakers and Hearers.* New York: Academic Press.

(1986). Audience diversity, participation and interpretation. *Text* 6(3): 283–316.

(1994). Professional vision. *American Anthropologist.*

Goodwin, Charles and Duranti, Alessandro, (1992). Rethinking context: an introduction. In A. Duranti and C. Goodwin, (eds.) *Rethinking Context: Language as an Interactive Phenomenon.* pp. 1–42. Cambridge: Cambridge University Press.

Goodwin, Charles and Goodwin, Marjorie Harness (1987a). Concurrent operations on talk: notes on the interactive organization of assessments. *IPrA Papers in Pragmatics* 1, no.1: 1–52.

(1992). Assessments and the construction of context. In A. Duranti and C. Goodwin (eds.) *Rethinking Context: Language as an Interactive Phenomenon,* pp. 147–90. Cambridge: Cambridge University Press.

(frth.). Formulating planes: seeing as a situated activity. In D. M. a. Y. Engeström, (ed.). *Distributed Cognition in the Workplace.* Newbury Park, CA: Sage.

Goodwin, Marjorie Hurness (1980). Processes of mutual monitoring implicated in the production of description sequences. *Sociological Inquiry* 50: 303–17.

(1990). *He-Said-She-Said: Talk as Social Organization among Black Children.* Bloomington: Indiana University Press.

Goodwin, Marjorie Harness and Goodwin, Charles (1987b). Children's arguing. In S. Philips, S. Steele, and C. Tanz (eds.) *Language, Gender, and Sex in Comparative Perspective.* pp. 200–48. Cambridge: Cambridge University Press.

Hanks, William F. (1990). *Referential Practice: Language and Lived Space Among the Maya.* Chicago: University of Chicago Press.

Heritage, John (1984a). A change-of-state token and aspects of its sequential placement. In J. M. Atkinson and J. Heritage (eds.) *Structures of Social Action,* pp. 299–345. Cambridge: Cambridge University Press.

(1984b). *Garfinkel and Ethnomethodology.* Cambridge: Polity Press.

Jefferson, Gail (1979). A technique for inviting laughter and its subsequent acceptance/declination. In G. Psathas, (ed.) *Everyday Language: Studies in Ethnomethodology.* pp. 79–96. New York: Irvington Publishers.

(1984). On the organization of laughter in talk about troubles. In J. M. Atkinson and J. Heritage (eds.) *Structures of Social Action*, pp. 346–69. Cambridge: Cambridge University Press.

Jefferson, Gail, Sacks, Harvey, and Schegloff, Emanuel A. (1987) Notes on laughter in the pursuit of intimacy. In G. Button and J. R. E. Lee, (eds.) *Talk and Social Organisation*, pp. 152–205. Clevedon, England: Multilingual Matters.

Lerner, Gene Howard (1987) Collaborative turn sequences: sentence construction and social action. Unpublished Ph.D. Dissertation, Psychology, University of California at Irvine.

(1993). Collectivities in action: establishing the relevance of conjoined participation in conversation. *Text* 13(2): 213–46.

Levinson, Stephen C. (1983). *Pragmatics.* Cambridge: Cambridge University Press.

(1987). Putting linguistics on a proper footing: explorations in Goffman's concepts of participation. In P. Drew and A. J. Wootton (eds.) *Goffman: An Interdisciplinary Appreciation*, pp. 161–227. Oxford: Polity Press.

Lyons, John (1972). Human language. In R. A. Hinde (ed.) *Non-Verbal Communication.* pp. 49–85. Cambridge: Cambridge University Press.

Nuckolls, Janis B. (1991). Quechua texts of perception. Abstract for the 90th Annual Meeting of the American Anthropological Association, Chicago, Nov. 20–4, 1991.

Ochs, Elinor (1986). From feelings to grammar: a Samoan case study. In B. B. Schieffelin and E. Ochs (eds.) *Language Socialization Across Cultures.* pp. 251–72. New York: Cambridge University Press.

Ochs, Elinor and Schieffelin, Bambi (1989). Language has a heart. *Text* 9(1): 7–25.

Ochs, Elinor, Schieffelin, Bambi B. and Platt, Martha (1979). Propositions across utterances and speakers. In E. Ochs, and B. B. Schieffelin (eds.) *Developmental Pragmatics.* pp. 251-68. New York: Academic Press.

Ochs, Elinor, Smith, Ruth and Taylor, Carolyn (1989). Dinner narratives as detective stories. *Cultural Dynamics* 2: 238–57.

Ochs, Elinor, Taylor, Carolyn, Rudolph, Dina, and Smith, Ruth (1992). Story-telling as a theory-building activity. *Discourse Processes* 15(1).

Quirk, R., Greenbaum, Leech G., and Svartik J. (1985). *A Comprehensive Grammar of the English Language.* New York: Longman, Inc.

Sacks, Harvey (1963). Sociological description. *Berkeley Journal of Sociology* 8: 1–16.

(1974). An analysis of the course of a joke's telling in conversation. In R. Bauman and J. Sherzer, (eds.) *Explorations in the Ethnography of Speaking*, pp. 337–53. Cambridge: Cambridge University Press.

(1992). *Lectures on Conversation*. Edited by Gail Jefferson, with an Introduction by Emanuel A. Schegloff. Oxford: Basil Blackwell.

Sacks, Harvey, Schegloff, Emanuel A. and Jefferson, Gail (1974). A simplest systematics for the organization of turn-taking for conversation. *Language* 50: 696–735.

Saussure, Ferdinand de (1959). *Course in General Linguistics*. Edited by Charles Bally and Albert Sechehaye, in collaboration with Albert Riedlinger, translated from the French by Wade Baskin. New York: Philosophical Library.

Schegloff, Emanuel A. (1968). Sequencing in conversational openings. *American Anthropologist* 70: 1075–95.

(1972). Notes on a conversational practice: formulating place. In D. Sudnow, (ed.) *Studies in Social Interaction*, pp. 75–119. New York: Free Press.

Schegloff, Emanuel A. and Sacks, Harvey (1973). Opening up closings. *Semiotica* 8: 289–327.

Schieffelin, Bambi B. (1983). Talking like birds: sound play in a cultural perspective. In E. Ochs and B. B. Schieffelin (eds.) *Acquiring Conversational Competence*, pp. 177–84. Boston: Routledge & Kegan Paul.

(1986). Teasing and shaming in Kaluli children's interactions. In B. B. Schieffelin and E. Ochs (eds.) *Language Socialization across Cultures*, pp. 165–81. Cambridge: Cambridge University Press.

(1990). *The Give and Take of Everyday Life: Language Socialization of Kaluli Children*. Cambridge: Cambridge University Press.

Shapin, Steven and Schaffer, Simon (1985). *Leviathan and the Air Pump: Hobbes, Boyle and the Experimental Life*. Princeton: Princeton University Press.

Suchman, Lucy (1992). Technologies of accountability: of lizards and airplanes. In G. Button, ed. *Technology in Working Order: Studies of Work, Interaction and Technology*, pp. 113–26. London: Routledge.

Whalen, Jack (1995). A technology of order production: computer-aided dispatch in public safety communications. In P. ten Have and G. Psathas (eds.) *Situated Order: Studies in the Social Organization of Talk and Embodied Action*. Washington DC: University Press of America.

Whorf, Benjamin (1956). *Language, Thought, and Reality*. Cambridge, MA: MIT Press.

(1968). Science and linguistics. In P. Gleeson and N. Wakefield (eds.) *Language and Culture: A Reader*, pp. 39-53.Columbus, Ohio: Charles E. Merrill. Reprinted from *Language, Thought and Reality* by Benjamin Whorf, MIT Press, Cambridge MA.

Wittgenstein, Ludwig (1958). *Philosophical Investigations*. Edited by G. E. M. Anscombe and R. Rhees. Translated by G. E. M. Anscombe, 2nd edition, Oxford: Blackwell.

9

Conversational signifying: grammar and indirectness among African American women[1]

MARCYLIENA MORGAN

9.1 Introduction

This paper examines conversational signifying, a practice fundamental to African American communication and identity. Though various forms of signifying have been previously investigated, no studies have explored how signifying is conversationally constructed through the systematic use of particular grammatical, prosodic and discursive structures to convey indirect messages. Women's interactions are the focus of this analysis not only because they have been largely ignored, but more importantly because women are often the innovators and connoisseurs of this empowering, artful practice.

9.2 Indirectness through signifying

In the following sections of the paper, the practice of signifying is introduced as part of the African American system of conversational indirectness. The discussion explores the ways in which language and interaction work together to create indirectness which in turn is a resource for mediating and realigning social relationships.

9.2.1 Forms of indirectness

Though African American interaction and communicative style have provided the scholarly community and public culture with numerous instances of the ways in which grammar and interaction reflect self, identity, and reality, African American language and discourse are often analyzed in terms of middle-class American language norms and practices (Kochman, 1981; Labov, 1972a). This paper views African American language and discourse as a multiconstructed and multitiered system which comprises norms of interaction which are both American and particularly African American. This system incorporates counterlanguage, especially forms of indirect discourse (cf. Morgan, 1989, 1991, 1993, 1994a).

Several analyses of African American interaction have suggested that indirectness is characteristic of, rather than one of a number of styles of African American speech. It is used among young children and adolescents in everyday play activities (Goodwin, 1988, 1990, 1992). Indirectness is also central to adolescent male verbal performances like the verbal game of signifying or sounding/the dozens (Abrahams, 1962; Kochman, 1972; Labov, 1972a; Garner, 1983), and it is a common component of interaction of adult women (Mitchell-Kernan, 1972, 1973; Morgan, 1989, 1991).

In the late 1980s, some of the portrayals of signifying which appeared in the 1970s (cf. Mitchell-Kernan, 1971, 1972, 1973; Kochman, 1972, 1981; Abrahams, 1976: Smitherman, 1977) were "rediscovered" and signifying was proclaimed the trope of tropes in African American speech styles (Gates, 1988). However, in spite of its recent attention, with few exceptions (Mitchell-Kernan, 1972), little is known about the way in which it is established and maintained within a system of indirectness. Mitchell-Kernan (1972) describes signifying as "the recognition and attribution of some implicit content or function which is obscured by the surface content or function" (317–18). This analysis explores the implicit and explicit functions of signifying and how it is constituted and constructed within the system of African American indirectness.

While African American indirectness can take many forms in discourse, there are essentially two forms which seem to be indicative of signifying:

(i)   pointed indirectness – when a speaker ostensibly says something to someone (mock receiver) that is intended for – and to be heard by – someone else and is so recognized.

(ii) baited indirectness - when a speaker attributes a feature to someone which may or may not be true or which the speaker knows the interlocutor does not consider to be a true feature.[2]

Pointed and baited indirectness can combine and are not mutually exclusive. The use of these forms assumes that members of the African American speech community consider speaker intentionality to be socially constructed or collaborated (cf. Duranti, 1993).

9.2.2 Signifying as pointed indirectness

Speakers use pointed indirectness to target interlocutors through mock receivers.[3] This type of indirectness is only successful if recognized by hearers who share prior knowledge about events or where the context has been established in such a way that the addressed target and those around can determine the identity of the intended target. Fisher (1976) uses the following example to describe this speech act, which is called remark dropping in Barbados.

A woman chose to wear an overly bright shade of lipstick to a party. She overheard a woman say, "Oh, I thought your mouth was burst" to a man whose lips were in perfect order. (1976: 231)

According to Fisher, the above indirect speech act is part of the communication system of Barbadian society. Though he considers remark dropping a common feature of interaction in this society, he reports that its use is assessed negatively by Barbadians as an indicator of the class and status of the speaker. In the United States African American community however, this form of indirectness is not associated with class or status as in the Caribbean. Rather, it is used by all classes to key signifying and, in contexts that include non-members, it can function to enact identity, solidarity and/or resistance, among speech community members participating in the interaction (Morgan, 1989, 1993, 1994).

Speakers who employ pointed indirectness focus on the context and plausibility of the mock receiver as the intended target. Typically, neither the mock receiver nor intended target responds since, for this form of indirectness, any response collaborates with the speaker. In the few cases that I have witnessed where the intended target responded to the speaker, the target was direct and argumentative. For example, while talking to a woman in her home about 1940s Chicago jazz clubs, she said, looking directly at me, "I don't have to tell you who's grown in here" when her teenage daughter entered the house later than expected. In this case the daughter responded: "I know you're my mother and you might as well get a life because I *am* grown!" The daughter was then given what her mother referred to as "extra" punishment for her "smart mouth."

If the mock receiver responds to the speaker and does not recognize that it is implausible that he or she is the target, the mock receiver runs the risk of embarrassment, especially if the comment is complimentary and the speaker and/or hearers believe that what is said is only true for the intended target. For example, at a middle-class social gathering I heard a woman say to a man who was not smiling and did not have dimples: "I like a man with a warm smile and deep dimples." Unfortunately, the man (mock target) responded with a flattered and beaming dimple-less smile and said "Thank you," which caused everyone, including the intended target, to laugh at the mock target.[4]

While pointed indirectness is accomplished by delivering a message to an intended target through a mock receiver, it can also lead to baited indirectness when a hearer believes a speaker means to talk about him or her by targeting attributes or features.

9.2.3 *Signifying as baited indirectness*

When baited indirectness is used in signifying, the speaker focuses on negative attributes of an unspecified target rather than mock receivers. This form of indirectness, which appears as circumlocution, often employs indefinite and personal pronouns, e.g. "something," "someone," that highlight that the attribute being discussed is distant from specific hearers. As in the case of pointed indirectness discussed above, any response by hearers is an indication that the baited indirectness is true.

This portrayal of baited and pointed indirectness suggests that when signifying is not part of a game (e.g. sounding/the dozens), it is unwanted indirectness. That is, when interlocutors signify, they put another person on the spot and everyone knows it. If the intended target, who is in the hot seat, responds to what is said in any direct way or becomes defensive, members consider the signifying to be true. The target of signifying's only recourse is to wait for the spotlight to move away from him or her.

As Figure 9.1 illustrates, pointed and baited indirectness are considered separate forms because in pointed, the speaker focuses on interlocutors who are not plausible targets to address the intended target. In baited indirectness, the speaker focuses on (usually negative) attributes or characteristics while in the target's presence, without directly addressing the target.

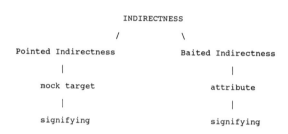

Figure 9.1

9.3 Grammatical and interactional resources for signifying

Before examining the architecture of signifying in women's interactions, it is necessary to outline some significant lexical, grammatical, prosodic and interactional resources that participants draw on in order to signify. The discussion will focus on the African American community's use of:

lexical and grammatical features that characterize dialect ambiguity and opposition between African American English (AAE) and American English (AE)

prosodic features such as loud talking, marking, pitch and timing/rhythm

interactional features such as eye gaze, parallelism and rights to a topic.

9.3.1 Reading dialect

This section introduces some of the lexical and grammatical features of signifying through a discussion of a larger practice which I will refer to as *reading dialect*. Reading dialect should be under-

stood in terms of the more general African American notion of
reading as an interpretive practice.

"Reading" occurs whenever a speaker denigrates another to his
or her face (Goffman, 1967) in an unsubtle and unambiguous manner. Though there may be self-reporting of reading having taken
place without witnesses (e.g. in a story, the narrator may simply
report "*I READ her!*"): reading only is legitimate when it is accomplished in the presence of other witnesses.[5] It is direct speech to the
point that it is often accusatory. When a target gets read, he or she
is verbally attacked for inappropriate or offensive statements or
what is perceived, by the reader, as the speaker's false representation of his or her beliefs, personal values, etc. It is not unusual to get
read for acting out class privileges, failing to greet friends, pretend-
ing to have beliefs that are not actually held, etc. For example, while
doing field work in Chicago, I was falsely read in a crowded waiting
area of a fried chicken "joint" by one of the cooks (I swear I never
saw him before that day!) who yelled, so everyone heard him, "See!
Yeah! You speak to me when there's nobody around and we're all
alone! But in front of people you're too good to speak!" The other
customers waiting for their fried chicken either looked at me in
disgust (shaking their heads), or didn't look at me at all. The
point here is not that a reader is correct or incorrect, but that the
reader is willing to jeopardize his or her own face (as well as that of
the target) by disclosing what the reader believes to be the target's
attempt to camouflage his or her beliefs, attitudes, etc.

Another aspect of reading that is common in the African
American community concerns the variety of language one uses in
interaction. *Reading dialect* occurs when members of the African
American community contrast or otherwise highlight obvious features of African American English (AAE) and American English
(AE) in an unsubtle and unambiguous manner to make a point.[6]
The point itself may or may not be a negative one. These lexical and
grammatical structures are very well known in the community and
are often the focus of verbal play, humor and irony. For example, to
stress a point members might say "It's not simply that I am cool. I
be cool. In fact, I been cool (a very long time)." In the African
American community, not only the two dialects of AAE and AE
but also varieties within those dialects are consistently read by
interlocutors.[7]

Within the framework proposed here, reading dialect involves a practice I refer to as *dialect opposition*. This practice highlights and exploits the forms which members consider to be different. When speakers employ dialect reading in interactions, they immediately signal to members that some form of signifying is in play. Since many features of AE and AAE are shared or structurally similar, it isn't always clear to members of the African American community when other members are using AE and when AAE. What reading dialect accomplishes is to transform the status of a lexical, prosodic, grammatical or discourse structure that could be either AAE or AE into one or the other dialect. This is achieved by the use of features or rules of AAE which are generally known and culturally marked. One of the most common forms of reading dialect concerns AAE lexical usage.[8]

Linguists have long observed that AAE attaches a variety of meanings to AE lexical items (McDavid and McDavid, 1951; Dillard, 1977; Dalby, 1972) and there are several dictionaries on the subject (Major, 1970, 1994; Smitherman, 1994; Freddy, 1992; Dillard, 1977). Lexical expansion in terms of meanings and/or parts of speech is a general principle in AAE where, for example, the verb *wack* becomes an adjective as in "That idea is wack" to mean incredibly stupid. There are also cases of lexical inversion (Holt, 1972) for words like *fat* (or *phat*) and *dope* which, for African American youth, often means extraordinarily good. It is also possible to have words like *bag*, which means to embarrass, that have no apparent relationship to the AE meaning. Similarly, bound and free morphemes can be manipulated so that the AAE verb *conversate* (instead of *converse*), as in "I just like to conversate" is derived from the noun *conversation*.[9] Whether members recognize the meanings attached to words or not, they recognize the practice as a culturally marked one.

Similar cases can be found for dialect opposition in syntax, prosody and discourse. For example, one can accomplish dialect opposition by responding to *what's up* with AAE *whazzup*! Among members who use these contrasts, *whazzup* serves as a put down mainly because it clearly represents a hip urban African American identity. Similarly, on a black situation TV comedy, an editor returned a writer's article and explained: "It needs work." He responded, "How much?" She responded with "A lot!" When he asked "How much is a lot?" the editor responded with "How about beaucoup?" (pronounced /buːku/ and /boːku/) a term from French adapted in the African American community as a quantifier which means a tremendous amount as in "There were beaucoup people at the party!" These examples reveal that many performances of dialect opposition index AAE and AE as socially constructed. Speakers often use dialect opposition to key conversational signifying episodes.

Reading dialect indicates that members of the African American community have knowledge of both AAE and AE dialect systems as well as a sense that the two systems are distinct. While the two dialects certainly overlap in grammar and lexicon and while members of the AAE community play on that overlap to create ambiguity, they also are constantly keying into what distinguishes the two dialects in order to interpret what is going on at any one interactional moment and thereby act on it. Members search for distinct forms and functions and contrast them with their possible linguistic counterparts in the other dialect. Members constantly mine the possible meanings implied by the particular forms and functions chosen.

It may well be that this awareness of dual dialect forms, meanings, and functions is not shared by *mono-AE* speakers. For example Rickford (1975) and Spears (1982) report that AE speakers overwhelmingly misinterpret utterances containing AAE forms such as stressed *been* and the modal semi-auxiliary *come* as in

(1)   Hey, I *BIN* know his name! (Rickford, 1975: 172)
(2)   He come walking in here like he owned the damn place.
        (Spears, 1982: 852)

In the first example, stressed *been BIN)* refers to the remote past and can be written as:

(1a)   I have known his name for a long time, and still do.

In the second case, Spears argues that *come* is not a motion verb but functions as a modal semi-auxiliary to signal the indignation of the speaker. Thus sentence 2 can be written as:

(2a)   I don't like him walking in here like he owned the damn place.

Spears uses the notion of *camouflage* to explain why AE speakers and researchers alike misread these forms:

> It is the form itself which provides the camouflage, and the meaning which is being camouflaged. In such a case, camouflage is the result of the formal trappings of the item. Word camouflage, then, has to do with meaning and function: they are camouflaged by the form that bears them. In the case of syntactic camouflage, meanings are camouflaged not only by the form that bears them, but also by their syntactic environment. Consequently, in such cases, it is the form-meaning unit itself that is camouflaged. Thus an utterance can pass as one generated by the grammar of the standard language, and only the language-wide pattern reveals that the camouflaged item is not part of the standard-language grammar. (1982: 869)

While AAE speakers may have a clear sense of meanings of statements, they are not always clear that AE speakers do not possess the skills to discern different meanings.

One way to fully explicate the sociolinguistic situation described above is to define the phenomenon of reading dialect as part of African American language ideology and contestation of perceived code/style mixing or shifting. In this regard, there has been a recent emergence of theories regarding codeswitching as well as the ways in which language constitutes identity or self fashioning. These new approaches have evolved in linguistic anthropology as well as cultural and women's studies (eg. Zentella, 1981; Anzaldua, 1987; Flores and Yudice, 1990; Gal, 1992, 1991; Kulick, 1992; Woolard, 1992; Schieffelin and Doucet, 1992; Schieffelin, 1994; Duranti, 1994) and explore the possibility that switching is not only between two linguistic systems, but can constitute a system in and of itself. Accordingly, in the African American community variation may simply be one system within which one may enact identity because, as in all communities, identity is socially constructed within contexts rather than theorized linguistic systems.[10] Thus the intricate integration of language norms and values associated with the symbolic and practical functions of AAE and AE constitutes linguistic and communicative practices.

For the most part, members of the African American community report that it is common to speak both AAE and AE.[11] To mark the context and discern what aspects of AAE pragmatics – including reading dialect – are in play, participants must decide if the interlocutor using AAE is mainly a monolingual speaker or not. A member's speech can be read as non-African American if he or she speaks only AE and as African American if he or she speaks AAE or both.[12] Thus, in terms of language choice, for members of the African American community, AE is read as the only variety which one can *choose* to speak and/or learn. In contrast, AAE is viewed as the language which one naturally speaks in the community. Consequently, mono-AE speech is read as a symbol of the American language "ideal" and "citizenship standard" and is therefore symbolic to the African American community of both the speaker's desire to be accepted as non-African American and an uncritical investment in the American social structure (cf. Bourdieu, 1977, 1991).

Since conversational signifying often occurs by contrasting the two dialects, it is often the case that one's identity is the subject of signifying.

9.3.2 Prosodic features of signifying

One indication that signifying is underway in interaction is through prosody, including *loud-talking*, *marking*, *high pitch*, and *timing/ rhythm*.

Loud-talking can only occur in the presence of an audience or over-hearers when someone talks about someone else at a volume which is either louder than necessary for the addressed target to hear or markedly different in volume (louder or quieter) from utterances which precede or follow. It can occur on a word or an entire segment. According to Mitchell-Kernan (1972),

Loud-talking often has the effect of unequivocally signalling the intent of the speaker from the perspective of the addressee. That is to say, it assures that intent will be imputed beyond the surface function of the utterance, which might be to seek information, make a request, make an observation, or furnish a reply to any of these (p. 329)

In contrast to loud-talking, marking is a mode of characterization where mannerisms are mimicked.

Rather than introducing personality or character traits in some summary form, such information is conveyed by producing or sometimes inserting aspects of speech ranging from phonological features to particular content which carry expressive value. (Mitchell-Kernan, 1972: 333)

Pitch and timing are also important resources for keying signifying. Members of the African American community associate high pitch with dishonest discourse and low pitch with honest or true discourse and AAE. Pitch contrast can occur across words or expressions and often co-occurs with other linguistic features involved in dialect opposition. Its appearance often reflects the attitude of the speaker toward the interlocutor or topic. Timing also signals speaker attitude in that rhythm is viewed as an important aspect of what is said. As in other communities (Sacks, Schegloff, and Jefferson, 1974: Levinson, 1983: Pomerantz, 1984), skipping a beat (or two) suggests that a speaker has a view or attitude which does not align with the other interlocutors. It can either be a preface to signifying as well as a component of ongoing signifying.

9.3.3 Interactional features and cultural norms relevant to signifying

Conversational signifying is keyed through the juxtaposition of interactional and broader cultural norms and expectations. For example, signifying is often keyed through eye gaze where the intended target is not necessarily the person at whom the speaker's gaze is directed. As suggested earlier, though all interlocutors may know the target, speakers select a mock receiver who is often well known to the intended target and speaker but who nevertheless must remain silent throughout the interaction.

Many occurrences of conversational signifying also include grammatical parallelism where interactors incorporate similar grammatical structures and word order while altering the meaning of the structure being copied (cf. Labov, 1972b). Grammatical parallelism can be ongoing and appear in immediate response sequences or throughout the conversation.

Whether or not signifying is being attempted is also related to rights of a speaker to the floor: in African American women's interactions, those rights are embedded in cultural norms and expectations concerning a speaker's right to speak or pass judgment about a topic.

Active participation in discourse is often based on the extent of the participant's personal involvement in the events being discussed. A striking difference in African American women's discourse is that if all major participants are not present during the telling of what happened, especially for events where what someone said is reported, the event is only marginally discussed. This is because innumerable recriminations may result when someone reports what someone said about someone else if the speaker is not there to address interpretations of what she meant. The importance adult women attach to the audience's right to determine intentionality, even when information is delivered behind the speaker's back, is vividly illustrated in instigating among young girls. Goodwin's (1980, 1990, 1992) analysis of he-said-she-said disputes among African American girls reveals the elaborate lengths to which they are willing to go in order to determine who said what behind someone's back and whether the person reporting is, in reality, an instigator who is attempting to start trouble. Being labeled either a "back stabber" or instigator results in social censure and public disgrace (Goodwin, 1990). Within women's interactions however, the main discourse focus is not whether someone instigates or back stabs but rather, whether the intentionality assessments made by the audience are reasonable considering the context and whether the original speaker had the opportunity to address them.

Adult women operate with two styles which are dialogic within the culture: "behind your back" and "to your face." In interactive contexts, this is often presented by the statement "I wouldn't say anything behind your back that I wouldn't say to your face."[13] Not surprisingly, interactions about people who are not present are often considered tactless and potentially divisive.[14] Therefore, talking about someone behind their back does not mean that someone says something derogatory: rather it means, at least for these women, that there is the risk that the teller's intentionality or actual words do not have the benefit of co-authorship and, as a result, the entire interaction may be misunderstood. Thus the behind your back/in your face dichotomy marks the interactive requirement that intentionality is socially constructed and anyone (e.g. the back stabber) who subverts the construction by reporting, actually intends to deprive the speaker of their discourse rights.

Consequently, with the exception of their children, the women in the interaction that we're about to examine never give details about other people's "business."[15] For example, a cousin named Marie was supposed to be at the taping session but did not appear. She is a close friend and relative of the women and has shared many of their childhood memories. In fact, all of the women have played a significant role in Cousin Marie's life (as she has in theirs): she has been a cancer survivor since the age of twenty-seven or – she has had six months to live at least ten times since the age of twenty-seven. Judy repeatedly said: "I sure wish Marie were here so she could tell you," but neither she nor any of the other women would provide detailed discussion of Cousin Marie's role in their stories. In contrast, in each other's presence/face, the women were very comfortable telling each other's stories, taking over the telling of personal narratives and assertively discussing many things, both positive and negative, about each other.

9.4 Constructing signifying in women's interactions

The analysis of signifying presented here is based on recordings made on a hot summer evening in Chicago at Judy's home in 1991. The video/audio taping session was initiated by Judy who wanted to cook an informal dinner for old friends and relatives and announced that it was "time" to tape. Those participating include three women who grew up together and are relatives: Ruby (age seventy-eight and an ex-jazz musician), Baby Ruby (a security guard, age sixty-three) and Judy (a retired data entry worker, age sixty-three). Ruby and Judy are sisters and Baby Ruby is their niece. Baby Ruby is not happy that she is still called by her childhood name and she is not happy that Ruby and Judy are her aunts. In fact, Baby Ruby consistently comments on the perpetual state of chaos that characterizes her life. Ruby joined the group approximately half an hour after the discussion began. Four of Judy's daughters (ages thirty-eight to forty-five), including the author of the paper (Marcyliena) and another sister of Judy's (Eva, age seventy), and eight grandchildren (ages two to eighteen) were also in the house. The setting for the talk was the dining room where the eldest granddaughter (eighteen years old) operated the camera and never spoke to the adults or commented on what they said. Judy's children occasionally spoke but mainly served as non-talking participants or overhearers. Two segments from this interaction will be analyzed for their relevance to conversational signifying. The first is taken from a narrative on "Teenage Days" and the second from a dispute ("Auntism") concerning family relationships.[16]

9.4.1 Teenage days

The narrative "Teenage Days" was told during the second hour of three hours of interaction. Throughout the evening, the women attempt to establish the social situation as well as their authority in the context (Lindstrom, 1992). MM's question, directed at Judy and Baby Ruby, begins the Teenage Days episode on shared activities during the teenage years.[17] Baby Ruby and Judy, with assistance from Ruby, establish who was the center of attention. MM (line 7) refers to Judy's tendency to describe her body during her teens as resembling the shape of a curved Coca Cola bottle.

```
     Teenage Days
     MM = Marcyliena
     JM = Judy
     BR = Baby Ruby
     R  = Ruby
     AL = ALL
1    MM:  What - what - what - I MEAN - what was teena - being a
2         teenager like I mean what was::
3    JM:  O:h I was:gor[geous
4    BR:              [OH well by that time HO:NEY? her hea:d was SO:
5                      big
6    R:               [O:H my GO:D O:H my GO:D
7         (.)
8    MM:  This is the Coca Cola pha:se?
9    BR:  O::H BABY The whole works
10        (.)
11        She was the only one
12        (.)
13        She ran in the Miss black WHAT ((high pitch)) EV?:ER thing
14        they was RUNNING in those da:ys=
15   R:   =Sure di:d
```

While assessments "make visible an agent evaluating an event in his or her phenomenal world" (Goodwin and Goodwin, 1992: 155), they can also frame forthcoming discussion or function to camouflage other discourse styles or speech acts. In this case, which employs both pointed and baited indirectness, the opinions

of Ruby and Baby Ruby have interactional value whether or not
Judy confirms their existence by reacting to them. While all three
women co-experienced teenage days (though Ruby not as a teen-
ager), Baby Ruby and Ruby transition into signifying on Judy in
lines 3–6 by directing their assessment of what Judy thought of
herself at MM rather than Judy herself. Yet the signification
begins ambiguously since in the African American community,
bragging about something that is true, and can be proven, is
not always viewed as conceit. So Judy could easily confirm that
she had every reason to think she was beautiful – because she
knows that she was (and she has the pictures and awards to
prove it).[18] Within these communicative norms, it is not immediately apparent that Ruby and Baby Ruby believe that Judy is
conceited. Judy's self fashioning as gorgeous (or believing that
she was gorgeous) may be only mockingly collaborated, as sig-
nalled by conversational overlap (lines 3–5), allusive nouns
("head"),[19] loud talking, repetition and marking (line 5), and
vowel length. Support that this episode is a case of conversational
signifying is provided from line 4 on, Judy does not respond to
what is being said about her. As mentioned in Section 9.2 on
indirectness, any response from Judy, positive or negative, auto-
matically aligns with Ruby and Baby Ruby's assessment.

That conversational signifying is actually in play is confirmed in
lines 4, 8 and 12 which contain linguistic features that index negative meanings.

```
4.   BR: OH well by that time HO:NEY? her hea:d was SO: big (that)

8.   BR: O::H BABY The whole works

12.  BR: She ran in the Miss black WHAT ((high pitch)) EV?:ER thing
         they was RUNNING in those da:ys=
```

In these conversational turns, Baby Ruby and Ruby initiate and
sustain conversational signifying by introducing dialect ambiguity
between AE and AAE readings of lexical items, grammatical structures and conversational acts. As discussed earlier, dialect ambiguity occurs when a speaker marks or performs the possibility that
some aspect of the linguistic system contains camouflaged AAE
usage. Baby Ruby successfully performs signifying by introducing
AAE lexical items and prosody that key negative assessment
among African American women. For example, in AE, "honey"

can be considered a term of affection or have sexist connotations (Brown and Levinson, 1979). The request: "Come here honey" is not necessarily demeaning or sexist when used by a parent to a child or reciprocally between lovers, but it is considered sexist when used by strangers or those in positions of power outside of personal relationships (i.e. coworkers). In AAE however, it is often used among women to introduce a gossip episode or an unflattering assessment: "Honey, let me tell you!" When "honey" begins a negative assessment it has a loud pronunciation and the vowels, especially the first, are usually long, ending with rising intonation: "HO:::NEY?". Thus Baby Ruby could be addressing MM affectionately in AE or, because of intonation and vowel length, introducing a negative assessment directed at Judy. However, because this pronunciation of "HO:NEY?" is also followed by the emphatic description of Judy's "head" (view of herself) as "so big," the ambiguity is marked and signifying is framed.

The transition from indirectness into signifying is furthered when in line 8, Baby Ruby uses the vocative "BABY," which like "HO:NEY?" has different meanings in AAE and AE. In AAE "BABY" can imply a negative assessment as well as address those present. (Baby Ruby is looking at Judy's granddaughter and daughter while she is talking.) Baby Ruby builds signifying by introducing the concessive noun phrase "WHATEV?:ER," which functions as an AAE negative quantifier of the noun "thing" (line 12). In AAE, *whatever* is used negatively as in "You can take your whatevers." It is also used as a response to indicate that a hearer is not interested in what a person is saying.[20] "Thing" in turn, is marked as AAE and can mean "the belief, life, style, attitude" as in the expression "It's a black thing" or "It's a G [gangster] thing."[21] That is, line 12 can be glossed in AAE as

12a.   She ran in the Miss black **WHATEV?:ER fit her ego**, (that)
         they was RUNNING in those da:ys=

An AAE reading of "thing" is favored by the co-occurrence in the same utterance of the AAE past copula "was" in agreement with third person plural subject "they." In fact, indirectness becomes "signifying" at the point it is actually performed through the juxtaposition of "WHATEV?:ER," which can have negative connotations in AAE, and "thing." It is reference to "thing" coupled with the negative "WHATEV?:ER" which: (1) creates readings dialect in the concessive noun phrase "WHATEV?:ER thing they was RUNNING," (2) foregrounds the AAE range of meanings of "thing" as attitude, belief or life and therefore (3) creates the layers of indirectness necessary to establish the occurrence of conversational signifying. Baby Ruby further highlights the indirectness and ambiguity by marking Judy in performing the utterance in line 12 using high pitch pronunciation associated with stereotyped white female shallowness and dishonesty. The signifying assessment is closed with Ruby's latched collaborative uptake of agreement in line 14 "Sure di:d."

In the Teenage Days episode, Baby Ruby's signifying is accomplished by contrasting or creating ambiguous functional grammatical categories and interactional strategies. Though the episode is triggered by a question from MM that Judy immediately responds to, Baby Ruby does not directly address Judy once the episode begins. Rather, she uses pointed indirectness by addressing Judy's daughter and then baited by assigning negative attributes to Judy. Baby Ruby also reads Judy by focusing on AAE grammatical and lexical usage. That conversational signifying is indeed occurring is confirmed by Judy's silence, since, as discussed earlier, any response confirms the negative assessment made by Baby Ruby.

9.4.2 Auntism

To further illustrate how signifying organizes African American women's interactions, let us consider another conversational segment taken from the same evening's interaction. In Auntism, Judy and Baby Ruby are involved in an interaction of pointed indirectness (see section 9.2.1) in which Baby Ruby's signifying includes directing some of her interaction about Judy to Judy's daughter.

Auntism

```
 1   MM:  NUMBER ONE uh - the First! question is:
 2        (.)
 3        now: in terms of growing up: right. you two were born
 4        (.)
 5        same year? right
 6        (.)
 7   BR:  =Six months apart and I'm in[I'm
 8   JM:                              [And she NEVER let me forget it.=
 9   MM:  =((laughs))
10        (.)
11   BR:  Right
12        (.)
13   BR:  [But I
14   JM:  [She's SIX months older than I am
15        (.)
16   BR:  But that's the aunt.
17        (.)
18   JM:  And I AM her aunt.
19        (.)
20   BR:  And I:: don't like it.
21        (.)
22   JM:  And I:: don't care=
23   MM:  =((laughs))
24        (.)
25   JM:  I am STILL the aunt
26        (.)
27   MM:  NOW: you have to understand we never knew::
28        (.)
29        that - you were her - she's your aunt
30        (.)
31   BR:  [YOU - you's
32   MM:  [WE WERE AL:WAYS:! confused?
33        (.)
34        Yeah we - we were like what's the reLA:tionship
35        (.)
36   BR:  ((gazes at MM)) You're KIDDIN?
37        (.)
38   BR:  That's my DAD'S si:ster ((nods head toward JM))
39        (.)
40        Aint THAT disGUSTtin?
```

```
41         (.)
42    JM:  Your bad what?
43         (.)
44    BR:  [My DA::D'S sister
45    MM:  [My DA::D"S sister
46         (.)
47    JM:  Right.
48         (.)
49    JM:  I AM her fa:ther's sister ((winks at granddaughter/camera))
50         (.)
51    JM:  My dad - father - And uh:: she - I don't know why: you all
52         didn't know it because she AL:ways sa::id: that I'm
53         [six months ol:der than you
54    BR:  [I SURE DID!
55         (.)
56    MM:  Well YEAH - But you - Yeah - I'm six months older than you:: -
57         than you doesn't mean:: [that
58    BR:                         [AH - DO -  AND YOUR AUNTISM DOESN'T
59                                  GO ANYWHERE
60    JM:                          [And she'd always call me (?)
61         (.)
62    JM:  She [A:Lways said it
63    BR:      [CAUSE I'M THE OLDEST
64         (.)
65    BR:  So your auntism: is: like nothing?
```

In Auntism, Judy and Baby Ruby offer competing perspectives concerning the true nature of their relationship and its entailments. In lines 1–14, an interactional sequence is initiated where Baby Ruby and Judy respond to MM's question about their being the same age, which for them is also a kinship question.[22] This interaction quickly becomes a competition over who will tell the story and Judy overlaps Baby Ruby (line 8) and completes Baby Ruby's point while overlapping with Baby Ruby again in line 14. Beginning line 16, Baby Ruby and Judy argue about their kinship and address each other as well as daughters and granddaughters, who function as mock receivers and overhearers. Judy and Baby Ruby did not use direct eye contact with each other, though they did manage a few side-way glances.

Judy does not overtake the telling as Baby Ruby does in Teenage Days. Rather, Baby Ruby and Judy signify on each other by reading dialect and using mock receivers. In particular Baby Ruby signifies through reading dialect (see 9.3.1) in line 16 when she draws the conversation into an AAE frame of reference by invoking the unambiguously AAE usage of the demonstrative pronoun "that" to refer to an animate entity, namely Judy, to convey a negative reading. In AAE "that" is frequently used to highlight the fact that a person is the target of the signifying. In these contexts "that" can be marked very negatively because many members of the African American community, especially older ones, interpret any use of an inanimate term in reference to a black person as a major insult, regardless of the race of the speaker (see also Duranti, 1984, for a similar meaning in Italian). "That" bears this additional significance because many older African Americans were raised in the South where white supremacists referred to black adults as children or objects.

Baby Ruby makes the statement "But that's the aunt" about Judy to MM (the mock receiver). Judy signifies back by also directing her comment to MM and reading dialect with the first person AE non contracted copula "AM" spoken loudly in line 18. "AM", which is spoken as part of loud talking, is thus marked as mono AE and represents authority since – Judy is the aunt.

This turn also begins a series of contrasting parallel statements which are conjoined by "and" (lines 20–25). These statements are part of signifying because the rhythm with which they are spoken and the rhythm between them are the same, causing the contrast to highlight lexical and grammatical relations (see 9.3.1 on opposition). Line 20 begins the assessment dispute over the nature of both the technical definition of "aunt" and the social norms and values associated with the term. In line 20 Baby Ruby offers her subjective negative assessment of either Judy being her aunt or the link between Judy as the subject ("I") and object ("aunt"). Judy responds with a parallel structure in line 22, conveying a negative comment regarding Baby Ruby's statement, and in line 25 she mirrors line 18, with the adverb "still" highlighting the fact that even though Baby Ruby doesn't like it, Judy is always going to be the aunt. However, the dispute over their relationship and who has the right to define it has not ended.

After MM (lines 27–29) attempts to offer an explanation for her initial question, Baby Ruby (line 38) initiates yet another signifying exchange about Judy's relationship to her by using a mock receiver (another one of Judy's daughters) and reading dialect using the negative demonstrative pronoun "that" to refer to Judy's relationship to Baby Ruby's father ("That's my DAD'S si:ster"). In the negative assessment that follows in line 40, the demonstrative pronoun "that" is repeated, referring ambiguously either to Judy directly or to Judy's relationship to Baby Ruby. Though this statement was made while looking at one of Judy's daughters, no daughter or granddaughter said a word (see 9.3.3 on mock receivers). Judy's question "Your bad what?" in line 42 results in both her daughter and Baby Ruby overlapping the statement "My DA::D'S sister." thus repairing the hearing problem. Judy (lines 47–49) confirms that Baby Ruby and her daughter are correct in line 47 ("Right") and she both reads dialect and uses a mock receiver by winking at her granddaughter and rewording Baby Ruby's description in line 38 ("That's my DAD'S si:ster") in the same AE syntactic frame used in lines 18 and 25 with the full form of the copula and the formal kin term "father" instead of "DAD'S" ("I AM her fa:ther's sister.")[23]

Though the signifying episode is interrupted by a topic change initiated by Judy (line 51), Baby Ruby has not finished her contestation over the right to define the relationship. In line 58, Baby Ruby further puts down the status of Judy as her aunt by recasting Judy's repeated assertion "I AM her aunt." "I am STILL the aunt" etc. as "YOUR AUNTISM." She changes the quality of the noun "aunt" by adding the suffix "ism" which denotes attitude and roles and responsibility of being an aunt (cf. Quirk et al., 1972). Thus Baby Ruby replaces Judy's insistence that their formal relationship is "aunt" and "niece" with her notion that Judy never had the duties, responsibilities, role and therefore status of an aunt. Baby Ruby therefore successfully closes the signifying sequence with the statement in line 65: "So your auntism: is: like Nothing?"

In Auntism, Judy and Baby Ruby accomplish conversational signifying by using the lexical, grammatical, prosodic and interactional resources available to members of the African American community. Signifying in this interaction centrally concerns how one negotiates authority/power identities contesting aunt/niece, age grading and friendship/peer relationships. In contrast to the Teenage Days episode above, Judy and Baby Ruby recognize when they are the intended targets (e.g. pointed indirectness) and verbally collaborate on the signifying by a turn for turn matching of comparative resources and introducing others. Judy is signifying that she is still the aunt but, Baby Ruby is signifying that she is a friend/peer and the "auntism means like nothing."

9.5 Conclusion

This analysis demonstrates the complexity of African American conversational signifying and the intricacies of verbal work accomplished by women. Figure 9.2 summarizes the relation of signifying to indirectness and the semiotic resources that members of the African American community employ in signifying.

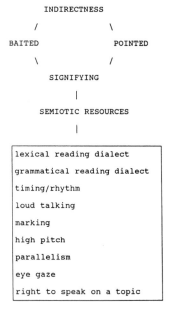

Figure 9.2

While any of the above features may index an attempt to signify, the features that have the most impact in a signifying interaction are those involved in reading dialect. Reading dialect involves AE and AAE lexical and grammatical practices, which invoke political and social meanings. Signifying through reading dialect transforms conversational interactions into interactions about identities – negotiating what constitutes and who has the right to define them. The linguistic and symbolic function of AE and AAE in signifying have been overlooked because the greatest analytic attention has been on the male-dominated verbal game of signifying (sounding/ the dozens) rather than on signifying in ordinary, extended interaction. Both conversational signifying and the verbal game are parts of an elaborate and multifaceted system of African American indirectness.

Notes

1 This paper is based on my ongoing fieldwork on women and language in the African diaspora, which covers Mississippi/Chicago and Jamaica/London. It includes discussion and analyses from fieldwork and ethnographic interviews conducted in Mississippi and Chicago between 1980 and 1992. This work was partly funded by the Academic Senate Committee on Research and the Interdepartmental Academic Program of the University of California, Los Angeles between 1990 and 1992. This analysis has greatly benefited from earlier comments from Valerie Smith, Juliette Morgan, Ruth Murray, Charles Goodwin and Marjorie Goodwin, and generous attention from Elinor Ochs, Emanuel Schegloff, and Sandra Thompson.
   Transcription conventions used in this paper are listed in the glossary, except for the following:

   ! An exclamation point indicates an animated tone, not necessarily an exclamation.
   - A single dash can indicate a (1) short untimed pause, (2) halting, abrupt cutoff, or, when multiple dashes hyphenate the syllables of a word or connect strings of words, the stream of talk so marked has (3) a stammering quality.
   (.) A period within parenthesis indicates a one-second pause.

2 These definitions are an expansion of Morgan (1989, 1993) where pointed and baited indirection were only defined structurally.
3 Pointed indirectness always involves a mock receiver. This style is often used in lectures where the speaker admonishes the whole audience when the target is only a segment of the audience. This technique was frequently used by Malcolm X (Breitman, 1965) when he addressed audiences that he believed contained non-supporters. He would often end his admonishment with "You know who you are."

4 This form is often manipulated in male/female street encounters where a man may say to a crowd of passing people "I love beautiful women!" and then says to the woman who turns to look at him "I didn't mean you!" An associated expression: "First one said it did it" is used when someone protests a negative assessment that does not directly name him or her.

5 Some people will use the term reading to mean "telling someone off." Since this can not be confirmed (no audience), it is not always considered proof that reading occurred.

6 I will use African American English (AAE) to refer to the range of language varieties used by people in the United States whose major socialization has been with United States residents of African descent. I will use American English (AE) to refer to the general discussion of varieties that are not considered socially marked or marked by class, region, gender, etc. Situations which refer to varieties of AE will be so designated. According to this definition, members of the African American community may speak either AE or AAE.

7 When reading occurs in formal contexts, it is usually considered inappropriate.

8 The lexical terms included here represent those widely used by urban youth at the time of the writing.

9 Smitherman (1994) uses this form in her introduction to her dictionary Black Talk. Between June and December 1993, I heard this word used repeatedly on three different talk shows which featured urban youth. During the same period, conversate was introduced as a dictionary entry during a humorous segment of Talk Soup, a cable program which reviews talk shows. In addition, no fewer than four middle-class women in their early twenties have used this term in my presence.

10 Of course, I don't mean to suggest that the system is simple. Rather, variation may not always respect linguistic systems and can constitute identity, especially in cases where identities are performed or enacted.

11 This statement is based on reported views of members (interviews, community publications and programs, television programs, etc.) where monolingual speakers of either variety are often the target of criticism and sometimes signifying. The question of what is AAE will not be considered here. While it is certain that members and linguists agree on linguistic categories, there is no agreement regarding the significance of distribution of these categories.

12 Of course speakers can be dominant in one variety and not the other. The social class of the speaker and whether his or her primary socialization occurred among African Americans of all classes greatly influences the use of AAE and AE.

13 Notice that, in hip hop culture, this has evolved to "In your face!" meaning a hostile directed statement or action.

14 In this respect they are similar to those among the Roadville working-class whites described by Heath (1983).

15 Children include adult children as well as children or adults raised by the women.

16 In the African American community, historicity and cultural knowledge are important and, because of white supremacist laws which greatly restricted the language use of African Americans (Morgan, 1994b), both the said and unsaid are thoroughly analyzed. This is especially true for older black women who were victimized in the south and on many occasions in the north. Familial relationships, childbirth, parentage, occupations, often reveal incredible injustices, are often a source of embarrassment as well as evoking anger and are seldom discussed. It is not surprising that many scholars, especially those socialized within the African American community eg. Gwaltney (1981), Jones (1982) and Morgan (1989), describe questions from researchers as problematic. For instance, when describing his field work among the African American community in Denver, Jones writes: "The only real problem with them (African Americans) is that some felt that answering my questions would somehow harm them. There was no specific bit of business which seemed threatening – merely the task of giving answers." (1982: 35)

17 I refer to myself and all of Judy's children (my sisters) as MM because in this interaction, Judy, Baby Ruby and Ruby consistently referred to Judy's daughters (all whose name begins with the letter M) by one another's name.

18 Perhaps the most publicized case of how this type of bragging is viewed in the African American community concerns the boxer Mohammed Ali who consistently bragged: "I am the greatest!" This seemed to irritate many outside of the African American community (especially sportscaster Howard Cosell). However, for members, these types of statements are usually met with some form of verbal exchange that can be best described as play, but they are not treated as conceit.

19 Allusion is used to refer to the process where a noun's meaning has been expanded to embody associated functions or meanings of the noun. It can also include the metaphorical context in which it may commonly occur. Thus "Mary is Chicago to me" can result in Mary simply being referred to as "Chicago." The noun is treated in terms of its referents as well as any product which it might produce. In the case of "head," it is the ego that is generated within the head that makes it large.

20 For example, to paraphrase a popular rap song of 1993, when a man tells a woman "You look beautiful" she responds "Yeah, whatever."

21 The word *thing* can be further highlighted with the pronunciation /the:ng/ which usually refers to mental or emotional state. Sometimes thing is pronounced /ting/, but this case is used to contrast AAE and Jamaican varieties.

22 On previous occasions, Baby Ruby made it clear that since she is the oldest, she should have been the aunt. She believes that it was unfair

that she never had the opportunity to enjoy the power (bullying) that comes with being the older child because Judy was her aunt.

23 The kin terms "father" and "mother" are widely discussed among members as formal, distant, and emotionless, terms. Though many people also use these terms affectionately, it is still common for children of all ages to refer to their mothers as "mom" or "mama" and fathers as "dad" or "daddy." My oldest sister was once punished for saying "Yes mother" to my mother after being told she had to be home by 11 p.m. My mother said she didn't like being called mother after telling my sister what to do.

References

Abrahams, Roger (1962). Playing the dozens. *Journal of American Folklore* 75: 209–18.

   (1976). *Talking Black*. Rowley, MA: Newbury.

Anzaldua, Gloria (1987). *Borderlands La Frontera: The New Mestiza*. San Francisco: Aunt Lute Books.

Bourdieu, Pierre (1977). The economics of linguistic exchanges. *Social Science Information* 16.6: 645–68.

   (1991). *Language & Symbolic Power*. Cambridge, MA: Harvard University Press.

Breitman, George (ed.) (1965). *Malcolm X Speaks*. New York: Grove Press.

Brown, Penelope and Levinson, Stephen (1979). Social structure, groups, and interaction. In K. Scherer and H. Giles (eds.) *Social Markers of Speech*, pp. 292–341. Cambridge: Cambridge University Press.

Dalby, David (1972). The African element in American English. In Kochman (ed.) *Rappin" and Stylin" Out*, pp. 170–86.

Dillard. J. L. (1977). *Lexicon of Black English*. New York: Seabury Press.

Duranti, Alessandro (1994). *From Grammar to Politics: Linguistic Anthropology in a Western Samoan Village*. Berkeley: University of California Press.

   (1993). Truth and intentionality: an ethnographic critique. *Cultural Anthropology* 8.2: 214–45.

   (1986). The audience as co-author: an introduction. *Text* 6.3: 239–47.

   (1984). The social meaning of subject pronouns in Italian conversation. *Text* 4.4: 277–311.

Fisher, Lawrence (1976). Dropping remarks and the Barbadian audience. *American Ethnologist* 3.2: 227–42.

Flores, Juan and George Yudice (1990). Living borders/Buscando America: languages of Latino self-formation. *Social Text* 8.2: 57–84.

Freddy, Fab 5 (aka Fred Brathwaite) (1992). *Fresh Fly Flavor: Words & Phrases of the Hip-Hop Generation*. Stamford, Ct: Longmeadow Press.

Gal, Susan (1991). Between speech and silence: the problematics of research on language and gender. In Micaela d. Leonarde (ed.) *Gender at the Crossroads of Knowledge: Feminist Anthropology in the Post Modern Era*, pp. 175–203. Chicago: University of Chicago Press.

(1992). Multiplicity and contention among ideologies: a commentary. *Pragmatics* 2.3: 445–50.

Garner, Thurmon (1983). Playing the dozens: folklore as strategies for living. *Quarterly Journal of Speech* 69: 47–57.

Gates, Henry Louis Jr. (1988). *The Signifying Monkey: A Theory of African-American Literary Criticism*. Oxford: Oxford University Press.

Goffman, Erving (1974). *Frame Analysis*. Harper Colophon: New York.

(1967). *Interaction Ritual: Essays in Face to Face Behavior*. Garden City, New York: Doubleday.

Goodwin, Charles and Goodwin, Marjorie Harness (1992). Assessments and the construction of context. In A. Duranti and C. Goodwin (eds.) *Rethinking Context Language as an Interactive Phenomenon*, pp. 101–24. Cambridge: Cambridge University Press.

Goodwin, Marjorie Harness (1988). Cooperation and competition across girls' play activities. In S. Fisher and A. Todd (eds.) *Gender and Discourse: The Power of Talk*. Norwood, New Jersey: Ablex.

(1990) *He-Said-She-Said: Talk as Social Organization Among Black Children*. Bloomington: Indiana University Press.

(1992). Orchestrating participation in events: powerful talk among African American girls. In K. Hall, M. Bucholtz, & B. Moonwomon (eds.) *Locating Power: Proceedings of the 1992 Berkeley Women and Language Group*, pp. 182–296. Berkeley: Berkeley Women and Language Group, Linguistics Department.

Gwaltney, John (1981). *Drylongso: A Self-Portrait of Black America*. New York: Vintage Books.

Heath, Shirley (1983). *Ways With Words: Language, Life, and Work in Communities and Classrooms*. Cambridge: Cambridge University Press.

Henley, Nancy (nd). Ethnicity and gender issues in language. In H. Landrine (ed.) *Handbook of Cultural Diversity in Feminist Psychology*.

Holt, Grace (1972). "Inversion" in black communication. In Kochman (ed.) *Rappin' and Stylin' Out*, pp. 152–9.

Hull, Gloria, Scott, Patricia Bell, and Smith, Barbara (1982). *All the Women are White, All the Blacks are Men, But Some of Us Are Brave*. Old Westbury, New York: The Feminist Press.

Hymes, Dell (1974). *Foundations in Sociolinguistics: An Ethnographic Approach*. Philadelphia, Pennsylvania: University of Pennsylvania Press.

Jones, Bessie & Hawes, Bess Lomax (1972). *Step It Down: Games, Plays, Songs & Stories From the Afro-American Heritage*. Athens, Georgia: University of Georgia Press.

Jones, Delmos (1988). Towards a native anthropology. In Johnetta Cole (ed.) *Anthropology for the Nineties*, pp. 30–41. New York: The Free Press.

Kochman, Thomas (ed.) (1972a). *Rappin' and Stylin' Out: Communication in Urban Black America*. Champaign, Illinois: University of Illinois Press.

(1972b). Toward an ethnography of black American speech behavior. In Thomas Kochman (ed.) *Rappin' and Stylin' Out: Communication in Urban Black America*, pp. 241–64. Champaign, Illinois: University of Illinois Press.

(1981). *Black and White Styles in Conflict*. Chicago: University of Chicago Press.

Kulick, Don (1992). Anger, gender, language shift and the politics of revelation in a Papua New Guinean Village. *Pragmatics* 2.3: 281–96.

Labov, William (1972a). Rules for ritual insults. In Thomas Kochman (ed.) *Rappin' and Stylin' Out: Communication in Urban Black America*, pp. 265–314. Champaign, Illinois: University of Illinois Press.

(1972b). *Language in the Inner City: Studies in the Black English Vernacular*. Philadelphia: University of Pennsylvania Press.

(1972c). *Sociolinguistic Patterns*. Philadelphia: University of Pennsylvania Press.

Labov, William, Cohen, Paul, Robins, Clarence, and Lewis, John (1968). A study of the non-standard English of Negro and Puerto Rican speakers in New York City, vol. I. Final Report, Cooperative Research Project 3288. Philadelphia: United States Regional Survey.

Labov, William and Waletzky, Joshua (1967). Narrative analysis. In *Essays on the Verbal and Visual Arts*, ed. June Helm, pp. 12-44. Seattle: University of Washington Press.

Levinson, Stephen (1983). *Pragmatics*. Cambridge: Cambridge University Press.

Lindstrom, Lamont (1992). Context contests: debatable truth statements on Tanna (Vanuatu). In A. Duranti and C. Goodwin (eds.) *Rethinking Context Language as an Interactive Phenomenon*, pp. 101-24. Cambridge: Cambridge University Press.

Major, Clarence (1994). *Juba to Jive: Dictionary of African-American Slang*. New York: International Publishers.

(1970). *Dictionary of Afro-American Slang*. New York: International Publishers.

McDavid, Raven and McDavid, Virginia (1951). The relationship of the speech of the American negroes to the speech of whites. *American Speech* 26: 3-17.

Mitchell-Kernan, Claudia (1971). *Language Behavior in a Black Urban Community*. Monographs of the Language-Behavior Laboratory University of California, Berkeley, Number 2.

(1972). Signifying, loud-talking, and marking. In Thomas Kochman (ed.) *Rappin' and Stylin' Out: Communication in Urban Black America*, pp. 315–35. Champaign, Illinois: University of Illinois Press.

(1973). Signifying. In A. Dundes (ed.) *Mother Wit from the Laughing Barrel*, pp. 310–28. New York: Garland Publishing.

Morgan, Marcyliena (1989). *From down South to up South: The Language Behavior of Three Generations of Black Women Residing in Chicago*. Diss. University of Pennsylvania.

(1991). Indirectness and interpretation in African American Women's discourse. *Pragmatics* 1(4): 421–51.

(1993). The Africanness of counterlanguage among Afro-Americans. In S. Mufwene (ed.) *Africanisms in Afro-American Language Varieties*. Athens, Georgia: University of Georgia Press.

(1994a). The African American speech community: reality and sociolinguistics. In Morgan (ed.) *Language and the Social Construction of Identity in Creole Situations*. Berkeley: Center for African American Studies.

(1994b). Just to have something: camouflaged narratives of African American life. Ms.

Mufwene, Salikoko (1992a). Ideology and facts on African American English. *Pragmatics* 2.2: 141–66.

(1992b). Why grammars are not monolithic. In Diane Brentari, Gary Larson, and Lynn A. MacLeod, (eds.) *The Joy of Grammar: A Festschrift in Honor of James D. McCawley*, pp. 225–50. Amsterdam: John Benjamins.

Pomerantz, Anita (1984). Agreeing and disagreeing with assessments: some features of preferred/dispreferred turn shapes. In J. Maxwell Atkinson and John Heritage (eds.) *Structures of Social Action*, pp. 57–101. Cambridge: Cambridge University Press.

Quirk, Randolph, Greenbaum, Sidney, Leech, Geoffrey, and Svartvik, Jan (1972). *A Grammar of Contemporary English*. London: Longman.

Rickford, John (1975). Carrying the new wave into syntax: the case of Black English *bin*. In Ralph W. Fasold and Roger W. Shuy (eds.) *Analyzing Variation in Language*, pp. 162–83. Washington, DC: Georgetown University Press.

Rossi-Landi, Ferruccio (1983). *Language As Work and Trade: A Semiotic Homology for Linguistics Economics*. South Hadley, Massachusetts: Bergin & Garvey Publishers, Inc.

Sacks, Harvey, Schegloff, Emanuel, and Jefferson, Gail (1974). A simplest systematics for the organization for turn-taking in conversation. *Language* 50.4: 696–735.

Schieffelin, Bambi (1994). Code-switching and language socialization: some probable relationships. In Judith Duchan, Lynne Hewitt, and Rae Sonnenmeier (eds.) *Pragmatics: From Theory to Practice*. Englewood Cliffs, New Jersey: Prentice Hall.

Schieffelin, Bambi and Doucet, Rachelle Charlier (1992). The "real" Haitian Creole: metalinguistics and orthographic choice. *Pragmatics* 2.3: 427–45.

Smitherman, Geneva (1994). *Black Talk: Words and Phrases From the Hood to the Amen Corner.* Boston: Houghton Mifflin.

(1977). *Talkin and Testifyin: The Language of Black American.* Boston: Houghton Mifflin.

Spears, Arthur (1982). The semi-auxiliary *come* in black English vernacular. *Language* 58: 850–72.

Williams, Brackette (1989). A class act: anthropology and the race to nation across ethnic terrain. *Annual Review of Anthropology* 18: 401–44.

Woolard, Kathryn (1992). Language ideology: issues and approaches. *Pragmatics* 2.2: 235–50.

Zentella, Ana Celia (1981). "Hablamos los dos": we speak both: growing up bilingual in el Barrio. Ph.D. dissertation, University of Pennsylvania.

10

Creating evidence: making sense of written
words in Bosavi*

BAMBI B. SCHIEFFELIN

Since their earliest contact with Europeans, the Kaluli people who
live at the foothills of Mt. Bosavi in the Southern Highlands
Province of Papua New Guinea have viewed books as powerful
and authoritative sources of information that white people use to
shape and control the behavior of others. In a narrative told to Steve
Feld and myself in 1990 about government contact in the early
1950s, an educated Kaluli man told us about his father who had
been selected by white patrol officers as the first local counsellor. As
he put it, "my father was given the black shirt with a red stripe, the
belt, knife, stick and *a book*, that book, people thought that if you
kill, the blood of a dead person will go inside in the book, and the
white man will know straight away and come and shoot you with a
gun; that fear, everywhere so, everyone got frightened when my
father got this."

This book, which was kept by the counsellor as part of his
responsibilities and taken out only during infrequent government
patrols made by white officers, listed the names of villagers. While
Kaluli people did not share an understanding of why their names
were written down by government people, they did not miss the fact
that this book and its meanings were created and owned by white
people, who used it as an instrument of control, authority, and
information. These early census and record keeping activities,
part of pacification efforts, were used to track and document
Kaluli people in order to discourage their periodic relocation to
new village sites, their solution to minimalizing the depletion of
local resources. This was one of the earliest experiences for
Kaluli people of what books could do, and what people did with
books.

In the mid 1960s two other changes occurred that would introduce additional ideas about books and literacy more generally – the
first, which I would like to think was relatively benign though not
inconsequential, was the arrival of anthropologists, first E. L.
Schieffelin, followed by myself and Steve Feld, whose visitations
of different durations would continue into the present. The second
change which has had far reaching consequences for Kaluli social
and ceremonial life, was the establishment of a fundamentalist mission and air strip which was managed by a Papuan National until
Australian missionaries arrived in the early 1970s.

This essay focuses on new communicative practices that emerged
as a result of interactions between Kaluli people and Australian
fundamentalist missionaries beginning in the early 1970s. To do
this I draw on ethnographic and linguistic fieldwork begun in
1967 that has continued intermittently into the present.
Taperecorded, transcribed analyses of social interaction over time
and across a wide range of situations and activities, in addition to
participant observation and informal interviews form the foundation of this analysis (Schieffelin, 1986, 1990). Additional ethnographic, sociolinguistic and ethnomusicological analyses have also
informed my assertions (Feld, 1988, 1990; Feld and Schieffelin,
1982; E. L. Schieffelin, 1976).

As Kaluli people were introduced to new forms and sources of
knowledge about their own and the outside world, their ideas about
truth, knowledge, and authority were challenged and changed,
affecting their communicative practices as well as their social structures. In such contact situations, new communicative practices
express the interests of both the missionized and the missionizers.
Kaluli people were active contributors to the linguistic and social
reorganization of their own society, as evidenced in the emergence
of several genres new to the area.

In such situations of social change, new language socialization
activities often develop. Particularly relevant for this essay are literacy lessons and sermons, both of which constitute important
activities for language socialization – socialization through the use
of language and socialization to use language – which continues
throughout the life cycle (Ochs and Schieffelin, 1984). From a
Kaluli perspective, lessons and sermons share interpretive frames
and participant structures as they originate from the same source,

the Christian mission. Combining spoken forms and written materials, both genres provide a new discursive space in which Kaluli people rethink their past, one consisting of particular social practices and beliefs – and distance themselves from it.

To accomplish this distancing, several techniques are deployed. In the literacy lesson and in the written text that it draws on, the terms *mo: lu tamina* "before," or "a long time ago, before" are systematically opposed to *o:go:* "today, now" to create narratives about how things used to be, in contrast to how things are and should be. Part of this contrast invokes the source of the difference: what "our fathers" believed is contrasted with what "this book shows us really well" and what "new words which really tell us." New facts, such as those drawn from health lessons and bible stories are used to revise boundaries or create new ones. For example, Kaluli people are reminded both in the written text and in the oral presentations that "before we didn't know," "we didn't understand," in contrast to "we now know," "we hear it really well." In classroom interaction, students are asked to register their agreement with these claims.

The practices of the past and the present/future are also coded by their assignment to gender roles; women's beliefs and activities are connected with the past, what was done before the mission was established, while men's beliefs and actions are seen as forward looking, progressive, taking up the new ideas. Not surprising is the evaluation associated with each of these positionings: women are negatively evaluated while men are viewed positively. These concepts are promoted in literacy materials and fortified through oral presentation and lessons by extensive linguistic means, including an innovation in the evidential system which further underscores an increased remoteness of the not very distant past.

10.1 Literacy and social change

This essay draws on a body of ethnographic work that views literacy practices and activities as historically contingent, ideologically grounded and culturally organized (Besnier, 1995; Collins, 1991; Duranti and Ochs, 1986; Gewertz and Errington, 1991; Guss, 1986; Heath, 1983; Kulick and Stroud, 1990; McKenzie, 1987; Street, 1984; Street and Besnier, 1994). This work demonstrates that societies "take up" or organize literacy practices in culturally variable ways depending on who is interested in literacy, and how literacy is viewed. As with other genres and activities, those involving literacy practices are constituted through specific interactional roles, arrangements, and sequences which use particular forms of language to enact social relationships and negotiate social identities. In situations where literacy is introduced as part of Christian missionization, literacy activities are often shaped by competing epistemological and cultural frameworks. These frameworks are encoded in the ways in which information is presented, knowledge is talked about, and analogies are drawn; they are also apparent in the connections that can *not* be made. Forms of resistance to literacy practices reflect not only linguistic ideology, but social and historical forces more broadly. Thus it is also useful to situate this work within current ethnohistorical accounts of competing language ideologies that have played a role shaping colonial and missionary encounters (Cohn, 1985; Comaroff and Comaroff, 1991; Fabian, 1986; Mignolo, 1992; Rafael, 1988).

10.2 Truth and evidence for it

Kaluli people, like many Papua New Guinean societies are concerned with the source and truth of what they and others know. They have well elaborated ideas of how truth is constituted, proven and linguistically marked. In the so-called "old" days, before missionaries, government patrols and anthropologists, sources of knowledge and proofs of truth were relatively stable – what the "fathers" said was what was known and believed by mature members of society. There was little reason to doubt the truthfulness of what had always been said about the natural and supernatural worlds that Kaluli people inhabited. Through direct experience, the spoken word and face-to-face interaction, cultural knowledge was orally represented, and authority and responsibility could be argued, and often were.

Through the mid-1970s and into the 1980s the missionaries introduced new facts about the world, ones they claimed to be either scientific or religious. These facts were soon represented through new words, genres, registers, and conventions for speaking. Literacy in the vernacular and Tok Pisin was introduced. The

Bosavi mission primary school used English as the language of instruction, but Kaluli people did not know either English or Tok Pisin. The few who successfully completed six years of primary school were drafted immediately into mission service: some were trained as pastors, store assistants or medical assistants. All became important players in the changing social order. With the exception of one individual whose narrative opened this essay, before the early 1980s no one had been educated beyond grade six.

The fundamentalist missionaries worked hard to establish their authority and took the view that conversion should move rapidly. Their evaluations of local cultural practices were echoed in Kaluli conversations, arguments, and sermons. By 1984 Kaluli people had given up traditional ceremonies and many "traditional" practices. With Christianity and its new material resources, the social organization of Kaluli society began to change: what had been a small-scale egalitarian society began to reshape itself into a loosely stratified society with new roles (jobs) such as pastor, deacon, aid post orderly, and trade store manager. Eventually, Christians and non-Christians took up residence in different parts of the village. Whatever power had been granted formerly to older men was now taken by those who had gained knowledge of how the mission, the mission store, and the missionary worked.

These social changes had linguistic consequences. Young men who acquired Tok Pisin extended their interactional range and could work as interpreters (*tanim tok*) for the government patrol officers and for the mission. The few young men who became literate in Tok Pisin and Kaluli, and were part of the mission effort, collaborated with the Australian missionary and translated texts from Tok Pisin (*Nupela Testamen*) or English (health booklets and literacy primers) into new varieties of the Kaluli language – varieties that were constructed by a powerful non-native speaker in conjunction with native speakers who wanted to acquire power. Of the four mutually intelligible dialects in the Bosavi area, one had been randomly selected earlier by a mission field linguist to be used for the orthography (Rule, 1966) and many features of dialect variation exist in the literacy materials, in addition to many spelling inconsistencies and syntactic simplifications and errors.

As a result of these collaborations, a new medium was created – booklets printed in a new variety of the vernacular. Written with the authority of the mission, they introduced several new types of evidence into Kaluli life; the first is the written Kaluli word. Simple but dramatic narratives urged social change. The motif here, and in sermons, was consistent: the past versus the present/future, articulated through examples of Kaluli ways of life which were depicted as backwards, wrong, and deriving from false beliefs, in contrast with European ways of doing things (from building houses, to health practices to hair styles) which were presented as new, right and good. Simple line drawings by the missionaries served as illustrations. Narratives took place in recognizable local places, and characters had Kaluli names. To make these narratives more believable, the missionary illustrated the more advanced booklets with black and white photographs of local people engaged in the activity described in the narrative. So in reading the texts, Kaluli could see themselves imaged, participating in the new practices being promoted. These graphic and photographic images were used as and became evidentials, that is, another new source of evidence for authority and truth. Combined with print, they became a source of knowledge that could be seen, referred to and reported on. Booklets introduced new information in new formats. They became the source of that information, and evidence for it. Those with access to these new sources of knowledge and truth, or those who could claim to understand them, became authorities themselves.

10.3 Evidentials

From a linguistic perspective as well as a social perspective, Kaluli people have always been concerned with evidence. Their language provides them with a range of evidentials, morphological and lexical means used by speakers to formally mark the source or evidence for the basis of their assertions, their attitudes towards knowledge, and the responsibility assumed in making a claim. Evidential particles, metalinguistic verbs (e.g., verbs of saying) and other sensory verbs indicating sources of knowledge (e.g., hearing, seeing), and reported speech are just some of the means by which speakers establish the "truth" of their assertions and take responsibility for them. For example, in Kaluli discourse, ranging from casual conversation to more formal arguments, speakers indicate through morphological or lexical means whether what they are saying derives from direct experience, visual, verbal or sonic information, speech reported to them or re-reported to them, common knowledge, or inference made from other secondary evidence:

Selected evidentials in Kaluli   *(recent innovations)

-lo:b   speaker's assertion is based on visible/visual evidence that can be shared by addressee. *Magu we mogago:lo:b* 'this banana is bad I see'; *Do:wo: ha:na:nigabo:lo:b* 'my father is about to go I see'.

-o:m   speaker's assertion is based on deduction or inference from something sensed aurally or through other senses, but without attribution of particular source. *To o:dowayo:m* 'there's talk around I'm hearing'; *No: mun o:dowayo:m* 'there is the smell of cooked meat I'm smelling'

-ko   indicates direction in which an event being talked about is taking place.

-a:le   used in interrogative forms to indicate doubt regarding accuracy of information, can elicit confirmation from addressee. *Dimia:iba:le?* 'I wonder if he will give it?'. Also used when wondering aloud to indicate uncertainty and possibly seek an opinion from addressee, *Ha:na:no:wa:le? mo:ha:na:no:wa:le?* 'I wonder will I go? Will I not go?'.

-le ~   indicates certainty of assertions, really/truly/only. *Hedele* 'it's really
-de   true;' *Ho:nde* 'it's really water and not anything else.'

-mala: ~   negative after inference indicating disappointment. *Ne*
-bala: *alima:no:mala:* 'I will not lie down' (seeing there is still more work to be done).

-malo: ~   affirmative emphasis after question or when answer is opposite to
-balo: what is expected. *Aoleya:le?* 'is it his real brother?' *aolemalo:!* 'it's truly his *real* brother!' but *aolemala:!* it's not his real brother!¹

-lo:do: emphasis with disappointment/sadness. *Ha:na:no:lo:do:* 'alas you are going away'.

*-lo:do: a:la:bo: 'we now know from this source, we did not know before' (used when referring to information from written sources)

*hia   extended use from the Tok Pisin 'here', visible/visual evidence, used to indicate meaning similar to *-lo:b*.

Evidence based on verbal sources use a range of forms, such as
-do: immediate repeat of direct quoting of someone else. For example, Speaker A ->B we! "here." Speaker C ->B wedo: ! "here" (he/
she said). The majority of evidentials for reporting speech, however,
are formed with a: la: ma or a:la: sama "say like that." Context and
pronouns clarify number and person. Such forms include:

a:la: siyo:	used for speaker self report or to report what another has said
a:la: sa:labeka:	'some one else recently said' (not used for lst person)
a:la: siyo:laleka	3rd hand reported speech
a:la: siyo:lo:bo:ka:	4th hand reported speech
a:la: sili sa:la:ingab	someone (sing/pl) is saying (duration)
a:la: sili sa:la:ingo:	someone (sing/pl) was saying (duration)
a:la: salan	generally said/one says (habitual)

Other sensory verbs are also used as evidentials, and the appropriate noun disambiguates or adds emphasis when needed. For example, dabuma "hear," but it can also mean "smell," goloma "touch,"
bo: ba "see," asuluma "think, feel, know, understand, experience."
    Emphatic markers, both lexical and morphological are used
extensively with evidentials. For example,

-ka:	emphasis when close to addressee - lst time or lst repeat
-a:	emphasis - 2nd repeat
-o	emphasis when calling out to addressee
mada	'really', 'very'
hede	'true'
hedele	'really truly'
made hedele	'really very truly'

In contrast to the more narrow linguistic view of evidentials
which tends to focus on categories of "truth" (Jakobson, 1957),
a broader social interactional perspective displays their multi-
functionality (Silverstein, 1985). Bybee describes evidentials as
"markers that indicate something about the source of the information in the proposition" (1985: 184). Willett has pointed out that
the notional boundaries of evidentiality are still unclear, but as a
semantic domain, evidentials "participate in the expression of the
speaker's attitude toward the situation his/her utterance describes"

(1988: 52). Bendix suggests that it is not enough to analyze the epistemological categories of evidentials, but one must view them as important resources used by speakers to manipulate claims of responsibility and evidence in strategic interaction (1993: 243). The social and historical context of the topic of talk, as well as the social relationship that holds between interlocutors can affect the choice of evidential marker, which, as Fox and Clifford point out, is sensitive to differences in claims to authority (1991).

Emphatic markers, affect markers and evidentials often co-occur in the same word or same utterance, and must be considered together. Analyses of evidentials in discourse highlight the importance speakers attach to establishing their authority with their audience, while acknowledging the dialogical nature of the production of meaning. Evidentials are used to convey affective and propositional meanings, and the same evidential markers may serve both functions. Haviland suggests "propositions ... live in a moral universe, which includes not only what participants take as true, or what they agree to think, but also agreements about *how* to think and feel about what they agree upon" (1989: 61). Persons not only exchange claims about the world, but their affective stances towards such claims. Givón (1982) has pointed out that speakers and hearers have an implicit contract to mark degrees of certainty in their propositions. Propositions that are to be taken for granted and viewed as unchallengeable by the hearer require no evidentiary justification by the speaker. Propositions that are asserted with relative confidence and are open to challenge by the hearer require evidentiary justification (ibid: 24). Furthermore, in situations of conflict, what may be contested is not the claim itself, but how someone knows it. Thus the use of an evidential is telling, and its choice is critical.

Drawing on linguistic examples, Chafe and Nichols suggest that an analysis of evidentials reveals a "natural epistemology" (1986: vii). I would like to suggest that when evidentials are examined in the context of their use in social interaction, such analysis reveals a "cultural epistemology." Everyday talk offers excellent opportunities to examine how individuals persuade, argue and make claims using evidentials. Activities of talk in situations of rapid social change often take up the topic of competing epistemologies, each differently valorized. Such cultural situations may result in linguistic innovations, expressed through evidentials as well as other linguistic means. I share a view with other linguistic anthropologists (e.g., Haviland, 1989; Hill and Irvine, 1993; Lucy, 1993) that the encoding of knowledge, authority and truth is a linguistic as well as a social phenomenon; the two must be viewed as interdependent.

10.4 The health lesson

My analysis of Kaluli literacy lessons, which introduce "scientific facts," shows innovations in morphological forms expressing epistemic stance, as well as in rhetorical and event structures. These linguistic changes are a notable response to missionization and underscore Kaluli concern with the sources and nature of knowledge and truth.

The particular event I draw from is a transcribed audio-taped literacy lesson that took place in 1984 at the Bosavi mission school. It is part of a larger project on Kaluli language use and social change with Steve Feld that draws on materials collected since 1967. In this new speech event, as in other innovated genres, all levels of language have been affected – the phonology, morphology, lexicon, syntax, semantics, pragmatics and of course, the cultural assumptions that organize speech activities. In spite of the fact that literacy instruction events draw on models of instruction imported from Western classrooms, there is clear evidence of local language ideology throughout. We will see how at a particular point in Kaluli history, written texts were granted authority as Kaluli people constructed linguistic means for entitling texts and making them authentic and authoritative sources of factual knowledge, even when there was no basis in fact for doing so.

The participants in this speech event are the instructor, Kulu Fuale, one of the few Kaluli Christians trained to teach vernacular literacy, and twenty-four teenaged male students in the 5th grade class. Kulu, who was fluent in Tok Pisin and spoke a little English called this a "health lesson." The lesson lasted forty-five minutes; most of the time was spent focused on a booklet about malaria.

Two printed texts that have been translated into the vernacular are used in this event. The first, a booklet about malaria, is based on an English script, and is widely used by missionaries in Papua New Guinea. The Kaluli version was created and translated by Keith

Briggs, the missionary in charge of the Bosavi station, collaboratively with Kulu Fuale. However, during the course of the lesson
Kulu repeatedly asserts that "Briggs wrote it." Kaluli people do not
take credit for the production of these materials. The remainder of
the lesson drew on a second written text, a selection of verses from
the New Testament translated from Tok Pisin into Kaluli by Kulu.
Both are presented as containing truths previously unknown. This
essay focuses on the first part of the health lesson.

I base my analysis on my transcription of the entire forty-five
minute long audiotaped event, during which time Kulu reads
from and talks about both written texts, writes on the board,
talks about other topics, and elicits class responses. The transcription and the printed texts must be considered together because of
two significant relationships: between the written texts and the oral
text (word-word relationship), and between the oral presentation
and the world that is represented, or misrepresented, through it.
Selections from the transcript will be used to illustrate how evidence
is marked in a variety of ways.

10.5 General participant and event structure

The introduction of Christian church services and adult literacy
classes exposed the Kaluli people to a radically different presenta-
tional and participation structure. Previously, in most Kaluli speech
situations, no single speaker controlled the floor, speakers self-
selected and many voices, some quite loud, made simultaneous
contributions to whatever topics were being entertained. In contrast, Christian speaking events can be characterized as those in
which a single speaker controls the floor and, in addition, has all
the relevant and correct information. There are no interruptions;
group response is elicited, coordinated and in unison, in response to
questions that seek one answer. Question/Answer sequences which
are used in local sermons are similar to those found throughout
lessons. They are unlike any other discourse sequence I have
recorded in over 150 hours of transcribed Kaluli speech. They
resemble the Western-style classroom Q/A sequence with one correct answer, which is searched for until it is reached. Furthermore,
Christian discussion is orderly and voices are never raised. Literacy
lessons are similar in this regard. In addition, they share framing

devices and the participant structure found in local sermons. This is
not surprising given the strong influence of and connection between
Christian activities and schooling, including vernacular literacy
classes. For example, in this literacy lesson, Kulu begins the class
with the directive that all will sing a song that uses a popular hymn
melody to which he has set new words. [2]

KF]   tambo

1   *everyone*

2   gisalowo: mo:la:bi

       will sing a song

3   (sings) ne o:ba: ganalabo: da:da:sen da:da:sen da:da:sen

       I hear   hear hear birds singing

4   okay

       okay

5   one two (class sings song in unison)

       one two

6   mada o:m

       thank you

                                    ##

After singing the first line of the song, Kulu uses "okay" (4) as a
discourse boundary marker, and counts in English, "one, two" so
that the students will all sing together. This introduced style of
singing departs from Kaluli song style which has a very different
aesthetic structure (Feld, 1988). After the students sing, Kulu thanks
them. The use of *mada o:m* "thank you" which is viewed by Kaluli
people as a mission-introduced concept and expression also marks
this as a Christian activity.

All of the students have copies of the booklet on malaria and its
prevention called *Hamule e walaf bo:lo:* "Hamule got sick" and
standing in the front of the class Kulu announces the topic (9)

"what mosquitoes do" and directs everyone's attention to the book, the source of the information.
Kulu is holding the booklet

##

9   o:go: kiso:wa:lo: dimidabo: ko:lo: kiso:wa:lo: dimidabo: ko:lo: agelema:niki

today   what the mosquitoes do, what the mosquitoes do that's what we are reading about

10-11 we bo:ba, Hamule we

look at this , Hamule here (re the booklet)

12   taminamiyo: kiso:wa:yo: a:la: dimidabo:**lo:do: a:la:bo:** niyo: mo:asulan
ko:sega

before, what mosquitoes do *we now know we did not know these things but

13   mo:lu nili doima:yo: ko:sega **o:go: dinafa asulab buko: wema: walasalab**

before our fathers (**erg**), *but now we really know this book* (**erg**) *shows/instructs*

14   a:la:fo: ko:lo: niliyo: **buko: wena ba:da:sa:ga:**

therefore when we look in this book

15   tif s/c taminamiyo: niyo: mo:asulo: ko:sega no niyo: nulu alifo:
alifo:labamiyo: kiso:wa:lo: nanog diabo: we aungabo:**lo:do: a:la:bo:**

*later s/c before we did not know but when we are sleeping at night the work mosquitoes do is
like this *we now know*

16   **buko: wenamilo: to salab we da:da:sa:ga: asuluma:niki**

listening to what the words in this book say makes us know/understand

##

Kulu (9) sets up a rhetorical framework of contrast that organizes much of the lesson: what was believed in the past as opposed to what is now known. In creating the contrast he uses an innovative evidential construction *-lo:do:a:la:bo:*. This form, used repeatedly throughout the text (for example, 15) has the meaning "known from this source/not known before," and marks information that is new, true and only known from the written word. This evidential does not appear in any traditional speech genres nor is it used in other relatively recent forms of Kaluli discourse, such as translation situations involving Tok Pisin. It is an innovation by Kaluli speakers to mark new information and its new source. Kulu further elaborates this theme of contrasting the past (13 and also 15), "what our fathers (knew) before" with the state of knowing in the present, "but now we really know," and makes the source lexically explicit, *buko: wema: walasalab* "this book shows/instructs." Note that "this book" is marked with an ergative/instrumental case marker, IT is the agent (or instrument) which instructs and shows, (*walasa:lab* "show and speak") and it is by looking at the book (14) and listening to what the words in this book say (16), that understanding or knowledge is obtained. This mode of achieving understanding is different from the ways Kaluli usually learn, which is by listening to what many others say, arguing with them, watching them, and being instructed while participating (Schieffelin, 1990). Source or evidence is made explicit, as is the sensory mode in which it is offered. The book has been granted an authoritative voice and becomes an authoritative source. This new evidential marker is only used in speaking. It never appears in written form. In fact, no evidential markers appear in secular written vernacular texts, a point I will return to.

In addition to this innovative evidential which we will see more of below, other evidential forms are used to indicate different sources of information. In directing the class's attention to the booklet, Kulu (KF) uses the evidential marker *-lo:b* "visually evident" to guide students to the top of the page, the place that they are to begin reading the text aloud as a group (27–28). He counts "one, two" in English to get them into vocal synchrony in the same way as when he instructed the group to sing in the opening of the class (5).

##

KF]   wa:la a:no: o:bo:**lo:bo**:? taminamilo: o:deyo: agela:bi one two

27   *what is it* (**obv**) *on the top* (of the page)? *read the firstpart, one two*

28   ha:ga a:no: agela:bi

       what's underneath,   read

Students slowly read aloud, syllable by syllable, a short text in Kaluli about preventing sickness in Bosavi.

```
KF]     okay
29      okay
```

Marking the end of the group reading with the boundary marker "okay" (29) which is used in Christian speech events, Kulu asks a number of questions which do not relate to the reading that has just been done. Instead, they relate to the cover of the literacy booklet which he is holding up and displaying to the class. The cover is simple: the words "Bosavi" and "Malaria" are typed in small letters at the top of the page. In the center of the page is a black and white line drawing of a mosquito (side view), which is encircled. Placed below the drawing and filling the bottom half of the page is the title written in large bolded capital letters, HAMULE E WALAF BO:LO: . It is apparent from the response of the students that the referent about which Kulu is speaking is not at all clear.

30   a:no: o:ba?

        what is it?

student] walaf

31   *sickness*

KF]   kalu wi o:ba?

32   *what is the person's name?*

class] Hamule

33

KF]   Hamule Hamule a:no:

34   *Hamule   it's Hamule*

35   e o:ba: walaf bo:lo:**lo:bo**:?

        *from what did he get sick (**obv**)?*

36   walafo: o:ba: walaf bo:lo:**lo:bo**:?

        *sickness, from what did he get sick (**obv**) ?*

36   walafo: o:ba: walaf bo:lo:**lo:bo**:?

      sickness, from what did he get sick (**obv**) *?*

37   walafo: o:b walaf bo:lo:**lo:bo**:?

      sickness, from what did he get sick (**obv**) *?*

student]   malalia

38   *malaria*

KF]   wa:la buko: a:no: bo:ba wa:la wa:lamilo: a:no: bo:ba

39   *look on the front of the book, on the front, look on the front* [drawing of mosquito]

student]   kiso:

40   *mosquito*

KF]   a:no: wiyo: o:b salaba? (pointing to title) Hamule e walaf bo:lo:

41   *what does the name say? Hamule he got sick*

42   a:no: piksa we o:bo:**lo:bo**:?

      this picture, what is it (**obv**)?

class] kiso:

43   *mosquito*

##

In lines 30–34 Kulu establishes that what he wants the group to focus on is the title of the booklet. Once that is established, he attempts to elicit a particular response to his question about the source of Hamule's sickness. His attempt to get the class to view the drawing of the mosquito above the title as visual evidence of the source is accomplished over several turns. Using the evidential marker *-lo:b*, Kulu asks the class three times (35–37) about Hamule's sickness, what caused it, what it was. What is visually obvious is the drawing of the mosquito and after receiving an answer to his third question, Kulu asks the class to look at the picture on the cover of the booklet (39) for the answer. His assumption is that the visual evidence is obvious. When only one student answers *kiso:* "mosquito," Kulu explicitly refers to the picture (42). Only then does he get the desired group response. Throughout his talk about the source of the sickness, malaria (25–37, 42 and elsewhere), he uses the evidential form *-lo:b* to indicate that the information is *visually* available.[3]

In contrast to this pattern of evidential choice, when Kulu refers to information, or wants the class to focus on information that is in the written texts, he shifts to evidentials that mark verbal evidence. In other words, the print and the book are classified as speaking subjects. Printed words do not have the same evidential status as graphic representations or as something visually evident. In addition Kulu marks these speaking subjects with ergative case marking, and uses verbs of speaking such as *a: la:ma* "say like that" and *sama* "speak/say" to provide evidence for what is in the text, as well as to give authority to the text, verbal authority. He extends this authority to himself at the same time.

##

52   **mada** a:la:sa:ga: kalu nowo: walaf bo:lo:wamiyo: kalu nowo: walaf

ba:labamiyo: o: walafdo: a:na diya:sa:ga: a:la:sa:ga: no ami dimian**ka: a:la:**

salabka: wema:

really after one man gets sick, another man gets sick, (the mosquito) *takes from the sick*

one and then gives it (malaria) *to another man it really says like that, this* (erg-book)

53   walafdo: a:na diya:sa:ga: nowa dimian**ka: a:la: salab** walafdo: a:no:

ho:bo:wo: wasuliya:sa:ga: nowa iliga:ifa:la:i **so:lo:lka:** e mulumudo: a

hononamilo: walaf ege owami a:na wa:ta:sa:ga: kalu amiyo: o:lan**ka:**

having taken from a sick one, it really gives to another it says, after mixing the blood of

the sick one it sends (the sickness) *to many I'm really saying, in the sickhouse over there,*

after drawing the sickness in the needle (stinger), (mosquito) *really shoots* (injects) *a man*

##

Kulu uses *wema: a:la: salabka:* "this one (the book, marked with the ergative casemarker) really says like that," (52) *buko: wema: ... walasalab* "this book instructs" (62), *a:la: salab* "it says like that" (53) in addition to variants of these expressions to locate the source of his assertions about mosquitoes. In addition he frequently adds *so:lo:ka:* "I"m really saying," combining a range of emphatics including *-ka:* and *-balo:* "emphatic counter to expected" (60) and other lexical items including *mada* "really," *hede* "truly," with their own emphatics to substantiate his own authoritativeness.

##

60   ni welo: nan**balo:** ko:lo: sab**ka:** ho:bo:wo: ko:sega ho:bo:wo: nan**balo:** a:no: noma:lo:wo: nowa a: dia:fa:na:lila wo:gelabamiyo:

they really drink from us that really live here, blood but they really drink blood, from one to another they keep on putting it in mixing it all up

61   o: walaf ko:li ko:lilo:wo: a:na fa:la:lowab**ka: a:la: salab**

all different sickness really comes up from that mixing it says like that

62   a:la:fo: ko:lo: o: walaf mo: a:no: o:go: **buko: wema:** iliki nimo: **walasalab** a:no:

therefore the sickness's beginning/cause now having this book (erg) instructs us about that

63   mo:wo: mada dinafa do:do:l

I really hear/understand the cause well

64   a:la:fo: ko:lo: ege buko: lidisi buko: wenami **wema:yo: mada nafa salab**

therefore uh book, in this literacy book this (erg) really says it well

##

Kulu's extensive use of emphatic markers intensifies his assertions about the "facts," their truthfulness, and how well they are stated. The literacy book not only instructs and really says it, but says it really well (64). These assertions are repeated throughout the lesson, and are not to be challenged.

Kulu not only presents the book as a speaking subject with its own voice, but talks about how Papua New Guineans only recently have seen them, and heard them speak.

##

57   Papua Nugini kalu we taminamiyo: **wengo:wo: mo:ba:ba:** ko:sega

      *PNG men **didn't see one like this** (book) before but*

58   no mada o:g Hamule **buko: wema:yo: kobale walasalab** nimo:wo: kiso:wo:
      nulu ya:sa:ga: alifo:lab ami e nanog diyaki a:namiyo: kalu ho:bo:wo:
      wo:gelaka: **a:la: salab**

      *really today **this Hamule book** (erg) **instructs us well** - mosquitoes having come at night*

      *while we sleep they do their work there really mixing men's blood **it says like that***

##

Books become the source of understanding through hearing them speak. Kulu asserts, "I hear/understand the reason from the book," (63) "we are really hearing new words spoken" (71) and reminds the class to think about and remember what they are hearing that is new.

##

67   wena asula:sa:ga:yo: go:no: gelo: alilabamiyo: nuluwo: asula:bi kiso:wa:yo:
      wengo: nanog diabo:**lo:bo:no: a:la:bo:**

      *when you think about this, when you are sleeping at night remember mosquitoes do this *we*

      now know don't forget

68   a:sa:ga: Papua Nugini us wenamiyo: taminamiyo: asula:leno:? gimo:
      a:dabu bo:do:lka: giliyo: sama asula:leno:? kiso:wa:yo: a:la: nanog diabami
      walafo:lo: kalu amiyo: a:la: kaluka:isale amiyo: a:la: balabo:**lo:b a:la:bo:**

      in the PNG interior here did we know this before? I'm asking you all again, you all say it

      did we know this before? that it was the mosquitoes work that made men sick, men and

      *women too *we now know**

class] mo:asula:len

69   *we didn't know*

KF]   mo:asula:len **hede salab**

70   *we didn't know, **that's truthfully said***

71   mo:asula:lenka: **a:la: salab** ko:lo: o: niliyo: **hedele ho:gi to salabo:lo:do:** a:la:

asula:sa:ga: dinafa asuluma:niki

*we didn't really know it says like that, we are really hearing new words spoken *we now*

know after thinking about them we will understand

10.6 The visual and the verbal: captioned photographs

The literacy booklet that is used in this lesson is illustrated with black and white photographs of Kaluli people that are captioned in the Kaluli language. These present an interesting site in which to examine evidential choice, that is, how particular evidentials mark particular aspects of the information Kulu is querying. At different points in the lesson Kulu asks the class to look at these captioned pictures as the source of information in order to answer his questions. For example, one picture shows Kaluli adults and children sitting around and eating. The caption reads:

Hamuleyo: walaf bulufo: ko:lo: eso:lo: kalukaisale ma:no: dowo:ta:sa:ga:

sagalaki mo:no:

When Hamule got well, men and women in his family cooked food and ate happily.

KF]   falelo: dowo: ko:lo: -- o: ba falelabiki sagalab -- a:no: wagaba? nodowa hono

153   so:wagaleno: sagala:li **o:siyo:** -- mo:wo: ha:h? sagalo: ilido: dowab a:no: --

walafo: dowo:**lo:bo:**?

because he got well -- because he is already well they are happy --what about it? on the

*other side there--the child is happy right there it **said**--what's the reason? they are*

*happy -- is there sickness (**obv**)? (from the picture)*

student] falele

154   *he got well*

KF]   falelo: ko:**lo:b** sagalab kelego: dima:daki a:la:fo:ko:lo: o:go: sagalab a:no:

155   o:bdo: miyo:wagaba?

*he got well (**obv**) (from the picture) so they are doing happy things, this happiness now,*

what brought it?

##

Kulu uses the same pattern of evidential marking in Q/A sequences where the focus of attention is captioned photographs. Here he carefully distinguishes between evidence which is visually evident (*-lo:b*) and that which is verbally evident (*o:siyo:*). For example, the caption says that men and women are happy and Kulu asks that the students produce the reason for that. This requires inferencing. When no response is forthcoming, he provides a possible answer, directing students to base their explanation on how people look in the photograph – *walafo: dowo:lo:bo:?* "is there obviously sickness?" After (154) the student provides the correct answer, Kulu reinforces it, using the evidential marker (*-lo:b*), which the student does not.

10.7 In and out of the text

While much of the information Kulu talks about is covered in the text, there are several places where Kulu's words radically depart from the text and from any general Kaluli or Western instructed notions about illness. Despite his extensive use of evidentials and emphatics, and assertions of telling the truth (74) there is considerable leeway for inventiveness. Kulu's words are never challenged by the class.

                                        ##

73   igo:wo: na:sa:ga:yo:lo: ka:yo: ka:yo: diniya o:lo:so:fa ko:lo: na:sa:ga:yo:lo:

        mada ge alifo:likiyo: mego:fo:lo: hononaka a:la: ko:la:liya: dia:ta ka

        alifo:mela:**ika:**

        *after eating wild pig too fish, fish cooked in a pot, having eaten those things, **really** while*

        *you are sleeping, into your mouth which is open, gets put in there when you are **really***

        sleeping

74   **mada hede so:lo:l**

        I'm really telling the truth

75   a:la:fo: ami eyo: o: egeyo: ko:lo: **mada** ege ko:li hinigan ilayamilo: ta:sa:ga:lo:

        a:namilo: gesinamilo: babido: a:no: no a:no: ko:lo: meyo:diliya: ya:ga: a:naka

        asifa: yaka

        then they (mosquitoes) the wachamacallit, really the wachamacallit different dirt from

        the shit house stays there on their claws (legs) sticking there and they (mosquitoes) come

        around smelling, come and sit there in the mouth

76   a:la:ta bes hononamiyo: nagalo:wo: a:na dimia:ni mogago: e gesinamilo:

      babidiliya:ga:lo: yab a:no: ge alifo:laba **mo:ba:daka: a:la: salab**

      then they give tooth aches in there, with bad stuff sticking on their claws they come when

      *you are sleeping you **really don't see it, it says like that***

                                      ##

Kulu is able to claim authority through asserting the existence of a
text that in fact is nonexistent. There is no text that talks about
mosquitoes and tooth decay, nor is this an idea that is shared
among Kaluli people. Kulu is listened to as a teacher and a
Christian, and he becomes a conveyer and interpreter of new
truth because he can read the words and mark them convincingly.

The literacy lesson closely resembles sermons with its essentially
monologic style, combining reading plus speaking by a knowledge-
able leader. The speaking takes place without the usual feedback
that organizes all other speech events and creates cohesion.
Throughout this event, Kulu proposes that the class trust the language to mean what it says, to take it as literal truth. Facts are made
into objects that can be pointed to in the texts, referenced through
particular language forms. The genre marks the activity as being
one in which only truthfulness is asserted, as in sermons, but in the
literacy lesson, particular evidentials help constitute a genre and an
interpretive framework for learning. It is monologic, without an
author present. Without an author there is no one with whom to
argue – Kaluli people have yet to have a dialogue, or an argument
with a printed text.

In this lesson, the written text and photographs are used to construct a reality that can henceforth become a material base for
changes in social and linguistic ideologies and practices. These
texts and their readings establish a new discursive orientation to
knowledge, truth, authority, and time itself. The written text explicitly denies that Bosavi people had reasons or beliefs before contact.
It presents a view that people can have control over their health if
they listen to the new words. In spite of this, many local concerns
are articulated throughout the lesson – and one is the Kaluli concern
with evidence. Printed text and photographs come to satisfy that
interest, while providing representations for re-imagining local life
as Kaluli people see themselves re-located in books. In contrast to

earlier fears about what white people would know about them from a book, today Kaluli names written in books take on a new meaning. Through collaboration between Kaluli and missionaries, not only have Kaluli people been re-imagined as modern Christians, but their linguistic resources have been adapted to accommodate this new view of themselves and their world. Without questioning the evidence,they come to believe that what is printed must be true.

Notes

*   I would like to thank the National Science Foundation and the Wenner-Gren Foundation for funding fieldwork in 1984 and 1990. Thanks also go to Steve Feld and Elinor Ochs for their always helpful comments. Finally, I would like to thank Sue Gal and Kit Woolard for their cogent written comments, as well as the other members of the Center for Transcultural Studies Working Group on Language and the participants in the School for American Research Seminar on Language Ideologies for asking tough questions.

    This essay is dedicated to the late Kulu Fuale; his patience and assistance in helping me understand the Kaluli language for over fifteen years was enriched by his unique linguistic curiosity.

1   The form -*mala:* has two distinct meanings which are disambiguated by stress/pitch differences in the language. These are not indicated in the orthography.

2   Inconsistencies in orthography are due to the preservation of the dialect features of speakers. Inconsistencies in the written texts are presented as they appear in the original materials. There are inconsistencies of spelling, as well as grammatical errors throughout the written literacy materials, and these sometimes cause difficulty in reading. There are discussions in the lesson of problems with the "writing" (spelling), but those discussions are beyond the scope of this paper.

    The transcription preserves the breath grouping of the speaker, and the numbers used throughout indicate those breath groups. However, in some lines, (153), breath groups are indicated as in the original transcript using the transcription convention – . Also used is s/c for self corrections by speakers. Selections from the transcript are used to illustrate particular points, but the sequential numbers of the complete transcript are retained to make this analysis usable with other analyses of the same transcript. A break in sequence is indicated by ##. There are no interruptions or overlaps in this speech event. Boldface is used to indicate the phenomena of interest.

3   Throughout the lesson, students do not use evidentials in their answers. In fact, their clipped one word responses here and throughout

the lesson have no morphological marking at all. In conversation, an answer would be marked with the evidential *-lo: b* to indicate that the hearer shares the same evidentiary base with the speaker. The only form produced by a student that resembles an evidential occurs in response to a question Kulu asks about how many students are in the class. One student responds using a codeswitched English and Tok Pisin utterance "twenty two *hia*" "twenty two here". This is the context in which *-lo: b* would be appropriate, but it is not used. I am currently examining the extent to which Tok Pisin *hia* is being used as an evidential in other types of Kaluli discourse.

References

Bendix, Edward (1993). The grammaticalization of responsibility and evidence: interactional manipulation of evidential categories in Newari. In Jane Hill and Judy Irvine (eds.) *Responsibility and Evidence in Oral Discourse*, pp. 226–47. Cambridge: Cambridge University Press.

Besnier, Niko (1995). *Literacy, Emotion, and Authority: Reading and Writing on a Polynesian Atoll.* New York: Cambridge University Press.

Bybee, Joan (1985). *Morphology: A Study of the Relation between Meaning and Form.* Amsterdam: John Benjamins.

Chafe, Wallace and Nichols, Joanna (eds.) (1986). *Evidentiality: The Coding of Epistemology in Language.* Norwood, NJ: Ablex.

Cohn, Bernard (1985). The command of language and the language of command. *Subaltern Studies* 4: 276–329.

Collins, James (1991). Hegemonic practice: literacy and standard language in public education. In C. Mitchell and K. Wesler (eds.) *Rewriting Literacy: Culture and the Discourse of the Other*, pp. 229–53. New York: Bergin and Garvey.

Comaroff, John and Comaroff, Jean (1991). *Of Revolution and Revelation: Christianity, Colonialism and Consciousness in South Africa*, vol. 1. Chicago: University of Chicago Press.

Duranti, Alessandro and Ochs, Elinor (1986). Literacy instruction in a Samoan village. In B. B. Schieffelin and P. Gilmore (eds.) *The Acquisition of Literacy: Ethnographic Perspectives*, pp. 213–32. Norwood, NJ: Ablex.

Fabian, Johannes (1986). *Language and Colonial Power.* Cambridge: Cambridge University Press.

Feld, Steven (1988). Aesthetics as iconicity of style, or, "lift-up-over-sounding": getting into the Kaluli groove. *Yearbook for Traditional Music* 20: 74–113.

(1990). *Sound and Sentiment.* 2nd edn. Philadelphia: University of Pennsylvania Press.

Feld, Steven and Schieffelin, Bambi (1982). Hard words: a functional basis for Kaluli discourse. In D. Tannen (ed.) *Georgetown University Roundtable on Languages and Linguistics 1981*, pp. 351–71. Washington, DC: Georgetown University Press.

Fox, Barbara and Clifford, Joseph (1991). Evidentiality and authority in English conversation. ms.

Gewertz, Deborah and Errington, Fredrick (1991). *Twisted Histories, Altered Contexts*. Cambridge: Cambridge University Press.

Givón, Talmy (1982). Evidentiality and epistemic space. *Studies in Language* 6,1: 23–49.

Guss, David (1986). Keeping it oral: a Yekuana ethnology. *American Ethnologist* 13, 3: 413–29.

Haviland, John (1989). "Sure, sure": evidence and affect. *Text* 9,1: 27–68.

Heath, Shirley (1983). *Ways with Words*. Cambridge: Cambridge University Press.

Hill, Jane and Irvine, Judith (eds.) (1993). *Responsibility and Evidence in Oral Discourse*. Cambridge: Cambridge University Press.

Jakobson, Roman (1957). Shifters, verbal categories, and the Russian verb. Russian Language Project, Dept of Slavic Languages and Literatures, Harvard University.

Kulick, Don and Stroud, Christopher (1990). Christianity, cargo and ideas of self. *Man* (n.s.) 25: 70–88.

Lucy, John (ed.) (1993). *Reflexive Language: Reported Speech and Metapragmatics*. Cambridge: Cambridge University Press.

McKenzie, D. F. (1987). The sociology of a text: oral culture, literacy and print in early New Zealand. In P. Burke and R. Porter (eds.) *The Social History of Language*. pp. 161–97. Cambridge: Cambridge University Press.

Mignolo, W. D. (1992). On the colonization of Amerindian languages and memories: Renaissance theories of writing and the discontinuity of the classical tradition. *Comparative Studies in Society and History* 32: 310–30.

Ochs, Elinor and Schieffelin, Bambi B. (1984). Language acquisition and socialization: three developmental stories and their implications. In R. Shweder and R. Levine (eds.) *Culture Theory: Essays on Mind, Self and Emotion*, pp. 276–320. Cambridge: Cambridge University Press.

Rafael, Vincente (1988). *Contracting Colonialism: Translation and Christian Conversion in Tagalog Society under Early Spanish Rule*. Ithaca: Cornell University Press.

Rule, Murray (1966). Customs, alphabet and grammar of the Kaluli people of Bosavi, Papua. Mimeo, Unevangelized Fields Missions.

Schieffelin, Bambi B. (1986). The acquisition of Kaluli. In Dan I. Slobin (ed.) *The Cross-Linguistic Study of Language Acquisition*, vol. 1, pp. 525–93. Hillsdale, N J : Lawrence Erlbaum Associates.

(1990). *The Give and Take of Everyday Life: Language Socialization of Kaluli Children*. New York: Cambridge University Press.

Schieffelin, Edward L. (1976). *The Sorrow of the Lonely and the Burning of the Dancers*. New York: St. Martins Press.

Silverstein, Michael (1985). The functional stratification of language and ontogenesis. In James V. Wertsch (ed.) *Culture, Communication, and Cognition: Vygotskian Perspectives*, pp. 205–35. New York: Cambridge University Press.

Street, Brian (1984). *Literacy in Theory and Practice*. New York: Cambridge University Press.

Street, Brian and Besnier, Niko (1994). Aspects of literacy. In T. Ingold (ed.) *Companion Encyclopedia of Anthropology*, pp. 527–62. London: Routledge.

Willett, Thomas (1988). A cross-linguistic survey of the grammaticalization of evidentiality. *Studies in Language* 12, 1: 51–97.

Appendix

Transcription conventions

1 Temporal and sequential relationships

     A Overlapping or simultaneous talk is indicated in a variety of ways.

[Separate left square brackets, one above the other on two succes-
[sive lines with utterances by different speakers, indicates a point of overlap onset, whether at the start of an utterance or later.

]   Separate right square brackets, one above the other on two suc-
]   cessive lines with utterances by different speakers indicates a point at which two overlapping utterances both end, where one ends while the other continues, or simultaneous moments in overlaps which continue.

//   In some older transcripts or where graphic arrangement of the transcript requires it, a double slash indicates the point at which a current speaker's utterance is overlapped by the talk of another, which appears on the next line attributed to another speaker. If there is more than one double slash in an utterance, then the second indicates where a second overlap begins, the overlapping talk appearing on the next line attributed to another speaker, etc. In transcripts using the // notation for overlap onset, the end of the overlap may be marked by a right bracket (as above) or by an

*   asterisk.

     So, the following are alternative ways of representing the same event: Bee's "Uh really?" overlaps Ava's talk starting at "a" and ending at the "t" of "tough."

```
Ava:      I 'av [a lotta  t]ough cou:rses.
Bee:            [Uh really?]

Ava:      I 'av // a lotta t*ough cou:rses.
Bee:      Uh really?
```

=   B Equal signs ordinarily come in pairs – one at the end of a line and another at the start of the next line or one shortly thereafter. They are used to indicate two things:

(1) If the two lines connected by the equal signs are by the same speaker, then there was a single, continuous utterance with no break or pause, which was broken up in order to accommodate the placement of overlapping talk. For example:

```
Bee:     In the gy:m? [(hh)
Ava:                  [Yea:h. Like grou(h)p
         therapy.Yuh know [half the grou]p thet=
Bee:                      [ O h : : : . ]`hh
Ava:     =we had la:s' term wz there en we [jus'=
Bee:                                       [`hh
Ava:     =playing arou:nd.
```

Ava's talk is continuous, but room has been made for Bee's overlapping talk (the "Oh").

(2) If the lines connected by two equal signs are by different speakers, then the second followed the first with no discernable silence between them, or was "latched" to it.

(0.5)   C Numbers in parentheses indicate silence, represented in tenths of a second; what is given here in the left margin indicates 5/10 seconds of silence. Silences may be marked either within an utterance or between utterances, as in the two excerpts below:

```
Bee:     `hhh Uh::, (0.3) I don'know I guess
         she's aw- she's awright she went to
         thee uh:: hhospital again tihda:y,
```

```
Bee:     Tch! .hh So uh I don't kno:w,
         (0.3)
Bee:     En:=
```

(.)   D A dot in parentheses indicates a "micropause," hearable but not readily measurable; ordinarily less than 2/10 of a second.

((pause))   E In some older or less carefully prepared transcripts, untimed silences may be indicated by the word "pause" in double parentheses.

2 Aspects of speech delivery, including aspects of intonation

.   A The punctuation marks are *not* used grammatically, but to indicate intonation. The period indicates a falling, or final, intonation contour, not necessarily the end of a sentence. Similarly, a

?   question mark indicates rising intonation, not necessarily a question, and a comma indicates "continuing" intonation, not necessarily a clause boundary. In some transcript fragments in these

?,   papers you may see a combined question mark and comma, which
         indicates a rise stronger than a comma but weaker than a question
         mark. Because this symbol cannot be produced by the
¿   computer, the inverted question mark (¿) is used for this purpose.

::   B Colons are used to indicate the prolongation or stretching of
         the sound just preceding them. The more colons, the longer the
         stretching. On the other hand, graphically stretching a word on the
         page by inserting blank spaces between the letters does *not* neces-
         sarily indicate how it was pronounced; it is used to allow align-
         ment with overlapping talk. Thus,

```
Bee:       Tch! (M'n)/(En ) they can't delay much
           lo:nguh they [jus' wannid] uh-`hhh=
Ava:                     [ O h  :  . ]
Bee:       =yihknow have anothuh consulta:tion,
Ava:       Ri::ght.
Bee:       En then deci::de.
```

         The word "ri::ght" in Ava's second turn, or "deci::de" in Bee's
         third are more stretched than "oh:" in Ava's first turn, even
         though "oh:" appears to occupy more space. But "oh" has only
         one colon, and the others have two; "oh:" has been spaced out so
         that its brackets will align with the talk in Bee's ("jus' wannid")
         turn with which it is in overlap.

-        C A hyphen after a word or part of a word indicates a cut-off or
         self-interruption, often done with a glottal or dental stop.

word   D Underlining is used to indicate some form of stress or empha-
         sis, either by increased loudness or higher pitch. The more under-
         lining, the greater the emphasis.
word   Therefore, underlining sometimes is placed under the first letter or
         two of a word, rather than under the letters which are actually
         raised in pitch or volume. Especially loud talk may be
WOrd   indicated by upper case; again, the louder, the more letters in
         upper case. And in extreme cases, upper case may be underlined.

°   E The degree sign indicates that the talk following it was mark-
         edly quiet or soft.
° °   When there are two degree signs, the talk between them is mark-
         edly softer than the talk around it.

         F Combinations of underlining and colons are used to indicate
         intonation contours, as follows:

_: If the letter(s) preceding a colon is underlined, then there is an "inflected" *falling* intonation contour (you can hear the pitch turn downward).

:   If a colon is itself underlined, then there is an inflected *rising* intonation contour (i.e., you can hear the pitch turn upward). So, in

```
Bee:        In the gy:m? [(hh)
Ava:                     [Yea:h. Like grou(h)p
            therapy.Yuh know [half the grou]p thet=
Bee:                         [ O h : : : . ]`hh
Ava:        =we had la:s' term wz there en we [jus'=
Bee:                                          [`hh
Ava:        =playing arou:nd.
Bee:        Uh-fo[oling around.
Ava:             [`hhh
Ava:        Eh-yeah so, some a' the guys who were
            bedder y'know wen' off by themselves so
            it wz two girls against this one guy en
            he's ta:ll.Y'know? [`hh
Bee:                            [ Mm hm?
```

the "Oh::::." in Bee's second turn has an upward inflection while it is being stretched (even though it ends with falling intonation, as indicated by the period). On the other hand, "ta:ll" at the end of Ava's last turn is inflected downward ("bends downward," so to speak), over and above its "period intonation."

↑   G The up and down arrows mark sharper rises or falls in pitch
↓   than would be indicated by combinations of colons and underlining, or may mark a whole shift, or resetting, of the pitch register at which the talk is being produced.

> <   H The combination of "more than" and "less than" symbols indicates that the talk between them is compressed or rushed. Used
< >   in the reverse order, they can indicate that a stretch of talk is
<   markedly slowed or drawn out. The "less than" symbol by itself indicates that the immediately following talk is "jump-started," i.e., sounds like it starts with a rush.

hhh   I Hearable aspiration is shown where it occurs in the talk by the letter "h" – the more h's, the more aspiration. The aspiration may
(hh)   represent breathing, laughter, etc. If it occurs inside the boundaries of a word, it may be enclosed in parentheses in order to set it apart
hh   from the sounds of the word (as in the turn shown below). If the aspiration is an inhalation, it is shown with a dot before it (usually a raised dot).

```
Bee:        [Ba::]sk(h)etb(h)a(h)ll? (h)(°Whe(h)re.)
```

3 Other markings

(( ))   **A** Double parentheses are used to mark transcriber's descriptions of events, rather than representations of them. Thus ((cough)), ((sniff)), ((telephone rings)), ((footsteps)), ((whispered)), ((pause)) and the like.

(word)   **B** When all or part of an utterance is in parentheses, or the speaker identification is, this indicates uncertainty on the transcriber's part, but represents a likely possibility.

( )   Empty parentheses indicate that something is being said, but no hearing (or, in some cases, speaker identification) can be achieved.

(try 1)/   **C** In some transcript excerpts, two parentheses may be printed,
(try 2)   one above the other; these represent alternative hearings of the same strip of talk. In some instances this format cannot be printed, and is replaced by putting the alternative hearings in parentheses, separated by a single oblique or slash, as in

Bee: °(Bu::t.)=/°(Goo:d.)=

Here, the degree marks show that the utterance is very soft. The transcript remains indeterminate between "Bu::t." and "Goo:d." Each is in parentheses and they are separated by a slash.

The core of this set of notational conventions was first developed by Gail Jefferson. It continues to evolve and adapt to the work of analysis, the developing skill of transcribers, and changes in technology. Not all symbols have been included here, and some symbols in some data sources are not used systematically or consistently. Papers in this volume may introduce additional conventions, especially for registering body behaviour in relation to the talk.

Subject index